Lenôtre's

Ice Creams and Candies

Lenôtre's Ice Creams and Candies

Gaston Lenôtre

Translated and Adapted by
Philip and Mary Hyman

Photos by Pierre Ginet

Barron's

Frontispiece, Frozen Cognac and Apricot Dessert, Recipe 82
Photography by Mr. P. Ginet.

All inquiries should be addressed to:
Barron's Educational Series, Inc.
113 Crossways Park Drive
Woodbury, New York 11797

Library of Congress Catalog Card No. 79-17809

International Standard Book No. 0-8120-5334-6

Library of Congress Cataloging in Publication Data
Lenôtre, Gaston.
    Lenôtre's ice creams and candies.
    Translation of Faites vos glaces et votre confiserie
comme Lenôtre.
    Includes index.
    1. Ice cream, ices, etc. 2. Desserts, Frozen.
3. Confectionery. I. Hyman, Philip. II. Hyman,
Mary. III. Title.
TX795.L4613   641.8'62   79-17809
ISBN 0-8120-5334-6

PRINTED IN HONG KONG
2345   041   9876543

Contents

Table of Measurements	vi
Foreword	vii
Preface	ix
Introduction	xi
Dictionary of Terms	xiii
Suggested Utensils	xviii
General Comments on Frozen Desserts	1
1 Sherbets and Granités	9
2 Ice Creams and Parfaits	41
3 Sundaes	73
4 Combination Desserts	91
5 Creams, Sauces, Pastries, and Fruit Preparations	145
6 Cooking Sugar, Jams, and Fruit Jellies	201
7 Candies	261
8 Chocolates	311
Cross Index of Basic Ingredients and Preparations	381
Alphabetical Index to Recipes	385

TABLE OF MEASUREMENTS

Basic American Measures

1 tablespoon = ½ fluid ounce
3 teaspoons = 1 tablespoon
1 cup = 8 fluid ounces
1 pint = 2 cups = 16 fluid ounces

Basic British Measures

1 tablespoon = ½ fluid ounce
4 teaspoons = 1 tablespoon
½ pint = 10 fluid ounces
1 pint = 20 fluid ounces

Weight Conversion to Metric

1 ounce = 28.35 grams (can be rounded off to 30 grams)
1 pound = 16 ounces = 454 grams (can be rounded off to 450 grams)

Weight Conversion from Metric

25 grams = ⅞ ounce
50 grams = 1¾ ounces
100 grams = 3½ ounces
125 grams = 4½ ounces

250 grams = 9 ounces
500 grams = 1 pound 1½ ounces
750 grams = 1 pound 10½ ounces
1 kilo (1000 g) = 2 pounds 3¼ ounces

Liquid Conversions

American		Metric		British
1 teaspoon	=	5 milliliter	=	1⅓ teaspoons
2 teaspoons	=	1 centiliter	=	2⅔ teaspoons
1 tablespoon	=	1.5 centiliter	=	1 tablespoon
3 tablespoons	=	½ decaliter	=	3 tablespoons
6½ tablespoons	=	1 decaliter	=	6½ tablespoons
1 generous cup	=	¼ liter	=	8¾ fl. oz. (scant ½ pint)
2 generous cups	=	½ liter	=	17½ fl. oz. (generous ¾ pint)
Scant 3¼ cups	=	¾ liter	=	26¼ fl. oz. (scant 1⅓ pints)
4¼ cups	=	1 liter	=	35 fl. oz. (1¾ pints)

FOREWORD

Lenôtre has done it again! After sharing pastry secrets in his first book, he now offers us his recipes for an unrivaled panorama of creative frozen desserts and confectionery. These recipes will come as revelations to many people who only know either the pale commercial versions of these desserts or have previously relied on recipes that produce results only vaguely related to the rich, exquisite ice creams and confections made by Lenôtre.

What makes Lenôtre's ice creams and sherbets so special? The answer is simple—these are *real* ice creams and sherbets, made the traditional way. Although the French didn't invent either ice creams or sherbets, many people believe that they are the masters of these frozen desserts. Once *all* ice creams were made with cream; in Lenôtre's recipes they still are. Once *all* sherbets were exquisite combinations of water, sugar, and fruit nothing more; Lenôtre's still are. Little by little, especially in the United States, both of these preparations became oddly distorted—gelatine and milk became standard ingredients in sherbets, and flour and whole eggs crept into ice creams (the cream all but disappeared) until finally an enormous confusion was created, and few people today actually know what ice cream or sherbet is. Lenôtre's ice creams and sherbets are what ice creams and sherbets used to be and ought to be—pure and rich, using the minimum number of ingredients for the maximum of flavor. Here, ice creams are made with egg yolks—*not* whole eggs, *not* dehydrated eggs, and certainly *no* flour! Here sherbets are simplicity itself—sugar syrup and fruit pulp, *no* milk, *no* gelatine, and of course only real fruit with real flavor, no artificial concoctions. The result is a clean, pure taste that is extraordinary. Americans may be surprised that Lenôtre doesn't include recipes for fruit ice creams, but this is because he, like most modern French chefs, believes that the natural fruit flavors are best in sherbets, where they are most pronounced—almost like essences—and that ice creams are best flavored with permeating tastes like vanilla, coffee, chocolate, etc.

But these two worlds meet in the combination desserts which are the most creative and exciting part of Lenôtre's work. Lenôtre will mold sherbet and ice cream together. A vanilla ice cream outside, for instance, will house a raspberry sherbet core, and the best of both worlds is the result. Indeed, all the molded frozen desserts and sundaes are remarkable. They are the result of first perfecting the basic sherbets and ice creams themselves, then testing and experimenting until just the right taste combinations are discovered, and it is in this work of experimentation that Lenôtre excells. The resulting combinations, like the Armagnac and Prune ice cream served with vanilla sauce or Nut Brittle ice cream served with caramel sauce or Lenôtre's superb Baked Alaska (to name only a very few), are absolutely exquisite.

All this is only half of Lenôtre's book! When he turns to confectionery, we realize that here too, many preconceptions (and past experiences) will have to be reexamined in the light of these recipes. The first surprise is how easy candies and chocolates are to make; the second is how good they taste. The reason for the first phenomenon is that Lenôtre, with his daughter Sylvie, has simplified procedures and described each step in detail so that even the novice will quickly be turning out boxes full of varied and delicious candies and chocolates. The second achievement, quality, is the result of Lenôtre's characteristic reliance on pure ingredients of the best possible quality—no skimping or cutting corners. You are told how to make everything you need, but only by using the best ingredients will you produce truly amazing results.

Indeed, it should be mentioned here that scattered throughout this book are numerous other recipes that make this a companion volume to Lenôtre's work on pastry. He has even included in this book several new pastry recipes that readers had asked for after the pastry book appeared. Jams, jellies, and home canning are explained in great detail, and brandied fruits as well as a delicious Cassis Liqueur are included to make this book as complete a complement to the pastry book as possible. The two volumes together are a must for anyone interested in French cooking, for they resume the art of making French desserts. All serious cooks owe Lenôtre a sincere "thanks" since he has now made it possible for them to produce at home splendid preparations like those that made the reputation of the master of desserts himself—Gaston Lenôtre.

Philip and Mary Hyman

PREFACE

This book is for people who like parties and who like to make special things for others. Every meal can be festive when your own homemade ice creams are in the freezer; children's snacks can turn into parties (they love to help make candies; and a family meal becomes a special occasion when you serve a frozen vacherin or frozen soufflé, then offer homemade candies to add to the feeling of festivity created by these simple treats. Candies and chocolates the ideal gift for friends and relatives—take on a very special importance when you make them yourself; they never go unappreciated.

The recipes in this book for ice creams, candies, and chocolates complete the first book I wrote on desserts and pastries. They are explained with the same precision as the pastry recipes, and I have included serving suggestions and comments on storing these desserts as I did in my other book. Don't think that making ice cream and candy is complicated. If you read the general comments which precede each section of this book, you should have no trouble whatever in following the recipes, and whether they be for ice creams, which you may have made before, or candies, such as chocolate cherries, chocolate thistles, or chocolate truffles, you'll be surprised at how quickly and easily you master the techniques involved.

Most important here, as in pastry, is the *quality of the ingredients*. You must first learn to know what you are buying and how to choose the best products: the taste of an ice cream or sherbet, whether it is good or bad, depends absolutely on the taste of the fruit or cream that went into it, so if the fruit you use is of the best quality, full of flavor, and perfectly ripe and your cream is fresh and sweet, you have all the chances in the world of making desserts everyone will rave about.

Always read a recipe through before starting, and be sure that you have all the utensils you need and that everything (utensils and ingredients) is set out and ready to use before you actually begin making the recipe itself. I have included not only a list of ingredients, but a list of utensils at the beginning of each recipe to help you prepare. For making ice creams and sherbets, it is extremely important that you have a good ice cream freezer; a detailed discussion of the advantages and disadvantages of various models is given in the section General Comments on Frozen Desserts.

The recipes in this book, whether for ice creams or confectionery, are those that are the easiest to make at home and that do not call for any specialized equipment. Two of my chefs are responsible for perfecting these recipes, and they deserve special thanks here: they are Alain Nadler, who specializes in making frozen desserts, and Jean-Claude Dudoit, who specializes in making pastry and confectionery. As was the case with the pastry book, my daughter Sylvie tried all of the recipes at her home, often making a recipe several times in order to make it as clear and simple as possible, so that even an inexperienced cook could understand the techniques involved and produce perfect results.

Because of these painstaking preparations, the recipes should be as clear and simple to follow as possible and should prove that ice creams and confectionery are no more difficult to make than the tarts or chocolate eclairs you learned to make with the pastry book.

Gaston Lenôtre

INTRODUCTION

Difficulty of the Recipes

Before choosing a recipe, you will know how difficult it is by consulting the following symbols placed after the name of each recipe in this book:

One chef's hat: This recipe is easy and can be made by a beginner.

Two chef's hats: This recipe is more elaborate, but most cooks should have few problems with it.

Three chef's hats: This recipe is more difficult and might not turn out if you are making it for the first time; it requires more skill and experience than the others, but don't be discouraged.

The Presentation of the Recipes and Illustrations

Each chapter starts with a list of the recipes it contains. This is followed by general comments concerning utensils, ingredients, and basic procedures used in that chapter.

The numerous photographs throughout the book show the desserts in finished as well as in preparatory stages. This should make certain techniques easier to understand. When the photo can be of help, there is a reference to it.

Preparation Times

The preparation time given at the beginning of each recipe takes into account *only* the time necessary to prepare that recipe itself, *not* the time it takes to prepare basic preparations that might be called for in the list of ingredients. It is advisable, therefore, that you prepare your basic ingredients (28° Sugar Syrup, Vanilla Ice Cream, pastry for pastry-based desserts, and so on) well in advance.

Cross Index of Basic Ingredients and Preparations

This index will help you decide what you can make with the ingredients you have available. For example, if you like pineapple, you will find under *Pineapple* all the recipes that use it: Molded Hawaiian Dessert, Champagne-Raspberry Sundae, Candied Pineapple Wedges, Gâtines Style Chocolate Truffles, and so on. Or if you prepared a lot of Nougatine Crumble, you can quickly find recipes that use it by looking under the heading *Nougatine Crumble*.

Storing

Frozen desserts and confectionery can usually be kept for several days, sometimes weeks, depending on the particular preparation involved. Since these are ideal things to prepare in advance, precise advice on storing is given after each recipe.

Utensils

In general, it is suggested that you use utensils made of either stainless steel or (for containers used in storing) plastic. All the other metals are corroded to some extent by the acids contained in many fruits. A list and accompanying photo of suggested utensils to be used are shown on pages xviii and xix.

Since the utensils for ice creams and other frozen desserts are completely different from those used in confectionery, specific comments are made at the beginning of each chapter regarding the utensils needed and their use.

Dictionary of Terms

A dictionary of terms and procedures has been included which not only defines certain cooking terms but also discusses problem utensils and ingredients (bain-marie, crème fraîche, egg size, butter, etc.). For best results, read the dictionary before doing any recipes. That way you will be familiar with the terms and will have no problem following the directions given.

DICTIONARY OF TERMS
Compiled for this translation by Philip and Mary Hyman

Bain-marie: This is a French term used when a substance in one container is placed in another which contains hot water for cooking. The effect is that produced by using a double boiler. It is a procedure that is always used when melting chocolate. Certain other preparations, such as parfaits flavored with alcohol, rely on it as well. Because ingredients are often mixed into the substance that was heated in the *bain-marie*, it is frequently more convenient to use than a double boiler. For this reason it is advisable to have several metal mixing bowls of different sizes that you can use to make your own *bain-marie* by placing them over a saucepan of water for heating.

Bowls: Generally speaking, mixing bowls can be made of virtually anything, but in making ice creams and confectionery, stainless steel, flat-bottomed bowls, such as the one pictured on page xix, are best. They heat and cool more quickly than glass, china, or earthenware would, which makes them ideal for use in a *bain-marie* or in an ice bath when the warming or chilling of a mixture is called for.

Whenever a large bowl is needed in this book, this will mean that when filled almost to the brim the bowl will hold 2 quarts (2 liters); a medium bowl holds 1½ quarts (1½ liters); and a small bowl holds 1 quart (1 liter).

Butter: Only the best unsalted butter should be used in these recipes. No substitutes for butter should ever be used. When butter is "softened" (or soft), this means that it is just soft enough to squeeze easily (usually an hour out of the refrigerator is sufficient).

Chestnut Cream and Chestnut Paste: Chestnut cream is made from fresh chestnuts, peeled and boiled with milk, sugar, and a little vanilla, and then mashed to form a sweet thick cream. It is sold in some specialty shops. In French it is called *crème de marrons*.

Chestnut paste (*pâte de marrons* in French) is a similar preparation, but it is much more compact than chestnut cream, being closer to the consistency of almond paste. It is generally less available than chestnut cream. Chestnut cream can sometimes be used instead of chestnut paste; this usually involves adjusting the measurements of the ingredients with which it is mixed, otherwise the resulting mixture will be too soft. (These adjustments are indicated in recipes where this substitution can be made.)

Crème fraîche: Crème fraîche is nothing more than natural heavy (whipping) cream in which the lactic acid is allowed to act until the cream thickens almost to the consistency of mayonnaise. Pasteurization prevents this reaction from taking place. In almost all recipes calling for crème fraîche, heavy cream can be used with equally good results. The choice of one over the other is basically one of taste, crème fraîche having a taste vaguely reminiscent of hazelnuts. Good, fresh crème fraîche does not have a sour taste, although it will eventually turn into "sour cream" if allowed to sit long enough.

If desired, 1 cup of crème fraîche can be made in the following way:

INGREDIENTS   1 cup fresh heavy (whipping) cream
2 tablespoons buttermilk

MAKING THE CREAM   Place the cream in a saucepan, stir in the buttermilk and heat until lukewarm to the touch—82 to 86°F (28 to 30°C) on a yoghurt thermometer. Allow to stand in a warm place—about 75°F (24°C)—for approximately 6 to 10 hours. The crème fraîche is ready when it is quite thick on top but liquid underneath—this will be discovered by stirring. Do not let the crème thicken too much at this stage or it will sour. When the crème has reached this stage, place it in a jar, stir it, cover the jar, and place in the refrigerator for at least 6 hours before using. The crème will thicken when it is chilled.

To Store: Crème fraîche will keep refrigerated for about 1 week before it starts to go sour.

Eggs: *All* the eggs used in this book should be medium. They should weigh approximately 1¾ ounces (49 g) each or 21 ounces (596 g) a dozen. Since actual egg sizes may vary slightly, it is a good idea to first measure the volume of the eggs. If broken into a measuring cup, one beaten egg of medium size measures a scant ¼ cup (50 m*l*). If eggs of this size are not used, the measurements for eggs given in these recipes will have to be adjusted accordingly.

Egg Whites: Egg whites may be refrigerated (or frozen) for later use. If they start to go bad, they have an unpleasant odor that is easily recognizable. For these recipes, 1 egg white equals 2½ tablespoons; 5 egg whites equal ¾ cup (155 g).

Egg whites are often beaten "until stiff." This means that the egg whites peak, and when held upright on the end of a beater or whisk, the peaks do not fall over. Egg whites should be beaten just before they are to be used; they have to be folded into other ingredients rather than beaten in. (See Fold.)

Flan Rings: These are thin, smooth, metal circles of differing heights and diameters, used mainly by professional bakers in France for making tarts and tartlets. They can also be used in making certain frozen desserts and frozen soufflés. Cardboard rings can easily be made to size by cutting a band of the necessary dimensions (indicated in specific recipes), wrapping it around the pastry base or the soufflé mold to be used, and taping the ends in place. The cardboard used for this should be perfectly smooth, quite thin, and pliable enough to be formed into a circle with no problem.

Flour: Either all-purpose or pastry flour may be used in the pastry recipes included in this book. *All measurements are for flour as it comes from the package.* If you wish to sift the flour, do so after measuring. (See Weights and Measures.) If preferred, a combination of all-purpose and pastry flour may be used instead of one alone.

Fold: This word is used primarily in connection with egg whites that have been beaten until very stiff, although it is also used with reference to whipped cream; when either of these preparations is to be mixed with other ingredients, it is "folded in." This requires the use of a flat, wooden spatula. Once the egg whites or whipped cream are in the same bowl as the ingredients they are to be mixed with, use the spatula to "cut" into the middle of the egg whites and scoop up or fold over half of the egg whites or cream onto the other half. Do this several times, turning the bowl as you do so. The cutting and folding should be done as carefully and quickly as possible. The airiness of the egg white or cream should not be lost nor should there be any unmixed particles in the final mixture, which should be perfectly homogenous.

Orange-Flower Water: This is a fragrant liquid produced by distilling orange blossoms. It is always used in very small doses and can be found in specialty shops. (It is often used in North African and Middle Eastern as well as in French cooking.) If orange-flower water is unavailable, vanilla extract, though completely different in taste, may be used instead if the recipe does not already call for vanilla in one form or another. Orange-flower water is not indispensable; it can be omitted altogether from most recipes without really harming the result.

Parchment Paper: Specially treated, nonstick parchment paper is often used in Lenôtre's recipes. When used as the surface on which to set partially finished candies, waxed paper can be used instead. When used in baking, the baking sheet can either be buttered or buttered and floured instead. In the latter case, instructions are given with the specific recipes.

Pastry Bag: Pastry bags are either plasticized (for easy cleaning) or made of cloth. Several different-sized pastry bags and a complete set of nozzles are indispensable for decorating certain frozen desserts and making certain chocolates. To fill the bag (it is easier if two people do this), place the nozzle in the bag, then bend the bag just above the nozzle by placing the nozzle on its side on a table and lifting the open end of the bag upward, perpendicular to the nozzle. This will prevent the cream or batter from coming out the nozzle as you fill the bag. When the bag is in this position, spoon the cream or batter into it.

When squeezing the batter onto a baking sheet, it is best to hold the nozzle with one hand, very close to, but not touching, the baking sheet. If filling paper cases in making chocolates, make sure the nozzle is pointing straight into the middle of the paper case at the beginning, otherwise the case will tip over. (The cream can then be squeezed in a decorative spiral as the case becomes full.) Squeeze the batter or cream out as evenly as possible with the hand not holding the nozzle. Squeeze very hard only toward the very end, when the bag appears to be empty—there is usually batter or cream left just behind the nozzle. Never use a syringe-type decorator instead of a pastry bag—the results could be disastrous.

Powdered (ground) almonds: Powdered almonds are what one would think they are—almonds that have been ground to a powder. Sold commercially in France, they are more difficult to obtain in the United States. Almonds can be powdered in a food processor or blender—they will generally be somewhat pasty when freshly ground because of the oil in them. Before grinding them, peel them as described in Recipe 171 for Almond Paste or simply use blanched almonds. Once ground, spread them out in a shallow dish and place in an oven at low heat for 1 to 2 hours—or leave them in a warm, dry place overnight. When dry, store the powdered almonds in a covered jar in a kitchen cabinet.

Ribbon: This term is used when a batter falls from a spoon or whisk in a smooth stream and piles up on itself like a ribbon before sinking into the rest of the batter.

Spatula: There are four kinds of spatulas used in this book.

The first (pictured on page xix) is a long, metal, flexible-blade spatula, used mainly for smoothing the surface of various preparations.

The second is a straight-edged, wooden spatula, used in making jams and fruit jellies for stirring and scraping along the bottom of a saucepan during cooking to keep the preparation from sticking.

The third is an ordinary wooden spatula, with a rounded end, used for folding beaten egg whites or whipped cream into various other ingredients. This type of spatula is often used as one would use a wooden spoon.

The fourth is a flexible rubber or plastic spatula, used for scraping creams, chocolate, and so on, out of mixing bowls to ensure that there is no waste.

Sugar Coffee Beans: These are candy coffee beans consisting of a hollow, hard, sugar shell filled with a coffee-flavored liquid. If these are not available from a confectionary supply house, a small raisin may be used for a different, but satisfying effect. For a more "exotic" taste, the raisins can be soaked for a ½ hour in rum and then patted dry in a towel before being used.

Thermometer: There are two types of thermometers called for in this book.

The first is a candy thermometer, used in making jams, certain candies, and any other preparation where cooking sugar is involved. It must be able to withstand temperatures as high as 392°F (200°C) without breaking.

The second is a yoghurt thermometer, used in controlling the temperature of melted chocolate and fondant. Any thermometer with a range of about 50 to 212°F (10 to 100°C) can be used. The important thing is that the middle range should fall between 75 and 95°F (24 and 35°C).

Unsweetened Cocoa Powder: This is also labeled as cocoa, pure cocoa, or bitter cocoa powder depending on the brand; it is always one hundred percent cocoa—no sugar added.

Weights and Measures: The exact gram weights have been retained in parentheses in this book. Scales are inevitably more accurate than cups and tablespoons. When measuring in cups, the ingredients should never be packed in unless specifically indicated. The cup should be filled and shaken gently *only* to level the ingredient so that the measurement can be read easily. Ingredients such as fondant or butter should be placed in the cup so that no air bubbles or pockets remain, and should be pressed until flat across the top. All spoon or cup measurements are level unless otherwise indicated. In referring to tablespoons or teaspoons, *generous* means that the contents of the spoon form a mound rather than being level with the edge of the spoon. *Scant* means that the spoon is not quite full but approaches the measurement given. When applied to cup measurements, *generous* means that the contents of the cup are to come slightly above the line indicating the measurement given but never more than 1 liquid ounce (⅛ cup) above it. *Scant* means that the contents are below the measurement given, but no more than 1 liquid ounce (⅛ cup) below it.

Whiten: When sugar is beaten with butter or egg yolks until very pale yellow, the mixture is said "to whiten." This term is often used in conjunction with the term "form a ribbon." (See Ribbon.)

Zest: This is a term used in connection with citrus fruits. The zest of an orange or lemon is the very thin, colored part of the peel, which can be removed either with a special utensil called a zester or with an ordinary vegetable peeler. The zest *never* includes the thick, whitish part of the peel.

The zest is used as a flavoring in several recipes. It is used either in strips and infused with a liquid or by being removed and finely chopped or else grated off the fruit with a fine-holed vegetable grater.

If orange or lemon *peel* is called for, this means the entire peel including the thick white part. The whole peel is used notably in making Half-Candied Orange Peel (Recipe 167).

SUGGESTED UTENSILS

UTENSILS PICTURED

1 Scale
2 Plastic cup cake or baba cases
3 Metal frame with movable "ruler"
4 Flan ring
5 Tartlet ring
6 Ice cream scoop (3 tablespoon capacity)
7 Wooden spoon
8 Metal mixing bowl
9 Round metal nozzles
   $\frac{1}{16}$ to ¾ inch (2 mm to 2 cm)
10 Star-shaped nozzle
11 Skimmer
12 Stainless steel wire whisk
13 Stainless steel pot
14 Timer
15 Plastic ice cream mold (square)
16 Plastic molds for frozen desserts (round)
17 Plastic molds for ice cream on a stick
18 Electric grater
19 Flexible-blade, metal spatula
20 Sieve
21 Pastry brush
22 Jam jar with screw-on lid
23 Sugar dredger
24 Electric mixer with several speeds
25 Food processor with blades
26 Rolling pin
27 Traditional ice–salt ice cream freezer
28 Freezer compartment ice cream freezer
29 Drum sieve
30 Candy thermometer
31 Measuring cup

UTENSILS NOT PICTURED

Soufflé molds
Plastic containers with covers for storage
Individual paper cases
(for serving candies and chocolates)
Electric juice extracter (juicer)
Deep freezer
Plastic scraper
Serrated knife
Sharp kitchen knife
Cookie cutter 1½ inch (4 cm) in diameter
Oven
Cake rack
Ladle
Cake pan 8 inches (20 cm) in diameter
Rectangular cake pan
8 × 12 inches (20 × 30 cm)
Madeleine mold
Food mill
Nonstick parchment paper
Cutting board
Pastry bag
Refrigerator
Straight edged, wooden spatula
Wooden spatula
Flexible rubber or plastic spatula
Yoghurt thermometer
Zester or vegetable peeler

GENERAL COMMENTS ON FROZEN DESSERTS

Choosing an Ice Cream Freezer

The perfect ice cream freezer for home use has yet to be invented, nevertheless great progress has been made in recent years, and if the public continues to demand improvements, manufacturers may work more energetically to solve the problems associated with these appliances.

There are basically two types of ice cream freezers: those that are placed directly into the freezer compartment of a refrigerator or deep freezer and then turned on to freeze the ice cream; and those bucket-like ice cream freezers that rely on ice and salt to freeze the contents of a metal canister placed in the bucket. The small ice cream freezers that are placed in the freezer compartment are appealing in many respects, but they will never produce the smooth, creamy, ice cream that can be made in the traditional ice–salt type ice cream freezer. Some freezer-cooled ice cream machines have dashers that are both too small and too light and will often lift out of the ice cream as it begins to thicken but has not finished freezing. Other machines avoid this problem but do not have a strong enough motor to keep turning as the ice cream stiffens, and the machine stops long before the ice cream is really thick. The worst machines of this type simply run for hours and, because of the heat of the machine's small motor, never freeze the ice cream or sherbet at all.

So, in general, these small, attractive machines all have disadvantages that make them undesirable compared to the traditional ice–salt freezers. To use these small machines, you often have to limit yourself to the specially conceived recipes that are suggested by their manufacturers, precisely because they are the most likely to freeze successfully in the appliance in question. This limits the variety and type of ice creams you can make, and often the best ice creams and sherbets simply won't work in this type of freezer. To make the recipes in this book, and for all ice cream and sherbet making in general, I advise the reader to pay the price of a traditional ice–salt-type ice cream freezer which will certainly cost more than the freezer compartment-type, but the result is excellent ice cream well worth the expense.

There are several versions of the ice–salt-cooled ice cream freezer on the market today. All consist of a bucket, made of wood or plastic, into which a tall metal canister is placed that holds the ice cream or sherbet. Inside the canister are the dashers which are the height of the canister itself, ensuring that all the ice cream or sherbet is evenly mixed as it is being frozen. These machines can be worked by hand but are generally powered by a motor placed either underneath or above the bucket. These ice cream freezers come in various sizes ranging from 2 to 20 quarts. For general home use the 2-quart (half-gallon) size is perfectly sufficient. Those who want to can still buy hand-cranked ice cream freezers, but, nostalgia aside, there is no reason to prefer them to their motor-operated cousins which make superb ice cream and require no physical exertion. I remember, as a young apprentice, pounding the ice and turning the crank on many an occasion when I first helped cater dinner parties. The ice cream had to be frozen while the dinner was being served, and when it was time for dessert, the ice cream was ready and served creamy and soft from the freezer—it was excellent. Today the same result can be achieved with motor-driven machines, and the ice cream can be prepared in advance and kept in the freezer compartment of the refrigerator until wanted.

Recently I have found that those machines with the motor placed underneath the ice bucket offer certain advantages to the more familiar freezer with the motor on top. This is because the motor is further removed from the canister containing the ice cream, and since the motor heats as it runs, this is an important consideration. More important, however, is the fact that in order to check the consistency of the ice cream as it stiffens inside the canister, you have to remove the motor from on top of the classic freezer, whereas in this case you simply remove the top of the canister on these machines with the motor placed underneath the bucket. In fact, at least one manufacturer has gone one step further and not only placed the motor underneath the bucket but made a clear plastic top for the canister so that you can see the ice cream as it freezes and never need to turn off the motor to tell if the ice cream has finished freezing (it's very pretty to watch as well).

Another improvement has been to make the bucket itself large enough to hold whole ice cubes, which can be piled around the canister, rather than having to use ice that has been coarsely crushed to a certain size (see comments on the use of the ice cream freezer).

Finally, although machines with wooden buckets and dashers are attractive and will always have a certain nostalgic appeal, there is no practical advantage to using them, while plastic buckets and dashers are in fact much easier to clean and equally efficient.

Using the Ice Cream Freezer

Here we are concerned only with the ice–salt-type ice cream freezer recommended in the preceding section. The comments that follow apply to all ice–salt-cooled freezers.

For the 2-quart (half-gallon) size freezer, which is recommended for most people, you will need four to six ordinary-sized trays of ice cubes. Always have plenty of ice on hand when you are planning to make ice cream or sherbet. Prepare the ice cream or sherbet mixture as described in the individual recipes and make sure that it is perfectly cold before pouring it into the canister for freezing.

2

Never pour a warm cream into the canister since this will take much too long to freeze, and all the ice will melt before the ice cream or sherbet is ready. The colder the ingredients that go into the canister, the sooner the ice cream will be frozen.

When the ice cream or sherbet is ready to go into the canister, remove the ice from the trays. Wear rubber gloves when working with the ice, since the cold ice will "burn" your fingers. Measure the salt that is to be mixed with the ice. Manufacturers' instructions vary on the use of salt, the kind, and the amount, but I recommend using only coarse salt (coarse sea salt, rock, bay, or kosher). Too much salt makes the ice cream or sherbet freeze too quickly, making it grainy, and too little makes it freeze too slowly. Generally speaking, it is better for the ice cream to freeze slowly rather than to try and speed things up and freeze it too quickly. I recommend using about two handfuls (3 tablespoons) of coarse salt for each tray of ice cubes, which means that a total of eight to twelve handfuls (approximately 1 cup) of coarse salt will be needed for the ice used with a 2-quart (half-gallon) ice cream freezer.

If your ice cream freezer has a bucket large enough to accommodate whole ice cubes in between the sides of the bucket and the canister, you can fill the canister with the cold sherbet or ice cream mixture, place it in the bucket, lock it into place and start filling the bucket with the ice cubes and salt. It should be noted that if the ice cubes are wrapped in a dish towel or piece of canvas as described below and hit just a few times with a rolling pin to break some of the pieces so that not all the ice cubes are whole and smooth, the ice cream will freeze more quickly than if only whole ice cubes are used. Place the ice in the bucket in about four layers, and sprinkle each layer with three handfuls (4½ tablespoons) of salt. When finished, the ice should come to the top of the canister. Most canisters have tops that close tightly, but some have holes in the top, and great care must be taken not to let any salt get into the canister. Once the ice and salt have been placed in the bucket around the canister, plug in the machine; the freezing time for the ice cream or sherbet now begins.

If the ice cream freezer is one that will not hold whole ice cubes, the ice must be coarsely crushed. Wear rubber gloves and use a large piece of canvas and a rolling pin to do this. Wrap the ice cubes in the canvas, making sure they are completely enclosed, and then pound them with the rolling pin until all the ice has been crushed to about the size of hazelnuts. Do not crush the ice too fine or it will melt too quickly and no longer be cold enough to freeze the ice cream. When the ice has been crushed, use it to fill the bucket as described for using whole ice cubes.

Depending on the temperature and consistency of the ingredients as they go into the canister, the freezing times for ice creams and sherbets can vary. Also important are the amount of salt used and the model of ice cream freezer employed. In any case, when the ice cream or sherbet thickens and then stiffens toward the end of the freezing time, the motor of the machine will begin to labor. Some machines have motors that will turn off automatically when the ice cream has finished freezing, but it is always better to watch the consistency of the ice cream or sherbet yourself and stop the motor when the ice cream looks ready. In general, ice creams and sherbets take from 20 to 40 minutes to

3

freeze—if it takes less than 20 minutes, there is too much salt in the ice–salt mixture in the bucket, and the resulting ice cream or sherbet will be grainy or icy. If it takes longer than 45 to 50 minutes, there is not enough salt. With practice, you will be able to adjust the amount of ice and salt to best suit your machine. Also, watch the level of ice in the bucket; if it drops below the level of the ice cream mixture in the canister, add more ice to the bucket and sprinkle in a little more salt as well.

When the ice cream or sherbet has finished freezing, it should be smooth and creamy, but stiff enough to have begun piling up and clinging, almost in a block, to the length of the dashers. It should be consistent enough to barely hold its shape when spooned but soft enough to "pour" in a thick mass into the mold or container in which it will be stored. Ice cream or sherbet can be served as it comes from the ice cream freezer, but it is generally softer at this stage than most people prefer. It is therefore best to make the ice cream well in advance, and then to mold it and keep it in the freezing compartment of a refrigerator to harden before serving (see *Turning Out and Serving Ice Creams, Sherbets, and Frozen Desserts*).

Once the ice cream has finished freezing, it should be poured into a mold (see *Ice Cream Molds*) that has been kept in the freezer while the ice cream or sherbet was being made. Unplug the ice cream freezer, unlock the canister, and remove it from the bucket. Carefully wipe off the ice water from the outside of the canister (the water is salty). Open the canister, remove the dasher, and with the aid of a spoon or wooden spatula, pour the ice cream or sherbet into the cold mold. If specific amounts of ice cream or sherbet are needed (see the recipes for Molded Desserts, etc.), measure them at this time. Generally, recipes call for a pint (½ quart or ½ liter) of ice cream or sherbet, so the simplest way to "measure" the ice cream is to pour it into ½-quart (½-liter) molds. Certain recipes call for other amounts, however; in these cases the ice cream should be poured from the canister into a measuring cup and then placed in a mold for storage. Label the mold, which will be only partially filled, so that you know how much ice cream is in it and what kind it is. Once the molds have been filled, press the ice cream or sherbet into it with a spoon if air pockets are visible, and tap the mold gently on the bottom. Then cover the mold and place it in the freezer.

Clean the ice cream freezer immediately after use, following the manufacturer's instructions.

Ice Cream Molds

The ice cream mold should be placed in the freezer compartment of the refrigerator while the ice cream is being made, and the ice cream or sherbet should be molded as soon as it comes from the ice cream freezer.

There are many different ice cream molds available; most are made of metal (stainless steel, tinned steel, or aluminum), but professionals in France store ice cream in discardable plastic molds that are easy to use and very inexpensive. When available, these plastic molds are preferable for home use as well. Ice cream molds can be almost any shape, but, in general, the square one is most commonly employed. All ice cream molds come with a cover, and the molded ice cream must always be kept covered in the freezer. If the ice cream or sherbet is to be turned out and served, you can mold it into any shape you like, but if it is simply being stored in a mold, it is preferable to use sized molds that are easy to scoop from and are graduated into easily recognizable quantities. For this reason, you should have square molds in different sizes for storing ice cream and sherbets. Generally a quart (liter) of ice cream or sherbet is stored in two ½-quart (½-liter) molds if it is later to be scooped or molded with another flavor. Consult the recipes using the ice cream or sherbet in question and mold the ice cream or sherbet so that when needed you will have the appropriate amount. The 1-quart (1-liter) molds are best if the ice cream or sherbet is to be served alone. You should also have some ½-pint (¼-liter) molds handy when there is a small amount of ice cream or sherbet you want to save. *Always measure ice cream or sherbet as it comes from the ice cream freezer and label the mold with the date made, the flavor, and the quantity.*

Ice cream molds are always stored with the top up, and they must be kept in a deep freezer or freezing compartment of a refrigerator, as described in the following section.

Note: If ice cream molds are unavailable, ordinary plastic containers with tops may be used instead, for either storing or molding ice creams or sherbets.

Storing Ice Creams, Sherbets, and Frozen Desserts

Ice creams, sherbets, and frozen desserts are generally stored in closed molds. The freezer must be kept at a temperature that is always at 0°F (-18°C) or less. Ice creams and frozen desserts can be kept in the freezer for 2 to 3 weeks if they are stored in closed molds. Sherbets and parfaits do not keep as well, and it is preferable to serve them no later than 2 weeks after they have been placed in the freezer. Never store sherbet-filled fruits (with the exception of pineapple) for any length of time in the freezer, since the bitterness of the peel affects the taste of the sherbet after 24 hours.

Turning Out and Serving Ice Creams, Sherbets, and Frozen Desserts

Once an ice cream, sherbet, or frozen dessert has been completely hardened in the freezer, it must be turned out and allowed to soften before being served or softened in the mold if being served in scoops. The time necessary to soften the ice cream or sherbet to the proper consistency for serving varies depending on the size and shape of the mold used for storing and the nature of the ice cream or sherbet in question. Generally speaking, the dessert should be taken from the freezer and placed in the refrigerator for 30 to 40 minutes before being served. In the refrigerator the dessert will soften slowly all the way through, whereas leaving it at room temperature would mean that the outside would melt quickly and the inside remain frozen. If you have placed the dessert in the refrigerator at the beginning or midway through a meal, let it sit for 15 to 20 minutes, and then check it periodically by inserting a knife into the center of the dessert. As soon as the knife goes in easily, the dessert is ready to serve. If the dessert softens too quickly, place it back in the freezer, and if it has not softened enough, leave it *but only for a short time* at room temperature. Once the dessert has softened enough, serve it immediately.

To turn out molded desserts, start at least ½ hour before you intend to place the dessert in the refrigerator to soften. Be sure to have the serving platter ready. First, fill a large bowl with barely lukewarm water. If using a discardable plastic mold, dip the mold in the water so that the water comes all the way up the sides of the mold *but not over the top edges*. It is advisable to remove the top of the mold before doing this. Hold the mold in the water for about 5 seconds. Then lift it out of the water and wipe off the bottom and sides of the mold. Turn the mold upside down over the platter, holding it as close to the platter as possible. With your fingers, pull out on opposite sides of the flexible mold to separate them from the ice cream or sherbet—if necessary rotate the mold and pull out on the other two sides as well—while pressing on the bottom of the mold with your thumbs to push the dessert out of the mold and onto the platter.

If using a metal mold, dip it into the water as described above, but hold it there for 10 seconds. Then lift the mold out of the water, wipe it dry, and run the blade of a knife between the side of the mold and the dessert, all around the mold. Place the platter upside down over the ice cream or sherbet, hold it in place, and then with a quick motion turn everything over as a unit. Shake the mold and platter in quick jerks from side to side and up and down. The dessert should slide from the mold and onto the platter. Lift the mold off. If the ice cream or sherbet sticks to the mold, lift the mold off the platter and turn it on its side. Give two or three very hard whacks with the heel of your hand against the side of the mold facing up, then rapidly turn the mold upside down over the platter, shaking it in little jerks to make the dessert fall onto the platter. Hold the mold as close to the platter as possible when doing this so that the ice cream doesn't have far to fall.

Whether using a plastic or metal mold, the turned-out dessert should be placed immediately back into the freezer so that the outside, which will have begun to melt, can harden again.

After it has been back in the freezer for at least 30 minutes, soften the dessert in the refrigerator as described earlier. Test it with a knife as described—the hole left in the ice cream or sherbet can easily be smoothed over with the back of a spoon.

Some frozen desserts are molded in a flan ring or by using a strip of cardboard to make a border inside which the dessert is built up. If a metal flan ring is used, rub it lightly with a sponge that has been dipped in hot water and then squeezed to remove any excess water. Be careful not to get any water on the dessert itself—the sponge should still be quite moist. Go all the way around the ring with the sponge and then lift the ring off. If a cardboard band was used, simply untape the ends of the band and peel it off.

Once an ice cream, sherbet, or frozen dessert is at room temperature, it will quickly begin to melt. Some desserts melt faster than others, but the general rule is to leave the dessert at room temperature the shortest time possible before serving. Keep desserts in the refrigerator for softening, leaving them at room temperature only while serving, then replace them in the freezer as soon as possible if there is any left.

Notes on Decorating

If the decorating instructions call for the use of a pastry bag, flexible-blade spatula, or other utensils, place these in the freezer for at least 15 minutes before they are needed. The dessert should be softened in the refrigerator before being decorated, unless otherwise indicated in the individual recipe. Once the dessert has been decorated, place it back in the freezer for about 15 minutes before serving. Certain desserts, however, are served immediately after being decorated; this is the case notably for those decorated with fresh or poached fruit, various sauces, or Chantilly cream.

Chapter 1

SHERBETS AND GRANITÉS

RECIPES

1. 28° Sugar Syrup (Sirop à 28° Baumé)
2. Apricot Sherbet I (Sorbet aux Abricots Frais)
3. Apricot Sherbet II (Sorbet aux Abricots au Sirop)
4. Pineapple Sherbet (Sorbet à l'Ananas au Sirop)
5. Banana Sherbet (Sorbet à la Banane)
6. Black Currant Sherbet (Sorbet au Cassis)
7. Lemon Sherbet (Sorbet au Citron)
8. Lime Sherbet (Sorbet au Citron Vert)
9. Orange or Tangerine Sherbet (Sorbet à l'Orange ou à la Mandarine)
10. Strawberry Sherbet (Sorbet aux Fraises)
11. Raspberry Sherbet (Sorbet aux Framboises)
12. Passion Fruit Sherbet (Sorbet aux Fruits de la Passion)
13. Red Currant Sherbet (Sorbet aux Groseilles)
14. Mango Sherbet (Sorbet aux Mangues)
15. Melon Sherbet (Sorbet au Melon)
16. Grapefruit Sherbet (Sorbet au Pamplemousse)
17. Peach Sherbet I (Sorbet aux Pêches Fraîches)
18. Peach Sherbet II (Sorbet aux Pêches au Sirop)

9

19. Pear Sherbet I (Sorbet aux Poires de Conserve Maison) ♨
20. Pear Sherbet II (Sorbet aux Poires au Sirop) ♨
21. Calvados Sherbet (Sorbet au Calvados) ♨
22. Champagne Sherbet (Sorbet au Champagne) ♨
23. Apple Cider Sherbet (Sorbet au Cidre) ♨
24. Port Sherbet (Sorbet au Porto) ♨
25. Coffee Granité (Granité au Café) ♨
26. Tea Granité (Granité au Thé) ♨

1
28° Sugar Syrup (Sirop à 28° Baumé)

This syrup, used in all sherbets, is called "28° sugar syrup," referring to its density on the Baumé scale (see Note). The technicalities need not concern most readers; what is important is to follow the instructions to the letter.

PREPARATION   5 minutes

INGREDIENTS   *For 6⅔ cups (1½ l) of 28° Sugar Syrup*
                   5 cups (1 kg) granulated sugar
                   4¼ cups (1 *l*) water

UTENSILS   Large saucepan
                   Wooden spoon
                   Large bowl or jar

Making the Syrup: Place the water and sugar in a large saucepan. Place over high heat, stirring with a wooden spoon until the sugar has dissolved. Continue heating until the syrup comes to a full boil. Then immediately remove the saucepan from the heat and pour the syrup into a large bowl or the jar in which you wish to store it. Leave to cool completely before using.

To Store: Once the syrup has cooled completely, cover the jar in which it is to be stored and place it in the refrigerator. This sugar syrup keeps for months, and it is always a good idea to have a jar of it in the refrigerator ready.

Note: The density of this syrup is very important; what is generally called a "light" syrup is one with a low density, while a "heavy" syrup is one with a high density. When cooking sugar, a candy thermometer is used to measure the temperature, but when density is involved, measurements are made on a simple instrument called a *hydrometer*. A hydrometer is about the size and shape of an ordinary medical thermometer, but it is a bit longer and has an enlarged, weighted end. To use this instrument, the sugar syrup in question is poured into a small narrow beaker and the hydrometer is lowered gently into the syrup. The hydrometer is graduated on its stem with the various densities; once in the syrup, the density is read at the point the floatation line crosses the hydrometer. For years, density was expressed in Baumé degrees, but hydrometers have recently switched to a decimal density system, even though the Baumé degrees are still often referred to. The sugar syrup used in making sherbets in this book is consistently referred to as a 28° sugar syrup, although its density could also be expressed as 1.241 on the modern decimal scale. Since only one sugar syrup is used in this book, you do not need a hydrometer when making it. The recipe is accurate and simple enough so that a 28° sugar syrup is automatically produced if it is followed scrupulously.

2
Apricot Sherbert I
(Sorbet aux Abricots Frais)

PREPARATION	10 minutes
COOKING TIME	10 minutes
COOLING TIME	Approximately 20 minutes on ice before freezing
FREEZING TIME	20 to 40 minutes
INGREDIENTS	*For approximately 1 quart (1 l) of sherbet* Generous 1⅔ cups (4 d*l*) cold 28° Sugar Syrup (Recipe 1) 4 cups (500 g) pitted fresh apricot halves
UTENSILS	Medium saucepan Electric blender 2 mixing bowls Wooden spoon Ice cream freezer Mold

Making the Sherbet: Heat the sugar syrup in a saucepan, add the apricots, and simmer for 10 minutes; the liquid must not boil. Pour the contents of the saucepan into an electric blender and blend until smooth. Pour into a bowl and leave the mixture to cool completely before freezing. To speed chilling, stand the bowl containing the fruit puree in another bowl filled with ice and water. Stir constantly and renew the ice water when necessary.

To Freeze: Once cold, pour the apricot puree into the ice cream freezer. Then freeze, mold, and serve (see pages 2 to 6).

3
Apricot Sherbet II
(Sorbet aux Abricots au Sirop)

(Photo page 17)

Apricot Sherbet I, made with fresh apricots, is much better than sherbet made with canned apricots. Nevertheless, since canned apricots (preferably home canned as in Recipe 122) can produce interesting results and must necessarily replace the fresh fruit in winter, this recipe is given using canned fruit.

PREPARATION	5 minutes
FREEZING TIME	20 to 40 minutes
INGREDIENTS	*For approximately 1 quart (1 l) of sherbet* 1½ quart (1½ l) can or jar of pitted apricot halves in light syrup (Recipe 122) Generous ¾ cup (2 dl) cold 28° Sugar Syrup (Recipe 1) *For decoration* 20 canned apricot halves
UTENSILS	Colander Electric blender Ice cream freezer Mold

Making the Sherbet: Drain the fruit; save the syrup they were packed in for making candies (see Fruit Jellies, Recipes 144–165). Place 2½ cups (500 g) of the drained fruit in a blender and blend until smooth; there should be 2 generous cups (5 dl) of puree after blending. Add the sugar syrup to this puree.

To Freeze: If all the ingredients were quite cold before being blended and mixed, the sweetened puree may be placed immediately in the ice cream freezer. Then freeze, mold, and serve (see pages 2 to 6).

To Decorate: Once the sherbet has been turned out for serving, decorate the top and sides with canned apricot halves as shown in the photo.

4
Pineapple Sherbet
(Sorbet à l'Ananas au Sirop)

PREPARATION	15 minutes
FREEZING TIME	20 to 40 minutes
INGREDIENTS	*For approximately 1 quart (1 l) of sherbet*
	15 slices of canned pineapple in light syrup
	6½ tablespoons (1 dl) cold 28° Sugar Syrup (Recipe 1)
	2 teaspoons kirsch
	½ cup (100 g) diced Half-Candied Pineapple (Recipe 166)
UTENSILS	Colander
	Large mixing bowl
	Electric blender
	Sieve
	Spoon
	Ice cream freezer
	Mold

Making the Sherbet: Drain the canned pineapple in a colander. Save 1 generous cup (2.5 dl) of syrup for making the sherbet and put the remaining syrup in a jar for use in candy making (see Fruit Jellies, Recipes 144–165). Cut the pineapple into wedges. You will need 3¾ cups (750 g) of drained pineapple wedges, which should be placed in a blender and blended to a smooth puree. Work the puree through a sieve to eliminate all the fibrous parts of the pineapple; then measure the result. You need 2 generous cups (5 dl) of sieved puree for making the sherbet. Add the 28° Sugar Syrup and the reserved syrup from the can to the sieved pineapple puree, stir well together, and pour into the ice cream freezer.

To Freeze: Freezing time is approximately 20 to 40 minutes. About 10 minutes before the sherbet is finished freezing, add the kirsch. When the sherbet is done, remove the dasher from the freezer canister and stir in the pieces of candied pineapple. Then freeze, mold, and serve (see pages 2 to 6).

Serving Suggestions: Pineapple Sherbet can be molded and served with Vanilla Parfait or Banana Ice Cream (see Chapter 4, Combination Desserts).

Note: To make fresh pineapple sherbet, see the Note after Recipe 90 for Sherbet-Filled Pineapple Desserts.

5
Banana Sherbet
(Sorbet à la Banane)

PREPARATION	10 minutes
FREEZING TIME	20 to 40 minutes
INGREDIENTS	*For approximately 1 quart (1 l) of sherbet*
	1 pound 10½ ounces (750 g) bananas (4 to 6 bananas, depending on size)
	Scant 1⅓ cups (3 dl) cold 28° Sugar Syrup (Recipe 1)
	Juice of ½ lemon
	Generous ¾ cup (2 dl) noneffervescent mineral water
	2 teaspoons rum (preferably white)
UTENSILS	Food mill *or* food processor
	Large mixing bowl
	Spoon
	Ice cream freezer
	Mold

Making the Sherbet: Peel the bananas and grind them through a food mill or puree them in a food processor to make a smooth puree. Do not use an electric blender because it will make the puree too foamy and sticky. Measure the puree; you need a generous 1⅔ cups (4 dl) for making the sherbet.

In a large bowl, mix the puree with the cold sugar syrup, lemon juice, mineral water, and rum. Then pour into the ice cream freezer and freeze until ready, then mold and serve (see pages 2–6).

Serving Suggestions: Serve banana sherbet with Fresh Pineapple Sauce (Recipe 98) or Hot Chocolate Sauce (Recipe 101).

Banana sherbet can be used to make numerous combination desserts; it can be molded and served with Coconut Ice Cream, Rum Parfait, Peanut Butter Ice Cream, or Chocolate Ice Cream (see Chapter 4, Combination Desserts).

Black Currant Sherbet
(Sorbet au Cassis)

PREPARATION	10 minutes
FREEZING TIME	20 to 40 minutes
INGREDIENTS	*For approximately 1 quart (1 l) of sherbet* Generous 1⅔ cups (4 dl) fresh or frozen black currant puree (see Recipe 125 for making the puree and the Comment given below if frozen puree is used). Generous 1⅔ cups (4 dl) 28° Sugar Syrup (Recipe 1) 6½ tablespoons (1 dl) red currant juice—puree (Recipe 125) 1½ tablespoons Black Currant Liqueur (Recipe 128)
UTENSILS	Large mixing bowl Spoon Ice cream freezer Mold

Making the Sherbet: Mix all the ingredients in a bowl, pour into the ice cream freezer, and freeze 20 to 40 minutes (see page 2).

To Mold: To mold and serve, see pages 4 to 6.

Comment: As described on page 190, black currants can be immediately frozen for later use once they are pureed. If frozen puree is used, do *not* thaw it; rather take it from the freezer and place it directly in the blender. Blend until smooth; then combine with the other ingredients and pour into the ice cream freezer. Freezing time will probably be shorter when starting with a frozen puree.

Serving Suggestions: Serve this sherbet with Red Currant Sauce (see Fresh Fruit Sauces, Recipe 98) or Vanilla Sauce (Recipe 99).

   Black Currant Sherbet can be molded with Vanilla Ice Cream for a delicious combination dessert (see Recipe 68). Or simply serve it in scoops on plates, decorated with canned litchis cut in half, with a little red currant sauce spooned over.

Home Canned Apricots in Light Syrup, Recipe 122; Fresh Fruit Sauce, Recipe 98;
Apricot Jam, Recipe 132; Apricot Jellies, Recipe 145;
Apricot Sherbet Recipe 2

7
Lemon Sherbet
(Sorbet au Citron)

PREPARATION	10 minutes
FREEZING TIME	20 to 40 minutes
INGREDIENTS	*For making approximately 1 quart (1 l) of sherbet* 1 generous cup (¼ *l*) lemon juice (see Note) 1 generous cup (¼ *l*) noneffervescent mineral water Generous 1⅓ cups (4 d*l*) cold 28° Sugar Syrup (Recipe 1) 1 fresh egg white
UTENSILS	Sieve Small mixing bowl Wire whisk Ice cream freezer Mold

Making the Sherbet: Pour the lemon juice through a sieve directly into the ice cream freezer, add the mineral water and sugar syrup, and begin freezing (see page 2).

To Freeze: Freezing time is approximately 20 to 40 minutes. About 10 minutes before the sherbet has finished freezing (it should just be beginning to catch and thicken), stop the machine and take out 2 tablespoons of the sherbet mixture. Place this in a bowl with the egg white and whisk vigorously until the mixture becomes thick and foamy, then pour back into the ice cream freezer and finish freezing. The egg white makes the sherbet creamier. (Industrial sherbet almost never contains egg white since sherbets made this way don't keep as well.)

To Mold: To mold and serve, see pages 4 to 6.

Serving Suggestions: Lemon Sherbet can be molded to make combination desserts with Strawberry or Raspberry Sherbet or used to make Sherbet-Filled Fruit (Recipe 91). Served with orange juice, Lemon Sherbet becomes part of the Pré Catelan Sundae (Recipe 57); or scoops of Lemon Sherbet can simply be served on a plate and garnished with several slices of fresh kiwi fruit or guava.

Note: When squeezing the lemons, don't press too hard since the whitish inner skin can give a bitter taste to the juice if squeezed into it.

8
Lime Sherbet
(Sorbet au Citron Vert)

PREPARATION	10 minutes
FREEZING TIME	20 to 40 minutes
INGREDIENTS	*For approximately 1 quart (1 l) of sherbet* 6½ tablespoons (1 d*l*) lime juice 6½ tablespoons (1 d*l*) lemon juice Scant 1⅓ cups (3 d*l*) noneffervescent mineral water Scant 2 cups (4.5 d*l*) cold 28° Sugar Syrup (Recipe 1) 1 fresh egg white
UTENSILS	Sieve Small mixing bowl Wire whisk Ice cream freezer Mold

Making the Sherbet: Combine the lime and lemon juices. Pour the juices through a sieve directly into the ice cream freezer, add the mineral water and sugar syrup, and begin freezing (see page 2).

To Freeze: Freezing time is approximately 20 to 40 minutes. About 10 minutes before the sherbet has finished freezing (it should just be beginning to catch and thicken), stop the machine and take out 2 tablespoons of the sherbet mixture. Place this in a bowl with the egg white and whisk vigorously until the mixture becomes thick and foamy, then pour back into the ice cream freezer and finish freezing. The egg white makes the sherbet creamier. (Industrial sherbet almost never contains egg white since sherbets made this way don't keep as well.)

To Mold: To mold and serve, see pages 4 to 6.

Note: When squeezing the fruit, don't press too hard since the whitish inner skin can give a bitter taste to the juice if squeezed into it.

Orange or Tangerine Sherbet
(Sorbet à l'Orange ou à la Mandarine)

PREPARATION	20 minutes
FREEZING TIME	20 to 40 minutes
INGREDIENTS	*For approximately 1 quart (1 l) sherbet* 2 cups (225 g) sugar cubes 8 nontreated oranges *or* 16 nontreated tangerines, washed in warm water and dried ⅔ cup (1.5 d*l*) noneffervescent mineral water ½ lemon 1 egg white (optional)
UTENSILS	Saucepan Wooden spoon Orange squeezer Strainer Large mixing bowl Medium mixing bowl Ice cream freezer Wire whisk Mold

Making the Sherbet: Rub the sugar cubes one by one on the orange or tangerine skins until all the sides of each sugar cube have yellowed. Do not rub any orange or tangerine in one place too long, and do not rub down to the whitish inner skin which has a bitter taste.

Place the sugar cubes in a saucepan with the mineral water, bring to a boil, stirring constantly with a wooden spoon to dissolve the sugar; then, as soon as the water boils, remove the pot from the heat.

Squeeze the oranges or tangerines, as well as the ½ lemon, and measure their juice; you will need a total of 2¾ cups (6.5 d*l*) of juice for the sherbet. Once this has been measured, pour the juice through a strainer into the saucepan containing the dissolved sugar and water. Mix with a wooden spoon.

To Freeze: Cool the mixture by placing it in a bowl inside another bowl that has been filled with ice and water and stir until completely cold, renewing the ice water when necessary. Pour the mixture into the ice cream freezer and freeze (see page 2). About 10 minutes before the sherbet is finished (it will just have begun to catch and thicken), stop the freezer and remove 2 tablespoons of sherbet, place it in a bowl with 1 egg white, and beat with a wire whisk until thick and foamy. Pour this back into the ice cream freezer and finish freezing the sherbet (this step is optional).

To Mold: Mold and serve as described on pages 4 to 6.

10
Strawberry Sherbet
(Sorbet aux Fraises)

PREPARATION	10 minutes
FREEZING TIME	20 to 40 minutes
INGREDIENTS	*For approximately 1 quart (1 l) of sherbet* 2½ pints (600 g) fresh strawberries (see Comment) Scant 2 cups (4.5 dl) cold 28° Sugar Syrup (Recipe 1) 1 tablespoon lemon juice (optional)
UTENSILS	Colander Electric blender Spoon Ice cream freezer Mold

Making the Sherbet: Stem and rapidly rinse the strawberries under cold running water. Place them in a blender and blend to make a puree. Measure the puree; you need 2⅓ cups (5.5 dl) for making the sherbet.

Mix the puree with the sugar syrup and pour into the ice cream freezer. (Lemon juice may be added before freezing to heighten the taste of the strawberries.)

To Freeze: Then freeze, mold, and serve (see pages 2 to 6).

Serving Suggestions: Strawberries Coated with Fondant (Recipe 178) can be used to decorate the sherbet before serving.

Strawberry Sherbet can be molded to make delicious combination desserts with Vanilla Ice Cream or Lemon Sherbet; it is also used in making Frozen Strawberry Vacherin, Cantaloupe or Muskmelon Sundae, or Melba Tulip Cookie Desserts.

Comment: Frozen Strawberry Puree (Recipe 125) can be used instead of fresh strawberries. Do *not* allow it to thaw. Take it from the freezer and place it directly in a blender with the sugar syrup. When blended, pour into the ice cream freezer and freeze. Freezing time will be slightly shorter using frozen fruit puree.

11
Raspberry Sherbet
(Sorbet aux Framboises)

PREPARATION   10 minutes

FREEZING TIME   20 to 40 minutes

INGREDIENTS   *For approximately 1 quart (1 l) of sherbet*
                          2¼ pints (550 g) fresh raspberries (see Comment)
                          Scant 2 cups (4.5 dl) cold 28° Sugar Syrup (Recipe 1)

UTENSILS   Electric blender
                          Bowl
                          Spoon
                          Ice cream freezer
                          Mold

Making the Sherbet: Place the raspberries in a blender and blend to make a puree; you need 2 generous cups (5 dl) of puree for making the sherbet. Mix the puree with the sugar syrup and pour into the ice cream freezer; then mold and serve (see pages 2 to 6).

Serving Suggestions: Raspberry Sherbet can be molded to make combination desserts with Vanilla Ice Cream or any of the following sherbets: pineapple, peach, red currant, or champagne. It is used in making Frozen Raspberry Vacherin, Cantaloupe or Muskmelon Sundae, or Melba Tulip Cookie Desserts.

Comment: Frozen Raspberry Puree can be used instead of fresh raspberries. Do *not* allow it to thaw. Take it from the freezer and place it directly in a blender with the sugar syrup. When blended, pour into the ice cream freezer and freeze. Freezing time will be slightly shorter using frozen fruit puree.

12
Passion Fruit Sherbet
(Sorbet aux Fruits de la Passion)

PREPARATION	20 minutes
FREEZING TIME	20 to 40 minutes
INGREDIENTS	*For approximately 1 quart (1 l) of sherbet* 2¼ pounds (1 kg) Passion Fruit (see Comment) 2 generous cups (½ *l*) cold 28° Sugar Syrup (Recipe 1) 1 generous cup (¼ *l*) noneffervescent mineral water
UTENSILS	Serrated knife Spoon Food mill, drum sieve, *or* electric juicer Sieve Mixing bowl Spoon Ice cream freezer Mold

Making the Sherbet: Cut each fruit in half and scoop out all the pulp and seeds with a spoon. Either run the pulp through an electric juicer or work it through a food mill or drum sieve and strain out any bits of seed through a sieve. The strained pulp and juice from the fruit should measure 1 generous cup (¼ *l*). Pour this into a bowl and mix it with the sugar syrup and water. Then pour it into the ice cream freezer, freeze, mold, and serve (see pages 2 to 6).

Serving Suggestions: Serve with Fresh Pineapple Sauce (Recipe 98) or Champagne Sabayon Sauce (Recipe 103).

Passion Fruit Sherbet can also be molded and served with Coconut Ice Cream (see Chapter 4, Combination Desserts) or simply scooped and served garnished with slices of fresh kiwi fruit.

Comment: The best passion fruits are those with red pulp; those with yellow pulp tend to be slightly more acid, although either can be used for this recipe. Do not be put off by the shriveled appearance of the fruit—this is a sign that it is perfectly ripe.

13
Red Currant Sherbet
(Sorbet aux Groseilles)

PREPARATION	15 minutes
FREEZING TIME	20 to 40 minutes
INGREDIENTS	*For approximately 1 quart (1 l) of sherbet* 3 pints (750 g) fresh red currants (measured with stems) Generous 1⅔ cup (4 dl) cold 28° Sugar Syrup (Recipe 1)
UTENSILS	Food mill Spoon Bowl Ice cream freezer Mold

Making the Sherbet: Remove the stems from the currants and work the fruit through a food mill equipped with a fine grill. Measure the resulting pulp; you need 2 generous cups (½ l) for making the sherbet. Stir the sugar syrup into the pulp and pour into the ice cream freezer. Then freeze, mold, and serve (see pages 2 to 6).

Serving Suggestions: Serve with red currant jelly or a few fresh red currants.

   Red Currant Sherbet can be molded and served with Vanilla Ice Cream or Raspberry Sherbet and is part of the Loire Valley Sundae (Recipe 65).

14
Mango Sherbet
(Sorbet aux Mangues)

PREPARATION	15 minutes
FREEZING TIME	20 to 40 minutes
INGREDIENTS	*For approximately 1 quart (1 l) of sherbet* 3 to 4 ripe mangos, weighing a total of 1¾ pounds (800 g) (see Comment) Scant 1⅓ cups (3 d*l*) cold 28° Sugar Syrup (Recipe 1) Juice of 1 lime
UTENSILS	Paring knife Electric blender Spoon Mixing bowl Ice cream freezer Mold

Making the Sherbet: With a paring knife peel off the skin of the mangos; then cut the flesh off the seed. Place the mango pulp in a blender and blend to a smooth puree; measure the resulting puree. You need 2 generous cups (5 d*l*) for making the sherbet.

Place the pulp in a bowl and stir in the sugar syrup and lime juice. Then pour into the ice cream freezer and freeze (see page 2).

To Mold: To mold and serve, see pages 4 to 6.

Serving Suggestions: Serve with Vanilla Sauce (Recipe 99).

Comment: Only completely ripe mangos should be used; when ripe, a mango is soft to the touch and gives easily when pressed. Mangos make a delicious, creamy, apricot-colored sherbet.

15
Melon Sherbet
(Sorbet au Melon)

PREPARATION	15 minutes
FREEZING TIME	20 to 40 minutes
INGREDIENTS	*For approximately 1 quart (1 l) of sherbet*
	1 large or 2 medium-sized muskmelons or cantaloupes, weighing a total of 2 pounds 10¼ ounces (1.2 kg)
	Generous 1⅔ cups (4 d*l*) cold 28° Sugar Syrup (Recipe 1)
UTENSILS	Paring knife
	Electric blender
	Spoon
	Mixing bowl
	Ice cream freezer
	Mold

Making the Sherbet: Cut the melon(s) in half and remove the seeds and stringy parts from the center(s). Scoop out the pulp, place it in a blender, and blend to a smooth puree. Measure the puree; you need 2½ cups (6 d*l*) for making the sherbet. Mix the melon puree with the sugar syrup and pour into the ice cream freezer. Then freeze, mold, and serve (see pages 2 to 6).

Serving Suggestions: Serve molded with Apricot Sherbet (see Chapter 4, Combination Desserts).

16
Grapefruit Sherbet
(Sorbet au Pamplemousse)

PREPARATION	10 minutes
FREEZING TIME	20 to 40 minutes
INGREDIENTS	*For approximately 1 quart (1 l) of sherbet* 3 large grapefruits 1½ cups (3.6 d*l*) cold 28° Sugar Syrup (Recipe 1)
UTENSILS	Lemon or orange squeezer Sieve Spoon Mixing bowl Ice cream freezer Mold

Making the Sherbet: Cut each grapefruit in half and squeeze out all the juice. Measure the juice; you need 2½ cups (6 d*l*) for making the sherbet. Strain the juice through a sieve into a bowl, mix with the sugar syrup, and pour into the ice cream freezer. Then freeze, mold, and serve (see pages 2 to 6).

Serving Suggestions: Like orange and lemon sherbets, Grapefruit Sherbet can be served in the hollowed out skin of the fruit. To prepare the fruit cut the grapefruits in half. Be careful in squeezing the juice to get the maximum amount of juice without damaging the peel. Use the juice to make the sherbet if it has not been prepared in advance.

Remove the thin membranes that fill the center and are attached to the insides of the peel; then rub the inside of each peel with a sugar cube. Do the same with the top part of each fruit. Make sure the hollowed-out bottom peel will stand upright—if not, cut a thin slice off the base to make it flat and stable. Place the hollowed-out bottoms and tops in the freezer for at least an hour before filling them with sherbet.

Fill each peel, either using a spoon or (if the sherbet is soft enough) a pastry bag. For grapefruits each half is filled with sherbet (see photo, page 136). Place the dessert immediately back in the freezer until ready to serve. Serve within 12 hours.

17
Peach Sherbet I
(Sorbet aux Pêches Fraîches)

PREPARATION	15 minutes
FREEZING TIME	20 to 40 minutes
INGREDIENTS	*For approximately 1 quart (1 l) of sherbet*
	1¾ pound (800 g) fresh peaches
	Scant 1⅓ cups (3 d*l*) cold 28° Sugar Syrup (Recipe 1)
	Juice of ½ lemon
UTENSILS	Electric blender
	Sieve (optional)
	Spoon
	Mixing bowl
	Ice cream freezer
	Mold

Making the Sherbet: Peel and seed the peaches. Place the pulp in a blender and blend to make a puree. Work the puree through a sieve to remove any fibers, then measure the puree. You need 2½ cups (6 d*l*) for making the sherbet.

   Place the puree in a bowl and stir in the sugar syrup and lemon juice. Then pour the mixutre into an ice cream freezer and freeze, mold, and serve (see pages 2 to 6).

Serving Suggestions: Serve molded with Raspberry Sherbet (see Chapter 4, Combination Desserts).

18
Peach Sherbet II
(Sorbet aux Pêches au Sirop)

Peach Sherbet I, made with fresh peaches, is better than sherbet made with canned peaches. Nevertheless, since canned peaches can produce interesting results, the following recipe is given using canned fruit.

PREPARATION	10 minutes
FREEZING TIME	20 to 40 minutes
INGREDIENTS	*For approximately 1 quart (1 l) of sherbet* 1 quart (1 *l*) can or jar of peaches in light syrup (see Recipe 124 for Home Canned Peaches) ⅔ cup (1.5 d*l*) cold 28° Sugar Syrup (Recipe 1) Juice of ½ lemon
UTENSILS	Colander Electric blender Spoon Ice cream freezer Mold

Making the Sherbet: Drain the fruit and place it in a blender (save the syrup for making candy; see Fruit Jellies, Recipes 144–165). Blend to a smooth puree, then measure the puree; you need 2 generous cups (5 d*l*) for making the sherbet.

Mix the puree with the sugar syrup and lemon juice. Then pour into the ice cream freezer and freeze (see page 2).

To Mold: To mold and serve, see pages 4 to 6.

19
Pear Sherbet I
(Sorbet aux Poires de Conserve Maison)

This recipe, made with homemade canned fruit, is much better than the next recipe made with commercial canned fruit. Nevertheless, since both can produce interesting effects, two recipes for Pear Sherbet are given.

PREPARATION	10 minutes
FREEZING TIME	20 to 40 minutes
INGREDIENTS	*For approximately 1 quart (1 l) of sherbet* 1 quart (1 *l*) jar of Home Canned Pears (Recipe 124) 1 generous cup (2.5 d*l*) syrup from the pears ⅔ cup (1.5 d*l*) cold 28° Sugar Syrup (Recipe 1) 2 teaspoons lemon juice
UTENSILS	Colander Electric blender Ice cream freezer Mold

Making the Sherbet: Drain the fruit in a colander and reserve 1 generous cup (2.5 d*l*) of their syrup for making the sherbet (save the rest for candy making; see Fruit Jellies, Recipes 144–165).

Place the fruit in a blender with the reserved syrup, the cold sugar syrup, and the lemon juice. Blend to a smooth puree and pour into the ice cream freezer. Then freeze, mold, and serve (see pages 2 to 6).

Serving Suggestions: Serve with fresh apricot sauce (see Recipe 98 for Fresh Fruit Sauces) to which 2 teaspoons of kirsch have been added for every 2½ cups (6.2 d*l*) of sauce.

Pear Sherbet is molded with Chestnut Ice Cream to make the Perigord Crown Dessert (Recipe 74).

The molded sherbet can simply be served decorated with Candy Chestnuts (Recipe 177).

20
Pear Sherbet II
(Sorbet aux Poires au Sirop)

This recipe is made with commercially canned pears.

PREPARATION	10 minutes
FREEZING TIME	20 to 40 minutes
INGREDIENTS	*For approximately 1 quart (1 l) of sherbet* 4 cups (550 g) drained canned pears in light syrup 6½ tablespoons (1 dl) syrup from the can ¾ cup (1.8 dl) cold 28° Sugar Syrup (Recipe 1) 2 teaspoons lemon juice
UTENSILS	Electric blender Ice cream freezer Mold

Making the Sherbet: Place the drained fruit in the blender with 6½ tablespoons (1 dl) of the syrup from the can, the sugar syrup, and the lemon juice. (Save the rest of the syrup in which the pears were packed for candy making; see Fruit Jellies, Recipes 144–165). Blend to make a smooth puree and pour into the ice cream freezer. Then freeze, mold, and serve (see pages 2 to 6).

Serving Suggestions: Serve with fresh apricot sauce (see Recipe 98 for Fresh Fruit Sauces) to which 2 teaspoons of kirsch have been added for every 2½ cups (6.2 dl) of sauce.

Pear Sherbet is molded with Chestnut Ice Cream to make the Perigord Crown Dessert (Recipe 74).

The molded sherbet can simply be served decorated with Candy Chestnuts (Recipe 177).

21
Calvados Sherbet
(Sorbet au Calvados)

This recipe uses 100 proof apple brandy. To use kirsch or weaker alcohols, see the comment at the end of the recipe.

PREPARATION	10 minutes
FREEZING TIME	20 to 40 minutes
INGREDIENTS	*For approximately 1 quart (1 l) of sherbet*
	6½ tablespoons (1 dl) of calvados (applejack or apple brandy) that is close to 100 proof (50°)
	Generous 1⅔ cup (4 dl) noneffervescent mineral water
	2 generous cups (½ l) cold 28° Sugar Syrup (Recipe 1)
UTENSILS	Ice cream freezer
	Mold

Making the Sherbet: Place all the ingredients listed in the ice cream freezer; they will mix together as the sherbet is being frozen. Then freeze, mold, and serve (see pages 2 to 6).

Comment: Any alcohol (brandy) between 80 and 100 proof (40° to 50°) can be used to make a sherbet. With brandies (like most kirsch) that are closer to 80 proof (40°), use only 1½ cups (3.5 dl) of mineral water instead of the generous 1⅔ cups (4 dl) demanded here for stronger alcohols.

Do Not Store: All sherbets made with alcohol are very fragile; they should not be saved, but always served the day they are made.

22
Champagne Sherbet
(Sorbet au Champagne)

PREPARATION	10 minutes
FREEZING TIME	20 to 40 minutes
INGREDIENTS	*For approximately 1 quart (1 l) of sherbet* Generous 1⅔ cups (4 dl) champagne (see Comment) Generous 1⅔ cup (1 dl) cold 28° Sugar Syrup (Recipe 1) ⅔ cup (1.5 dl) noneffervescent mineral water Juice of 1 lemon or ½ orange
UTENSILS	Ice cream freezer Mold

Making the Sherbet: Place all the ingredients listed in the ice cream freezer; they will mix together as the sherbet is being frozen. Then freeze, mold, and serve (see pages 2 to 6).

Serving Suggestions: Serve with a Champagne Sabayon Sauce (Recipe 103) or mold with Raspberry Sherbet (Recipe 11).

Comment: Use a very good, full-bodied champagne for making this sherbet (preferably a pink champagne from a vintage year).

Do Not Store: All sherbets made with alcohol are very fragile; they should not be saved, but always served the day they are made.

23
Apple Cider Sherbet
(Sorbet au Cidre)

PREPARATION   10 minutes

FREEZING TIME   20 to 40 minutes

INGREDIENTS   *For approximately 1 quart (1 l) of sherbet*
2½ cups (6 d*l*) hard apple cider (very dry)
1½ cups (3.5 d*l*) cold 28° Sugar Syrup (Recipe 1)

UTENSILS   Ice cream freezer
Mold

Making the Sherbet: Place all the ingredients listed in the ice cream freezer; they will mix together as the sherbet is being frozen. Then freeze, mold, and serve (see pages 2 to 6).

Variation: Apple Cider Granité

Using a scant 3¼ cups (¾ *l*) hard apple cider and ¾ (160g) granulated sugar, an apple cider granité can be made, following the instructions for making and serving Coffee Granité (Recipe 25).

Juanita Banana Sundae, Recipe 60; Coffee Liégeois Sundae, Recipe 53;
Ivory Coast Sundae, Recipe 51

24
Port Sherbet
(Sorbet au Porto)

PREPARATION	10 minutes
FREEZING TIME	20 to 40 minutes
INGREDIENTS	*For approximately 1 quart (1 l) of sherbet* 1 cup (2.3 d*l*) red port about 36 proof (18°) Scant 3¼ cups (7.5 d*l*) cold 28° Sugar Syrup (Recipe 1)
UTENSILS	Ice cream freezer Mold

Making the Sherbet: Place all the ingredients listed in the ice cream freezer; they will mix together as the sherbet is being frozen. Then freeze, mold, and serve (see pages 2 to 6).

Serving Suggestions: Serve with fresh cantaloupe or muskmelon.

Comment: Sherbets can be made in this way with all alcoholic beverages that are about 36 proof (18°) such as madiera or sherry.

25
Coffee Granité
(Granité au Café)

PREPARATION	10 minutes
FREEZING TIME	3 hours
INGREDIENTS	*For approximately 1½ pints (¾ l) of granité* Scant 3¼ cups (¾ l) unsweetened, strong, black coffee ¾ cup (160 g) granulated sugar
UTENSILS	Coffee pot Mixing bowl *or* tray (see Comment) Spoon

Making the Granité: Pour the black coffee into a bowl (see Comment) with the sugar, mix well, and leave to cool completely. This can be speeded up by placing the bowl containing the coffee and sugar in another bowl previously filled with ice and water. Once cold, place the bowl in the freezer or freezing compartment of a refrigerator.

To Freeze: After about an hour, the coffee mixture should begin to freeze and form crystals. Stir the mixture, being careful to scrape off the icy parts that stick to the sides of the bowl, and mix gently so that the frozen and unfrozen elements are evenly combined. Replace the bowl in the freezer, removing and mixing about every 30 minutes until all the contents of the bowl have about the consistency of soft crushed ice. This consistency is usually reached after about 3 hours in the freezer.

To Serve: Once the granité is ready, it should be served within the following hour; otherwise it will continue freezing and finally turn into a block of ice.

Serve the granité in tall tulip-shaped champagne or other wine glasses that have been previously iced by placing them in the freezer for 30 minutes.

Comment: The size of the receptacle used to make a granité has a great deal of influence on the time it takes to freeze. Using a wide shallow one (a shallow metal baking dish or large ice trays, for example) will mean that the granité will freeze faster than the same mixture in a bowl.

Never use a plastic receptacle for making granités, since plastic is a poor conductor of heat and cold and the granité will take too long to freeze.

26
Tea Granité
(Granité au Thé)

PREPARATION	10 minutes
FREEZING TIME	3 hours
INGREDIENTS	*For approximately 1 quart (1 l) of granité* 4¼ cups (1 *l*) water 1½ to 2 tablespoons (10 to 15 g) Orange Pekoe tea leaves ¾ cup (160 g) granulated sugar
UTENSILS	Saucepan Tea pot Strainer Mixing bowl *or* tray (see Comment) Spoon

Making the Granité: Make the tea using the amounts of tea and water given here. When it has finished steeping, pout it through a strainer onto the sugar, mix well, and leave to cool completely. This can be speeded up by placing the bowl containing the tea and sugar in another bowl previously filled with ice and water. Once cold, place the bowl in the freezer or freezing compartment of a refrigerator.

To Freeze: After about an hour, the tea mixture should begin to freeze and form crystals. Stir the mixture, being careful to scrape off the icy parts that stick to the sides of the bowl, and mix gently so that the frozen and unfrozen elements are evenly combined. Replace the bowl in the freezer, removing and mixing about every 30 minutes until all the contents of the bowl have about the consistency of soft crushed ice. This consistency is usually reached after about 3 hours in the freezer.

To Serve: Once the granité is ready, it should be served within the following hour; otherwise it will continue freezing and finally turn into a block of ice.

Serve the granité in tall tulip-shaped champagne or other wine glasses that have been previously iced by placing them in the freezer for 30 minutes.

Comment: The size of the receptacle used to make a granité has a great deal of influence on the time it takes to freeze. Using a wide shallow one (a shallow metal baking dish or large ice trays, for example) will mean that the granité will freeze faster than the same mixture in a bowl.

Never use a plastic receptacle for making granités, since plastic is a poor conductor of heat and cold and the granité will take too long to freeze.

Passion Fruit Sundae in Half Coconuts, Recipe 52; Sherbet-Filled Fruits, Recipe 91

Chapter 2

ICE CREAMS AND PARFAITS

RECIPES

27. Vanilla Ice Cream (Glace à la Vanille)

28. Almond Ice Cream (Glace aux Amandes)

29. Banana Ice Cream (Glace à la Banane)

30. Peanut Butter Ice Cream (Glace aux Cacahuètes)

31. Lenôtre's Special Caramel Ice Cream (Glace au Caramel Lenôtre)

32. Chocolate Ice Cream (Glace au Chocolat)

33. Coffee Ice Cream (Glace Fin Moka)

34. Chestnut Ice Cream (Glace aux Marrons)

35. Honey Ice Cream (Glace au Miel)

36. Coconut Ice Cream (Glace à la Noix de Coco)

37. Pistacio Ice Cream (Glace à la Pistache)

38. Nut Brittle Ice Cream (Glace au Praliné Noisettes)

39. Armagnac and Prune Ice Cream (Glace aux Pruneaux d'Agen)

40. Vanilla Parfait (Parfait à la Vanille)

41. Coffee-Flavored Vanilla Parfait (Parfait à la Vanille Parfumé au Café)

42. Coffee Parfait (Parfait au Café)

43. Chocolate Parfait (Parfait au Chocolat)

44. Alcohol-Flavored Parfait (Parfait à l'Alcool)

41

GENERAL COMMENTS ON ICE CREAMS

The following recipe for Vanilla Ice Cream illustrates the basic procedure used in making the other ice creams in this book. The method is carefully described here for future reference. When making other ice creams, the ingredients may differ from those given below but the basic procedure remains the same.

27
Vanilla Ice Cream
(Glace à la Vanille)

PREPARATION	15 to 20 minutes
COOKING TIME	Approximately 10 minutes for cooking the cream
COOLING TIME	Approximately 30 minutes on ice before freezing
FREEZING TIME	20 to 40 minutes
INGREDIENTS	*For approximately 1 quart (1 l) of ice cream* 2 generous cups (½ l) milk 1 vanilla bean split open lengthwise 1 generous cup (210 g) granulated sugar 6 egg yolks 1 generous cups (¼ l) heavy cream or crème fraîche (see Dictionary of Terms)
UTENSILS	1 medium-sized saucepan with cover 2 mixing bowls Electric mixer *or* wire whisk Wooden spoon *or* spatula Candy thermometer (optional) Ice cream freezer Molds

Sweetening and Flavoring the Milk: Place the milk, vanilla bean, and half the sugar in a sauce pan and bring to a boil. Once the milk boils, cover the pot and remove from the heat. Let the mixture stand for 10 minutes before proceeding with the recipe.

Note 1:   In many other ice creams the flavoring is not added to the milk at this stage. When the flavoring (i.e., chocolate, fruit puree, etc.) is added later–

generally after the cream has been cooked–the milk and half of the sugar must still be brought to a boil to dissolve the sugar but need not be left to stand before proceeding with the recipe.

Preparing the Egg Yolk–Sugar Mixture: Place the egg yolks and remaining sugar in a bowl and beat with an electric mixer or wire whisk until the mixture whitens and forms a ribbon.

Making the Cream: Place the saucepan containing the milk, vanilla bean, and sugar over high heat and bring back to a boil. Pour a little of the boiling milk into the bowl with the egg yolk–sugar mixture, whisking constantly as the liquid is added. Remove the saucepan of milk from the heat and pour the contents of the bowl into it, stirring constantly with a wooden spoon or spatula.

Cooking the Cream: Place the saucepan back over low heat, using a candy thermometer to watch the temperature of the cream as it cooks. Stir the cream constantly—it should never be allowed to boil. As it cooks, the cream will thicken perceptibly, especially toward the end of the cooking time. If using a candy thermometer, cook the cream until the thermometer registers 185°F (85°C), then remove from the heat and continue stirring for 1 to 2 minutes more before cooling the cream.

Although it is preferable to use a candy thermometer when cooking the cream, it is not absolutely necessary. As the cream cooks and thickens, it will begin to lightly coat the wooden spatula used to stir it. Lift the spatula periodically out of the cream and hold it at a tilt so that the excess cream will fall from the spatula back into the saucepan. Use your finger to draw a line in the thin film of cream that adheres to the spatula. If the cream needs to be cooked longer, the line will quickly lose its shape and the cream on the spatula will look as thin as milk. When sufficiently cooked, the cream will nicely coat the spatula and the top edge of the line will hold its shape. When the cream is cooked, it should immediately be removed from the heat.

Cooking the cream generally takes about 5 to 10 minutes (see Comment).

Cooling the Cream: Once the cream is cooked, lift out the vanilla bean and pour the cream into a bowl. Add the crème fraîche or heavy cream to the bowl, stirring constantly to mix well (see Note 2). The addition of the chilled cream both enriches and starts cooling the cooked ingredients. The finished cream must now be allowed to cool *completely* before being placed in the ice cream freezer. To speed cooling, place the bowl containing the cream in a slightly larger bowl that has previously been filled with ice cubes and water. Stir the cream frequently as it cools, and test the temperature using your finger. The cream should feel cold to the touch when finished cooling, which takes about 30 minutes in ice water.

Note 2:   Not all ice creams in this book add chilled crème fraîche or heavy cream to the cooked ingredients. Cooking and cooling instructions apply to all ice creams with or without the addition of chilled cream at this stage of the preparation. If whipped cream is called for, it is always folded in after the cooked cream has cooled completely.

43

To Freeze the Cream: Once the cream is completely cold, pour it into the ice cream freezer and start the machine. Then freeze, mold, and serve (see pages 2 to 6).

Comment: Great care must be taken when cooking the cream. If heated too much, the egg will curdle and the cream will look grainy. If this happens, remove the saucepan from the heat, take out the vanilla bean, immediately add 1 tablespoon of cold milk or cream to the pot, and pour the cream into an electric blender. Blend until smooth; then proceed as described under the heading "Cooling the Cream."

Serving Suggestions: The wonderfully subtle taste of Vanilla Ice Cream makes it the perfect partner to various other flavors when making molded desserts (Chapter 4). It can be served alone or with a scoop of Chocolate Ice Cream (Recipe 32), Coffee Ice Cream (Recipe 33), Nut Brittle Ice Cream (Recipe 38), Caramel Ice Cream (Recipe 31), Raspberry Sherbet (Recipe 11), or Strawberry Sherbet (Recipe 10).

It can also be served simply topped with a Fresh Fruit Sauce (Recipe 98), Hot Chocolate Sauce (Recipe 101), or Caramel Sauce (Recipe 102).

All of the recipes that use Vanilla Ice Cream are listed in the Cross Index of Basic Ingredients.

To Store: This ice cream may be stored in the freezer for 2 weeks (see Storing Ice Creams, page 5).

28
Almond Ice Cream
(Glace aux Amandes)

PREPARATION	15 to 20 minutes
COOKING TIME	Approximately 10 minutes for cooking the cream
COOLING TIME	Approximately 30 minutes on ice before freezing
FREEZING TIME	20 to 40 minutes
INGREDIENTS	*For approximately 1 quart (1 l) of ice cream* ½ cup (1.2 dl) heavy cream Scant 3¼ cups (¾ l) milk 1¼ cups (150 g) ground almonds 1 generous cup (210 g) granulated sugar 6 egg yolks
UTENSILS	3 bowls 2 medium saucepans 1 cover for saucepan Strainer Electric mixer *or* wire whisk Wooden spoon *or* spatula Candy thermometer (optional) Ice cream freezer Molds

Preliminary Preparations: Place the heavy cream in a bowl and chill in the refrigerator while preparing the ice cream.

Sweetening and Flavoring the Milk: Place the milk, ground almonds, and half of the sugar in a saucepan, stir, and bring to a boil. Once the milk boils, cover the pot and remove from the heat. Let the mixture stand for 10 minutes before proceeding with the recipe.

Preparing the Egg Yolk–Sugar Mixture: Place the egg yolks and remaining sugar in a bowl and beat with an electric mixer or a wire whisk until the mixture whitens and forms a ribbon.

Making the Cream: Once the milk–almond mixture has finished infusing, pour it through a strainer into a clean saucepan. Place the strained liquid over high heat and bring to a boil. Pour a little of the boiling liquid into the bowl with the egg yolk–sugar mixture, whisking constantly as the liquid is added. Remove the saucepan from the heat and pour the contents of the bowl into it, stirring constantly with a wooden spoon or spatula.

Cooking the Cream: Place the saucepan back over low heat, using a candy thermometer to watch the temperature of the cream as it cooks. Stir the cream constantly—it should never be allowed to boil. As it cooks, the cream will thicken perceptibly, especially toward the end of the cooking time. If using a candy thermometer, cook the cream until the thermometer registers 185°F (85°C), then remove from the heat and continue stirring for 1 to 2 minutes more before cooling the cream.

Although it is preferable to use a candy thermometer when cooking the cream, it is not absolutely necessary. As the cream cooks and thickens, it will begin to lightly coat the wooden spatula used to stir it. Lift the spatula periodically out of the cream and hold it at a tilt so that the excess cream will fall from the spatula back into the saucepan. Use your finger to draw a line in the thin film of cream that adheres to the spatula. If the cream needs to be cooked longer, the line will quickly lose its shape and the cream on the spatula will look as thin as milk. When sufficiently cooked, the cream will nicely coat the spatula and the top edge of the line will hold its shape. When the cream is cooked, it should immediately be removed from the heat.

Cooking the cream generally takes about 5 to 10 minutes.

Cooling the Cream: Once the cream is cooked, pour it into a bowl. Add the crème fraîche or heavy cream to the bowl, stirring constantly to mix well. The addition of the chilled cream both enriches and starts cooling the cooked ingredients. The finished cream must now be allowed to cool *completely* before being placed in the ice cream freezer. To speed cooling, place the bowl containing the cream in a slightly larger bowl that has previously been filled with ice cubes and water. Stir the cream frequently as it cools, and test the temperature using your finger. The cream should feel cold to the touch when finished cooling, which takes about 30 minutes in ice water.

Adding the Whipped Cream: Once the cooked ingredients have cooled completely, remove the heavy cream from the refrigerator and whip as described in Recipe 106 for Whipped Cream. Fold the whipped cream into the other ingredients. Then pour the mixture into the ice cream freezer.

To Freeze: Freeze, mold, and serve (see pages 2 to 6).

29
Banana Ice Cream
(Glace à la Banane)

PREPARATION	15 minutes
COOKING TIME	Approximately 10 minutes for cooking the cream
COOLING TIME	Approximately 30 minutes on ice before freezing
FREEZING TIME	20 to 40 minutes
INGREDIENTS	*For approximately 1 quart (1 l) of ice cream* 2 generous cups (½ l) milk ⅔ cup (140 g) granulated sugar 4 egg yolks 4 to 5 bananas, weighing about 1 pound 5 ounces (600 g) when purchased 2 teaspoons white rum (optional)
UTENSILS	1 medium-sized saucepan with cover Electric mixer *or* wire whisk Wooden spoon *or* spatula Food mill *or* food processor Candy thermometer (optional) 3 bowls Ice cream freezer Molds

Making the Ice Cream: Using the amounts of milk, sugar, and egg yolks given here, make the cream, cook it, and allow to cool as described in Recipe 27 for Vanilla Ice Cream. Once the cream is cold, peel the bananas and grind them through a food mill or puree them in a food processor. (Do not use an electric blender; it makes the pulp too foamy and sticky.) Measure the puree to be sure you have 1½ cups (350 g). Then pour it into a bowl and add the cold cooked cream to it little by little. Whisk constantly to combine the cream with the banana pulp and make a smooth mixture.

To Freeze: Pour the mixture into the ice cream freezer and freeze (see page 2). If desired, 2 teaspoons of white rum may be added to the ice cream about 10 minutes before it has finished freezing. To mold and serve, see pages 4 to 6.

Serving Suggestions: Banana Ice Cream can be used to make numerous combination desserts; it is especially good with pineapple, raspberry, or strawberry sherbets. An interesting dessert can be made with a scoop of Banana Ice Cream next to a scoop of Pineapple Sherbet placed in a wide champagne glass or a dish on top of a slice of Candied Pineapple.

Banana Ice Cream can be served with Vanilla Sauce (Recipe 99), Hot Chocolate Sauce (Recipe 101), or Pineapple Sauce (Recipe 98).

Variant: Frozen Banana Mousse (Mousse Glacée à la Banane)

This dessert can be made without an ice cream freezer. Simply proceed as in this recipe for Banana Ice Cream, but instead of putting the banana cream mixture in the ice cream freezer, place it in a blender and blend for 2 to 3 minutes. Then place it in a mold and freeze in the freezer compartment of a refrigerator; the result is a delicious frozen mousse.

30
Peanut Butter Ice Cream (Glace aux Cacahuètes)

PREPARATION	20 minutes
COOKING TIME	Approximately 10 minutes for cooking the cream
COOLING TIME	Approximately 30 minutes on ice before freezing
FREEZING TIME	20 to 40 minutes
INGREDIENTS	*For approximately 1 quart (1 l) of ice cream*

Scant 3¼ cups (¾ *l*) milk
1 generous cup (210 g) granulated sugar
6 egg yolks
4 tablespoons (75 g) peanut butter

For decoration (optional)
Generous ½ cup (100 g) crumbled Disneyland Peanut
    Brittle (Recipe 186)

UTENSILS	

1 medium-sized saucepan with cover
3 mixing bowls
Electric mixer *or* wire whisk
Wooden spoon *or* spatula
Candy thermometer (optional)
Ice cream freezer
Molds

Making the Ice Cream: Using the milk, sugar, and egg yolks, make and cook the cream as described in Recipe 27 for Vanilla Ice Cream. Before cooking the cream, place the peanut butter in a mixing bowl. When the cream has finished cooking but is still hot, add it a tablespoon at a time to the peanut butter. Stir constantly as the cream is being added. As the mixture becomes thinner, progressively add more hot cream at a time until it has all been added and a smooth mixture has been made.

To Freeze: Allow the flavored cream to cool completely before placing it in the ice cream freezer, then mold and serve (see pages 2 to 6).

Serving Suggestions: Serve molded with Banana Sherbet (see Chapter 4, Combination Desserts), or mold and serve alone decorated with crumbled Disneyland Peanut Brittle (Recipe 186).

31
Lenôtre's Special Caramel Ice Cream
(Glace au Caramel Lenôtre)

PREPARATION	15 minutes once caramel is prepared (20-25 minutes to prepare caramel)
COOKING TIME	Approximately 10 minutes for the cream
COOLING TIME	Approximately 30 minutes on ice before freezing
FREEZING TIME	20 to 40 minutes
INGREDIENTS	*For approximately 1 quart (1 l) of ice cream* 2 generous cups (½ l) milk 6 egg yolks ½ cup (100 g) granulated sugar 1 generous cup (¼ l) heavy cream or crème fraîche (see Dictionary of Terms) Generous ½ cup (100 g) small Nougatine Crumble (Recipe 197) *For the caramel* 1 cup (200 g) granulated sugar 10 drops lemon juice
UTENSILS	1 medium-sized saucepan with cover 1 heavy-bottomed, small pot 2 mixing bowls Electric mixer *or* wire whisk Wooden spoon *or* spatula Candy thermometer (optional) Ice cream freezer Mold

Making the Ice Cream: Make the caramel as described in Recipe 198 for Lenôtre's Caramel.

When the caramel has finished cooking, heat the milk in a saucepan. Bring the milk to a boil and pour it into the pot with the hot caramel, stirring as the milk is being added. Continue stirring the mixture over low heat until all the caramel has dissolved.

Place the egg yolks and sugar in a bowl and beat with an electric mixer or wire whisk until the mixture whitens and forms a ribbon. Bring the caramel–milk mixture to a boil and pour a little of it into the bowl with the egg yolks, whisking

51

constantly. Remove the pot from the heat and pour the ingredients from the bowl into it. Stir constantly so that all the ingredients are well combined.

Cooking the Cream: Place the saucepan back over low heat, using a candy thermometer to watch the temperature of the cream as it cooks. Stir the cream constantly—it should never be allowed to boil. As it cooks, the cream will thicken perceptibly, especially toward the end of the cooking time. If using a candy thermometer, cook the cream until the thermometer registers 185°F (85°C), then remove from the heat and continue stirring for 1 to 2 minutes more before cooling the cream.

Although it is preferable to use a candy thermometer when cooking the cream, it is not absolutely necessary. As the cream cooks and thickens, it will begin to lightly coat the wooden spatula used to stir it. Lift the spatula periodically out of the cream and hold it at a tilt so that the excess cream will fall from the spatula back into the saucepan. Use your finger to draw a line in the thin film of cream that adheres to the spatula. If the cream needs to be cooked longer, the line will quickly lose its shape and the cream on the spatula will look as thin as milk. When sufficiently cooked, the cream will nicely coat the spatula and the top edge of the line will hold its shape. When the cream is cooked, it should immediately be removed from the heat.

Cooking the cream generally takes about 5 to 10 minutes.

Cooling the Cream: Once the cream is cooked, pour it into a bowl. Add the crème fraîche or heavy cream to the bowl, stirring constantly to mix well. The addition of the chilled cream both enriches and starts cooling the cooked ingredients. The finished cream must now be allowed to cool *completely* before being placed in the ice cream freezer. To speed cooling, place the bowl containing the cream in a slightly larger bowl that has previously been filled with ice cubes and water. Stir the cream frequently as it cools, and test the temperature using your finger. The cream should feel cold to the touch when finished cooling, which takes about 30 minutes in ice water.

To Freeze: Pour the mixture into the ice cream freezer. When the ice cream has finished freezing, remove the dasher from the freezer canister and stir the Nougatine Crumble into the ice cream. Then mold and serve as described on pages 4 to 6.

Serving Suggestions: Serve alone or accompanied by Vanilla Sauce (Recipe 99). This ice cream is used in making the Auteuil-Style Frozen Caramel Dessert (Recipe 85).

32
Chocolate Ice Cream
(Glace au Chocolat)

PREPARATION	10 minutes
COOKING TIME	Approximately 10 minutes for the cream
COOLING TIME	Approximately 30 minutes on ice before freezing
FREEZING TIME	20 to 40 minutes
INGREDIENTS	*For approximately 1 quart (1 l) of ice cream* Scant 3¼ cups (¾ *l*) milk 1 generous cup (210 g) granulated sugar 6 egg yolks 6 tablespoons (60 g) unsweetened cocoa powder
UTENSILS	1 medium-sized saucepan with cover Electric mixer *or* wire whisk Wooden spoon *or* spatula Candy thermometer (optional) 3 mixing bowls Ice cream freezer Molds

Making the Ice Cream: Using the milk, sugar, and egg yolks, make and cook the cream as described in Recipe 27 for Vanilla Ice Cream.

Once the cream is cooked but before it is allowed to cool, place the cocoa powder in a bowl and whisk in the hot cream, a tablespoon at a time at the beginning; more cooked cream can be progressively added to the cocoa each time. Whisk constantly until all the cream has been added and a smooth mixture has been formed. Cool the cream as described in Recipe 27.

To Freeze: Pour the mixture into the ice cream freezer and freeze, then mold and serve (see pages 2 to 6).

Serving Suggestions: Chocolate Ice Cream is delicious when served with either Vanilla or Pistachio Ice Cream. It can also be used to fill cream puffs when making Profiteroles (Recipe 95).

33

Coffee Ice Cream (Glace Fin Moka)

PREPARATION	20 minutes
COOKING TIME	Approximately 10 minutes for the cream
COOLING TIME	Approximately 30 minutes on ice before freezing
FREEZING TIME	20 to 40 minutes
INGREDIENTS	*For approximately 1 quart (1 l) of ice cream* Generous ½ cup (50 g) coarsely ground coffee beans 2 generous cups (½ l) milk 1 generous cup (210 g) granulated sugar 6 egg yolks 1 generous cup (¼ l) heavy cream or crème fraîche 20 sugar coffee beans (optional) (see Dictionary of Terms)
UTENSILS	2 medium saucepans Wooden spoon *or* spatula 1 cover for saucepan Candy thermometer 2 mixing bowls (optional) Fine sieve Ice cream freezer Electric mixer *or* wire whisk Molds

Making the Ice Cream: Place the ground coffee in a saucepan with the milk and half of the sugar. Stir and bring to a boil, then cover and remove the pot from the heat. Let the ingredients stand for 10 minutes. Then pour the contents of the saucepan through a fine sieve into another saucepan.

Combine these ingredients with the other half of the sugar, the egg yolks, and the heavy cream; finish making, cooking, and cooling the cream as described in Recipe 27 for Vanilla Ice Cream. Pour the finished, chilled cream into an ice cream freezer and freeze (see page 2).

To Mold: Coffee Ice Cream should be molded and covered as soon as it comes from the ice cream freezer since it has a tendency to discolor when exposed to the air. To mold and serve, see pages 4 to 6.

If desired, sugar coffee beans can be stirred into the ice cream just before it is molded and stored.

Serving Suggestions: Coffee Ice Cream can be served in sundaes or used to make molded desserts with Vanilla Ice Cream (Recipe 68), Nut Brittle Ice Cream (Recipe 38), Vanilla Parfait (Recipe 40), or Chocolate Parfait (Recipe 43).

34
Chestnut Ice Cream
(Glace aux Marrons)

PREPARATION	10 minutes
COOKING TIME	Approximately 10 minutes for the cream
COOLING TIME	Approximately 30 minutes on ice before freezing
FREEZING TIME	20 to 40 minutes
INGREDIENTS	*For approximately 1 quart (1 l) of ice cream* 2 generous cups (½ l) milk Generous ⅓ cup (70 g) granulated sugar 4 egg yolks 1 cup (300 g) chestnut cream (see Dictionary of Terms)
UTENSILS	1 medium-sized saucepan with cover 2 medium-sized mixing bowls 1 large mixing bowl Electric mixer *or* wire whisk Wooden spoon *or* spatula Candy thermometer (optional) Ice cream freezer Molds

Making the Ice Cream: Make and cook the cream as described in Recipe 27 for Vanilla Ice Cream. Once the cream is cooked, but before it is allowed to cool, place the chestnut cream in a bowl and begin stirring in the cooked cream, a tablespoon at a time in the beginning. The liquid can be added in progressively larger quantities as the chestnut cream is diluted. Stir constantly until all the hot cream has been added. Then whisk until a smooth mixture is formed.

To Freeze: Cool the cream as described in Recipe 27. Then pour it into the ice cream freezer and freeze, then mold and serve (see pages 2 to 6).

Serving Suggestions: Chestnut Ice Cream can be molded and served with Pear Sherbet (see Recipe 69; see also Recipe 74 for Perigord Crown Dessert).
   It is also excellent served in scoops with fresh pear sauce to which 2 teaspoons of pear brandy has been added (Recipe 98 for Fresh Fruit Sauces).

35
Honey Ice Cream
(Glace au Miel)

PREPARATION	10 minutes
COOKING TIME	Approximately 10 minutes for the cream
COOLING TIME	Approximately 30 minutes on ice before freezing
FREEZING TIME	20 to 40 minutes
INGREDIENTS	*For approximately 1 quart (1 l) of ice cream* 2 generous cups (½ l) milk ⅓ cup (100 g) high-quality honey 6 egg yolks Generous ⅔ cup (150 g) granulated sugar 1 generous cup (¼ l) heavy cream or crème fraîche (see Dictionary of Terms)
UTENSILS	1 medium-sized saucepan with cover 2 mixing bowls Electric mixer *or* wire whisk Wooden spoon *or* spatula Candy thermometer (optional) Ice cream freezer Molds

Sweetening and Flavoring the Milk: Place the milk and honey in a saucepan and slowly bring to a boil, stirring to dissolve the honey.

Preparing the Egg Yolk–Sugar Mixture: Place the egg yolks and all of the sugar in a mixing bowl and beat with an electric mixer or wire whisk until the mixture whitens and forms a ribbon.

Making the Cream: When the milk and honey mixture begins to boil, pour a little of the hot liquid into the bowl with the egg yolk–sugar mixture, whisking constantly. Remove the saucepan of milk from the heat and pour the contents of the bowl into it, stirring constantly with a wooden spoon or spatula.

Cooking, Cooling, and Freezing the Cream: Proceed as described in Recipe 27 for Vanilla Ice Cream.

⚜

36
Coconut Ice Cream
(Glace à la Noix de Coco)

PREPARATION	20 minutes
COOKING TIME	Approximately 10 minutes for the cream
COOLING TIME	Approximately 30 minutes on ice before freezing
FREEZING TIME	20 to 40 minutes
INGREDIENTS	*For approximately 1 quart (1 l) of ice cream*
	2 generous cups (½ l) milk
	1 cup (75 g) grated coconut
	1 generous cup (210 g) granulated sugar
	6 egg yolks
	1 generous cup (¼ l) heavy cream or crème fraîche
	(see Dictionary of Terms)
UTENSILS	1 medium-sized saucepan with cover
	2 mixing bowls
	Electric mixer *or* wire whisk
	Wooden spoon *or* spatula
	Candy thermometer (optional)
	Ice cream freezer
	Molds

Making the Ice Cream: Using these ingredients, make the ice cream following Recipe 27 for making Vanilla Ice Cream. All of the coconut should be added to the milk in the beginning and allowed to stand. Do *not* strain the milk before combining it with the egg yolk–sugar mixture, since it is pleasant to have the grated coconut in the finished ice cream.

Serving Suggestions: Serve scoops of Coconut Ice Cream in a coconut shell that has been emptied of its milk and split in half—do not remove the pulp from the coconut shell (see photo, page 38). Decorate with a Chocolate Palm (Recipe 119).

Coconut Ice Cream can be molded to make combination desserts with Passion Fruit Sherbet (Recipe 12) or Banana Sherbet (Recipe 5).

This ice cream can also be served simply with Fresh Pineapple Sauce (Recipe 98) and coconut cookies.

Raspberry Tulip, Recipe 66; Melba Tulip Cookie Desserts with Apricots, Recipe 63;
Loire Valley Sundae, Recipe 65

37
Pistacio Ice Cream (Glace à la Pistache)

PREPARATION	40 minutes
COOKING TIME	Approximately 10 minutes for the cream
COOLING TIME	Approximately 30 minutes on ice before freezing
FREEZING TIME	20 to 40 minutes
INGREDIENTS	*For approximately 1 quart (1 l) of ice cream* 3 tablespoons (30 g) blanched almonds ¾ cup (120 g) shelled pistacios 1 generous cup (210 g) granulated sugar Scant 3¼ cups (¾ *l*) milk 6 egg yolks 1½ teaspoons kirsch
UTENSILS	1 medium-sized saucepan with cover 2 mixing bowls Electric mixer *or* wire whisk Electric blender *or* food processor Wooden spoon *or* spatula Strainer Candy thermometer (optional) Ice cream freezer Mold

Sweetening and Flavoring the Milk: Place the almonds and pistacios in an electric blender or food processor with half of the granulated sugar. Grind for several seconds until a coarse, grainy powder is formed. Pour this into a saucepan and add the milk; whisk to mix the ingredients over high heat and bring to a boil. Cover the pot and remove from the heat. Let the mixture stand for 30 minutes before proceeding with the recipe.

Preparing the Egg Yolk–Sugar Mixture: Place the egg yolks and remaining sugar in a mixing bowl and beat, using an electric mixer or a wire whisk, until the mixture whitens and forms a ribbon.

Making the Cream: Once the milk and nuts have finished infusing, pour the mixture through a strainer into a clean saucepan. Bring the strained liquid to a boil and pour a little of it into the bowl with the egg yolk–sugar mixture, whisking constantly as the liquid is being added. Remove the saucepan of milk from the heat and pour the contents of the bowl into it, stirring constantly with a wooden spoon or spatula.

Cooking the Cream: Place the saucepan back over low heat, using a candy thermometer to watch the temperature of the cream as it cooks. Stir the cream constantly—it should never be allowed to boil. As it cooks, the cream will thicken perceptibly, especially toward the end of the cooking time. If using a candy thermometer, cook the cream until the thermometer registers 185°F (85°C), then remove from the heat and continue stirring for 1 to 2 minutes more before cooling the cream.

Although it is preferable to use a candy thermometer when cooking the cream, it is not absolutely necessary. As the cream cooks and thickens, it will begin to lightly coat the wooden spatula used to stir it. Lift the spatula periodically out of the cream and hold it at a tilt so that the excess cream will fall from the spatula back into the saucepan. Use your finger to draw a line in the thin film of cream that adheres to the spatula. If the cream needs to be cooked longer, the line will quickly lose its shape and the cream on the spatula will look as thin as milk. When sufficiently cooked, the cream will nicely coat the spatula and the top edge of the line will hold its shape. When the cream is cooked, it should immediately be removed from the heat.

Cooking the cream generally takes about 5 to 10 minutes.

Cooling the Cream: Once the cream is cooked, pour it into a bowl. Add the crème fraîche or heavy cream to the bowl, stirring constantly to mix well. The addition of the chilled cream both enriches and starts cooling the cooked ingredients. The finished cream must now be allowed to cool *completely* before being placed in the ice cream freezer. To speed cooling, place the bowl containing the cream in a slightly larger bowl that has previously been filled with ice cubes and water. Stir the cream frequently as it cools, and test the temperature using your finger. The cream should feel cold to the touch when finished cooling, which takes about 30 minutes in ice water.

To Freeze and Mold the Cream: Once the cream is completely cold, pour it into the ice cream freezer, start the machine, and freeze (see page 2). Just before molding stir in the kirsch. To mold and serve, see pages 4 to 6.

Serving Suggestions: Pistacio Ice Cream can be molded and served with Chocolate Ice Cream (Recipe 32) to make a delicious combination dessert (see Chapter 4, Molded Combination Desserts).

Comment: The very pale greenish-brown color of this ice cream is a proof of its quality. The delicate taste of the almonds and pistacios is by far preferable to the more "attractive" green ice cream which is called pistacio ice cream but which is generally nothing more than bitter almond extract and green food coloring.

38
Nut Brittle Ice Cream
(Glace au Praliné Noisettes)

PREPARATION	20 minutes
COOKING TIME	Approximately 10 minutes for the cream
COOLING TIME	Approximately 30 minutes on ice before freezing
FREEZING TIME	20 to 40 minutes
INGREDIENTS	*For approximately 1 quart (1 l) of ice cream* 2 generous cups (½ l) milk Generous ¾ cup (170 g) granulated sugar 6 egg yolks 1 generous cup (¼ l) heavy cream or crème fraîche (see Dictionary of Terms) ⅔ cup (100 g) finely ground Nut Brittle made with hazelnuts (Recipe 196)
UTENSILS	1 medium-sized saucepan with cover 2 mixing bowls Electric mixer *or* wire whisk Wooden spoon *or* spatula Candy thermometer (optional) Ice cream freezer Molds

Making the Ice Cream: Using these ingredients, make the ice cream following the procedure described in Recipe 27.

The powdered nut brittle should be stirred into the cooked cream during the cooling time, after the chilled heavy cream has been added. The pieces of nut brittle will be mixed evenly throughout the ice cream as it freezes in the ice cream freezer.

Serving Suggestions: This ice cream can be molded with Coffee Ice Cream (Recipe 33) or Coffee Parfait (Recipe 42) to make a combination dessert (see Chapter 4, Molded Combination Desserts). It is also used in other frozen desserts, such as Sylvie Lenôtre's Success Sundae (Recipe 62) or the Frozen Nut Brittle Delight (Recipe 70).

Nut Brittle Ice Cream is also delicious served alone with either a Caramel Sauce (Recipe 102) or a Vanilla Sauce (Recipe 99).

39
Armagnac and Prune Ice Cream
(Glace aux Pruneaux d'Agen)

PREPARATION	1¼ hours
COOKING TIME	Approximately 10 minutes for the cream
COOLING TIME	Approximately 30 minutes on ice before freezing
FREEZING TIME	20 to 40 minutes
INGREDIENTS	*For approximately 1 quart (1 l) of ice cream* 2 generous cups (½ l) milk Scant ⅔ cup (120 g) granulated sugar 4 egg yolks *For the prune cream* Scant ⅓ cup (7 cl) Armagnac Scant ⅓ cup (7 cl) 28° Sugar Syrup (Recipe 1) 1½ cup (200 g) pitted prunes
UTENSILS	2 medium-sized saucepans with covers 2 medium-sized mixing bowls 1 large mixing bowl Electric mixer *or* wire whisk Electric blender *or* food processor Wooden spoon *or* spatula Candy thermometer (optional) Ice cream freezer Molds

Preliminary Preparations: Place the Armagnac and sugar syrup in a saucepan and bring to a boil; add the prunes, bring back to a boil, and remove from the heat. Cover the saucepan and leave the prunes to infuse in the liquid for 1 hour. Then pour the contents of the saucepan into an electric blender or food processor and blend to make a smooth cream. Pour the prune cream into a mixing bowl and reserve.

Sweetening and Flavoring the Milk: Place the milk and half the sugar in a saucepan and bring to a boil. Once the milk boils, cover the pot and remove from the heat. Let the mixture stand for 10 minutes before proceeding with the recipe.

Preparing the Egg Yolk–Sugar Mixture: Place the egg yolks and remaining sugar in a bowl and beat with an electric mixer or wire whisk until the mixture whitens and forms a ribbon.

Making the Cream: Place the saucepan containing the milk and sugar over high heat and bring back to a boil. Pour a little of the boiling milk into the bowl with the egg yolk–sugar mixture, whisking constantly as the liquid is added. Remove the saucepan of milk from the heat and pour the contents of the bowl into it, stirring constantly with a wooden spoon or spatula.

Cooking the Cream: Place the saucepan back over low heat, using a candy thermometer to watch the temperature of the cream as it cooks. Stir the cream constantly—it should never be allowed to boil. As it cooks, the cream will thicken perceptibly, especially toward the end of the cooking time. If using a candy thermometer, cook the cream until the thermometer registers 185°F (85°C), then remove from the heat and continue stirring for 1 to 2 minutes more before cooling the cream.

Although it is preferable to use a candy thermometer when cooking the cream, it is not absolutely necessary. As the cream cooks and thickens, it will begin to lightly coat the wooden spatula used to stir it. Lift the spatula periodically out of the cream and hold it at a tilt so that the excess cream will fall from the spatula back into the saucepan. Use your finger to draw a line in the thin film of cream that adheres to the spatula. If the cream needs to be cooked longer, the line will quickly lose its shape and the cream on the spatula will look as thin as milk. When sufficiently cooked, the cream will nicely coat the spatula and the top edge of the line will hold its shape. When the cream is cooked, it should immediately be removed from the heat.

Cooking the cream generally takes about 5 to 10 minutes.

Making the Ice Cream: Once cooked, pour a little of the cream into the bowl with the prune cream, stirring constantly as the hot liquid is being added. Continue adding the cooked cream to the bowl, progressively increasing the amount added each time, until all the hot cream has been stirred into the prune cream. Whisk the resulting mixture until it is smooth.

Cool and freeze the cream as described in Recipe 27.

Serving Suggestions: Serve with Vanilla Sauce (Recipe 99) flavored with 2 teaspoons of Armagnac for every generous 1⅔ cups (4 d*l*) cold vanilla sauce.

Note: This ice cream never hardens completely like most ice creams. It should be placed in the refrigerator no more than 10 minutes to soften before serving—if eaten within 24 hours of being made, even this is unnecessary. Prune ice cream should not be turned out, but served in scoops, and it should be made at least half a day in advance. Nevertheless, this delicious ice cream keeps its soft, creamy consistency for quite a long time before melting.

GENERAL COMMENTS ON PARFAITS

The following parfait recipes can be made without the use of an ice cream freezer. A parfait is a preparation made either with egg yolks and milk (much like ice cream) or with egg yolks and 28° Sugar Syrup (for alcohol-flavored parfaits). In either case, an important quantity of whipped cream is involved; it is added to the other ingredients after they have been cooked and beaten.

Parfaits generally resemble ice creams when served, but they are richer, lighter in texture, and creamier; they are delicious served alone, but are often used in molded combination desserts, pastry-based frozen desserts, and frozen soufflés.

Recipe 40 for Vanilla Parfait is given in great detail since it serves as a basic recipe for all egg yolk–milk-based parfaits.

40
Vanilla Parfait (Parfait à la Vanille)

PREPARATION	15 to 20 minutes
COOKING TIME	Approximately 10 minutes for the cream
COOLING TIME	Approximately 20 to 25 minutes (beating) and 1 hour refrigerated
FREEZING TIME	3 hours before serving
INGREDIENTS	*For approximately 1 quart (1 l) of parfait serving 6 to 8* 1 generous cup (¼ *l*) milk 1 cup (200 g) granulated sugar 1 vanilla bean, split open lengthwise 6 egg yolks *For the whipped cream* ½ cup (1.2 d*l*) heavy cream (Recipe 106)
UTENSILS	2 large bowls 2 saucepans with covers Wooden spatula Electric mixer *or* wire whisk (see Comment) Candy thermometer Mold

Preliminary Preparations: Place the cream for making the whipped cream in a bowl and refrigerate before starting to make the parfait.

Sweetening and Flavoring the Milk: Place the milk, half of the sugar, and the vanilla bean in a saucepan. Bring to a boil, then cover the saucepan, and remove from the heat. Leave to infuse for 10 minutes before proceeding with the recipe. with the recipe.

Note 1:   In some parfaits (e.g., Chocolate Parfait), no flavoring is added to the milk at this stage. The milk and half of the sugar must still be brought to a boil but need not be left to infuse before proceeding with the recipe.

Preparing the Egg Yolk–Sugar Mixture: Place the egg yolks and the remaining sugar in a mixing bowl and beat with an electric mixer or wire whisk until the mixture whitens and forms a ribbon.

Making the Cream: Place the saucepan containing the milk, sugar, and vanilla bean over high heat and bring back to a boil. Pour a little of the boiling milk mixture into the bowl with the egg yolk–sugar mixture, whisking constantly as the liquid is being added. Remove the saucepan of milk from the heat and pour the contents of the bowl into it, stirring constantly with a wooden spoon or spatula.

Cooking the Cream: Place the saucepan containing the cream on the stove and heat gently, using a candy thermometer to watch the temperature as the cream cooks. Stir the cream constantly—it should never be allowed to boil. As it cooks, the cream will thicken perceptibly, especially toward the end of the cooking time. If using a candy thermometer, cook the cream until the thermometer registers 189°F (87°C)—because of the large number of egg yolks, this cream can be cooked to a slightly higher temperature than the cream used in vanilla ice cream. Once this temperature is reached, remove the cream from the heat and continue stirring for 1 to 2 minutes longer before proceeding.

Note 2:   It is preferable to use a candy thermometer when cooking the cream, but it can be cooked without one, following the instructions given under "Cooking the Cream" in Recipe 27 for Vanilla Ice Cream.

Cooling the Cream: Once the cream is cooked, pour it into a large mixing bowl and remove the vanilla bean. Beat the cooked cream using an electric mixer, first on a medium-slow speed for about 4 to 6 minutes to cool the mixture and then on a very slow speed for approximately 10 to 15 minutes more. The mixture must be beaten until it has cooled completely and thickened enough to form a ribbon. This is very important, as is the type mixer you have (see Comment); beating times will vary, but the cream must be beaten until it is the consistency of a sponge cake batter before baking: that is, it should grow considerably in volume, be thick and foamy, and form a ribbon as it falls from a spatula. Be careful not to beat it longer than necessary; if beaten too long, the cream will eventually "fall" and become liquid again (see Comment).

Once the cream has been sufficiently beaten, place it in the refrigerator for about 1 hour or until it is as cold as the heavy cream previously refrigerated for making the whipped cream. When this point is reached, make the whipped cream and fold it little by little into the bowl with the vanilla cream. Once the ingredients are homogenously mixed, the parfait is ready to be molded.

Molding the Parfait: The parfait must be kept refrigerated until being molded, and it must be molded within 2 hours of the time it is made. Once molded, it must be placed in the freezer for 3 hours to harden before serving.

To Store: Once molded, the parfait can be kept for up to 2 weeks in the freezer.

Serving Suggestions: Vanilla Parfait is used in a number of frozen desserts. It is delicious molded with Pineapple Sherbet (Recipe 4), with molded combination desserts (Chapter 4), and in making the Snowball (Recipe 75) and several frozen soufflés (Recipes 78–81).

Comment: The type of mixer used in beating this type of parfait is very important. It must have *at least* 3 speeds, and the slowest speed must be *very* slow. The best are those equipped with a single, large beater. Most machines with 2 beaters will not beat slowly enough and they do not incorporate enough air. As a result, the batter will not rise and thicken properly but will either begin thickening and then fall or else never thicken at all but remain liquid.

If this happens, the cream can still be mixed with the whipped cream and frozen, but the result is more like vanilla ice cream than a parfait. However, it should not be used to make either a frozen soufflé or any other dessert that is built up inside a ring as it will not hold its shape. A successful parfait is nearly as thick as whipped cream, so it will not "leak" out under a metal or cardboard ring as would a parfait that did not thicken properly.

Therefore, if you do not have the right kind of mixer, the only way to be sure of having the parfait thicken properly is to use a wire whisk. Beat for the times indicated, relatively quickly for the first 4 to 6 minutes, then very slowly with a lazy, relaxed circular motion of the wrist, raising the whisk well out of the cream each time you beat, to incorporate air into the cream. If done in a relaxed way, the 20 to 25 minutes total beating time is not at all tiring.

41
Coffee-Flavored Vanilla Parfait
(Parfait à la Vanille Parfumé au Café)

PREPARATION	10 minutes after preparing Vanilla Parfait (Recipe 40)
FREEZING TIME	3 hours before serving
INGREDIENTS	*For 1 dessert serving 6 to 8* 4½ teaspoons coffee extract 4½ teaspoons instant coffee 1 quart (1 *l*) Vanilla Parfait (Recipe 40), but not frozen
UTENSILS	Double boiler Bowl Wooden spatula Mold

Flavoring the Vanilla Parfait: Place the coffee extract and the instant coffee in a double boiler and stir until the instant coffee dissolves. Remove from the heat and leave to cool.

When cold, stir 2 tablespoons of the vanilla parfait into the coffee and then pour this mixture into the rest of the vanilla parfait and combine by folding the ingredients together. Pour the finished parfait into a soufflé mold or other mold and place immediately in the freezer.

Serving Suggestions: A frozen soufflé can be made with this parfait following the instructions for molding on page 108.

If desired, rather than flavor all of the Vanilla Parfait, half of it can be flavored as described here and molded with the remaining unflavored half to make a Combination Frozen Soufflé like the one pictured on page 115, and described in Recipe 81 for Combination Frozen Soufflés.

42
Coffee Parfait
(Parfait au Café)

PREPARATION	20 minutes
COOKING TIME	Approximately 10 minutes for the cream
COOLING TIME	Approximately 20 to 25 minutes (beating) and 1 hour refrigerated
FREEZING TIME	3 hours before serving
INGREDIENTS	*For one quart (1 l) of parfait serving 6 to 8* 1½ teaspoons coarsely ground coffee 1 generous cup (¼ l) milk 1 cup (200 g) granulated sugar 3 tablespoons instant coffee or 2 teaspoons coffee extract 6 egg yolks *For the whipped cream* ½ cup (1.2 dl) heavy cream (see Recipe 106)
UTENSILS	2 large bowls 2 saucepans with covers Wooden spatula Electric mixer *or* wire whisk (see Comment after Recipe 40) Sieve Candy thermometer Mold

Making the Parfait: Using the ingredients listed here, make the parfait following the instructions given in Recipe 40 for Vanilla Parfait.

When sweetening and flavoring the milk, add the ground coffee to the pot with the milk and half of the sugar. After infusing for 10 minutes, strain the liquid and add the coffee extract (or the instant coffee) to it; this will intensify both the taste and color. Finish as described in Recipe 40.

Serving Suggestions: Coffee Parfait can be used to make a frozen soufflé with Vanilla Parfait (see Recipe 81 for Frozen Soufflés) and it can be molded with Nut Brittle Ice Cream (Recipe 38) to make Frozen Nut Brittle Delight (Recipe 70).

43
Chocolate Parfait (Parfait au Chocolat)

PREPARATION	10 minutes
COOKING TIME	Approximately 10 minutes for the cream
COOLING TIME	Approximately 20 to 25 minutes for beating
FREEZING TIME	3 hours before serving
INGREDIENTS	*For 2½ pints (1.2 l) of parfait serving 8 to 10*
	1 generous cup (¼ l) milk
	1 cup (200 g) granulated sugar
	6 egg yolks
	10½ ounces (300 g) semi-sweet chocolate broken into small pieces
	For the whipped cream
	1 generous cup (¼ l) heavy cream (see Recipe 106)
UTENSILS	2 large bowls
	2 saucepans with covers
	Wooden spatula
	Electric mixer *or* wire whisk (see Comment following Recipe 40)
	Candy thermometer
	Mold

Making the Parfait: Using the ingredients listed here, make and cook the parfait cream as described in Recipe 40 for Vanilla Parfait.

After the cream has finished cooking, remove the saucepan from the heat and add the pieces of chocolate to the hot cream a handful at a time, beating constantly with a wire whisk as the chocolate is being added. The cream must then be beaten to cool, thicken, and form a ribbon, but unlike the Vanilla Parfait it should *not* be refrigerated before adding the whipped cream, since the chocolate will harden too quickly. Therefore, simply fold in the whipped cream after the chocolate cream has formed a ribbon. Then mold, freeze, and serve.

Serving Suggestions: Chocolate parfait can be used to make many delicious desserts. It can be molded with Vanilla Ice Cream (Recipe 68, Molded Combination Desserts) or Vanilla Parfait (Recipe 81) and is an ingredient in both the Medicis Frozen Pistacio Dessert (Recipe 84) and the Frozen Chocolate and Orange Dessert (Recipe 83).

44
Alcohol-Flavored Parfait (Parfait à l'Alcool)

PREPARATION	10 minutes
COOKING TIME	20 minutes
COOLING TIME	7 to 10 minutes (beating) and 1 hour refrigerated
FREEZING TIME	3 hours before serving
INGREDIENTS	*For a little less than 1 quart (1 l) serving 4 to 5* ¾ cup (1.7 d*l*) 28° Sugar Syrup (Recipe 1) 4 egg yolks 1 tablespoon alcohol (see Note) *For the whipped cream* 1 generous cup (2.5 d*l*) heavy cream (see Recipe 106)
INGREDIENTS	*For approximately 2½ pints (1¼ l) serving 7 to 8* 1 generous cup (2.5 d*l*) 28° Sugar Syrup (Recipe 1) 6 egg yolks 1½ tablespoons alcohol (see Note) *For the whipped cream* Generous 1½ cups (3.75 d*l*) heavy cream (see Recipe 106)
UTENSILS	2 large mixing bowls 1 small saucepan Yoghurt thermometer Wire whisk Wooden spatula Double boiler *or* mixing bowl and saucepan (*bain-marie*) Electric mixer Mold

Preliminary Preparations: Place the cream for making the whipped cream in a bowl and refrigerate before starting to make the parfait.

Sweetening and Cooking the Egg Yolks: Heat the sugar syrup in a small saucepan over low heat; use a yoghurt thermometer and heat to between 86°F (30°C) and 104°F (40°C). If you do not have a yoghurt thermometer, test the temperature with your finger—the syrup should be lukewarm.

In a small bowl, beat the egg yolks well. Then, little by little, pour the warm sugar syrup onto them, whisking vigorously.

Pour the sweetened egg yolks into the top of a double boiler or a *bain-marie* and cook over low heat for 20 minutes, stirring the mixture every 3 or 4 minutes with a wooden spatula. When stirring, great care should be taken to detach any parts of the mixture sticking to the sides or bottom of the double boiler or the mixing bowl used in the *bain-marie*. The mixture will thicken as it cooks. Cook very slowly over low heat so that the water in the bottom of the double boiler or *bain-marie* simmers but does not boil.

Beating and cooling: Pour the egg yolk mixture into a mixing bowl and beat with an electric mixer on high speed for 1 minute. Continue beating on medium speed for 3 minutes and then on low speed for a final 3 to 5 minutes. Mixing times vary, but when beaten, the egg yolk mixture will thicken and grow in volume; it should be beaten until it forms a ribbon when it falls from a spoon or spatula.

When finished mixing, place the bowl in the refrigerator for 1 hour so that its contents will cool to approximately the same temperature as the heavy cream used in making the whipped cream.

Note: If the parfait does not thicken properly when being beaten, your mixer is at fault. See Comment after Recipe 40 for Vanilla Parfait.

Adding the Whipped Cream and Alcohol: Make the whipped cream as described in Recipe 106, and fold it into the cooled egg yolk mixture little by little. Halfway through, add the alcohol; it will be mixed into the parfait as the rest of the whipped cream is folded in (see Note).

To Mold: Once the cream and alcohol have been added, the parfait must be molded immediately and placed in the freezer for at least 3 hours before serving.

To Store: Once molded, the parfait can be kept in the freezer for 2 weeks.

Serving Suggestions: The following are desserts using different alcohol-flavored parfaits: kirsch-flavored parfait (molded with or served in scoops with pineapple sherbet); cognac-flavored parfait (Recipe 82); Grand Marnier-flavored parfait (Recipes 76 and 78); rum-flavored parfait (Recipe 80); frozen Martinique Dessert (Recipe 77), and combination dessert molded with Banana Sherbet.

Note: This parfait mixture can be flavored with almost any alcohol; the most frequently used are rum, kirsch, cognac, or Grand Marnier.

When making alcohol-flavored parfaits, it is often a good idea to flavor part of the preparation with one alcohol and the rest with another. This can be done by dividing the parfait in half after the whipped cream has been added and then folding a different alcohol into each half. If the parfait is divided in this way, only half the amount of alcohol called for in the list of ingredients is added to flavor each half of the parfait.

Chapter 3

SUNDAES

RECIPES

45. Auteuil Sundae (Coupe Auteuil)

46. Red Currant Sundae (Coupe aux Groseilles)

47. Belle Hélène Pear Sundae (Poire Belle Hélène)

48. Tropical Fruit Sundae (Coupe aux Fruits Exotiques)

49. Chocolate Liégeois Sundae (Chocolat Liégeois)

50. Concorde Sundae (Coupe Concorde)

51. Ivory Coast Sundae (Coupe Côte-d'Ivoire)

52. Passion Fruit Sundae (Coupe aux Fruits de la Passion)

53. Coffee Liégeois Sundae (Café Liégeois)

54. Armagnac Sundae (Coupe à l'Armagnac)

55. Hawaiian Sundae (Coupe Hawai)

56. Cardinal Sundae (Coupe Cardinal)

57. Pré Catelan Sundae (Coupe Fruitée du Pré Catelan)

58. Champagne and Raspberry Sundae (Coupe Champagne-Framboises)

59. Cantaloupe or Muskmelon Sundae (Melon de Cavaillon)

60. Juanita Banana Sundae (Coupe Juanita Banana)

61. Vanilla Meringue Sundae (Meringue Glacée)

62. Sylvie Lenôtre's Success Sundae (Succès Glacé Sylvie Lenôtre) 🎩

63. Melba Tulip Cookie Dessert (Tulipe de Fruits Melba) 🎩 🎩

64. Whipped Cream Tulip Cookie Dessert (Tulipe à la Chantilly) 🎩 🎩

65. Loire Valley Sundae (Coupe Val de Loire) 🎩

66. Raspberry Tulip (Tulipe Framboisée) 🎩 🎩

67. Ruby Sundae (Coupe Rubis) 🎩

Snowball, Recipe 75

GENERAL COMMENTS ON SUNDAES

Sundaes are desserts made with scoops of one or more flavors of ice cream, sherbet, parfait, or a combination of any or all three. Sundaes are always served with a sauce and are often served with small pieces of fruit, pastry, or meringue to garnish them. The ice cream or sherbet used in making a sundae can be prepared hours, even days, in advance but the sauce and garnishing elements are added only at the last minute.

Included with the sundaes are several desserts served in cup-like pastry shells called tulip pastries (*tulipes* in French). The pastry here replaces the glass in these sundae-like desserts (see photo, page 58).

Most of the sundaes in this book are small, delicately arranged, and subtly flavored. Unlike American versions of this type of dessert, French sundaes are often composed of only a few elements, many times using a sauce the same flavor as the ice cream or sherbet to intensify the taste experience.

One quart (1 *l*) of ice cream or sherbet will make about 20 scoops if using an ice cream scoop of a 3-tablespoon (5-c*l*) capacity, which is the size I suggest using. When you have to prepare a lot of sundaes, it is convenient to scoop the ice cream being used a day ahead of time and freeze the scoops as follows. Remove the stored ice cream or sherbet from the freezer and place it in the refrigerator to soften as described in General Comments on Storing and Serving Ice Creams and Sherbet (pages 5 to 7). Place a piece of nonstick parchment paper on a large plate in the freezer and turn the freezer down to its lowest setting. Leave the plate in the freezer for at least 15 minutes.

When the ice cream has softened enough, remove the plate from the freezer and scoop the ice cream onto the paper. Put the plate back into the freezer, and when the scoops have hardened, place them in a freezer bag or a box that can be tightly closed. In this way, the scoops can be kept in the freezer for up to 10 days. When needed, the scoops should be arranged in the serving dishes or glasses and allowed to thaw in the refrigerator until soft enough to serve in the same way as any stored ice cream.

The following recipes for sundaes are only a sampling of the many desserts that can be made in the same way. Many of the flavor combinations used in the Molded Combination Desserts (see Chapter 4) can be used to make sundaes. Sundaes are generally served either in a tall narrow glass or a wide champagne-style one. Of course, special sundae glasses or any small dish or bowl can be used when making this type dessert. In any case, the receptacle used for the sundae should be placed in the freezer for at least 15 minutes before being filled with the ice cream, sauce, and garnish.

Important: All of the following sundae recipes are for making 1 sundae, that is, 1 serving. By simply multiplying the amounts of the ingredients given with each sundae, you can easily calculate what you need to make 4, 5, 6, or 10 identical sundaes.

Perigord Crown Dessert, Recipe 74, decorated with Ardèche-Style Truffles,
Recipe 225

45
Auteuil Sundae (Coupe Auteuil)

PREPARATION

5 minutes

INGREDIENTS

For 1 serving
2 scoops of Vanilla Ice Cream (Recipe 27)
3 tablespoons (½ dl) Caramel Sauce (Recipe 102)

For decoration
Chantilly Cream (Recipe 104)
Large Nougatine Crumble (Recipe 197)

Making the Dessert: (See the General Comments on Sundaes.) Place the scoops of ice cream in a cold serving glass or dish, spoon over the caramel sauce, then decorate with a little Chantilly cream, sprinkle a little nougatine crumble over the cream, and serve.

46
Red Currant Sundae (Coupe aux Groseilles)

PREPARATION

5 minutes

INGREDIENTS

For 1 serving
2 scoops of Vanilla Ice Cream (Recipe 27)
3 tablespoons (½ dl) Red Currant Sauce (see Recipe 98 for
    Fresh Fruit Sauce)
1 small bunch of fresh red currants

Making the Dessert: (See the General Comments on Sundaes.) Place the scoops of ice cream, one on top of another, in a cold serving glass or dish. Spoon over the red currant sauce and place a bunch of fresh currants in the glass to decorate. Serve immediately.

47
Belle Hélène Pear Sundae (Poire Belle Hélène)

PREPARATION   5 minutes

INGREDIENTS   *For 1 serving*
                   2 scoops of Vanilla Ice Cream (Recipe 27)
                   ½ pear in light syrup (Recipe 124)
                   3 tablespoons (½ dl) Hot Chocolate Sauce (Recipe 101)

                   For decoration
                   Slivered almonds

Making the Dessert: (See the General Comments on Sundaes.) Place the scoops of ice cream in a cold serving glass or dish and cover the ice cream with the pear half. Spoon the hot chocolate sauce over the pear and sprinkle with slivered almonds. Serve immediately.

Note: This classic dessert can be varied by using either half a peach or two apricot halves in light syrup instead of the pear.

48
Tropical Fruit Sundae (Coupe aux Fruits Exotiques)

PREPARATION   5 minutes

INGREDIENTS   *Fo. serving*
                   2 scoops of Vanilla Ice Cream (Recipe 27)
                   A few thin slices of mango or papaya
                   3 tablespoons (½ dl) Fresh Apricot Sauce (see Recipe 98
                       for Fresh Fruit Sauce)

Making the Dessert: (See the General Comments on Sundaes.) Place the scoops of ice cream in a cold serving glass or dish, cover the ice cream with the thin slices of fruit, and spoon over the apricot sauce. Serve immediately.

49
Chocolate Liégeois Sundae (Chocolat Liégeois)

PREPARATION   5 minutes

INGREDIENTS   *For 1 serving*
4½ teaspoons unsweetened or sweet cocoa powder
3 tablespoons (½ d*l*) cold water or cold milk
2 scoops of Chocolate Ice Cream (Recipe 32)

For decoration
1 generous tablespoon Chantilly Cream (Recipe 104)
Grated chocolate

Making the Dessert: (See the General Comments on Sundaes.) Depending on your own taste preference, use either unsweetened or sweet cocoa powder, and mix it with either cold milk or cold water to make a cold chocolate sauce.

Place the scoops of ice cream in a cold tall glass, pour the chocolate sauce into the glass, and top with a generous spoonful of Chantilly Cream. Decorate the whipped cream with a little grated chocolate and serve immediately.

50
Concorde Sundae (Coupe Concorde)

PREPARATION   5 minutes

INGREDIENTS   *For 1 serving*
2 scoops of Chocolate Ice Cream (Recipe 32)
3 tablespoons (½ d*l*) Orange Sauce (Recipe 100)

For decoration
Swiss Meringue Chocolate Fingers or grated chocolate

Making the Dessert: (See the General Comments on Sundaes.) Place the ice cream in a cold serving glass or dish and spoon over the Orange Sauce. Decorate with Swiss Meringue Chocolate Fingers or with grated chocolate. Serve immediately.

51
Ivory Coast Sundae (Coupe Côte-d'Ivoire)

(Photo page 35)

PREPARATION   5 minutes

INGREDIENTS   *For 1 serving*
                   1 scoop of Chocolate Ice Cream (Recipe 32)
                   1 scoop of Banana Sherbet (Recipe 5)
                   3 tablespoons (½ d*l*) Vanilla Sauce (Recipe 99)

                   For decoration
                   1 Chocolate Palm (Recipe 119)

Making the Dessert: (See the General Comments on Sundaes.) Place the scoop of ice cream and the scoop of sherbet next to each other in a cold serving glass or in a previously refrigerated calabash shell. Spoon over the Vanilla Sauce, decorate with the Chocolate Palm, and serve immediately. (The Vanilla Sauce can also be served under the ice cream as shown in the photograph.)

52
Passion Fruit Sundae (Coupe aux Fruits de la Passion)

(Photo page 38)

PREPARATION   5 minutes

INGREDIENTS   *For 1 serving*
                   1 scoop of Coconut Ice Cream (Recipe 36)
                   1 scoop of Passion Fruit Sherbet (Recipe 12)
                   ½ a coconut or ½ a calabash
                   3 tablespoons (½ d*l*) Vanilla Sauce (Recipe 99)

                   For decoration
                   Chocolate Palm (Recipe 119—optional)

Making the Dessert: (See the General Comments on Sundaes.) Place a scoop of ice cream and a scoop of sherbet in the half coconut or calabash, spoon over the vanilla sauce, decorate with the chocolate palm, and serve immediately.

53
Coffee Liégeois Sundae (Café Liégeois)

(Photo page 35)

PREPARATION   5 minutes

INGREDIENTS   *For 1 serving*
                       2 scoops of Coffee Ice Cream (Recipe 33)
                       3 tablespoons (½ dl) very sweet, cold, black coffee

                       For decoration
                       1 generous tablespoon Chantilly Cream (Recipe 104)
                       3 sugar coffee beans (optional)
                         (see Dictionary of Terms)

Making the Dessert: (See the General Comments on Sundaes.) Place the ice cream in a tall cold glass, pour over the cold, sweetened coffee, and top with a generous spoonful of Chantilly Cream. Sprinkle a few sugar coffee beans over the Chantilly to decorate and serve immediately.

54
Armagnac Sundae (Coupe à l'Armagnac)

PREPARATION   5 minutes

INGREDIENTS   *For 1 serving*
                       3 tablespoons (½ dl) Vanilla Sauce (Recipe 99), flavored
                         with Armagnac (to taste)
                       2 scoops of Armagnac and Prune Ice Cream (Recipe 39)

                       For decoration
                       Either 1 Stuffed Prune (Recipe 179)
                         or thin strips of Half-Candied Orange Peel (Recipe 167)

Making the Dessert: (See the General Comments on Sundaes.) Place the ice cream in a cold serving glass or dish, spoon over the sauce, and decorate either with a Stuffed Prune or with a few strips of Half-Candied Orange Peel. Serve immediately.

55
Hawaiian Sundae (Coupe Hawai)

PREPARATION   35 minutes

INGREDIENTS   *For 1 serving*
6½ tablespoons (1 dl) Kirsch-Flavored Parfait, unfrozen
    (Recipe 44)
1 scoop of Pineapple Sherbet (Recipe 4)

For decoration
Half-Candied Pineapple Slices (Recipe 166)
3 tablespoons (½ dl) kirsch (optional—see Note)

Making the Dessert: (See the General Comments on Sundaes.) Place the parfait in a tall serving glass and place the glass in the freezer for 30 minutes. Remove from the freezer and place the scoop of sherbet on top of the parfait, pressing it lightly so that it will sink into the parfait a bit. Decorate with a few small pieces of Half-Candied Pineapple Slices and serve immediately.

Note: The pineapple can be left to soak for 1 hour in kirsch if desired.

To Store: This dessert can be made and kept in the freezer for 24 hours before adding the pineapple and serving.

56
Cardinal Sundae (Coupe Cardinal)

PREPARATION   5 minutes

INGREDIENTS   *For 1 serving*
1 scoop of Black Currant Sherbet (Recipe 6)
1 scoop of Vanilla Ice Cream (Recipe 27)
3 tablespoons (½ dl) Black Currant Sauce (Recipe 98)
    or 1 tablespoon black currant jelly

For decoration
Chantilly Cream (Recipe 104)

Making the Dessert: (See the General Comments on Sundaes.) Place the ice cream and sherbet in a cold serving glass or dish, spoon over either the black currant sauce or the jelly, decorate with Chantilly Cream, and serve immediately.

57
Pré Catelan Sundae (Coupe Fruitée du Pré Catelan)

PREPARATION   5 minutes

INGREDIENTS   *For 1 serving*
                   2 scoops of Lemon Sherbet (Recipe 7)
                   3 tablespoons (½ d*l*) orange juice sweetened with sugar

                   For decoration
                   Half-Candied Orange Slice (Recipe 168)

Making the Dessert: (See the General Comments on Sundaes.) Place the sherbet in a cold serving glass or dish, pour over the orange juice, and top with the half-candied orange slice. Serve immediately.

58
Champagne and Raspberry Sundae
(Coupe Champagne-Framboises)

(*Photo page 55*)

PREPARATION   5 minutes

INGREDIENTS   *For 1 serving*
                   2 scoops of Raspberry Sherbet (Recipe 11)
                   1 scoop of Champagne Sherbet (Recipe 22)
                   3 tablespoons (½ d*l*) Fresh Raspberry Sauce (Recipe 98)

                   For decoration
                   A few Half-Candied Pineapple Slices (Recipe 166)
                   Fresh raspberries

Making the Dessert: (See the General Comments on Sundaes.) Place the scoops of sherbert on top of each other in a tall cold glass, spoon over the fresh raspberry sauce, and decorate with the Half-Candied Pineapple Slices and fresh raspberries. Serve immediately.

59

Cantaloupe or Muskmelon Sundae
(Melon de Cavaillon)

PREPARATION	5 to 10 minutes
INGREDIENTS	*For 1 serving* ½ cantaloupe or muskmelon

Either
2 scoops of Melon Sherbet (Recipe 15)
3 tablespoons (½ d*l*) Fresh Strawberry Sauce (Recipe 98)

or
1 scoop of Melon Sherbet (Recipe 15)
1 scoop of Strawberry Sherbet (Recipe 10)
3 tablespoons (½ d*l*) Fresh Strawberry Sauce (Recipe 98)

or
1 scoop Melon Sherbet (Recipe 15)
1 scoop Port Sherbet (Recipe 24)
3 tablespoons (½ d*l*) red port

For decoration
3 fresh strawberries

Making the Dessert: (See the General Comments on Sundaes.) It is best to cut and scoop out the seeds from the melon just before you are ready to fill and serve it.

Place any one or a combination of the sherbets listed above into the half melon and spoon over the sauce or the port depending on your choice of sherbets. Decorate with a few fresh strawberries and serve immediately.

60
Juanita Banana Sundae (Coupe Juanita Banana)
(Photo page 35)

PREPARATION   5 minutes

INGREDIENTS   *For 1 serving*
                     2 scoops of Vanilla Ice Cream (Recipe 27)
                     ½ banana (split lengthwise)
                     3 tablespoons (½ dl) Hot Chocolate Sauce (Recipe 101)

                     For decoration
                     Chantilly Cream (Recipe 104)

(See the General Comments on Sundaes.) In a crescent-shaped serving dish (see photo) or on a plate, place the ice cream and the half banana. Spoon over the Hot Chocolate Sauce and decorate with a little Chantilly Cream squeezed from a pastry bag to make a rose-like mound. Serve immediately.

   As shown in the photo, the chocolate sauce can be put in the serving dish before the other ingredients, if desired.

61
Vanilla Meringue Sundae (Meringue Glacée)

PREPARATION   5 minutes

INGREDIENTS   *For 1 serving*
                     2 oval meringues (Recipe 109)
                     1 large scoop of Vanilla Ice Cream (Recipe 27)

                     To decorate
                     Chantilly Cream (Recipe 104)
                     Grilled Slivered Almonds (Recipe 118)
                     or
                     3 tablespoons (½ dl) Hot Chocolate Sauce (Recipe 101)
                     Grated chocolate

Making the Dessert: (See the General Comments on Sundaes.) In a small dish or large, cup-cake-type plastic mold, place the two meringues facing each other; hold the meringues apart and place the ice cream between them. Decorate with either Chantilly Cream sprinkled with grilled slivered almonds or Hot Chocolate Sauce sprinkled with grated chocolate. Serve immediately.

62

Sylvie Lenôtre's Success Sundae (Succès Glacé Sylvie Lenôtre)

PREPARATION   5 minutes

INGREDIENTS   *For 1 serving*
2 individual Success Pastries (Recipe 110)
1 scoop of Nut Brittle Ice Cream (Recipe 38)

Either 3 tablespoons (½ dl) Vanilla Sauce (Recipe 99)
  or 3 tablespoons (½ dl) Caramel Sauce (Recipe 102)

For decoration
Large Nut Brittle Powder (Recipe 196)

Making the Dessert: (See the General Comments on Sundaes.) In a wide, low dish or large, cup-cake-type plastic mold, place one of the Success Pastries. Place the ice cream on top and cover with the second Success Pastry. Spoon over either sauce and sprinkle with the powdered nut brittle. Serve immediately.

63

Melba Tulip Cookie Dessert (Tulipe de Fruits Melba)

(*Photo page 58*)

PREPARATION   5 minutes

INGREDIENTS   *For 1 serving*
1 Tulip Pastry (Recipe 117)
2 scoops of Vanilla Ice Cream (Recipe 27)
A few pieces of fresh or canned fruit

For decoration
1 tablespoon Red Currant Jelly (Recipe 143)
Slivered almonds

Making the Dessert: (See the General Comments on Sundaes.) Place the tulip pastry on a serving plate, put the ice cream into it, and decorate with fruit. Spoon over the currant jelly, sprinkle with slivered almonds, and serve immediately.

Note: As shown in the photo, Fresh Fruit Sauce (made from the same fruit served around the ice cream) can be used instead of jelly with the dessert.

64
Whipped Cream Tulip Cookie Dessert (Tulipe à la Chantilly)

PREPARATION   5 minutes

INGREDIENTS   *For 1 serving*
1 Tulip Pastry (Recipe 117)
2 scoops of Vanilla Ice Cream (Recipe 27)

For decoration
Chantilly Cream (Recipe 104)
Grilled Slivered Almonds (Recipe 118)

Making the Dessert: (See the General Comments on Sundaes.) Place the tulip cookie on a plate, put the scoops of ice cream into it, decorate with the Chantilly Cream and Slivered Almonds. Serve immediately.

65
Loire Valley Sundae (Coupe Val de Loire)

PREPARATION   5 minutes

INGREDIENTS   *For 1 serving*
2 scoops of Raspberry Sherbet (Recipe 11)
1 Tulip Pastry (Recipe 117—optional)
3 tablespoons (½ dl) Fresh Strawberry Sauce (Recipe 98)

For decoration
4 Brandied Cherries (Recipe 126)
   or 4 Home Canned Cherries (Recipe 123)
Slivered almonds (optional)

Making the Dessert: (See the General Comments on Sundaes.) Place the scoops of sherbet either in a cold, tall glass or in a tulip pastry. Spoon over the strawberry sauce, decorate with the cherries, and sprinkle with slivered almonds if desired. Serve immediately.

66
Raspberry Tulip (Tulipe Framboisée)

(Photo page 58)

PREPARATION   5 minutes

INGREDIENTS

For 1 serving
1 Tulip Pastry (Recipe 117)
2 scoops of Raspberry Sherbet (Recipe 11)
3 tablespoons (½ d*l*) Fresh Raspberry Sauce (Recipe 98)

For decoration
1 small bunch of fresh red currants

Making the Dessert: (See the General Comments on Sundaes.) Place the tulip pastry on a plate and fill with the scoops of sherbet, spoon over the raspberry sauce, and decorate with a bunch of fresh red currants. Serve immediately.

67
Ruby Sundae (Coupe Rubis)

PREPARATION   5 minutes

INGREDIENTS

For 1 serving
2 scoops of Red Currant Sherbet (Recipe 13)
1 Tulip Pastry (Recipe 117—optional)
3 tablespoons (½ d*l*) Red Currant Jelly (Recipe 143)

For decoration
4 Brandied Cherries (Recipe 126)
   or 4 Home Canned Cherries (Recipe 123)

Making the Dessert: (See the General Comments on Sundaes.) Place the scoops of sherbet either in a tall, cold glass, dish, or tulip pastry. Spoon over the jelly and decorate with the cherries. Serve immediately.

Chapter 4

COMBINATION DESSERTS

RECIPES

68. Molded Vanilla Desserts (Glaces Panachées à la Vanille)

69. Molded Chestnut and Pear Dessert (Glace Marrons-Poires)

70. Frozen Nut Brittle Delight (Glace Praliné-Délices)

71. Molded Apricot and Raspberry Dessert (Sorbet Abricots-Framboises)

72. Molded Hawaiian Dessert (Bombe Hawai)

73. Molded Raspberry and Champagne Dessert (Sorbet Champagne-Framboises)

74. Perigord Crown Dessert (Couronne Périgourdine)

75. Snowball (Boule de Neige)

76. Frozen Grand Marnier Dessert (Rosace Glacée au Grand Marnier)

77. Frozen Martinique Dessert (Rosace Glacée de la Martinique)

78. Frozen Grand Marnier Soufflé (Soufflé au Grand Marnier)

79. Individual Frozen Grand Marnier Soufflés (Soufflé au Grand Marnier Individuel) 🍳🍳

80. Port Royal Frozen Soufflé (Soufflé Port-Royal) 🍳🍳🍳

81. Two-Flavored Frozen Soufflés (Soufflés Panachés à la Vanille) 🍳🍳

82. Frozen Cognac and Apricot Dessert (Biscuit Glacé de Cognac) 🍳🍳🍳

83. Frozen Chocolate and Orange Dessert (Biscuit Glacé du Roussillon) 🍳🍳

84. Médicis Frozen Pistacio Dessert (Biscuit Glacé Médicis) 🍳🍳

85. Auteuil-Style Frozen Caramel Dessert (Biscuit Glacé d'Auteuil) 🍳🍳

86. Frozen Strawberry or Raspberry Vacherin (Vacherin aux Fraises ou aux Framboises) 🍳🍳

87. Frozen Coffee Vacherin (Vacherin Fin Moka) 🍳🍳

88. Baked Alaska (Omelette Norvégiènne) 🍳🍳🍳

89. Individual Chocolate Parfait Desserts (Parfait au Chocolat Individuel) 🍳

90. Sherbet-Filled Pineapple Dessert (Sorbet à l'Ananas dans le Fruit) 🍳🍳🍳

91. Sherbet-Filled Fruits (Fruits Givrés) 🍳🍳

92. Frozen Coffee Dessert (Café Frappé) 🍳🍳

93. Frozen Chocolate Dessert (Chocolat Frappé) 🍳🍳

94. Frozen Rice Pudding with Apricots (Riz du Mas du Juge) 🍳

95. Profiteroles (Profiteroles) 🍳🍳

96. Chocolate-Coated Ice Cream on a Stick (Sucettes Glacées) 🍳🍳

97. Baked Alaskan Banana Dessert (Banane à la Norvégiènne) 🍳🍳

GENERAL COMMENTS ON MOLDED
COMBINATION DESSERTS

The following desserts are only a sampling of the many that can be made by molding and serving two or more flavors of ice cream, sherbet, or parfait in the same mold. Using a little imagination, you can create your own molded combination desserts following the principles outlined here. The number of combinations is endless: sherbets can be molded with sherbets, ice creams, or parfaits; ice creams with other ice creams, and so on.

The introductory comments to the first recipe (Molded Vanilla Desserts), as well as storing information apply to all similar desserts unless otherwise indicated.

68
Molded Vanilla Desserts
(Glaces Panachées à la Vanille)
(*Photo page 95*)

Ice creams, sherbets, and parfaits used in making molded combination desserts must be of a "newly made" consistency; that is, they should be about the softness of ice cream or sherbet when it comes from the ice cream freezer (see the coffee ice cream pictured in the photo). Parfaits should be the consistency they are after having the whipped cream folded into them but before freezing—it is best to make them at the last minute for this reason.

Ideally, ice creams or sherbets used in molded desserts should be molded immediately or within 1 or 2 hours of the time they come from the ice cream freezer, when they will be of the perfect consistency for lining or pouring into a mold. If previously frozen, ice cream, sherbet, or parfaits must be softened to the "newly made" consistency described above before being used as an element in a molded combination dessert. This softening is simply done by removing it from the freezer and placing it in the refrigerator for approximately 45 minutes to 1 hour, or until softened to the proper consistency.

PREPARATION	15 minutes
COOLING TIME	2 to 3 hours
FREEZING TIME	3 hours before serving

For a 1-quart (1-l) mold serving 6

To line the mold
½ quart (½ *l*) Vanilla Ice Cream (Recipe 27)

To fill the center of the mold
½ quart (½ *l*) Strawberry Sherbet (Recipe 10) *or* Raspberry Sherbet (Recipe 11) *or* Coffee Ice Cream (Recipe 33) *or* Chocolate Parfait (Recipe 43)

UTENSILS   1-quart (1-*l*) ice cream mold with cover
Flexible-blade, metal spatula or spoon

Preliminary Preparations: Place the mold and cover in the freezer for at least 15 minutes before lining it.

Lining the Mold: Take the mold from the freezer and pour the Vanilla Ice Cream into the mold. Work quickly, using a flexible-blade metal spatula or a metal spoon to push the ice cream around and up the sides of the mold. The ice cream should cover the bottom and the sides of the mold. Don't worry about neatness or the fact that the ice cream will not line the mold evenly at this stage; this will be done later.

Place the mold back into the freezer for 30 to 40 minutes, after which time the ice cream will have stiffened enough to allow you to even out the lining of the mold. The ice cream should still be soft enough to push, so that it will cover the sides and bottom of the mold in one equally thick, smooth layer, and cold enough so that once pushed up and smoothed out it will hold its shape. If after this second smoothing the ice cream is still too soft to hold its shape when pushed up the sides, it should be refrigerated for another 30 minutes to an hour and the lining completed at that time. (The time in the freezer varies depending on the stiffness of the ice cream to start with and the temperature of your freezer.)

Filling the Center of the Mold: Once the mold has been lined (see photo), place it immediately back into the freezer for 1 hour if it is to be filled with either another ice cream or a sherbet. However, if it is filled with a parfait, the parfait should be poured into the center immediately after the lining has been completed and the filled mold then placed in the freezer. Once the mold is filled, it must be left in the freezer for at least 3 hours before turning out and serving.

To Turn Out and Serve: See comments on turning out and serving molded ice creams and sherbets (page 5).

To Store: In a closed mold, molded combination desserts made with vanilla ice cream may be kept in the freezer for up to 2 weeks.

94

♕ ♕

69

Molded Chestnut and Pear Dessert
(Glace Marrons-Poires)

PREPARATION	15 minutes
COOLING TIME	3 to 4 hours
FREEZING TIME	3 hours before serving
INGREDIENTS	*For a 1-quart (1-l) mold serving 6*
	½ quart (½ *l*) Chestnut Ice Cream (Recipe 34)
	¼ cup (80 g) chestnut cream
	(see Dictionary of Terms)
	½ quart (½ *l*) Pear Sherbet (Recipe 19 or 20)
UTENSILS	1-quart (1-*l*) ice cream mold with cover
	Flexible-blade, metal spatula or spoon

Preliminary Preparations: Place the mold and cover in the freezer for at least 15 minutes before lining it.

Lining the Mold: Take the mold from the freezer and pour the Chestnut Ice Cream into the mold. Work quickly, using a flexible-blade metal spatula or a metal spoon to push the ice cream around and up the sides of the mold. The ice cream should cover the bottom and the sides of the mold. Don't worry about neatness or the fact that the ice cream will not line the mold evenly at this stage; this will be done later.

Place the mold back into the freezer for 30 to 40 minutes, after which time the ice cream will have stiffened enough to allow you to even out the lining of the mold. The ice cream should still be soft enough to push, so that it will cover the sides and bottom of the mold in one equally thick, smooth layer, and cold enough so that once pushed up and smoothed out it will hold its shape. If after this second smoothing the ice cream is still too soft to hold its shape when pushed up the sides, it should be refrigerated for another 30 minutes to an hour and the lining completed at that time. (The time in the freezer varies depending on the stiffness of the ice cream to start with and the temperature of your freezer.)

Making the Dessert: After the mold has been lined with the Chestnut Ice Cream and placed in the freezer for 1 hour, spread the chestnut cream evenly over the Chestnut Ice Cream and place in the freezer for 1 hour more before filling the center with the Pear Sherbet. Once the dessert is made, it must be left in the freezer for at least 3 hours before turning out and serving (see page 5).

Frozen Grand Marnier Dessert, Recipe 76

Frozen Nut Brittle Delight (Glace Praliné-Délices)

PREPARATION	15 minutes
COOLING TIME	2 to 3 hours
FREEZING TIME	3 hours before serving
INGREDIENTS	*For a 1-quart (1-l) mold serving 6* ½ quart (½ *l*) Nut Brittle Ice Cream (Recipe 38) ½ quart (½ *l*) Coffee Parfait (Recipe 42) 38 sugar coffee beans (optional)
UTENSILS	1-quart (1-*l*) mold with cover Flexible-blade, metal spatula or spoon

Preliminary Preparations: Place the mold and cover in the freezer for at least 15 minutes before lining it.

Lining the Mold: Take the mold from the freezer and pour the Nut Brittle Ice Cream into the mold. Work quickly, using a flexible-blade metal spatula or a metal spoon to push the ice cream around and up the sides of the mold. The ice cream should cover the bottom and the sides of the mold. Don't worry about neatness or the fact that the ice cream will not line the mold evenly at this stage; this will be done later.

Place the mold back into the freezer for 30 to 40 minutes, after which time the ice cream will have stiffened enough to allow you to even out the lining of the mold. The ice cream should still be soft enough to push, so that it will cover the sides and bottom of the mold in one equally thick, smooth layer, and cold enough so that once pushed up and smoothed out it will hold its shape. If after this second smoothing the ice cream is still too soft to hold its shape when pushed up the sides, it should be refrigerated for another 30 minutes to an hour and the lining completed at that time. (The time in the freezer varies depending on the stiffness of the ice cream to start with and the temperature of your freezer.)

Filling the Center of the Mold: Place the mold in the freezer for 1 hour before filling the center with the Coffee Parfait. If using the sugar coffee beans, add them to the Coffee Parfait after the filled mold has been in the freezer for 1 hour more; stir them delicately into the parfait that has begun to stiffen (this will keep them from falling to the bottom). Place the finished dessert in the freezer for at least 3 hours more before turning out and serving (see page 5).

Serving Suggestions: Serve with a sauceboat of cold Caramel Sauce (Recipe 102).

71

Molded Apricot and Raspberry Dessert
(Sorbet Abricots-Framboises)

PREPARATION	15 minutes
COOLING TIME	2 to 3 hours
FREEZING TIME	3 hours before serving
INGREDIENTS	*For a 1-quart (1-l) mold serving 6*
	½ quart (½ *l*) Apricot Sherbet (Recipe 2 or 3)
	½ quart (½ *l*) Raspberry Sherbet (Recipe 11—see Note)
UTENSILS	1-quart (1-*l*) mold with cover
	Flexible-blade, metal spatula or spoon

Preliminary Preparations: Place the mold and cover in the freezer for at least 15 minutes before lining it.

Lining the Mold: Take the mold from the freezer and pour the Apricot Sherbet into the mold. Work quickly, using a flexible-blade metal spatula or a metal spoon to push the sherbet around and up the sides of the mold. The sherbet should cover the bottom and the sides of the mold. Don't worry about neatness or the fact that the sherbet will not line the mold evenly at this stage; this will be done later.

Place the mold back into the freezer for 30 to 40 minutes, after which time the sherbet will have stiffened enough to allow you to even out the lining of the mold. The sherbet should still be soft enough to push, so that it will cover the sides and bottom of the mold in one equally thick, smooth layer, and cold enough so that once pushed up and smoothed out it will hold its shape. If after this second smoothing the sherbet is still too soft to hold its shape when pushed up the sides, it should be refrigerated for another 30 minutes to an hour and the lining completed at that time.

Filling the Center of the Mold: Once the mold has been lined, place it immediately back into the freezer for 1 hour before filling it with the Raspberry Sherbet. Once the mold is filled, it must be left in the freezer for at least 3 hours before turning out and serving (see page 5).

Serving Suggestions: Serve decorated with fresh raspberries and a sauceboat of Fresh Raspberry Sauce (Recipe 98).

Note: Strawberry sherbet (Recipe 10) can be used instead of raspberry sherbet to make an equally delicious dessert. In this case, decorate with fresh strawberries and serve with Strawberry Sauce.

72

Molded Hawaiian Dessert (Bombe Hawai)

PREPARATION	15 minutes
COOLING TIME	2 to 3 hours
FREEZING TIME	3 hours before serving
INGREDIENTS	*For a 1-quart (1-l) mold serving 6* ½ quart (½ l) Pineapple Sherbet (Recipe 4) ½ quart (½ l) Kirsch-Flavored Parfait (Recipe 44) ½ cup (100 g) diced Half-Candied Pineapple Slices (Recipe 166)
UTENSILS	1-quart (1-l) ice cream mold with cover Flexible-blade, metal spatula or spoon

Preliminary Preparations: Place the mold and cover in the freezer for at least 15 minutes before lining it.

Lining the Mold: Take the mold from the freezer and pour the Pineapple Sherbet into the mold. Work quickly, using a flexible-blade metal spatula or a metal spoon to push the sherbet around and up the sides of the mold. Don't worry about neatness or the fact that the sherbet will not line the mold evenly at this stage; this will be done later.

   Place the mold back into the freezer for 30 to 40 minutes, after which time the sherbet will have stiffened enough to allow you to even out the lining of the mold. The sherbet should still be soft enough to push, so that it will cover the sides and bottom of the mold in one equally thick, smooth layer, and cold enough so that once pushed up and smoothed out it will hold its shape. If after this second smoothing the sherbet is still too soft to hold its shape when pushed up the sides, it should be refrigerated for another 30 minutes to an hour and the lining completed at that time.

Filling the Center of the Mold: Once the mold has been lined place it immediately back into the freezer for 1 hour before filling it with the Kirsch-Flavored Parfait. Delicately stir the pieces of candied pineapple into the parfait once the mold has been filled. Place the dessert in the freezer for at least 3 hours before turning out and serving (see page 5).

Serving Suggestion: Serve with a sauceboat of Fresh Pineapple Sauce (Recipe 68).

73

Molded Raspberry and Champagne Dessert
(Sorbet Champagne-Framboises)

(Photo page 55)

PREPARATION	15 minutes
COOLING TIME	2 to 3 hours
FREEZING TIME	3 hours before serving
INGREDIENTS	*For a 1-quart (1-l) mold serving 6*
	½ quart (½ l) Raspberry Sherbet (Recipe 11)
	½ cup (100 g) diced Half-Candied Pineapple Slices (Recipe 166)
	½ quart (½ l) Champagne Sherbet (Recipe 22)
UTENSILS	1-quart (1-l) ice cream mold with cover
	Flexible-blade, metal spatula or spoon

Preliminary Preparations: Place the mold and cover in the freezer for at least 15 minutes before lining it.

Lining the Mold: Take the mold from the freezer and pour the Raspberry Sherbet into the mold. Work quickly, using a flexible-blade metal spatula or a metal spoon to push the sherbet around and up the sides of the mold. Don't worry about neatness or the fact that the sherbet will not line the mold evenly at this stage; this will be done later.

Place the mold back into the freezer for 30 to 40 minutes, after which time the sherbet will have stiffened enough to allow you to even out the lining of the mold. The sherbet should still be soft enough to push, so that it will cover the sides and bottom of the mold in one equally thick, smooth layer, and cold enough so that once pushed up and smoothed out it will hold its shape. If after this second smoothing the sherbet is still too soft to hold its shape when pushed up the sides, it should be refrigerated for another 30 minutes to an hour and the lining completed at that time.

Filling the Center of the Mold: Once the mold has been lined, place it immediately back into the freezer for 1 hour; then stir the pieces of Half-Candied Pineapple into the Champagne Sherbet and fill the center of the mold with this mixture. Place the finished dessert in the freezer for at least 3 hours before turning out and serving (see page 5).

Note: This dessert does not save well and should be served within 24 hours of the time it is made.

74

Perigord Crown Dessert
(Couronne Périgourdine)

(Photo page 77)

PREPARATION	15 minutes
COOLING TIME	3 to 4 hours
FREEZING TIME	3 hours before serving
INGREDIENTS	*For a 1-quart (1-l) mold serving 6 to 8* ½ quart (½ l) Chestnut Ice Cream (Recipe 34) Generous ⅓ cup (120 g) chestnut cream (see Dictionary of Terms) ½ quart (½ l) Pear Sherbet (Recipe 19 or 20) *For decoration* 30 Ardèche-Style Truffles (Recipe 225)
UTENSILS	1 decorated ring mold with a 1-quart (1-l) capacity (see Note) Flexible-blade, metal spatula or spoon

Making the Dessert: Proceed as described in Recipe 68 for Molded Vanilla Desserts, using the Chestnut Ice Cream to line the mold. After the mold has been lined with the Chestnut Ice Cream and placed in the freezer for 1 hour, spread the Chestnut Cream evenly over the ice cream and place back in the freezer for 1 hour more before filling the center with the Pear Sherbet (see photo). Place the finished dessert in the freezer for at least 3 hours before turning out and serving (see page 5).

Once the dessert has been turned out onto a serving platter, decorate it with Ardèche-Style Truffles as shown in the photo.

Note: This dessert is prettiest if made in a decorative ring mold like the one in the photo. However, it can be made in any mold or ring, ribbed or smooth, as long as the mold chosen is no larger than the one used in the recipe. If a flat-bottomed mold or a ring mold with a large central opening is used, place the truffles on top of the dessert and around the sides (do not try to fill a large center with them).

75
Snowball
(Boule de Neige)

(Photo page 75)

PREPARATION	45 minutes
COOLING TIME	2 to 3 hours
FREEZING TIME	4 hours before serving
INGREDIENTS	*For making 1 dessert serving 8* ½ quart (½ *l*) Vanilla Ice Cream (Recipe 27) Generous 1⅔ cups (4 d*l*) Strawberry Sherbet (Recipe 10) ⅓ cup (50 g) Large Nut Brittle Powder (Recipe 196) 5 candied cherries cut into halves or quarters ½ quart (½ *l*) Vanilla Parfait (Recipe 40) *For decoration* 2 generous cups (½ *l*) Chantilly Cream (Recipe 104) 18 to 20 Candied Violets 8 to 10 candied cherries cut in half
UTENSILS	1 flat- or round-bottomed bowl with an approximately 5-cup (1¼-*l*) capacity Flexible-blade, metal spatula or spoon Pastry bag with a star-shaped nozzle

Preliminary Preparations: Place the mold and cover in the freezer for at least 15 minutes before lining it.

Lining the Mold: Take the mold from the freezer and pour the Vanilla Ice Cream into the mold. Work quickly, using a flexible-blade metal spatula or a metal spoon to push the ice cream around and up the sides of the mold. Don't worry about neatness or the fact that the ice cream will not line the mold evenly at this stage; this will be done later.

   Place the mold back into the freezer for 30 to 40 minutes, after which time the ice cream will have stiffened enough to allow you to even out the lining of the mold. The ice cream should still be soft enough to push, so that it will cover the sides and bottom of the mold in one equally thick, smooth layer, and cold enough so that once pushed up and smoothed out it will hold its shape. If after this second smoothing the ice cream is still too soft to hold its shape when pushed up the sides, it should be refrigerated for another 30 minutes to an hour and the lining completed at that time. (The time in the freezer varies depending

103

on the stiffness of the ice cream to start with and the temperature of your freezer.)

Filling the Center of the Mold: Once the mold has been lined, place it immediately back into the freezer for 1 hour. Then remove it from the freezer and spread the strawberry sherbet evenly over the vanilla ice cream. Replace it immediately in the freezer and leave for 1 hour more.

Shake the nut brittle to make the largest pieces come to the surface—save these for decorating the dessert. Mix the remaining nut brittle powder with the vanilla parfait, add 2½ candied cherries and stir gently to mix well. Pour this mixture into the center of the mold when it comes from the freezer, then place the remaining 2½ cherries on top of the vanilla parfait mixture (see photo). Replace the filled mold in the freezer for at least 4 hours before turning out and decorating.

To Decorate: Turn out the molded dessert at least 1½ hours before serving and place back in the freezer (see General Comments on Turning Out and Serving Ice Cream, page 5). Make the Chantilly Cream as described in Recipe 104. About 30 to 40 minutes before serving, pour the Chantilly Cream into a cold pastry bag fitted with a star-shaped nozzle, remove the dessert from the freezer, and squeeze out a little cream at a time to cover the surface of the ice cream with a star-like pattern. Decorate the Chantilly Cream with the halves of candied cherries, candied violets, and sprinkle with the powdered nut brittle reserved earlier. Place the finished Snowball in the refrigerator for 20 to 30 minutes before serving. (If placed back in the freezer, the Chantilly Cream will harden.)

To Store: Once the mold is filled, it can be kept in the freezer for up to 2 weeks before turning out and decorating.

76

Frozen Grand Marnier Dessert
(Rosace Glacée au Grand Marnier)

(Photo page 97)

PREPARATION	25 minutes
COOLING TIME	50 minutes
FREEZING TIME	3 hours before serving

INGREDIENTS	*For 1 dessert serving 8*
	14 Half-Candied Orange Slices (Recipe 168)
	½ quart (½ *l*) Grand Marnier-Flavored Parfait
	    (Recipe 44)
	1½ pints (¾ *l*) Orange Sherbet (Recipe 9)
	
	For decoration
	2 to 3 large pieces Half-Candied Orange Peel
	    (Recipe 167—optional)

UTENSILS	1 circular, ribbed mold with a 1½-quart (1½-*l*) capacity (see Note) Flexible-blade, metal spatula or spoon Knife Large, round nozzle from pastry bag

Making the Dessert: Read the instructions for making molded desserts given in Recipe 68 for Molded Vanilla Desserts; comments made there about preliminary preparations and the consistency of the sherbet and parfait apply equally to this recipe.

Line the walls of the mold with 10 of the Half-Candied Orange Slices as shown in the photo. Then place the mold in the freezer for 30 minutes. Finely chop the remaining orange slices and stir them into the Grand Marnier-Flavored Parfait.

Remove the mold from the freezer and pour the Orange Sherbet into it. Using a flexible-blade, metal spatula or spoon, gently spread the sherbet around the sides and bottom of the mold, taking care not to disturb the positions of the orange slices. As in all molded desserts, the sherbet should be of "newly made" consistency (see Recipe 68 for Molded Vanilla Desserts) so that it will spread easily. Once the sides and bottom of the mold have been covered with an even layer of orange sherbet, place the mold back in the freezer for 30 minutes. Next, pour the Grand Marnier-Flavored Parfait into the center to fill the mold. Smooth the surface of the parfait and sherbet—the mold may not be completely filled.

Place the dessert back in the freezer for at least 3 hours before serving, leaving the mold uncovered so that it will freeze more quickly. Once the dessert has hardened, cover the mold, unless planning to serve the same day.

To Decorate and Serve: See General Comments on Turning Out and Serving Ice Creams, page 5.

Using a sharp knife and the nozzle from a pastry bag, cut strips, circles, and semi-circles in the candied orange peel. Use this to decorate the top of the dessert as pictured in the photo. Once the dessert has been turned out and decorated, it should be served that day. Bring the dessert to the table on a serving platter and cut it as you would a cake, using a knife that has been quickly dipped in hot water and wiped dry.

To Store: In a closed mold, this dessert can be kept for up to 2 weeks in the freezer.

Note: Any mold that is of the same capacity as the one employed in this recipe [i.e., 1½ quarts (1½ *l*)] can be used instead of the particular model shown in the photo. A flat- or round-bottomed, metal bowl may be used if no mold is available. In this case, cover the bowl with a plate if planning to store the dessert.

77

Frozen Martinique Dessert
(Rosace Glacée de la Martinique)

PREPARATION   20 minutes

COOLING TIME   50 minutes

FREEZING TIME   3 hours before serving

INGREDIENTS   *For 1 dessert serving 8*
                        9 (200 g) Half-Candied Pineapple Slices (Recipe 166)
                        ½ quart (½ *l*) Rum-Flavored Parfait (Recipe 44)
                        1½ pints (¾ *l*) Pineapple Sherbet (Recipe 4)
                            or 1½ pints (¾ *l*) Vanilla Ice Cream (Recipe 27)

                        For decoration
                        10 candied cherries cut in half (optional)

UTENSILS   1 circular, ribbed mold with a 1½-quart (1½-*l*) capacity
                        Flexible-blade, metal spatula or spoon
                        Knife
                        Large, round nozzle from pastry bag

Making the Dessert: Cut each slice of candied pineapple in half through the middle, making two very thin rings out of each slice.

Proceed as described in Recipe 76 for Frozen Grand Marnier Dessert, using the pineapple slices instead of orange slices to line the mold. Finely chop the remaining pineapple and stir it into the Rum-Flavored Parfait.

Cover the sides and bottom of the mold with either the Pineapple Sherbet or the Vanilla Ice Cream and fill the center with the Rum-Flavored Parfait, as described in the Frozen Grand Marnier Dessert. Freeze for at least 3 hours before turning out and serving (see page 5).

To Decorate and Serve: Once the dessert has been turned out, place half a candied cherry in the center of each ring of pineapple all around the dessert and serve.

To Store: Before turning out, this dessert may be kept in a closed mold in the freezer for up to 2 weeks.

GENERAL COMMENTS ON FROZEN SOUFFLES

A frozen soufflé should always look like a perfectly risen baked soufflé. To achieve this effect, the soufflé mold is wrapped with a strip of thin cardboard or stiff paper so that the cardboard border sticks up above the actual edge of the soufflé mold itself (see photo, page 117).

Cut the cardboard so that it is long enough to wrap easily around the full circumference of the mold and high enough to not only stick up above the edge of the mold but to handle easily as well [i.e., the strip of cardboard can be the height of the soufflé mold plus 1¼ inches (3 cm) in width]. Wrap the cardboard around the mold and attach the ends together with a piece of tape. Place the soufflé mold, thus wrapped, on a plate for easy handling when taking it in and out of the freezer. Fill the mold as described in the following recipes or with frozen soufflés of your own invention. (For simple frozen soufflés with two or more flavors, see Recipe 81 for the Chocolate and Vanilla Frozen Soufflé.) The cardboard band is never removed until just before serving.

Important: The parfait used in making frozen soufflés must be of "newly made" consistency, that is, the consistency after having the whipped cream folded into them but before being frozen. It is best to make them at the last minute for this reason. However, especially when two flavors are involved, this is not always possible. A previously frozen parfait may be used in a frozen soufflé if allowed to soften to this "newly made" consistency by removing it from the freezer and placing it in the refrigerator for approximately 45 minutes to 1 hour or until soft enough to spread very easily.

78

Frozen Grand Marnier Soufflé (Soufflé au Grand Marnier)

PREPARATION	30 minutes
COOLING TIME	30 minutes
FREEZING TIME	3 hours before serving
INGREDIENTS	*For 1 soufflé serving 6 to 8*
	½ cup (100 g) finely diced mixed candied fruit
	3 tablespoons (½ d*l*) Grand Marnier
	If using pastry
	1 quart (1 *l*) Grand Marnier-Flavored Parfait (Recipe 44)
	1 Almond Pastry (Recipe 111)
	or 1 Orange-Almond Pastry (Recipe 112)
	6 inches (15 cm) across and ¾ inch (2 cm) thick

Without pastry
2½ pints (1¼ *l*) Grand Marnier-Flavored Parfait
(Recipe 44)

For decoration
Generous ¼ cup (50 g) Large Nougatine Crumble
(Recipe 197)
or 8 Candied Orange Wedges (Recipe 174)

UTENSILS

Knife
Small bowl
6-inch-wide (15 cm) soufflé mold
Strip of cardboard, approximately 20 × 4 inches (51 × 10 cm)
Pastry brush
Flexible-blade, metal spatula or spoon

Preliminary Preparations: Place the diced candied fruit in a bowl with the Grand Marnier and leave to soak for 30 minutes.

Wrap the band of cardboard or stiff paper around the outside of the soufflé mold as shown in the photo on page 117 (see the General Comments on Frozen Soufflés). Put the wrapped mold on a plate and place in the freezer for 15 to 30 minutes.

Making the Dessert

If Using Pastry: Drain the candied fruit and keep the Grand Marnier which was used to soak them. Take a pastry brush and brush the pastry with the Grand Marnier until it is lightly dampened.

Pour the Grand Marnier-Flavored Parfait into the cold soufflé mold until it is a third full; then place the pastry in the mold on top of the parfait. Mix the candied fruit with the remaining parfait and pour it into the mold. Smooth the top of the parfait if necessary with a spatula or spoon.

Without the Pastry: Drain the candied fruit and mix them with the Grand Marnier-Flavored Parfait; pour this into the soufflé mold and smooth the top if necessary.

To Freeze: Once the mold has been filled, place it in the freezer for at least 3 hours before serving.

To Decorate and Serve: Remove from the freezer and decorate the top of the soufflé with the pieces of Nougatine Crumble or the Candied Orange Wedges. Take off the cardboard just before serving.

To Store: The soufflé can be kept in the freezer for up to 1 week before decorating and serving.

79

Individual Frozen Grand Marnier Soufflés
(Soufflé au Grand Marnier Individuel)

PREPARATION	30 minutes
COOLING TIME	30 minutes
FREEZING TIME	3 hours before serving
INGREDIENTS	*For 6 individual soufflés* ½ cup (100 g) finely diced mixed candied fruit 3 tablespoons (½ dl) Grand Marnier 2½ pints (1¼ l) Grand Marnier-Flavored Parfait (Recipe 44) *For decoration* Generous ¼ cup (50 g) Large Nougatine Crumble (Recipe 197) *or* 6 Candied Orange Wedges (Recipe 174—optional)
UTENSILS	Knife Small bowl 6 ramekins approximately 3 inches (7.5 cm) wide, each with a capacity of about ½ cup (1.2 dl) 6 cardboard strips, 11 × 3 inches (28 × 7.5 cm) Metal spoon

Making the Individual Desserts: Using the strips of cardboard to wrap the ramekins and raise up the edges, make and fill the molds following the general instructions in Recipe 78 for Frozen Grand Marnier Soufflé (without pastry).

80

Port Royal Frozen Soufflé
(Soufflé Port-Royal)

(Photo page 117)

PREPARATION	30 minutes
COOLING TIME	30 minutes
FREEZING TIME	3 hours before serving
INGREDIENTS	*For 1 dessert serving 6 to 8*
	8 Half-Candied Pineapple Slices cut into ½ inch (1.2 cm) wedges (Recipe 166)
	½ candied cherry
	1 quart (1-*l*) Rum-Flavored Parfait (Recipe 44)
	Generous ¾ cup (180 g) drained Home Canned Apricots (Recipe 122)
	6½ tablespoons (1 d*l*) syrup from the apricot can or jar
	½ cup (100 g) granulated sugar
UTENSILS	Nonstick parchment paper
	Thin cardboard
	Plate *or* the bottom of a spring form cake pan
	Flexible-blade, metal spatula or spoon
	Saucepan
	Soufflé mold, 6 inches (15 cm) in diameter

Preparing the Top of the Soufflé: In this dessert the decorative top of the soufflé is made separately and then placed on top of the rest which is frozen in a mold.

To make the decorative top, cut a piece of cardboard into a strip that is 1 inch (2.5 cm) wide and long enough so that when the two ends are taped together, a circle is formed that just fits the inside dimensions of the soufflé mold. Place this cardboard circle on a piece of nonstick parchment paper; for easy handling, place the paper on a large plate or the bottom of a spring form cake pan.

Inside the circle all around the edge and in the center, place as many wedges of the candied pineapple as necessary to make the decorative pattern shown in the photo; save the remaining wedges for later use. Place half a candied cherry, cut side down, in the center, as shown in the same photo. Fill the cardboard circle with Rum-Flavored Parfait, smooth the surface with a flexible-blade, metal spatula or a metal spoon, and place in the freezer for 3 hours before removing the cardboard and placing the decoration on the rest of the dessert.

Preparing the Body of the Soufflé: Place the drained apricots and 6½ table-spoons (1 dl) of the syrup in which they were canned in a saucepan with the granulated sugar. Cook over moderate heat for about 15 minutes or until the liquid thickens to about the consistency of a marmalade; stir frequently to avoid sticking. Once cooked, remove from the heat, stir in the remaining pieces of candied pineapple, and place the saucepan in a bowl of ice cubes and water so that the marmalade will cool rapidly. Stir until cold; then place the marmalade mixture in the refrigerator until it has cooled to 39°F (4°C).

Fill the soufflé mold by first pouring in about a third of the remaining Rum-Flavored Parfait, on which you place half of the marmalade mixture (see photo). Then pour in another third of the parfait, distribute the remaining marmalade mixture over it, and finish filling the mold with the parfait. Place the mold in the freezer for 3 hours before decorating with the top and serving.

Assembling the Soufflé: After both elements of the soufflé have hardened in the freezer, turn the top upside down onto the soufflé mold; remove the cardboard band and the parchment paper to expose the decorative design.

To Store: This soufflé can be kept for up to 1 week in the freezer once assembled, but the cardboard band must not be removed until ready to serve.

Two-Flavored Frozen Soufflés
(Soufflés Panachés à la Vanille)

(Photo page 115)

PREPARATION	1 hour
FREEZING TIME	4 to 6 hours
INGREDIENTS	*For 1 dessert serving 8*
	2¾ cups (6.5 d*l*) Vanilla Parfait (Recipe 40)
	2¾ cups (6.5 d*l*) Coffee Parfait (Recipe 42)
	or 2¾ cups (6.5 d*l*) Chocolate Parfait (Recipe 43)
	For decoration (optional)
	1 generous cup (¼ *l*) Chantilly Cream (Recipe 104)
	9 sugar coffee beans *or* chocolate bits
UTENSILS	Soufflé mold, 6 inches (15 cm) in diameter
	Cardboard strip, 20 × 4 inches (51 × 10 cm)
	2 rigid cardboard rectangles, approximately 6 × 4 inches (15 × 10 cm) (optional)
	Pastry bag and star-shaped nozzle (optional)

Dividing the Mold into Compartments: Cut and wrap a strip of cardboard around the soufflé mold so that the top of the cardboard is 1¼ inches (3 cm) above the edge of the mold (see General Comments on Frozen Soufflés, page 108).

Cut some very rigid cardboard into two rectangles that are each 6 × 4 inches (15 × 10 cm). Trim the edges of each one so that it will fit inside the soufflé mold. Cut a line in the center of each rectangle, going about two-thirds of the way up, so that the two rectangles can be slipped into each other, interlocking at right angles. Place the cardboard inside the mold (see photo).

To Fill the Mold (see Note): When the cardboard is in place, decide which compartments are for vanilla and which are for the other parfait. The two parfaits used should fill the mold as illustrated in the photo. To help support the cardboard when the first parfait is poured in, place weights against the sides of the cardboard that will later be occupied by the second parfait; then pour the first parfait into the two empty compartments, as shown in the photo. (The picture shows two compartments after being filled with the first of the parfaits being used and after the first freezing period; the weights needed to support the cardboard walls are not shown in the picture, but they would occupy the empty compartments.) Place the mold in the freezer for 2 to 3 hours before finishing to fill it with the second parfait.

Remove the mold from the freezer, take out the cardboard used to form the compartments, and pour the second parfait into the spaces left to fill the mold. Place back into the freezer for 2 to 3 hours before serving.

To Decorate and Serve: When ready to serve, remove the strip of cardboard from around the soufflé mold and decorate the top of the soufflé with swirls of Chantilly Cream made with a pastry bag and a star-shaped nozzle; candied coffee beans or little chocolate bits can be placed on each swirl of cream if desired.

To Store: This soufflé can be kept in the freezer for up to 1 week.

Note: A simplified version of this recipe can be made by simply pouring one of the two parfaits into the built up soufflé mold, allowing it to harden in the freezer, and then filling the mold with the second parfait. The result is just as tasty, but not as attractive as when the compartments are made.

GENERAL COMMENTS ON CAKE OR PASTRY-BASED FROZEN DESSERTS

Important: Ice creams, sherbets, and parfaits used in these desserts must always be of a "newly made" consistency; that is, they should be about the same softness as ice cream or sherbet when it comes from the ice cream freezer or as a parfait when the whipped cream has been folded into it but before it has frozen. (For more details, see Recipe 68.)

The technique used in making most of the following desserts is a combination of that used in molded combination desserts and in frozen soufflés. A typical pastry-based dessert is built up inside a flan ring, frozen, and then the ring is removed before serving. A flan ring is a circular strip of metal, generally used on a baking sheet instead of a pie pan when making pies or flans. In the following recipes a flan ring with a diameter of 8 inches (20 cm) and a height of 2 inches (5 cm) is required (see flan ring pictured in the photo for Frozen Cognac and Apricot Dessert, page ii). Before filling, the ring is always placed on a flat rigid piece of cardboard, a plate, or the bottom of a spring form cake pan slightly larger than the ring itself, so that the dessert can be easily handled.

Flan rings are sold in stores specializing in baking equipment, but if they are not available, you can improvise a substitute with thin, smooth cardboard, cut into a band, and taped to form a circle of the appropriate dimensions.

When making desserts with a pastry base, use cakes and pastry that are thin and just the size of the ring employed; when filling a flan ring that is 2 inches (5 cm) high, the general rule is to use a cake or meringue that is no more than ¾ inch (2 cm) high. The cake is generally placed in the ring and then the ring is filled with parfait, ice cream, sherbet, or a combination of two or three things.

Comments on Serving: Desserts made with flan rings are always frozen before the ring is removed. To remove a metal flan ring, carefully rub it with a sponge that has been dipped in hot water and squeezed to remove the excess water, being careful not to touch the dessert itself. Wipe the ring dry with a cloth and lift it off, pushing very gently on the dessert if the ring does not lift off easily. If a cardboard ring is used, it is simply untaped and "peeled off."

Before removing the flan ring or cardboard band, place the frozen dessert on the serving platter and leave it in the freezer for 30 minutes to cool the platter. Then remove the ring or band and place the dessert in the refrigerator for 10 to 15 minutes to soften if only parfaits are being used; if any combination using ice cream or sherbet is used, place the dessert in the refrigerator for 20 to 30 minutes to allow the sherbet or ice cream to soften (this extra time will not hurt the parfaits if they are combined with ice cream or sherbet).

Frozen Cognac and Apricot Dessert
(Biscuit Glacé de Cognac)

(Photo page ii)

PREPARATION	20 minutes
COOLING TIME	40 minutes
FREEZING TIME	3 hours before serving
INGREDIENTS	*For 1 dessert serving 8* 1 Almond Pastry (Recipe 111), 8 inches (20 cm) wide and ¾ inch (2 cm) high ½ quart (½ *l*) Apricot Sherbet (Recipe 2 or 3) Half of a 1-pound (500-g) jar of Apricot Jam (Recipe 132) ½ quart (½ *l*) Cognac-Flavored Parfait (Recipe 44) *For decoration* Candied angelica Slivered almonds ½ cup (1.2 d*l*) Chantilly Cream (Recipe 104—optional)
UTENSILS	1 metal flan ring, 8 inches (20 cm) wide and 2 inches (5 cm) high *or* a cardboard strip approximately 24 × 2 inches (61 × 5 cm) 1 rigid cardboard circle, plate, or bottom of spring form cake pan, 9 inches (23 cm) in diameter Plastic scraper

Making the Dessert: (See the General Comments on Cake or Pastry-Based Frozen Desserts, page 116). Place the flan ring on a piece of cardboard, plate, or the bottom of a spring form cake pan that is slightly wider than the ring is. Put the Almond Pastry inside the ring, or make a ring of cardboard to go around it, and place it in the freezer for 20 minutes before filling the ring with the other ingredients. Place the jam in the refrigerator so that it will be cool when used.

Take the ring containing the cake from the freezer, pour in the Apricot Sherbet, spread it evenly over the cake, and place the ring back in the freezer for another 20 minutes.

Spoon the jam out onto a plate and separate the whole pieces of fruit from the rest; you will need a scant ½ cup (125 g) of apricots once separated. Save two nice apricots for decorating the dessert and cut the rest into small pieces. Stir the pieces of apricot into the Cognac-Flavored Parfait; then pour the parfait into

118

the ring to fill it and place it back in the freezer for at least 3 hours before serving.

To Decorate and Serve: Remove the ring and decorate the top of the dessert with the pieces of apricot reserved earlier, some slivered almonds, and candied angelica to make a flower design as shown in the photo. Canned apricot halves can be used for decorating if the pieces from the jam are not whole, and the top of the dessert can be spread with a thin layer of Chantilly Cream before decorating if desired.

Serving Suggestions: Serve with Apricot Sauce (Recipe 98).

To Store: This dessert can be kept in the freezer for up to 2 weeks before decorating and serving.

83

Frozen Chocolate and Orange Dessert
(Biscuit Glacé du Roussillon)

PREPARATION	20 minutes
COOLING TIME	40 minutes
FREEZING TIME	3 hours before serving
INGREDIENTS	*For 1 dessert serving 8*

For 1 dessert serving 8
1 Almond Pastry (Recipe 111) *or* 1 Orange-Almond Pastry (Recipe 112), 8 inches (20 cm) wide and ¾ inch (2 cm) high
½ quart (½ *l*) Orange Sherbet (Recipe 9)
½ quart (½ *l*) Chocolate Parfait (Recipe 43)

For decoration
Chocolate nonpareils
2 to 3 large pieces Half-Candied Orange Peel (Recipe 167—optional)

UTENSILS

1 metal flan ring, 8 inches (20 cm) wide and 2 inches (5 cm) high *or* a strip of cardboard about 24 × 2 inches (61 × 5 cm)
1 cardboard circle, plate, *or* bottom of spring form cake pan, 9 inches (23 m) in diameter
Flexible-blade, metal spatula *or* spoon

Making the Dessert: (See the General Comments on Cake or Pastry-Based Frozen Desserts, page 116). Place the flan ring on a piece of cardboard, a plate, or the bottom of a spring form cake pan, slightly wider than it is. Put the pastry into the ring or make a ring around the pastry with the cardboard, and place it in the freezer for 20 minutes before filling the ring with the other ingredients.

Remove from the freezer and spoon the orange sherbet into the ring, spread it evenly over the pastry bottom with a spatula or spoon, and replace in the freezer for 20 minutes more; then pour in the parfait to fill the ring. Sprinkle the surface of the dessert generously with the chocolate nonpareils and place back in the freezer for at least 3 hours before serving.

To Decorate and Serve: Remove the ring and decorate the surface of the dessert with candied orange peel cut into decorative shapes. Serve with a sauceboat of Orange Sauce (Recipe 100).

To Store: This dessert can be kept in the freezer for a week before decorating and serving; once it has been decorated, it can be kept only 12 hours.

120

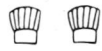

84

Médicis Frozen Pistacio Dessert (Biscuit Glacé Médicis)

PREPARATION	20 minutes
COOLING TIME	20 minutes (1 flavor) or 40 minutes (2 flavors)
FREEZING TIME	3 hours before serving
INGREDIENTS	*For 1 dessert serving 8* 1 French-Meringue (Recipe 109) *or* 1 Success Pastry (Recipe 110) 8 inches (20 cm) wide and ¾ inch (2 cm) high Generous 3⅓ cups (8 d*l*) Pistacio Ice Cream (Recipe 37) *or* Generous 1⅔ cups (4 d*l*) Pistacio Ice Cream (Recipe 37) Generous 1⅔ cups (4 d*l*) Chocolate Parfait (Recipe 43) *For decoration* 3½ ounces (100 g) semi-sweet chocolate
UTENSILS	1 flan ring 8 inches (20 cm) wide and 2 inches (5 cm) high *or* a strip of cardboard 24 × 2 inches (61 × 5 cm) 1 cardboard circle, plate, or bottom of a spring form pan Flexible-blade, metal spatula or spoon Vegetable grater with large holes

Making the Dessert: (See the General Comments on Cake or Pastry-Based Frozen Desserts, page 116). Place the flan ring on a piece of cardboard, a plate, or the bottom of a spring form cake pan slightly wider than it is. Put the meringue in the ring or make a ring around it with the cardboard, and place it in the freezer for 20 minutes before filling the ring with the other ingredients.

Remove from the freezer and fill the ring either entirely with pistacio ice cream or by making two layers, one of pistacio ice cream and one of chocolate parfait. (If two layers are made, first pour in and smooth out the pistacio ice cream with a metal spatula or spoon so that it evenly covers the meringue, then place in the freezer for 20 minutes before finishing to fill the ring with the chocolate parfait.) Once filled, place in the freezer for 3 hours.

To Decorate and Serve: Remove the ring and decorate the surface of the dessert with slivers of chocolate made by grating a bar or squares of chocolate; if the chocolate is softened slightly by holding it about 1 foot (30 cm) from a source of heat for only 1 second, the shavings will be more attractive. Serve with Hot Chocolate Sauce (Recipe 101).

To Store: This dessert can be kept in the freezer for up to 2 weeks before decorating and serving; once decorated, it should be served within 12 hours.

85

Auteuil-Style Frozen Caramel Dessert
(Biscuit Glacé d'Auteuil)

PREPARATION	20 minutes
COOLING TIME	20 minutes
FREEZING TIME	3 hours before serving

INGREDIENTS

For 1 dessert serving 8
1 French Meringue (Recipe 109) *or* 1 Success Pastry (Recipe 110), 8 inches (20 cm) wide and ¾ inch (2 cm) high
Generous 3⅓ cups (8 d*l*) Lenôtre's Special Caramel Ice Cream (Recipe 31)

For decoration
1 generous cup (¼ *l*) Chantilly Cream (Recipe 104)
8 squares Nougatine (Recipe 197)

UTENSILS

1 flan ring 8 inches (20 cm) wide and 2 inches (5 cm) high *or* a strip of cardboard 24 × 2 inches (61 × 5 cm)
1 cardboard circle, plate, *or* bottom of a spring form cake pan, 9 inches (23 cm) in diameter
Flexible-blade, metal spatula *or* spoon
Pastry bag with star-shaped nozzle

Making the Dessert: (See the General Comments on Cake or Pastry-Based Frozen Desserts, page 116). Place the flan ring on a piece of cardboard, a plate, or the bottom of a spring form cake pan slightly wider than it is. Put the meringue in the ring or make a ring around it with the cardboard, and place it in the freezer for 20 minutes before filling the ring with the other ingredients.

Remove from the freezer and fill the ring with the caramel ice cream; smooth the surface and place the dessert back in the freezer for at least 3 hours before decorating and serving.

To Decorate and Serve: At least 1½ hours before serving, remove the ring. Place the Chantilly Cream in a pastry bag fitted with a star-shaped nozzle and squeeze out 8 rose-like circles of cream on top of the dessert. Place a small piece of nougatine on each mound of cream. Place the dessert back in the freezer until ready to soften in the refrigerator and serve. Once decorated, the dessert should not be kept for more than 12 hours before serving. Serve with a sauceboat of Vanilla Sauce (Recipe 99).

To Store: This dessert can be kept in the freezer up to 2 weeks before being decorated and served.

86

Frozen Strawberry or Raspberry Vacherin
(Vacherin aux Fraises ou aux Framboises)

(Photo page 155)

PREPARATION	20 minutes
COOLING TIME	1 hour 20 minutes
FREEZING TIME	3 hours before serving

INGREDIENTS	*For 1 dessert serving 10*
	1 French Meringue (Recipe 190),
	    8 inches (20 cm) wide and ¾ inch (2 cm) high
	½ quart (½ *l*) Vanilla Ice Cream (Recipe 27)
	    or ½ quart (½ *l*) Apricot Sherbet (Recipe 2 or 3)
	2½ cups (6 d*l*) Strawberry Sherbet (Recipe 10)
	    or 2½ cups (6 d*l*) Raspberry Sherbet (Recipe 11)
	
	For decoration
	2 generous cups (½ *l*) Chantilly Cream
	    (Recipe 104)
	10 oval meringues (Recipe 109)
	24 fresh strawberries *or* 32 fresh raspberries
	Generous 1⅔ cups (4 d*l*) Fresh Fruit Sauce made with
	    either strawberries or raspberries (Recipe 98)

UTENSILS	1 flan ring 8 inches (20 cm) wide and 2 inches (5 cm) high
	    or a strip of cardboard 24 × 2 inches (61 × 5 cm)
	1 cardboard circle, plate, or bottom of a spring form cake
	    pan, 9 inches (23 cm) in diameter
	Flexible-blade, metal spatula or spoon
	Pastry bag with star-shaped nozzle

Making the Dessert: (See the General Comments on Cake or Pastry-Based Frozen Desserts, page 116). Place the flan ring on a piece of cardboard, a plate, or the bottom of a spring form cake pan slightly wider than it is. Put the meringue circle into the ring or make a ring of cardboard to go around it, and place it in the freezer for 20 minutes before filling the ring with the other ingredients.

Remove from the freezer and pour either the vanilla ice cream or the apricot sherbet into the ring to make the first layer. Smooth the surface with a metal spatula or spoon to cover the meringue evenly, and then place back into the freezer for 1 hour before finishing to fill the ring. Remove from the freezer and fill the ring with either strawberry or raspberry sherbet to form the second layer. Smooth the surface of the dessert and place it back in the freezer for at least 3 hours before decorating and serving.

To Decorate and Serve: At least 2 hours before serving, remove the ring. Using a flexible-blade spatula, spread a third of the Chantilly Cream evenly over the top and sides of the dessert; the cream should form a thin, even layer about ¼ inch (½ cm) thick. Place the remaining cream in a pastry bag fitted with a star-shaped nozzle. Decorate the sides of the dessert with the oval meringues by placing them against the sides of the dessert as shown in the photo. Leave a little space in between the meringues; then, using the cream in the pastry bag, decorate these areas as well as the circumference of the top of the dessert (see photo). Put the dessert back into the freezer until ready to soften in the refrigerator and serve.

Just before taking the dessert to the table, fill the space in the center of the top of the meringue shell with the fresh fruit and spoon over a little fresh fruit sauce made with the same fruit. Serve immediately with a sauceboat of the fresh fruit sauce to accompany the dessert.

To Store: This dessert can be kept in the freezer for up to 2 weeks before decorating and serving; once decorated, the dessert should be served within 12 hours.

Note: A classic when made with Vanilla Ice Cream as a first layer, this dessert is even more enticing when the Apricot Sherbet is used instead.

87

Frozen Coffee Vacherin
(Vacherin Fin Moka)

PREPARATION	10 minutes
COOLING TIME	20 minutes
FREEZING TIME	3 hours before serving

INGREDIENTS	*For 1 dessert serving 8*
	⅛ French Meringue (Recipe 109)
	   or 1 Success Pastry (Recipe 110) 8 inches (20 cm) wide
	   and ¾ inch (2 cm) high
	Generous 3⅓ cups (8 d*l*) Coffee Ice Cream
	   (Recipe 33)
	57 (60 g) sugar coffee beans (optional)
	
	For decoration
	2 generous cups (½ *l*) Coffee-Flavored
	   Chantilly Cream (Recipe 105)
	   or ½ quart (½ *l*) Coffee Ice Cream
	   (Recipe 33)
	8 sugar coffee beans (optional)

UTENSILS	1 flan ring 8 inches (20 cm) wide and 2 inches (5 cm) high
	   or a strip of cardboard 24 × 2 inches (61 × 5 cm)
	1 cardboard circle, plate, *or* bottom of a spring form cake
	   pan, 9 inches (23 cm) in diameter
	Flexible-blade, metal spatula *or* spoon
	Pastry bag with star-shaped nozzle

Making the Dessert: (See the General Comments on Cake and Pastry-Based Frozen Desserts, page 116). Place the flan ring on a piece of cardboard, a plate, or the bottom of a spring form cake pan slightly wider than it is. Put the meringue or success pastry in the ring or make a ring out of cardboard to go around it, and place it in the freezer for 20 minutes before filling the ring.

Remove from the freezer and fill the ring with the Coffee Ice Cream. Then gently stir in the sugar coffee beans. Smooth the surface of the ice cream and place back into the freezer for at least 3 hours before decorating and serving.

To Decorate and Serve: There are two distinct ways of decorating this dessert: either with Coffee-Flavored Chantilly Cream or with more Coffee Ice Cream. The second possibility is the trickier of the two since the ice cream melts quickly and must be applied rapidly (as discussed below). In either case the ring is removed before decorating the dessert, and the dessert should be decorated at least 1½ hours before serving.

Coffee-Flavored Chantilly Cream Decoration: Fill a pastry bag fitted with a star-shaped nozzle with the Chantilly Cream. With the cream, draw vertical lines all around the sides of the dessert. Then, starting from the center of the top of the dessert, draw eight lines that radiate out from the center and end in a spiral or curlicue at the edge, thus indicating the eight slices that will be made of the dessert. Squeeze a little rose-like mound of cream in the center of the dessert and place a sugar coffee bean on each of the spirals around the top. Place the dessert back into the freezer until ready to soften in the refrigerator and serve.

Coffee Ice Cream Decoration: The ice cream used in decorating must be of a soft "newly made" consistency. Place it in a cold pastry bag fitted with a cold star-shaped nozzle and quickly decorate the cake as just described. Once decorated, the dessert must be placed in the freezer at least 1½ hours before softening in the refrigerator and serving.

To Store: This dessert may be kept in the freezer for up to 2 weeks before decorating; once decorated it should be served within 12 hours.

88

Baked Alaska
(Omelette Norvégiènne)

(Photo page 138)

PREPARATION	1 hour
COOLING TIME	1 hour
COOKING TIME	1 or 2 minutes
FREEZING TIME	4 hours before decorating (see Note)
INGREDIENTS	*For 1 dessert serving 6 to 8* 1 Génoise (Recipe 107) 12 × 8 inches (30 × 20 cm) ½ cup (1.2 dl) 28° Sugar Syrup (Recipe 1) ⅓ cup (8 cl) kirsch ½ cup (100 g) chopped mixed candied fruits 1 quart (1 l) Vanilla Ice Cream (Recipe 27) *For the meringue* 6 egg whites 3 tablespoons granulated sugar Generous ⅔ cup (150 g) granulated sugar 1 cup (150 g) confectioner's sugar *For decoration* Generous ½ cup (50 g) slivered almonds 2 tablespoons (20 g) confectioner's sugar
UTENSILS	Long serrated knife Oval, metal or oven-proof serving platter, 14 inches (36 cm) long Several cardboard "rulers" Pastry brush Large plate or sheet of aluminum foil Flexible-blade, metal spatula Large mixing bowl Electric mixer or wire whisk Sifter Wooden spatula Pastry bag with star-shaped nozzle (optional)

Preparing and Filling the Cake: Using a serrated knife, cut off the corners and trim the end of the génoise so that it will be oval shaped and fit easily on the serving platter. Cut the génoise in half, forming two layers. To do this, pile up strips or "rulers" of cardboard on both sides of the cake and about half the height of the cake, lay the blade of the serrated knife on these "rulers" and begin cutting; the rulers will guide the blade of the knife and keep it parallel to the table as you cut.

Lift off the top half of the cake carefully and place it on a large plate or a sheet of aluminum foil. Place the bottom half of the cake on the metal serving platter. Combine the sugar syrup with the kirsch and measure out ⅔ cup (1.5 dl) of the kirsch-flavored syrup. Brush both halves of the cake equally with it; then place both halves in the freezer for at least 1 hour before proceeding to fill the cake with the ice cream.

While the cake is in the freezer, place the candied fruit in a bowl with the remaining kirsch-flavored sugar syrup and let stand.

The Vanilla Ice Cream can be made at this time, or if made previously, it should be placed in the refrigerator to soften so that once the cake comes from the freezer the ice cream will be softened to a "newly made" consistency.

When the ice cream is ready, drain the candied fruit and stir it gently into the ice cream. Take the two halves of the cake from the freezer and spread all of the Vanilla Ice Cream evenly over the bottom half that is on the serving platter. Once this is done, place the other half of the cake on top of the ice cream and place the dessert back in the freezer for at least 4 hours before decorating and serving (see Note).

To Decorate and Serve: Preheat the oven to its maximum temperature or light the broiler, half an hour in advance.

Beat the egg whites until stiff, adding the 3 tablespoons of granulated sugar half way through the beating time. Once the egg whites are stiff, put the remaining granulated sugar and the confectioner's sugar into a sifter and sift onto the beaten whites. Use a spatula to cut and fold the sugar into the egg whites. This step may be done 30 to 45 minutes in advance and the meringue placed in the refrigerator.

Remove the dessert from the freezer and use a flexible blade spatula to spread three quarters of the meringue over the top and sides of the dessert. The dessert should be evenly coated with meringue. Place the remaining meringue in a pastry bag fitted with a star-shaped nozzle and decorate the surface with swirls and lines like those shown in the photo; a simpler solution to decorating is to spread all of the meringue over the top and sides of the dessert, lifting it here and there with the spatula to make peaks. The dessert may be decorated, then placed back in the freezer up to 1 hour before serving.

When ready to serve, sprinkle the dessert with slivered almonds and 2 tablespoons of sifted confectioner's sugar and place in the oven or under the broiler for 1 to 2 minutes before the dessert is to be served. Watch it carefully while it is in the oven; the meringue should be golden brown and the dessert should be served immediately as it comes from the oven.

Note: The success of this dessert depends on the cake and ice cream being very hard before the decoration is added and the dessert is browned; if not hard enough, the ice cream will melt in the oven. For this reason, it is often best to leave the cake and ice cream, once assembled, in the freezer overnight or even several days before it is to be decorated and served.

Variations: When fresh strawberries or raspberries are in season, sprinkle a few over the meringue just before it goes in the oven.

The ice cream filling that is placed inside the cake can be varied for interesting results; here are some ideas for replacing the vanilla ice cream and candied fruit used in this recipe: Apricot Sherbet (Recipe 2) mixed with pieces of Canned Apricot (Recipe 122) that have previously been soaked for an hour in cognac; Coffee Ice Cream (Recipe 33) to fill the cake and sugar coffee beans to decorate the meringue; Caramel Ice Cream (Recipe 31) to fill the cake and Large Nougatine Crumble (Recipe 197) to decorate the meringue; Vanilla Ice Cream (Recipe 27) flavored with coarsely powdered nut brittle to fill the cake and pieces of nut brittle (Recipe 196) to decorate the meringue.

89

Individual Chocolate Parfait Desserts
(Parfait au Chocolat Individuel)

PREPARATION	1 hour
FREEZING TIME	3 hours before serving
INGREDIENTS	*For 8 desserts* 8 small Orange-Almond Pastries (Recipe 112) about 3 inches (7.5 cm) in diameter 2½ pints (1.2 *l*) Chocolate Parfait (Recipe 43) 8 Half-Candied Orange Slices (Recipe 168)
UTENSILS	8 small ramekins, 3 inches (7.5 cm) in diameter 8 small flan rings the same diameter as the ramekins *or* 8 strips of cardboard, 9 inches wide by 3 inches high (23 × 7.5 cm)

Making the Desserts: Place a small flan ring on top of each ramekin or build up the sides of each ramekin by wrapping them in a strip of cardboard as when making frozen soufflé desserts (see General Comments on Frozen Soufflés, page 108); once built up, the top of the flan ring or cardboard should be about 1¼ inches (3 cm) above the edge of the ramekin itself. Once each ramekin has been built up in this manner, place a small Orange-Almond Pastry in the bottom of each, trimming the edges of each pastry if necessary. Then fill the ramekins to the brim with the Chocolate Parfait. Place the desserts in the freezer for at least 3 hours before serving. To serve, remove the flan ring or cardboard used to surround the ramekins, and decorate the surface of each dessert with a Half-Candied Orange Slice which has been cut into quarters (to make it easier to eat) and then put back together in the shape of a whole slice on top of the dessert.

To Store: These desserts can be kept in the freezer for 4 days before serving.

90
Sherbet-Filled Pineapple Dessert
(Sorbet à l'Ananas dans le Fruit)

(Photo page 136)

PREPARATION	1 hour
FREEZING TIME	20 to 40 minutes for the sherbet 3 hours for the dessert
INGREDIENTS	*For 1 dessert serving 10* 2 pineapples, 3 pounds 5 ounces (1½ kg) each Scant 2 cups (4.5 dl) 28° Sugar Syrup (Recipe 1) ½ cup (100 g) chopped Half-Candied Pineapple Slices (Recipe 166) *For decoration* 2 Half-Candied Pineapple Slices (Recipe 166) 6 candied cherries cut in half
UTENSILS	Large serrated knife Ordinary knife Metal spoon Electric blender, juicer, or food mill Fine mesh sieve Wooden spoon Pastry bag with ¾ inch (2 cm) nozzle (optional) Strip of cardboard approximately 15¾ × 1½ inches (40 × 4 cm) (for upright presentation only)

Preparing the Fruit to be Decorated and Filled: The pineapple used to serve the sherbet can either be prepared for serving on its side or standing upright; the first option is the most convenient for serving. Select the more attractive pineapple for hollowing out and serving (see photo).

Lengthwise Presentation: Lay the pineapple on its side and use a large serrated knife to cut off the upper third of the fruit. Using an ordinary knife, cut around the inside of the pineapple's skin to loosen the pulp; leave about ⅜ inch (1 cm) of pulp and skin around the sides of the fruit.

Cut out the pulp or use a spoon to scoop it out, being careful in either case not to damage or puncture the skin. Reserve all the pulp for use in making the sherbet used to fill the fruit; place the hollowed-out skin in the freezer while making the sherbet.

Upright Presentation: Stand the pineapple upright and cut off the top of the fruit about a third of the way down from the leaves. Save the top and place it in

131

the freezer; it will be used in decorating the finished dessert later. You may need to cut off a little of the base of the fruit so that it will stand upright by itself.

Using the serrated knife, cut around the inside of the skin to detach the pulp; be careful to leave at least ⅜ inch (1 cm) between the knife and the skin of the fruit, and do not cut all the way to the bottom of the fruit, since this might mean puncturing the skin at the bottom. After having loosened the pulp all around the pineapple, cut a small horizontal slit in the skin of the fruit about ¾ inch (2 cm) up from the bottom of the pineapple, and insert the serrated knife; work the knife gently from side to side in a fan-like motion to detach the pulp from the bottom of the pineapple. Remove the pulp in one block from the fruit and use it for making the sherbet that will fill the fruit. Place the hollowed-out skin in the freezer while making the sherbet.

Making the Sherbet: Peel the second pineapple by cutting off the skin deep enough to remove the little "eyes" that dot the surface of the pulp. Cut out the hard central core from each pineapple and cut the pulp into chunks. Put the pulp in a blender, grind it through a food mill using a medium grill, or place it in an electric juicer (this last method is by far the most convenient). Using your hands, squeeze the skin of the second pineapple over a bowl to extract the maximum amount of juice. If the pulp was pureed in a blender or food mill, it must be worked through a sieve to remove any fibrous parts of the pineapple; if the juicer was used, this step is unnecessary.

Measure the strained pineapple pulp and juice, mixed together; you will need a generous 3⅓ cups (8 d*l*) of puree for making the sherbet. Add the sugar syrup to the puree, mix together, and pour into the ice cream freezer. Freezing time is approximately 20 to 40 minutes (see General Comments on Using the Ice Cream Freezer, pages 2 to 4).

Decorating and Filling the Fruit

Lengthwise Presentation: Take a quarter of the Pineapple Sherbet and reserve it in a bowl in the freezer. Mix the remaining sherbet with the chopped pieces of Half-Candied Pineapple Slices; spoon this into the hollowed-out pineapple and pack it down. Place the reserved sherbet in a cold pastry bag (if the sherbet is consistent enough) or use a flexible-blade, metal spatula to dress it artistically over the top of the filled pineapple, mounding it as shown in the photo. Cut the 2 remaining slices of half-candied pineapple into four pieces each and lay them across the top of the dessert, placing the candied cherries in between the slices on top of the dessert or around the sides as shown in the photo. Place the dessert back in the freezer for at least 3 hours before serving (see General Comments on Serving Ice Cream, Sherbet, etc., pages 5 to 7).

Upright Presentation: Mix three-quarters of the sherbet with the chopped pieces of half-candied pineapple and pour this into the hollowed-out pineapple skin. Reserve the extra sherbet in a bowl in the freezer while making the border for the top. Place the filled pineapple in the freezer and leave for at least 3 hours before decorating and serving.

132

Make the decorative border for the top of the fruit by cutting a piece of cardboard to form a circle the size of the top of the pineapple and 1½ inches (4 cm) high. Place this on a plate and line the sides with alternating wedges cut from the half-candied slices of pineapple and halves of candied cherries (cut side against the cardboard—see photo). Place this in the freezer for 15 minutes; then remove from the freezer and fill the cardboard circle to the rim with the Pineapple Sherbet reserved earlier, adding the sherbet slowly so as to fill the spaces between the fruit around the edges, then the middle (use a spoon or spatula to smooth the sherbet against the sides, being careful not to disturb the fruit). Place the filled cardboard circle back into the freezer for at least 3 hours before using to decorate and serving. When ready to serve, place the circle containing the decoration on top of the filled fruit, untape and peel off the cardboard, place the top of the fruit with its leaves back in place, and serve (see photo).

Note: A little less than 1 quart (1 *l*) of fresh Pineapple Sherbet may be made by using the pulp of one pineapple plus the juice from its skin and reducing all the measurements by half. In this case, the chopped half-candied pineapple is simply mixed into the finished sherbet, which is molded and placed in the freezer for storage.

91

Sherbet-Filled Fruits (Fruits Givrés)

(Photo page 38)

This recipe is for oranges, tangerines, lemons, and grapefruits.

PREPARATION	30 minutes
COOLING TIME	1 hour

INGREDIENTS	*For 8 servings*
	8 oranges
	    or 16 tangerines
	    or 8 large lemons
	    or 4 grapefruits
	Sugar cubes
	1 quart (1 *l*) of sherbet made from the juice of the fruit employed or made in advance with other fruit (see Index for specific sherbet recipes)
	
	For decoration (optional)
	Green Almond Paste leaves (Recipe 171)
	Candied cherries

UTENSILS	Sharp knife Lemon or orange squeezer Spoon or pastry bag with a star-shaped nozzle (optional)

General Comments: Sherbet used for filling citrus fruit skins can be prepared well in advance but must be softened to a "newly made" consistency before use.

The hollowed-out skin may be frozen and kept in the freezer for up to 4 days before being filled with the sherbet. Once the sherbet has been placed in the skin, however, the dessert should be served within 12 hours or the skin will impart a bitter taste to the sherbet.

For these desserts, always select somewhat thick-skinned fruit (nontreated, if possible). Wash and dry the fruit well before scooping out the pulp and freezing the skins.

Making Sherbet-Filled Fruits: (See Note). Cut off the tops of the lemons, oranges, or tangerines two-thirds up from the bottom; grapefruits are cut in half. Using a lemon or orange squeezer, squeeze the fruit carefully to get the maximum amount of juice without damaging the peel. Use the juice to make the sherbet if it has not been prepared in advance.

Remove the thin membranes that fill the center and are attached to the insides of the peel; then rub the inside of each peel with a sugar cube. Do the same with the top part of each fruit. Make sure the hollowed-out bottom peel will stand upright—if not, cut a thin slice off the base to make it flat and stable. Place the hollowed-out bottoms and tops in the freezer for at least an hour before filling them with sherbet.

Fill each peel, either using a spoon or (if the sherbet is soft enough) a pastry bag. Cover the sherbet with the top of the fruit except in the case of grapefruits, in which case each half is simply filled with sherbet (see photo). Place the dessert immediately back in the freezer until ready to serve. Serve within 12 hours (see General Comments on Serving Ice Cream, Sherbet, etc., pages 5 to 7).

Note: All sherbet-filled fruits are made in the same way; they differ only in that you should serve two tangerines, one orange or lemon, and half a grapefruit per person.

The finished desserts may be decorated either with little leaves made of green almond paste or with candied cherries, or served simply as they are (see photo).

92

Frozen Coffee Dessert (Café Frappé)

PREPARATION	10 minutes
FREEZING TIME	1 to 2 hours before serving
INGREDIENTS	*For approximately 1 quart (1 l) serving 6* Generous 3⅓ cups (8 d*l*) Coffee Ice Cream (Recipe 33) Generous ¾ cup (2 d*l*) Coffee Granité (Recipe 25)
UTENSILS	Mixing bowl Spoon A 1-quart (1-*l*) ice cream mold

Making the Dessert: Place the mold in the freezer 15 minutes before it is to be filled.

The ice cream must be soft, either newly made or softened, so that the granité will mix into it. If the ice cream was in the freezer, place it in the refrigerator to soften for 30 minutes to 1 hour before stirring in the granité. Once the granité has been stirred in, pour the mixture into the cold ice cream mold and place in the freezer for 1 to 2 hours. This dessert should be creamy when served.

To Serve: Spoon into tall, tulip-shaped glasses or wine glasses.

To Store: Once molded, this dessert can be kept in the freezer for up to 2 days. In this case, it should be softened in the refrigerator for 30 minutes to an hour before serving.

93

Frozen Chocolate Dessert (Chocolat Frappé)

PREPARATION	10 minutes
FREEZING TIME	1 to 2 hours before serving
INGREDIENTS	*For approximately 1 quart (1 l) serving 6* 2¾ cups (6.5 dl) Chocolate Ice Cream (Recipe 32) 1½ cups (3.5 dl) Coffee Granité (Recipe 25)
UTENSILS	Mixing bowl Spoon A 1-quart (1-l) ice cream mold

Making the Dessert: Place the mold in the freezer 15 minutes before it is to be filled.

The ice cream must be soft, either newly made or softened, so that the granité will mix into it. If the ice cream was in the freezer, place it in the refrigerator to soften for 30 minutes to 1 hour before stirring in the granité. Once the granité has been stirred in, pour the mixture into the cold ice cream mold and place in the freezer for 1 to 2 hours. This dessert should be creamy when served.

To Serve: Spoon into tall, tulip-shaped glasses or wine glasses.

To Store: Once molded, this dessert can be kept in the freezer for up to 2 days. In this case, it should be softened in the refrigerator for 30 minutes to an hour before serving.

Frozen Rice Pudding with Apricots (Riz du Mas du Juge)

PREPARATION	15 minutes
COOKING TIME	45 minutes
COOLING TIME	1 hour
FREEZING TIME	2 hours before serving
INGREDIENTS	*For 1 dessert serving 8 to 10* 2 generous cups (½ *l*) milk ⅓ cup (60 g) rice ⅓ cup (60 g) granulated sugar A 1-pound (500-g) jar of Apricot Jam (Recipe 132) 1 quart (1-*l*) Vanilla Ice Cream (Recipe 27)—see Note
UTENSILS	2 saucepans with covers Strainer 2 mixing bowls Ice cream thermometer (optional) Ring mold or other mold with 6⅓-cup (1½-*l*) capacity

Making the Dessert: Sprinkle the rice into 2 generous cups (½ *l*) of rapidly boiling water and boil for 20 seconds; pour into a sieve, hold under cold running water to cool, and then drain.

In a large saucepan, bring the milk to a boil, add the rice and sugar, stir well, then cover the pot and cook slowly for 45 minutes. Check the rice as it cooks to be sure it doesn't stick to the bottom of the pot; stir it occasionally to avoid sticking. When finished cooking, the rice should have absorbed all the milk.

Pour the cooked rice into a bowl and allow to cool. To speed cooling, place the bowl in a larger bowl filled with ice and water and stir until the rice is cold. Place the rice in the refrigerator if necessary to cool it to 39°F (4°C). (If you do not have a thermometer that registers these low temperatures, test the rice with your finger—it should be as cold as ice water.)

Remove ½ cup (150 g) of apricot pieces from the apricot jam and cut them into small squares (save the remaining jam for other uses). Mix these pieces with the cold rice; then stir the mixture into the softened Vanilla Ice Cream (see Note). Pour into the mold and place in the freezer for 2 hours before turning out and serving (see Comments on Turning out and Serving, pages 5 to 7). Serve with a sauceboat of Fresh Apricot Sauce (Recipe 98).

Note: The ice cream must be of "newly made" consistency. If the ice cream was stored in the freezer, place it in the refrigerator for about 30 to 45 minutes to soften before stirring in the other ingredients.

95
Profiteroles (Profiteroles)

PREPARATION	15 minutes
INGREDIENTS	*For 8 servings* 40 Cream Puff Pastries (Recipe 108) 1½ pints (¾ *l*) Vanilla Ice Cream (Recipe 27) Generous 1⅔ (4 d*l*) cups Hot Chocolate Sauce (Recipe 101)
UTENSILS	Small spoon Serrated knife

Making the Dessert: The cream puff pastries should be baked the day the dessert is made or at the earliest the day before, so that they will be rich and tasty; do not freeze them.

Using a serrated knife, cut each little pastry almost in half through the middle, forming a top and bottom still attached at one side, and fill each one with a spoonful of ice cream just before serving. Spoon over the hot chocolate sauce and serve immediately.

Variations: It is sometimes fun to reverse the flavors and fill the cream puffs with Chocolate Ice Cream and spoon over Vanilla Sauce or fill them with Coffee Ice Cream and serve them with Hot Chocolate Sauce.

96

Chocolate-Coated Ice Cream on a Stick (Sucettes Glaceés)

PREPARATION	1 hour
COOKING TIME	5 minutes
FREEZING TIME	3 hours before serving
INGREDIENTS	*For 10 individual servings*
	2½ cups (6 d*l*) of the ice cream or sherbet of your choice
	10½ ounces (300 g) semi-sweet dark chocolate or white chocolate
	2 tablespoons (30 g) tasteless cooking oil or vegetable shortening
UTENSILS	10 molds for ice cream on a stick (see utensil photo, page xix and Comment, pages 5 to 7)
	10 ice cream sticks
	Nonstick parchment paper
	Plate
	Double boiler or mixing bowl and saucepan *(bain-marie)*
	Yoghurt thermometer
	Large glass

Making the Desserts: The ice cream or sherbet used must be of "newly made" consistency; if made in advance and stored in the freezer, place it in the refrigerator to soften for 30 to 45 minutes before using it in this recipe.

Place the ice cream molds in the freezer for 1 hour before filling them with the ice cream or sherbet.

Pour the ice cream or sherbet into the molds, filling them completely; pour slowly to avoid the formation of air bubbles.

Stick an ice cream stick into each one so that it goes about halfway into the ice cream; or if the stick is incorporated in the cover, place the cover on and then place the molds in the freezer for at least 2 hours before unmolding. When hardened, unmold the ice creams and place them on a plate that has been covered with nonstick parchment paper. Put them back into the freezer for at least 1 hour longer before coating them with chocolate.

Melt the chocolate in a double boiler with the oil or shortening; use a yoghurt thermometer to be sure that the chocolate is not heated to more than 104°F (40°C) when it is melted.

Pour the melted chocolate into a glass or other container that is slightly taller and slightly wider than the molded ice cream. Remove the ice creams from the freezer and dip each one quickly into the glass of chocolate, then remove, allow

142

the excess chocolate to drip off, and place the coated ice cream back on the nonstick paper. Continue in this manner until all of the ice creams have been coated. Then place them all back in the freezer for 2 hours before serving.

Note: The chocolate coating can be flavored in many ways, according to the ice cream used; some suggestions are offered here. With Nut Brittle (Recipe 38) or Caramel Ice Cream (Recipe 31), add a scant ¼ cup (30 g) of powdered Nut Brittle (Recipe 196) or Nougatine Crumble (Recipe 197) to the melted chocolate.

With Coconut Ice Cream (Recipe 36), add a generous ⅓ cup (30 g) of grated coconut to the melted chocolate.

With Vanilla or Chocolate Ice Cream (Recipe 27 or 32), after coating the ice cream with the chocolate, quickly sprinkle the chocolate with large pieces of Nougatine Crumble (Recipe 197) before it hardens.

With Strawberry or Raspberry Sherbet (Recipe 10 or 11), use white chocolate and add 4 drops of red food coloring to it when it is melted.

To Store: Before coating with the chocolate, the molded ice cream or sherbet can be kept in the freezer for up to 2 weeks, but once unmolded and coated with chocolate, the desserts must be served within 3 days.

97

Baked Alaskan Banana Dessert
(Banane á la Norvégiènne)

PREPARATION	30 minutes
FREEZING TIME	30 minutes for the skins 3 hours before serving
COOKING TIME	1 or 2 minutes
INGREDIENTS	*For 8 servings* 8 bananas 1 quart (1 *l*) Banana Ice Cream (Recipe 29) French Meringue (Recipe 109)
UTENSILS	Knife Pastry bag (optional) Baking sheet

Making the Dessert: Lie each banana on its side and cut out a long strip of the skin about ½ inch (1.5 cm) wide so that once it is removed, the banana itself can be taken out of its skin. (Part of the pulp can be used to make the banana ice cream if it has been prepared in advance.) Place the banana skins in the freezer for at least 30 minutes before proceeding to fill them.

The ice cream must be of "newly made" consistency; if made in advance and stored in the freezer, it should be placed in the refrigerator to soften for about 30 to 45 minutes.

Take the banana skins from the freezer and place them on a baking sheet or plate that will fit in your freezer. Using a spoon, fill the banana skins with the banana ice cream and place them back in the freezer for at least 3 hours (the ice cream must be very hard when it next comes from the freezer).

One hour before serving, prepare the meringue and use it to completely cover the ice cream that is visible inside the skin of the banana. (A pastry bag may be used for this.) After the meringue has been added, replace the bananas in the freezer.

Heat the broiler for at least 15 minutes before serving the dessert. When ready to serve, place the bananas on a baking sheet and leave under the broiler for 1 to 2 minutes maximum, to color the meringue; then serve immediately.

Chapter 5

CREAMS, SAUCES, PASTRIES AND FRUIT PREPARATIONS

RECIPES

98. Fresh Fruit Sauce (Coulis de Fruits)
99. Vanilla Sauce (Sauce à la Vanille)
100. Orange Sauce (Sauce à l'Orange)
101. Hot Chocolate Sauce (Sauce à Profiteroles)
102. Caramel Sauce (Sauce au Caramel)
103. Champagne Sabayon Sauce (Sabayon au Champagne)
104. Chantilly Cream (Chantilly)
105. Coffee-Flavored Chantilly Cream (Chantilly au Café)
106. Whipped Cream (Crème Fouettée)
107. Génoise
108. Cream Puff Pastry (Pâte à Chou)
109. French Meringue (Meringue Française)
110. Success Pastry (Fond de Succès)
111. Almond Pastry (Biscuit aux Amandes)
112. Orange-Almond Pastry (Biscuit Orange aux Amandes)
113. Provencal Petit Fours (Biscuits de Provence)
114. Vanilla Wafer Batter (Pâte à Langue de Chat)

145

115. Finger Wafers (Langues de Chat)   🍳

116. Wafer Rounds Filled with Truffle Cream (Petits Fours en Caissettes)   🍳

117. Tulip Pastries (Tulipes)   🍳 🍳 🍳

118. Grilled Slivered Almonds (Amandes Effilées et Grillées)   🍳

119. Chocolate Palms and Other Chocolate Ornaments (Décors en Chocolat)   🍳 🍳 🍳

120. Madeleines   🍳

121. Gatines-Style Spice Cake (Pain d'Épices des Gatines)   🍳

122. Home Canned Apricots in Light Syrup or "au Naturel" (Abricots au Sirop ou au Naturel)   🍳

123. Home Canned Cherries in Light Syrup or "au Naturel" (Cerises au Sirop ou au Naturel)   🍳

124. Home Canned Pears or Peaches in Light Syrup (Pêches ou Poires au Sirop)   🍳

125. Frozen Fruit Purees (Purée de Fruits)   🍳

126. Brandied Cherries (Cerises à l'Eau-de-Vie)   🍳

127. Brandied Raspberries (Framboises à l'Eau-de-Vie)   🍳

128. Black Currant Liqueur (Liqueur de Cassis)   🍳

129. Tropical Fruit Salad (Salade de Fruits Exotiques)   🍳

98
Fresh Fruit Sauce
(Coulis de Fruits)

PREPARATION   10 minutes

INGREDIENTS   *For 5¼ cups (1¼ l) of sauce serving 10 to 12*
                   2¼ pounds (1 kg) prepared fresh fruit (see Comment and
                       Note)
                   3 cups (600 g) granulated sugar (see Comment)

                   For a generous 2½ cups (6.2 dl) of sauce serving 4 to 6
                   1 pound 2 ounces (500 g) prepared fresh fruit (see Com-
                       ment and Note)
                   1½ cups (300 g) granulated sugar (see Comment)

UTENSILS   Electric blender

Making the Sauce: This sauce can be made with any fruit you like. Many fruits
will have to be peeled, seeded, and quartered (pears, peaches, apricots, etc.);
others can simply be washed and used whole (strawberries, raspberries, etc.).

Place the fruit in a blender with the sugar and blend at medium speed for 2
minutes or until well combined and smooth.

Comment: When fresh fruit is not available, canned or frozen fruit can be used
instead. Drain off any syrup from canned fruit and place it in the blender
without adding any sugar.

If using frozen fruit, allow it to thaw and then make the sauce as described for
using fresh fruit.

To Store: Fruit sauce can be kept refrigerated in a tightly closed container for
up to a week. It can also be frozen for up to 6 months but must be whisked while
thawing to restore its texture and original smoothness.

However, if frozen fruit was used when making the sauce, the sauce should
not be frozen for storing.

Note: Since this recipe calls for the weight of prepared fruit (i.e., peeled,
seeded, etc.), it is preferable to have a kitchen scale on which to weigh it. For
those who have no scale, it is advisable to puree the fruit alone and then measure it. For 3¾ cups (9 dl) of puree, use 3 cups (600 g) of granulated sugar; For a
scant 2 cups (4.5 dl) of puree, use 1½ cups (300 g) sugar. The sugar can then be
added to the puree and whisked or beaten with an electric mixer until the sauce
is well blended.

99
Vanilla Sauce
(Sauce à la Vanille)

PREPARATION	15 to 20 minutes
COOKING TIME	10 minutes
COOLING TIME	30 minutes
INGREDIENTS	*For a generous 3⅓ cups (8 dl) of sauce serving 8 to 12* 2 generous cups (½ *l*) milk 1 vanilla bean split in half lengthwise 1 generous cup (210 g) granulated sugar 6 egg yolks *For a generous 1⅔ cups (4 dl) of sauce serving 4 to 6* 1 generous cup (¼ *l*) milk ½ vanilla bean split open lengthwise ½ cup (105 g) granulated sugar 3 egg yolks
UTENSILS	1 medium-sized saucepan with cover 2 bowls Electric mixer Wire whisk Wooden spoon *or* spatula Candy thermometer (optional)

Making the Sauce: To make the sauce, proceed exactly as described in Recipe 27 for Vanilla Ice Cream. The procedure and ingredients are the same, the only difference being that when making the sauce, no crême fraîche or heavy cream is added when cooling.

   Once the sauce has cooled completely, it should be placed in the refrigerator until called for.

Uses: See the Cross Index of Basic Ingredients and their uses.

To Store: This sauce can be kept refrigerated for up to 48 hours.

100

Orange Sauce (Sauce à l'Orange)

PREPARATION   15 to 20 minutes

COOKING TIME   10 minutes

COOLING TIME   30 minutes

INGREDIENTS   *For a generous 3⅓ cups (8 dl) of sauce serving 8 to 12*
                         2 medium-sized nontreated oranges
                         2 generous cups (½ l) milk
                         1 generous cup (210 g) granulated sugar
                         6 egg yolks

INGREDIENTS   *For a generous 1⅔ cups (4 dl) of sauce serving 4 to 6*
                         1 medium-sized nontreated orange
                         1 generous cup (¼ l) milk
                         ½ cup (105 g) granulated sugar
                         3 egg yolks

UTENSILS   2 mixing bowls
                         Electric mixer
                         Wire whisk
                         1 medium-sized saucepan with cover
                         1 small saucepan
                         Wooden spoon *or* spatula
                         Vegetable peeler
                         Strainer
                         Candy thermometer (optional)

Making the Sauce: Use a vegetable peeler or "zester" to remove the colored zest from the orange peel. (Do not remove the whitish inner skin just underneath the zest since this has a bitter taste.)

Crop the pieces of zest into a small pot of rapidly boiling water, leave there for a few seconds, and then drain in a strainer and hold under cold running water to cool. Drain completely.

Making orange sauce is identical to making Vanilla Sauce (Recipe 99) but the vanilla bean is replaced by the orange zest prepared as just described. The orange zest is strained out before cooling the sauce.

Uses: This sauce is served with Chocolate Ice Cream (Recipe 32), Concorde Sundae (Recipe 50), and Frozen Chocolate and Orange Dessert (Recipe 83).

To Store: This sauce can be kept refrigerated for up to 24 hours.

101
Hot Chocolate Sauce
(Sauce à Profiteroles)

PREPARATION	Approximately 10 minutes
COOKING TIME	5 minutes
INGREDIENTS	*For a generous 1⅔ cups (4 dl) sauce serving 4 to 6* Scant ½ cup (60 g) unsweetened cocoa powder Generous ¾ cup (2 dl) water 1 scant cup (180 g) granulated sugar 6½ tablespoons (100 g) crème fraîche or heavy cream (see Dictionary of Terms)
UTENSILS	Large mixing bowl Saucepan Wire whisk

Making the Sauce: Place the cocoa powder in the mixing bowl.

Place the water and sugar in a saucepan and bring to a boil, stirring constantly. Once the sugar has dissolved and the water is boiling, pour it into the bowl containing the cocoa, whisking constantly as the liquid is being added. Pour the combined ingredients back into the saucepan and place over low heat.

Whisking constantly, add the cream and bring the sauce to a boil. (Be careful, since the sauce tends to rise like milk when boiled.) As soon as the sauce comes to a boil, remove it from the heat and serve immediately.

This sauce is always served hot.

Uses: In addition to numerous ice creams, sherbets, and various sundaes, Hot Chocolate Sauce is served on

> Profiteroles (Recipe 95)
> Vanilla Ice Cream (Recipe 27)
> Caramel Ice Cream (Recipe 31)

To Store: The sauce can be kept in a tightly sealed container in the refrigerator for up to 4 days. It must always be heated to boiling before serving.

102

Caramel Sauce (Sauce au Caramel)

PREPARATION   20 minutes after making the caramel

INGREDIENTS   *For 1 cup (2.4 dl) of cold sauce serving 6 or ⅔ cup (1.5 dl)*
                   of hot sauce serving 4

                   For the caramel
                   1 cup (200 g) granulated sugar
                   10 drops lemon juice

                   For the sauce
                   Generous ¾ cup (2 dl) crème fraîche or heavy cream
                   Generous ½ cup (1.25 dl) milk (if sauce is to be served
                   cold)

UTENSILS   2 saucepans
                   Wooden spoon *or* spatula

Making the Sauce: Make the caramel as described in the recipe for Lenôtre's
Special Caramel Ice Cream (Recipe 31). Once it is made, remove the saucepan
from the heat for 5 minutes before incorporating the cream as described below
(since the caramel forms at an extremely high temperature, it must cool to approximately the same temperature as the boiling cream when the two are combined to make the sauce).

When the caramel has cooled for 5 minutes, bring the cream to a boil and add
it to the caramel little by little, stirring as you do so. Place the pot back over low
heat and stir until any lumps of caramel have melted (see Note).

When the sauce is smooth, it is ready to serve hot.

If the sauce is to be served cold, allow it to cool completely. Bring the milk to
a boil and allow it to cool completely as well. Then stir it into the cool sauce (the
milk is added because as it cools, the caramel sauce thickens considerably).

Uses: This sauce is equally good hot or cold on Vanilla Ice Cream (Recipe 27),
Chocolate Ice Cream (Recipe 32), or Nut Brittle Ice Cream (Recipe 38), as well
as on numerous sundaes.

To Store: The sauce can be kept refrigerated in a tightly sealed container for
up to 4 days.

Note: If a large lump of caramel forms, pour off the sauce and melt the lump
over low heat, stirring constantly. When melted, add the sauce, still stirring,
bring to a boil to keep lumps from reforming, then strain the sauce into a bowl.

103
Champagne Sabayon Sauce
(Sabayon au Champagne)

PREPARATION	20 minutes
COOKING TIME	10 minutes
INGREDIENTS	*For 3¾ cups (9 dl) of sauce serving 9* 5 egg yolks 1 generous cup (¼ *l*) champagne (white or pink) Scant ¾ cup (140 g) granulated sugar
UTENSILS	Double boiler *or* mixing bowl and saucepan (*bain-maire*) Wire whisk Yoghurt thermometer Mixing bowl Electric mixer

Making the Sauce: This delicious sauce is somewhat fragile, so it must be made no more than 30 minutes before being served.

Place the egg yolks and champagne in the top of a double boiler or in a mixing bowl placed over a pot of simmering water (*bain-marie*). In either case, the water beneath the egg yolk–champagne mixture should simmer but not boil so as to heat but not cook these ingredients (the water should not touch the receptacle containing the ingredients).

Whisk the egg yolks and champagne gently for 8 to 10 minutes; the mixture should not expand and the temperature of the ingredients should be kept at a constant 113°F (45°C)—use a yoghurt thermometer to check it.

After whisking, pour the ingredients into a mixing bowl and add the sugar. Beat with an electric mixer on medium speed for 5 minutes, then beat on low speed for 5 minutes more; or continue using a wire whisk.

The sauce is now ready; it is always served at room temperature, never chilled.

Uses: Serve this sauce with

> Pistacio Ice Cream (Recipe 37)
> Passion Fruit Sherbet (Recipe 12)
> Champagne and Raspberry Sundae (Recipe 58)
> Frozen Rice Pudding with Apricots (Recipe 94)

104
Chantilly Cream
(Chantilly)

PREPARATION	2 to 4 minutes
COOLING TIME	1 hour
INGREDIENTS	*For 2 generous cups (½ l) of Chantilly Cream* 1 generous cup (2.5 dl) heavy cream 3 tablespoons confectioner's sugar or granulated sugar
UTENSILS	Large mixing bowl Wire whisk *or* electric mixer

Making the Chantilly Cream: (See Note). Place the cream and sugar in a mixing bowl; then place the bowl in the refrigerator for 1 hour or in the freezer for 20 minutes before beating.

Beat energetically with a wire whisk or on the highest speed when using a mixer to make the cream expand. After beating for about 2 to 4 minutes, the cream should have doubled in volume and formed soft but definite peaks when the whisk or beaters are lifted out of it. When this point is reached, stop beating immediately—if beaten too much, the cream will become liquid and grainy.

Chantilly is usually poured into a pastry bag and squeezed out to decorate ice cream or parfait-based desserts, or else it is spread like an icing over the desserts as part of their decoration.

To Store: If not used immediately, the Chantilly Cream can be placed in a tightly closed container or a covered bowl and kept in the refrigerator for up to 24 hours. If stored in this manner, it should be whisked lightly when taken from the refrigerator before using.

Note: This recipe is a simplified version of the one given in *Lenôtre's Desserts and Pastries.*

Uses: Chantilly cream can be used to decorate many ice creams and sundaes, but it is rarely used with sherbets; fresh fruit sauces are better with sherbets (specific recommendations for their use are given throughout this book).

105
Coffee-Flavored Chantilly Cream
(Chantilly au Café)

PREPARATION	2 to 4 minutes
COOLING TIME	1 hour
INGREDIENTS	*For 2 generous cups (½ l) of cream* 1 tablespoon instant coffee 1 tablespoon hot water 1 generous cup (2.5 d*l*) heavy cream 3 tablespoons confectioner's sugar or granulated sugar
UTENSILS	Small mixing bowl Medium-sized mixing bowl Electric mixer *or* wire whisk

Making the Cream: Place the instant coffee in a small bowl and stir in a tablespoon of hot water to dissolve it. Leave the coffee to cool; then pour it into a medium-sized bowl with the cream and sugar.

Place the bowl in the refrigerator for 1 hour or in the freezer for 20 minutes before beating.

Beat energetically with a wire whisk or on the highest speed when using a mixer to make the cream expand. After beating for about 2 to 4 minutes, the cream should have doubled in volume and formed soft but definite peaks when the whisk or beaters are lifted out of it. When this point is reached, stop beating immediately—if beaten too much, the cream will become liquid and grainy.

Chantilly is usually poured into a pastry bag and squeezed out to decorate ice cream or parfait-based desserts, or else it is spread like an icing over the desserts as part of their decoration.

Uses: Use in decorating the Frozen Coffee Vacherin (Recipe 87) or other coffee-flavored desserts.

To store: If not used immediately, the Chantilly Cream can be placed in a tightly closed container or a covered bowl and kept in the refrigerator for up to 24 hours. If stored in this manner, it should be whisked lightly when taken from the refrigerator before using.

Frozen Raspberry Vacherin, Recipe 86

106
Whipped Cream
(Crème Fouettée)

PREPARATION	2 to 4 minutes
COOLING TIME	1 hour
INGREDIENTS	*For 1 generous cup (¼ l) of whipped cream* Generous ½ cup (1.25 d*l*) heavy cream
	For 2 generous cups (½ l) of whipped cream 1 generous cup (¼ *l*) heavy cream
	For 4¼ cups (1 l) of whipped cream 2 generous cups (½ *l*) heavy cream
UTENSILS	Mixing bowl Electric mixer *or* wire whisk

Making the Whipped Cream: Place the cream in a mixing bowl and refrigerate for 1 hour or place in the freezer for 20 minutes before beating.

Beat the cream with a wire whisk or an electric mixer for about 2 to 4 minutes or until it has doubled in volume and thickened enough to form soft but definite peaks when the whisk or beaters are lifted out of it. When this point is reached, immediately stop beating and use the cream as described in the recipe that calls for it. If beaten too long, the cream will become liquid and grainy.

Always add whipped cream to other ingredients little by little, generally by cutting and folding the cream in to mix it smoothly. When cooked creams (as in making parfaits) are combined with whipped cream, they should be the same temperature as the whipped cream; this is achieved by refrigerating the cooled, cooked cream at the same time as the cream used for whipping—this way, when the cream is whipped, you can be sure the other elements with which it is to be mixed are at the same temperature as the whipped cream itself—this avoids lumps from forming.

Uses: Whipped cream is used in making some ice creams [for example, Almond Ice Cream (Recipe 28)] and all parfaits.

Whipped cream can also be added to any sherbet to make an eggless ice cream which is very light and creamy. To make approximately 1 quart (1 l) of creamy sherbet, mix the fruit pulp and 28° Sugar Syrup (Recipe 1) as described in the specific recipe. Then measure the mixture. Use a scant 3¼ cups (7.5 dl) fruit–syrup mixture and fold into it a generous ¾ cup (190 ml) whipped cream. When perfectly mixed, place in the ice cream freezer and freeze.

Brandied Cherries, Recipe 126; Brandied Raspberries, Recipe 127;
Fondant, Recipe 194; Chocolate Cherries, Recipe 201;
Chocolate Raspberries, Recipe 202

107
Génoise

PREPARATION   20 minutes

BAKING TIME   30 to 35 minutes

INGREDIENTS   *For 2 round cakes 8 inches (20 cm) in diameter or 1*
                            rectangular cake 8 × 12 inches (20 × 30 cm)
                        Generous ⅔ cup (155 g) granulated sugar
                        5 whole (1 cup) eggs
                        3 tablespoons (45 g) butter
                        Scant 1¼ cup (155 g) flour
                        1½ teaspoons (8 g) vanilla sugar

                        For 1 round cake 8 inches (20 cm) in diameter
                        Generous ⅓ cup (78 g) granulated sugar
                        3 whole (½ cup) eggs
                        1½ tablespoons (23 g) butter
                        Generous ½ cup (78 g) flour
                        1 scant teaspoon (4 g) vanilla sugar

UTENSILS   Mixing bowl
                        Electric mixer
                        Wire whisk
                        Large saucepan
                        Small saucepan
                        Wooden spatula
                        Flour sifter
                        1 or 2 round cake pans 8 inches (20 cm) in diameter
                            or 1 rectangular cake pan 8 × 12 inches (20 × 30 cm)
                        Cake rack

Making the Batter: Preheat the oven to 350°F (175°C). Place the eggs and sugar in a mixing bowl and set the bowl over a saucepan of boiling water; the water should not touch the bowl. Beat the eggs and sugar together for 1 minute with the wire whisk. Then, with the bowl away from the heat, beat with the mixer at high speed for 2 minutes and then for 5 minutes more at low speed or until the mixture is very pale and falls from a wooden spatula in a smooth ribbon.

Clarify the butter in a small saucepan. Sift the flour and vanilla sugar; then fold into the egg–sugar mixture. Fold in the warm butter. Stop mixing as soon as all of the ingredients are well blended. This step should be done quickly and the cake should be baked right away.

Baking the Cake: Pour the batter into the buttered and floured cake pan(s) and bake for 30 to 35 minutes or until the cake is golden brown and beginning to pull away from the sides of the pan. Let the cake cool for about 10 minutes; then turn out onto a cake rack while still warm. Allow to cool completely before using.

Note: Do not overheat the egg mixture in the double boiler or the cake will dry out too fast when baking.

To Store: The cake will keep fresh for a week in the refrigerator if well wrapped in plastic wrap or aluminum foil.

To Freeze: The cake will keep for 1 month if well wrapped, but be sure to allow it to thaw completely for 24 hours in the refrigerator before use.

To Layer: Génoise cakes often are cut in half or into three or four layers after baking. To do this properly, you need a very long serrated knife and several strips of cardboard. It is essential that the blade of the knife be several inches longer than the diameter of the Génoise. Pile the cardboard strips on opposite sides of the Génoise so that they make two piles of equal height. The height of these piles is very important and depends on how many layers the cake has to be cut into. Use a ruler to measure the height of your Génoise. If you want to cut the cake into four equal layers, make the strips of cardboard into piles whose height is ¼ that of the Génoise (e g , for a cake two inches tall, the piles of cardboard strips should be ½" high). Place the blade of the knife flat against the two piles of cardboard strips and saw into the cake, keeping the knife in contact with the strips, which will guide the blade. Lift off the top section of the cake and remove this first, bottom slice from between the strips. Replace the remaining cake in between the cardboard strips and cut through the cake again. Repeat this procedure once more, and the Génoise will be cut into four equal layers. The same procedure is used with cutting a Génoise into two, three, four, or five layers.

♕

<h1 style="text-align:center">108
Cream Puff Pastry
(Pâte à Choux)</h1>

Do not work this dough too long or else the puffs will not rise correctly.

PREPARATION	15 minutes
BAKING TIME	20 to 30 minutes per baking sheet
INGREDIENTS	*For approximately 1⅓ cups (600 g) dough (to make 30 to 40 small cream puffs)* 4 to 5 eggs = 1 generous cup (¼ *l*), beaten 1 generous cup (¼ *l*) of half milk/half water ¾ teaspoon (5 g) salt 1 teaspoon (5 g) granulated sugar 7½ tablespoons (110 g) butter 1 cup (140 g) flour Granulated sugar (preferably coarse grained) to sprinkle on top
UTENSILS	Large, heavy-bottomed saucepan Mixing bowl Wooden spoon Wire whisk Pastry bag with ⅝-inch (1.5-cm) nozzle 2 baking sheets

Making the Dough: Preheat the oven to 425°F (220°C). Measure the eggs, since their volume can be more or less than the actual amount required by the recipe.

Place the milk/water mixture in the saucepan and add the salt, sugar, and butter. Bring slowly to a boil, then remove from the heat, and add all the flour at one time. Beat the dough vigorously with a wooden spoon, replace the saucepan on the heat, and beat the dough for 1 minute or until it comes away from the sides of the pan and no longer sticks to the spoon.

Transfer the dough to a warmed mixing bowl. Add a third of the beaten egg, beating the dough all the while with the spoon. When the egg is mixed in, add half the remaining egg, still beating the dough; finally add the remaining egg and continue to beat until the dough is smooth.

Baking the Puffs: Fill the pastry bag with the dough. Butter and flour the baking sheets or line them with nonstick parchment paper, sticking each corner of the paper to the baking sheet with some of the dough.

Make little mounds, about 1½ inches (4 cm) in diameter, 15 to 20 per baking sheet. Sprinkle the mounds of dough with granulated sugar.

Put in the oven as soon as the dough is ready. Bake at 425°F (220°C) for the first 15 minutes; then lower the heat to 400°F (200°C) for the next 15 minutes. This change in temperature will prevent the puffs from cracking open, but after turning the oven down, keep the oven door ajar with a wooden spoon. Watch the baking to see that the puffs brown but remain slightly moist; if they dry out too much, they will not be good.

To Store: If used for profiteroles, the cream puffs should be made no more than a day in advance so that they will be perfectly moist inside.

For other uses, such as those mentioned in *Lenôtre's Desserts and Pastries*, the puffs can be easily kept for a week if placed in tightly closed bags in the refrigerator or for 1 month in the freezer. If frozen, be sure to defrost the puffs for 24 hours in the refrigerator before using (do not freeze the puffs if using them for profiteroles).

109
French Meringue
(Meringue Française)

Save your egg whites in the refrigerator to make meringues; once baked, they keep very well.

PREPARATION	15 minutes
BAKING TIME	1 hour 15 minutes
INGREDIENTS	*For 1 circle 8 inches (20 cm) in diameter and 10 to 12 small ovals*
	3 egg whites—½ cup (90 g)
	Scant ½ cup (90 g) granulated sugar
	Scant ⅔ cup (90 g) confectioner's sugar
UTENSILS	Mixing bowl
	Electric mixer
	Baking sheet
	Nonstick parchment paper (optional)
	Pastry bag with ¾-inch (2-cm) nozzle

Making the Batter: Preheat the oven to 275°F (135°C).

Beat the egg whites until very stiff; halfway through, add 2 tablespoons of the granulated sugar. When the egg whites are very stiff, mix the remaining granulated sugar and the confectioner's sugar together and sift little by little into the egg whites, folding it into them.

Note: To fold dry ingredients into the beaten egg whites proceed as follows. Sift a little of the sugar mixture over the beaten egg whites and incorporate it into them by cutting and folding the egg whites with a wooden spatula. To do this, "cut" through the middle of the egg whites with the edge of the spatula; then lift and fold half of the whites up and over the other half. Work carefully but quickly, turning the bowl itself a quarter of a turn each time you cut and fold, until the other ingredients have been completely incorporated into them. Once this has been done, sprinkle more of the dry mixture (sugar and confectioner's sugar) over the egg whites and continue cutting and folding in this way until all the sugar has been mixed with the whites and a completely homogenous mixture has been formed.

Baking the Meringue: Line the baking sheet with nonstick parchment paper or butter and flour the sheet. If using parchment paper, stick the corners down with a little of the meringue batter. Draw an 8-inch (20-cm) circle on the baking

162

sheet or paper. Then, using a pastry bag fitted with a ¾-inch (2-cm) nozzle, fill the circle with the batter, making a tight spiral starting from the center of the circle.

When the circle has been filled in, make 10 to 12 ovals measuring 1½ × 2 inches (3.5 × 5 cm). This is done by simply drawing the pastry bag in a straight line 2 inches (5 cm) long; the meringue will spread while baking and the proper width will be attained in this way (see photo for Frozen Strawberry Vacherin, page 155). Because the meringues will "grow," do not place them too close together on the baking sheet.

Bake the meringues for approximately 1 hour 15 minutes; the small ovals may be done after an hour, so check them. When the meringue is done, it should be a very pale pinkish brown color, and dry on both the top and bottom. If the meringues color too quickly, turn the oven down.

Uses: The small oval meringues can be served with any ice cream, as an accompaniment. The large circle is used as a base in the frozen meringue shells and in other frozen desserts.

To Store: Once baked and cooled, the meringues can be kept in a tightly closed metal or plastic box in a dry place for 3 weeks.

110
Success Pastry
(Fond de Succès)

PREPARATION	15 minutes
BAKING TIME	1 hour 20 minutes
INGREDIENTS	*For 2 pastries 8 inches (20 cm) in diameter and 20 small pastries*
	5 egg whites = ¾ cup (155 g)
	1 generous tablespoon (20 g) granulated sugar
	¾ cup (170 g) granulated sugar
	Scant ⅔ cup (90 g) confectioner's sugar
	⅔ cup (90 g) powdered (ground) almonds
	3 tablespoons (5 d*l*) milk
	Confectioner's sugar to sprinkle on top
	For 1 pastry 8 inches (20 cm) in diameter and 10 small pastries
	3 egg whites = ½ cup (95 g)
	2½ teaspoons (12 g) granulated sugar
	½ cup (100 g) granulated sugar
	⅓ cup (55 g) confectioner's sugar
	Generous ⅓ cup (55 g) powdered (ground) almonds
	2 tablespoons (3 c*l*) milk
	Confectioner's sugar to sprinkle on top
UTENSILS	2 large mixing bowls
	Electric mixer
	Wooden spatula
	Nonstick parchment paper (optional)
	2 pastry bags: one with a ¾-inch (2-cm) nozzle and one with a ⅜-inch (1-cm) nozzle
	2 baking sheets
	Sugar dredger

Making the Batter: Preheat the oven to 275°F (135°C).

Beat the egg whites until stiff; halfway through add the smaller amount of granulated sugar.

In a separate bowl, mix the larger amount of granulated sugar with the confectioner's sugar. Add the powdered almonds and the milk; then fold in a few spoonfuls of egg white. Pour this mixture on top of the remaining egg whites, and fold it in with a wooden spatula. Work carefully but quickly; there should be no particles of unblended egg white in the finished batter.

Butter the baking sheets and dust them lightly with flour or line them with parchment paper, sticking each corner of the paper down with a dab of batter.

Baking

For Large Pastries: With a pencil, draw 1 or 2 circles 8 inches (20 cm) each on a baking sheet. Squeeze out the batter in a continuous, tight spiral to fill the circles using a pastry bag with a ¾-inch (2-cm) nozzle. Dust the batter with confectioner's sugar and bake for 1 hour 20 minutes.

For Small Pastries: With the pastry bag equipped with a ⅜-inch (1-cm) nozzle, make 10 or 20 mounds, 1½ inches (4 cm) in diameter. These may be placed on the same sheet as a large circle or on a separate baking sheet. Dust the batter with confectioner's sugar and bake for 45 to 50 minutes. (If using two baking sheets, switch their position in the oven after 20 to 25 minutes so that the pastries on both sheets will brown evenly.)

Watch the browning of the success pastries; you might have to lower the oven temperature because you find that they are browning too rapidly.

Uses: Success pastries are used in making Sylvie Lenôtre's Success Sundae (Recipe 62), the Auteuil-Style Frozen Caramel Dessert (Recipe 85), and the Medicis Frozen Pistacio Dessert (Recipe 84).

To Store: Success pastries can be kept in a tightly closed box in a dry place for 2 weeks. Don't hesitate to prepare them in advance.

111
Almond Pastry
(Biscuit aux Amandes)

PREPARATION	15 to 20 minutes
BAKING TIME	30 minutes
INGREDIENTS	*For 2 round pastries 8 inches (20 cm) in diameter*
	⅓ cup (80 g) butter
	6 to 7 egg whites = generous ¾ cup (200 g)
	3 tablespoons granulated sugar (for the egg whites)
	4 tablespoons (40 g) flour
	Generous ½ cup (80 g) powdered (ground) almonds
	1 scant cup (180 g) granulated sugar
	For 1 round pastry 8 inches (20 cm) in diameter
	2½ tablespoons (40 g) butter
	3 to 4 egg whites = ½ cup (100 g)
	4½ teaspoons granulated sugar (for the egg whites)
	2 tablespoons (20 g) flour
	Generous ¼ cup (40 g) powdered almonds
	Scant ½ cup (90 g) granulated sugar
UTENSILS	1 round cake pan 8 inches (20 cm) in diameter for each pastry
	Saucepan *or* double boiler
	2 large mixing bowls
	Wire whisk *or* electric mixer
	Wooden spatula

Making the Batter: Preheat the oven to 350°F (175°C).

Lightly butter the cake pan(s) and generously dust it (them) with flour. Then turn the pan(s) upside down and tap it (them) to remove any excess flour. (Slivered almonds may be sprinkled to adhere to the sides of the mold at this time if desired, but this is only done when the pastry is to be served alone.)

Melt the butter over very low heat or in a double boiler. Beat the egg whites using a wire whisk or an electric mixer; halfway through, add half of the sugar indicated for the egg whites. Continue beating until the egg whites are very stiff and hold a firm peak; then beat in the remaining sugar indicated for the egg whites.

Note: To fold dry ingredients into beaten egg whites proceed as follows. Sift the flour and mix in a bowl with the powdered almonds and remaining sugar.

166

Sprinkle a little of this mixture over the beaten egg whites and incorporate it into them by cutting and folding the egg whites with a wooden spatula. To do this, "cut" through the middle of the egg whites with the edge of the spatula; then lift and fold half of the whites up and over the other half. Work carefully but quickly, turning the bowl itself a quarter of a turn each time you cut and fold, until the other ingredients have been completely incorporated into them. Once this has been done, sprinkle more of the dry mixture (sugar, almonds, flour) over the egg whites and continue cutting and folding in this way until all the sugar–flour mixture has been mixed with the whites and a completely homogenous mixture has been formed.

Baking the Pastry: Remove two tablespoons of the egg white mixture and place them in a bowl with the butter melted earlier; mix rapidly together. Then pour this into the whites and cut and fold rapidly but carefully to combine with the rest. Pour the batter immediately into the buttered and floured cake pan(s), filling each pan no more than half full, and place immediately in the oven. Bake for 30 to 40 minutes or until the cake is golden brown and beginning to pull away from the sides of the pan.

This pastry will never rise as much as a Génoise because it is much richer and heavier; the middle of the pastry will remain soft after baking.

Once finished baking, turn the pastry out while still hot and leave to cool on a cake rack.

Uses: This pastry is used in making the Frozen Chocolate and Orange Dessert (Recipe 83), the Frozen Grand Marnier Soufflé (Recipe 78), and the Frozen Cognac and Apricot Dessert (Recipe 82).

To Store: Once baked, the pastry can be placed in a plastic bag and frozen; this way it can be kept for 1 month. Otherwise, wrapped in aluminum foil, it can be kept in the refrigerator for up to 1 week.

♔

112
Orange–Almond Pastry
(Biscuit Orange aux Amandes)

PREPARATION	15 to 20 minutes
BAKING TIME	30 minutes
INGREDIENTS	*For 2 pastries 8 inches (20 cm) in diameter*

INGREDIENTS

For 2 pastries 8 inches (20 cm) in diameter
2 oranges (preferably nontreated)
3 tablespoons (30 g) flour
1 cup (200 g) granulated sugar
1½ cup (200 g) powdered (ground) almonds
6 egg whites = ¾ cup (180 g)
3 drops red food coloring
Confectioner's sugar to sprinkle on top

For 1 pastry 8 inches (20 cm) in diameter
1 orange (preferably nontreated)
4½ teaspoons (15 g) flour
½ cup (100 g) granulated sugar
Generous ⅔ cup (100 g) powdered (ground) almonds
3 egg whites = scant ½ cup (90 g)
2 drops red food coloring
Confectioner's sugar to sprinkle on top

UTENSILS

1 or 2 flan rings or cake pans 8 inches (20 cm) wide and ¾ inch (2 cm) high
Baking sheet
Nonstick parchment paper (optional)
Vegetable peeler
Knife
Small mixing bowl
Large mixing bowl
Wooden spatula
Flexible-blade, metal spatula
Sugar dredger *or* sifter
Cake rack

Making the Batter: Preheat the oven to 350°F (175°C).

Lightly butter the flan rings and place them on a baking sheet which has either been lined with parchment paper or buttered and lightly floured; or butter and lightly flour the cake pans.

Use a vegetable peeler to remove the colored outside zest from the orange(s);

do not remove the whitish inner skin with the zest since this has a bitter taste. Finely chop the zest with a knife.

Place the flour, granulated sugar, and powdered almonds in the small bowl and stir to combine.

Using an electric mixer or a wire whisk, beat the egg whites and food coloring together until stiff in the large bowl. Then add the chopped orange zest, followed by the flour–sugar–almond mixture which is added a little at a time.

Note: To fold dry ingredients into beaten egg whites proceed as follows. Sift the flour and mix in a bowl with the powdered almonds and remaining sugar. Sprinkle a little of this mixture over the beaten egg whites and incorporate it into them by cutting and folding the egg whites with a wooden spatula. To do this, "cut" through the middle of the egg whites with the edge of the spatula; then lift and fold half of the whites up and over the other half. Work carefully but quickly, turning the bowl itself a quarter of a turn each time you cut and fold, until the other ingredients have been completely incorporated into them. Once this has been done, sprinkle more of the dry mixture (sugar, almonds, flour) over the egg whites and continue cutting and folding in this way until all the sugar–flour mixture has been mixed with the whites and a completely homogenous mixture has been formed.

Baking the Pastry: When all the ingredients have been combined, pour the batter immediately into the flan ring(s) or cake pan(s) and smooth the surface of a batter with a flexible-blade, metal spatula. Using a sugar dredger or sifter, sprinkle the surface lightly with confectioner's sugar and place in the oven for 20 to 30 minutes or until the cake begins to pull away from the sides of the ring or pan. Remove from the oven and leave to cool on a cake rack; remove the flan ring(s) or turn the pastry out while still warm.

Uses: This pastry is used in making the Frozen Grand Marnier Soufflé (Recipe 78), the Frozen Chocolate and Orange Dessert (Recipe 83), and individual parfait desserts.

To Store: Placed in a tightly closed freezer bag, this pastry can be frozen and kept for 1 month; wrapped in aluminum foil, it can be kept in the refrigerator for up to 4 days.

113
Provencal Petit Fours
(Bicuits de Provence)

PREPARATION	15 minutes
BAKING TIME	15 minutes
INGREDIENTS	*For 70 to 80 petit fours*
	2½ tablespoons (40 g) butter
	⅓ cup (50 g) shelled, unsalted pistacios
	½ cup (100 g) granulated sugar
	⅓ cup (50 g) powdered (ground) almonds
	3 egg whites = scant ½ cup (90 g)
	2 teaspoons granulated sugar (for the egg whites)
	Confectioner's sugar to sprinkle on top
	For 35 to 40 petit fours
	4 teaspoons (20 g) butter
	2 generous tablespoons (25 g) shelled, unsalted pistacios
	¼ cup (50 g) granulated sugar
	2 generous tablespoons (25 g) powdered (ground) almonds
	1½ egg whites = 3½ tablespoons (45 g)
	1 teaspoon granulated sugar (for the egg whites)
	Confectioner's sugar to sprinkle on top
UTENSILS	1 or 2 baking sheets
	Nonstick parchment paper (optional)
	Electric blender
	Small saucepan
	Large mixing bowl
	Small mixing bowl
	Electric mixer or wire whisk
	Wooden spatula
	Pastry bag with ⅜-inch (1-cm) nozzle
	Sugar dredger

Making the Batter: Preheat the oven to 350°F (175°C).

   Line the baking sheet(s) with parchment paper or lightly butter and flour it (them).

   Place the butter in a small saucepan, heat gently until it melts, then remove from the heat, and leave to cool.

170

Place the pistacios and half of the granulated sugar in the electric blender and blend until ground fine but not pasty. Mix this in a bowl with the powdered almonds and the remaining sugar.

Using an electric mixer or wire whisk, beat the egg whites until very stiff, adding the sugar indicated for them halfway through. Add the nut–sugar mixture to the beaten egg whites by folding them in, little by little. Once this has been done, fold in the cool, melted butter.

Note: To fold dry ingredients into beaten egg whites proceed as follows. Sprinkle a little of the nut-sugar mixture over the beaten egg whites and incorporate it into them by cutting and folding the egg whites with a wooden spatula. To do this, "cut" through the middle of the egg whites with the edge of the spatula; then lift and fold half of the whites up and over the other half. Work carefully but quickly, turning the bowl itself a quarter of a turn each time you cut and fold, until the otehn ingredients have been completely incorporated into them. Once this has been done, sprinkle more of the dry mixture over the egg whites and continue cutting and folding in this way until all the nut-sugar mixture has been mixed with the whites and a completely homogenous nut-sugar mixture has been formed.

Baking the Pastry: Pour the batter immediately into a pastry bag fitted with a ⅜-inch (½-cm) nozzle, and squeeze it out onto the prepared baking sheet(s), making little, high, mounds of batter. The batter can also be simply spooned out of the bowl with a teaspoon and placed over the baking sheet(s) in high little mounds if you do not wish to use a pastry bag. About 1 inch (2.5 cm) should be left between the mounds of batter.

Use a sugar dredger to sprinkle the batter with confectioner's sugar, which will keep the petit fours from spreading too much when baking. Place the baking sheet(s) in the oven and bake for 15 minutes. (If using two baking sheets, switch their positions in the oven after 7 minutes for even browning.)

Serving Suggestions: These petit fours are particularly good served with either Pistacio Ice Cream (Recipe 37) or Caramel Ice Cream (Recipe 31), as well as all the molded combination desserts that use Vanilla Ice Cream.

To Store: The petit fours can be kept in a tightly sealed container for up to a week in a dry place.

♟

114
Vanilla Wafer Batter
(Pâte à Langues de Chat)

(Photo page 175)

PREPARATION	15 minutes
SOFTENING TIME	2 hours
INGREDIENTS	*For approximately 1½ cups (400 g) of batter that make 16 tulip pastries or 80 wafers* 7 tablespoons (110 g) butter ⅔ cup (130 g) granulated sugar 4 egg whites = ⅔ cup (130 g) 1 vanilla bean *or* 4 drops vanilla extract 1 scant cup (130 g) flour *For approximately ¾ cup (200 g) of batter that makes 8 tulip pastries or 40 wafers* 3½ tablespoons (55 g) butter ⅓ cup (65 g) granulated sugar 2 egg whites = ⅓ cup (65 g) ½ vanilla bean or 2 drops vanilla extract Scant ½ cup (65 g) flour
UTENSILS	Knife Small mixing bowl Saucepan *or* double boiler Yoghurt thermometer (optional) Large mixing bowl Electric mixer *or* wire whisk Wooden spatula Sifter

Making the Batter: Take the butter and egg whites from the refrigerator and leave at room temperature for 2 hours before proceeding with the recipe.

Split open the vanilla bean lengthwise and, using the tip of a knife, scrape the dark "filling" out of it and into a bowl containing the sugar; if using the vanilla extract, simply add the extract to the sugar.

Place the egg whites in a bowl or the top of a double boiler; then place some hot (not boiling) water in a saucepan into which the bowl will fit or in the bottom of a double boiler. The bottom of the bowl should not touch the water, which should be very hot, but not burning to the touch [it should register no more than 122°F (50°C) on a yoghurt thermometer]. Allow the egg whites to warm

172

over the water until they are lukewarm. This warming is done away from the heat to avoid cooking the egg whites.

Rinse a mixing bowl out with very hot water and wipe it dry. Place the softened butter in the bowl and beat it with an electric mixer or a wooden spoon until it is creamy. Add the sugar–vanilla mixture to the butter, beating constantly but slowly; then start adding the warmed egg whites a tablespoon at a time (if working by hand, begin beating the mixture with a wire whisk when adding the egg whites). When the egg whites have been added and the batter is perfectly homogenous, stop beating and sift the flour into the bowl, cutting and stirring it into the other ingredients with a wooden spatula (work quickly but gently when mixing in the flour).

The batter is now ready for use. If not used immediately, it can be kept in the refrigerator for several hours, but it should be used the day it is made.

Uses: To bake the batter, see Finger Wafers (Recipe 115), Tulip Pastries (Recipe 117), and Wafer Rounds Filled with Truffle Cream (Recipe 116).

115
Finger Wafers
(Langues de Chat)

(Photo page 175)

PREPARATION	5 minutes
BAKING TIME	10 minutes
INGREDIENTS	*For 80 to 90 wafers* 1½ cups (400 g) Vanilla Wafer Batter (Recipe 114) *For 40 to 45 wafers* ¾ cup (200 g) Vanilla Wafer Batter (Recipe 114)
UTENSILS	1 to 2 baking sheets Nonstick parchment paper (optional) Large pastry bag with ¼-inch (6-mm) nozzle

Baking the Batter: Preheat the oven to 400°F (200°C).

Lightly butter and flour the baking sheet(s) or line it (them) with parchment paper, sticking the corners of the paper down with a little of the batter.

Pour the batter into a pastry bag fitted with a ¼-inch (6-mm) nozzle. Squeeze the batter out into very thin finger length lines, as one would if making lady fingers (see Note). Leave a good inch (2.5 cm) between the "fingers," since the batter spreads a lot when baking (see photo). When all the batter has been used up, place the baking sheet(s) in the oven and bake for 10 minutes. Watch the cooking carefully; the finger wafers should be colored around the edges but not in the middle (see photo).

To Store: The wafers can be kept for up to 2 weeks in a tightly closed container kept in a dry place.

Note: Round vanilla wafers can be made by simply squeezing the batter out into little mounds rather than "fingers."

Finger Wafers, Recipe 115; Wafer Rounds Filled with Truffle Cream, Recipe 116;
Tulips, Recipe 117; Vanilla Wafer Batter, Recipe 114

116

Wafer Rounds Filled with Truffle Cream
(Petits Fours en Caissettes)

(Photo page 175)

PREPARATION	30 minutes
BAKING TIME	12 minutes
INGREDIENTS	*For 50 to 60 petits fours* ¾ cup (200 g) Vanilla Wafer Batter (Recipe 114) Scant 1½ cups (400 g) Norman-Style Truffle Cream (Recipe 219)
UTENSILS	60 individual paper cases (preferably brown nonstick parchment paper) Baking sheet Pastry bag A ⅛-inch (3-mm) round nozzle A star-shaped nozzle

Baking the Wafer Rounds and Filling the Cases: Preheat the oven to 400°F (200°C).

If brown nonstick parchment paper cases are not available, use ordinary white paper cases and brush each one with a little melted butter; place the paper cases on a baking sheet.

Fill a pastry bag fitted with a ⅛-inch (3-mm) nozzle with the wafer batter and squeeze enough batter into each cut, using a spiral motion, to fill it by about a third. Place the baking sheet in the oven and bake for 12 minutes (the paper will straighten up around the batter when baking).

When done, remove the wafers from the oven and leave to cool in their cups before filling them (see photo). To fill the cups, pour the truffle cream into a pastry bag fitted with a star-shaped nozzle and squeeze enough truffle cream into each cup to fill it.

To Store: Once baked, but before filling the paper cases with the truffle cream, the wafer rounds can be kept in their cases in a cookie box for up to a week, but once the truffle cream has been added, the chocolates can be kept for only 24 hours in the refrigerator.

Bitter Orange Marmalade, Recipe 139; Caramel-Apple Sauce, Recipe 142

Tulip Pastries (Tulipes)

(Photo pages 58 and 175)

PREPARATION	30 minutes
BAKING TIME	10 minutes
INGREDIENTS	*For 16 tulip pastries* 1½ cups (400 g) Vanilla Wafer Batter (Recipe 114) *For 8 tulip pastries* ¾ cup (200 g) Vanilla Wafer Batter (Recipe 114)
UTENSILS	1 circular or square piece of stiff cardboard 8 inches (20 cm) wide (see Note) Tape measure Compass *or* 6-inch (15-cm) wide plate Scissors Nonstick parchment paper (optional) Flexible-blade, metal spatula Baking sheet 8 small mixing bowls *or* 4 small brioche molds with a 1-cup (¼ *l*) capacity

Baking and Shaping the Tulip Pastries: Preheat the oven to 350°F (175°C).

Take a flat cardboard circle or square 8 inches (20 cm) across and draw a smaller circle in the center of it that is only 6 inches (15 cm) wide using a compass or a small plate. With a pair of scissors, cut out this circle and discard. Place the cardboard [now with a 6-inch (15-cm) hole in the middle] in one corner of a baking sheet which has either been lined with a sheet of parchment paper or buttered and lightly floured.

Fill the hollow center of the cardboard with a tablespoon of wafer batter, spreading the batter out with a spatula so that it fills the central circle completely and evenly (see photo, page 175). Once this is done, carefully lift the cardboard from around the batter and repeat this operation, placing the cardboard successively in each corner of the baking sheet, filling the center and lifting off the "mold" until there are 4 very thin circles of batter on the baking sheet ready to bake. Place the baking sheet in the oven and bake for 10 minutes; when the edges of each baked disk have colored, but the center is still a cream color (photo, page 175), the circles are done.

Molding the Batter: Once the batter has been baked, it must be removed from the oven and molded *immediately*. There are two ways of doing this.

Method 1:   Take 8 small mixing bowls all the same size and place 4 of them upside down on a table. As soon as the batter is baked, take the baking sheet from the oven and, using a flexible-blade spatula, lift off the baked circles of batter. Place each circle on one of the upside down bowls, and immediately cover it with another bowl (see photo, page 58). This must be done very quickly because as the batter cools it becomes brittle and impossible to shape.

Method 2:   Remove each wafer circle from the baking sheet as soon as it comes from the oven, and place each circle immediately into a small ribbed brioche mold. The baked batter will quickly cool to the shape of the mold into which you have put it. This method makes for a very pretty tulip shape with nice pleats all around it (see photo, page 58).

To Store: The tulip pastries can be stacked inside each other and kept in a cookie box or cake box for up to 2 weeks. They must be placed in the box as soon as they are completely cool; if left out in the open for even a few hours, they become "stale" and rubbery.

Note: The cardboard backing of a pad of paper or the cardboard with which men's shirts are packed are excellent for making this "mold."

Grilled Slivered Almonds (Amandes Effilées et Grillées)

PREPARATION	10 minutes
BAKING TIME	5 to 10 minutes
INGREDIENTS	*For 1 generous cup (100 g) almonds* 4½ teaspoons granulated sugar 2 tablespoons water 1 generous cup (100 g) slivered almonds 1 teaspoon orange-flower water (see Dictionary of Terms)
UTENSILS	Baking sheet Nonstick parchment paper Small saucepan Wooden spoon Mixing bowl Fork Serving platter or baking sheet (for cooling)

To Flavor and Brown the Almonds: Preheat the oven to 350°F (175°C).

Line a baking sheet with nonstick parchment paper.

Place the sugar and water in a small saucepan and heat enough to dissolve the sugar.

Place the almonds in a mixing bowl, add the orange-flower water, and then pour over the sugar syrup, stirring gently so as not to break the almonds.

Pour the coated almonds out onto the baking sheet and spread them out with the aid of a fork or spoon as much as possible, so that they form an even layer on the baking sheet. Place them in the oven and, after 5 minutes have passed, check to see that the almonds are browning properly. Not all ovens brown evenly, so check often, and as soon as any of the almonds have browned, remove them from the oven with a fork; continue baking the remaining almonds, removing them as they brown.

As they come from the oven, spread the almonds onto a cold baking sheet or a serving platter to cool; detach them from one another as much as possible so that they do not stick together when cooling.

Uses: Grilled slivered almonds are used to sprinkle over and decorate numerous ice cream desserts; they are also used in some of our chocolate recipes.

To Store: Once they have cooled completely, the almonds can be kept in a tightly sealed container in a dry place for up to 1 month.

119

Chocolate Palms and Other Chocolate Ornaments
(Décors en chocolat)

(Photo page 35)

PREPARATION	1 hour
COOLING TIME	15 minutes per strip
INGREDIENTS	*For 8 to 10 chocolate palms* 7 ounces (200 g) semi-sweet chocolate 2 teaspoons vegetable shortening
UTENSILS	A sheet of ordinary writing or typing paper Pencil Ruler Transparent plastic sheet approximately 8 × 12 inches (20 × 30 cm) Scissors A piece of nonstick parchment paper Double boiler *or* mixing bowl and saucepan *(bain-marie)* Wooden spoon Yoghurt thermometer Box with cover (for storing)

Making the Chocolate Palms: On a piece of paper, use a pen or pencil to draw a palm tree that is no more than 4 inches (10 cm) tall; don't make the trunk of the tree too narrow, otherwise it will break too easily when the chocolate hardens (see photo).

Take a sheet of plastic (the kind used for making "sleeves" or folders for protecting documents or any other fairly thick plastic) and cut it into three strips 8 × 4 inches (20 × 10 cm).

Place the drawing of the palm on a flat surface and cover it with one end of the strip of plastic.

Make a "pastry bag" by rolling a piece of nonstick parchment paper into a cone shape. Use a piece of tape to attach the edges of the paper where they overlap. The tip of the cone should be quite pointed, and the whole thing made neatly so that when the melted chocolate is poured into it, it will not leak out.

Heat the chocolate and shortening in a double boiler or a *bain-marie*, using a yoghurt thermometer to be sure that the temperature does not exceed 95°F (35°C). Once the chocolate and shortening have melted, mix them together and pour the mixture into the paper "pastry bag."

Hold the bag near the drawing of the palm and cut off the very tip of the paper cone, making a tiny hole so that the chocolate will flow out in a thin but even stream. As it does so, use it to draw around the outside edges of your palm tree, on the plastic; then fill in the middle of your chocolate "drawing" until you have a solid chocolate palm. Carefully slide the plastic over to reveal the drawing on the paper again, and make another chocolate palm in the same manner; generally you can make 3 to 4 chocolate palms on each strip of plastic.

Once the palms on any strip of plastic are completed, place the plastic immediately in the refrigerator so that the palms on it can harden. Then continue making palms in the same way on the other strips of plastic.

Wait no longer than 15 minutes once the chocolate has been refrigerated before checking it to see if it has hardened enough to handle. If it has, place the palms immediately into a tightly closing container, where they should be kept until wanted.

Uses: Chocolate palms are used to decorate sundaes, particularly those using tropical fruits, like the Ivory Coast Sundae pictured on page 35.

To Store: Chocolate palms can be kept refrigerated in a tightly closed container for up to 2 weeks.

Other Decorations: Other chocolate ornaments can be made in the same way as the palms: chocolate swans, stars, or christmas trees are only a few of the ideas you might like to try. Once the technique of working with the chocolate in this way is mastered, whole scenes can be drawn and used to decorate the tops of frozen desserts.

Note: Once the palms (or other chocolate ornaments) have hardened in the refrigerator, they can be decorated with little dots or lines of white chocolate, squeezed from the "pastry bag" in the same way as the dark chocolate.

120

Madeleines (Madeleines)

This recipe and the recipe for Spice Cake that follows have nothing to do with the other recipes in this book. They are given here as a belated supplement to my previous book on Desserts and Pastries, since numerous readers requested my recipes for these very popular pastries.

PREPARATION	15 to 20 minutes
REFRIGERATION	15 minutes minimum
BAKING TIME	10 minutes per tray of small madeleines (see Note)
INGREDIENTS	*For 40 small or 20 large madeleines* ¾ cup (180 g) butter Scant 1½ cups (200 g) flour 1½ teaspoons (6 g) baking powder 1 cup (200 g) granulated sugar 5 eggs 1 vanilla bean split in half lengthwise *or* 4 drops vanilla extract ½ finely grated lemon zest (optional)
UTENSILS	Small saucepan Sifter 3 mixing bowls Electric mixer or wire whisk Wooden spatula Large madeleine mold (see Note) Pastry brush Spoon Knife Cake rack

Making the Batter: Melt the butter in a small saucepan over very low heat; once melted, pour it into a bowl to cool—the butter should be barely lukewarm when added to the other ingredients used for making the batter.

Sift the flour and place it in a bowl with the baking powder; stir together so that the two will be combined when called for in making the batter.

In a mixing bowl, place the sugar and whole eggs; if using a vanilla bean, use the tip of a knife to scrape the inside flavorful "filling" out of the bean into the bowl with the sugar and eggs; otherwise simply add the drops of vanilla extract (if lemon peel is being used, it should be added at this time as well). Using an electric mixer or wire whisk, beat these ingredients together for a minute or two until they whiten and form a ribbon. Sprinkle the flour–baking powder mixture onto the egg yolk–sugar–vanilla mixture and use a wooden spatula to cut and fold in the flour (see instructions for folding dry ingredients into beaten egg whites in the note to Recipe 111 for Almond Pastry). When the ingredients are almost perfectly mixed, pour the barely warm butter into the batter and continue cutting and folding gently until a perfectly smooth batter is formed (make sure that there are no lumps left in it). Place the batter in the refrigerator for at least 15 minutes before proceeding to mold and bake. Once made, the batter can be kept in the refrigerator for several hours before baking.

Baking the Madeleines: Preheat the oven to 400°F (200°C).

Use a pastry brush to lightly coat each madeleine mold with a little melted butter. Then dust the molds lightly with flour, tapping them to make the excess flour fall out before the batter is added.

Using an ordinary spoon, spoon enough batter into each mold to fill them three-quarters full. Once the molds have been filled appropriately, place them in the oven and bake for 10 to 15 minutes; check the madeleines as they are baking to see that they don't color too quickly, and before removing them from the oven, stick the blade of a knife into one to be sure that they are completely cooked through; the knife blade should come out dry and clean if the madeleines are done.

Large madeleines take a little longer to bake than small ones. Always test the pastries with a knife before removing them from the oven; if they begin to darken too much, simply lay a sheet of aluminum foil across them to prevent further browning. Once the madeleines have finished baking, remove them from the oven and turn out immediately onto a cake rack to cool.

To Store: Madeleines can be stored in a tightly closed container for up to a week in the refrigerator.

Note: Madeleine molds are typically one sheet of metal into which elongated shell shapes for the madeleines have been stamped. These madeleine tins come in different sizes, and the size of the madeleines themselves can vary enormously, depending on the mold employed, so anywhere from 20 to 40 madeleines can be made with the measurements given here.

Other molded cookies or cookie-like pastries can be made with madeleine batter. If madeleine molds are not available, very small ribbed brioche molds or cupcake molds can be used for baking the batter. Whatever the mold used, the batter should be no more than ½ inch (1.2 cm) deep, and the cookies should always be checked for doneness as described above before being removed from the oven.

121

Gatines-Style Spice Cake
(Pain d'Épices des Gatines)

See the general comments on Recipe 120 for Madeleines.

PREPARATION	30 minutes
BAKING TIME	1 hour 30 minutes
INGREDIENTS	*For 2 cakes serving 8 each (see To Store)* 1⅓ cups (3 d*l*) or 400 g) light-colored honey 1¼ cups (250 g) granulated sugar ⅔ cup (150 g) butter Generous 1⅔ cups (4 d*l*) hot water Zests of 1 orange and 1 lemon (see Dictionary of Terms) Peel of 1 orange 2 teaspoons anis seed *or* 3 tablespoons (5 cl) anis syrup 1 generous cup (100 g) slivered almonds Scant 4 cups (550 g) ordinary flour *or* generous 4½ cups (550 g) rye flour 4 tablespoons (45 g) baking powder
UTENSILS	2 rectangular pound-cake molds, each 12 inches (30 cm) long Waxed paper *or* parchment paper Small saucepan 2 mixing bowls Food processor *or* blender (optional) Knife Electric mixer with dough hook, paddle, *or* wooden spoon

Making the Dough and Baking: Preheat the oven to 400°F (200°C).

Lightly butter the cake molds and line them with waxed paper or parchment paper that sticks up an inch or more above all the sides of the mold.

Place the honey, sugar, butter, and water in a saucepan and heat gently to dissolve and mix all these ingredients.

Finely chop the orange and lemon zests, either by hand or using a food processor or electric blender.

Dice the orange peel by hand and combine it in a bowl with the chopped zests, the anis seed or syrup, and the slivered almonds.

Place the flour and baking powder in a mixing bowl and begin beating slowly with an electric mixer or wooden spoon, adding the warm ingredients from the saucepan little by little. Beat constantly until all the contents of the saucepan have been added; then sprinkle in the chopped orange–almond mixture, continuing to beat gently until all the ingredients are well combined to form the dough. Divide the dough evenly between the two cake pans and place them in the oven. Bake for 30 minutes; then lower the heat to 350°F (175°C) and continue baking for 1 hour longer. Check to see that the cakes do not brown too much when baking; if they darken too much and risk burning, lay a sheet of aluminum foil across them to prevent further coloring. When the cakes are done, remove them from the oven and leave to cool in the molds for 24 hours before turning out and serving.

To Store: Since these cakes store well and it is no more difficult to make two of them than one, the recipe is given for 2 cakes—of course, you can cut the ingredients in half and make only 1 cake if you prefer.

Spice cakes improve in taste and are easier to cut and serve if allowed to sit for 2 to 3 days after being baked. To store them, simply wrap them in a clean towel; they can be kept like this in the refrigerator for up to 2 weeks.

122

Home Canned Apricots in Light Syrup or "Au Natural"
(Abricots au Sirop ou au Naturel)

(Photo page 17)

PREPARATION   20 minutes

STERILIZATION   30 minutes in a sterilizer or 15 minutes in a pressure cooker

INGREDIENTS   *For each 1-quart (1-l) jar used*
1¾ pounds (800 g) fresh apricots
1 generous cup (¼ *l*) 28° Sugar Syrup (Recipe 1)
     or 2 tablespoons granulated sugar

UTENSILS   1-quart (1-*l*) jars for canning (preferably those with wire latch closing systems pictured in the photo)
Sterilizer *or* very large pressure cooker

Filling the Jars: Wash the apricots, cut them in half lengthwise, and remove the pits.

Carefully wash and dry each jar. Then fill them with the apricot halves; don't pack the fruit in tightly but fill the jars to the very top rim. If making apricots in syrup, pour in the Sugar Syrup and seal the jars; if simply making apricots "au natural" add only the granulated sugar and then seal the jars.

Sterilizing: Sterilizing fruits at home can either be done in a pressure cooker or in a large pot called a sterilizer. If you have a sterilizer, follow the instructions that come with it for placing the jars in it and using it. As a general rule, the jars are held in place inside the sterilizer by a system of clips that prevent the jars from shaking, hitting each other, and possibly breaking during their sterilization. An old-fashioned method for preventing breakage is to wrap each jar in a towel before placing it in the pot to be sterilized.

Jars are generally placed on a perforated piece of metal that sits on the bottom of the sterilizer or else on towels that have been folded and placed in the bottom of the pot. Enough water is added to the sterilizer to cover the jars by about 1 inch (2.5 cm); the water is brought to a boil, and sterilization occurs after the water has boiled continuously for 30 minutes. (If a pressure cooker is used, sterilization occurs 15 minutes from the time the pot begins to "whistle".)

After the sterilization time is up, turn off the source of heat and leave the jars in the pot to cool. *Always leave the jars in the pot immersed in the water until they have cooled at least to luke warm.* Once the jars have cooled, remove them from the pot, wipe them dry, and store them in a kitchen cabinet (if left in the light, the fruit will discolor).

Once the jars have cooled completely, check to see whether or not sterilization has been achieved by unlatching the jars; if the top is sealed onto the neck of the jar, sterilization has been successful, but if unlatching releases the top or the jar opens easily, then the sterilization did not occur. (See the instructions that come with the jars sold for home canning equipment for more detailed instructions.)

To Store: Home canned fruit can be kept in a kitchen cabinet for up to a year. Once a jar has been opened, it must be kept in the refrigerator and treated like freshly stewed fruit.

123

Home Canned Cherries in Light Syrup or "Au Natural" (Cerises au Sirop ou au Naturel)

PREPARATION	30 minutes
STERILIZATION	30 minutes in a sterilizer *or* 15 minutes in a pressure cooker
INGREDIENTS	*For each 1-quart (1-l) jar used* 2¼ pounds (1 kg) cherries (preferably "tart" or sour cherries) 1 generous cup (¼ *l*) 28° Sugar Syrup (Recipe 1) *or* 2 tablespoons granulated sugar
UTENSILS	1-quart (1-*l*) jars for canning Sterilizer *or* very large pressure cooker

Filling the Jars: Pit the cherries by either gently pulling on their stems to remove the seed or else by slitting them open with a small knife (cherry-pitting utensils tend to bruise the fruit). Place the pitted cherries in a jar and add either the Sugar Syrup (for fruit in light syrup) or simply the sugar (for fruit "au natural"). Seal the jars.

To Sterilize: Follow the instructions given in Recipe 122 for Home Canned Apricots.

124

Home Canned Pears or Peaches in Light Syrup
(Pêches ou Poires au Sirop)

PREPARATION	40 minutes
STERILIZATION	30 minutes in a sterilizer *or* 15 minutes in a pressure cooker
INGREDIENTS	*For each 1-quart (1-l) jar* 2½ pounds (1 kg 125 g) pears or peaches 1 generous cup (¼ l) 28° Sugar Syrup (Recipe 1) ¼ vanilla bean
UTENSILS	1-quart (1-*l*) jars for canning Sterilizer *or* very large pressure cooker

Preparing the Fruit: Peel and pit the peaches or peel and core the pears as follows.

To peel and pit peaches, drop them into rapidly boiling water for 10 seconds; then remove them with a skimmer or slotted spoon and hold them under cold running water or place them in a bowl of ice water to cool. The skin will then come off easily.

If using freestone peaches, the pit will come out easily when the peach is cut in half lengthwise. If the pit does not come out easily, you have clingstone peaches and the flesh must be cut off the pit.

Peel pears with a vegetable peeler. Cut them in half lengthwise and scoop out their seeds with a spoon-like utensil used for making melon balls. If you do not have such a utensil, cut each half in two lengthwise and cut out the core with a knife.

Filling the Jars: Fill each jar with the prepared fruit; do not pack the fruit in tightly but fill the jars to the brim. Place the piece of vanilla bean in the jar, pour in the sugar syrup, and seal the jar.

Sterilizing: Follow the instructions given in Recipe 122 for Home Canned Apricots.

125

Frozen Fruit Puree (Purée de Fruits)

In the individual sherbet and ice cream recipes, most fruits are pureed in the blender or with a food mill before being mixed with other ingredients. Fruit purees are also made in some of the candy recipes, notably the fruit jellies (pâtes de fruit). Whenever fruit is blended to make a puree, it is generally stemmed and seeded and only the pulp is pureed. Best results in sherbet and candy making are always obtained when fresh fruit is used for making the fruit puree, and specific amounts of fresh fruit are given in the individual sherbet recipes. Some fruits, however, lend themselves to freezing, and these frozen purees can be used when the fruit is out of season.

Not all fruits can be pureed and frozen with equally good results, and the following four fruits were chosen precisely because they give the best results when treated in this manner. Only perfectly ripe and undamaged fruit should be used in making fruit purees, especially when the puree is to be frozen.

PREPARATION | 10 to 30 minutes

INGREDIENTS | *For approximately 1 quart (1 l) of fruit puree (see Note)*
3 quarts (1.5 kg) fresh ripe red or black currants *or* 2
    quarts (1 kg) fresh ripe raspberries or strawberries
Granulated sugar (optional)

UTENSILS | Electric blender *or* food processor,
Food mill *or* electric juicer
Large pot
Spoon
Colander
Freezer bags and labels

To Make and Freeze Black Currant Puree: Remove the stems from the fruit. Bring about 3 quarts (3 *l*) of water to a boil in a large pot. Drop the black currants into the boiling water and stir gently over high heat until the water comes back to a boil; then pour the contents of the pot into a colander to drain the fruit.

Place the softened black currants in a food mill or juicer, a third at a time, to extract the juice (do not use a food processor or blender). There will be a lot of waste (skin, seeds, etc.) which should be discarded. If desired, the puree can be sweetened with sugar, but no more than ½ cup (100 g) of sugar should be added per quart (*liter*) of puree produced.

To freeze, pour the puree immediately into freezer bags (small bags are preferable since only small amounts of puree will be wanted at a time—see Note); seal the bags and place them in the freezer. Label the bags clearly with the name of their contents and the date of freezing. The puree can be kept frozen for up to 6 months.

When the puree is needed for making sherbets or fruit jellies (pâtes de fruit), use it *without thawing*. Take the bag from the freezer and place its frozen contents directly in the blender. Blend until smooth; then use the puree immediately to make a sherbet or candy. When making sherbets with frozen puree blended this way, the freezing time for the sherbet is often cut in half. Blending the frozen puree without thawing means that the fruit will keep the maximum amount of its flavor and aroma. *Never leave the frozen puree to thaw in the refrigerator or at room temperature.* Once the frozen puree comes from the blender, it can be immediately placed in the refrigerator and kept for up to 24 hours, but it is best employed as soon after blending as possible.

To Make and Freeze Red Currant Puree: Do not stem the fruit, but remove the leaves and grind the fruit through a food mill or use an electric juicer (do not use a blender or food processor) to extract the juice puree.

To freeze and use after freezing, follow the instructions given for Black Currant Puree.

Whole red currants on their stems can also be frozen. Simply place them in freezer bags and place the open bags in the freezer. When the fruit has hardened, seal the bags. To use the fruit, remove the bags from the freezer and thaw for 2 hours before using the whole fruit to decorate sundaes or for candy or jelly making.

To Make and Freeze Raspberry Puree: Stem the raspberries if necessary and place them in a blender or food processor to make the puree.

To freeze, follow the instructions given for Black Currant Puree.

Whole fresh raspberries can be rolled in granulated sugar and frozen by placing them on a plate in the freezer until hard and then placing them in freezer bags, sealing the bags, and storing them in the freezer. They must be allowed to thaw for about 2 hours before using to decorate frozen desserts.

To Make and Freeze Strawberry Puree: Wash and remove the stems from the fruit. Place the fruit in a blender or food processor to make the puree.

To freeze and use the frozen puree, follow the instructions given for Black Currant Puree.

I am against the idea of freezing whole strawberries since they not only look unpleasant once thawed but are too soft and have lost much of their juice.

Note: Measure the puree before freezing and label the bags with the amounts of puree they contain. It is best to consult individual sherbet and candy-making recipes before freezing the puree so that you will know the exact amounts needed and can freeze bags containing the appropriate amount of puree.

126

Brandied Cherries (Cerises à l'Eau-de-Vie)

(Photo page 157)

PREPARATION	15 minutes
MACERATION	About 10 weeks
INGREDIENTS	*For a 1-quart (1-l) jar* 1½ pounds (700 g) "tart" or sour cherries 2 generous cups (½ *l*) pure, 90 to 120 proof (45° to 60°) grain alcohol (see Note 1) ½ cup (100 g) granulated sugar (see Note 2) 6½ tablespoons (1 d*l*) cherry liqueur
UTENSILS	A 1-quart (1-*l*) jar, preferably with a wire latch (see photo) Mixing bowl

Making the Brandied Cherries: Discard any bruised or damaged fruit; then rinse the remaining, healthy cherries rapidly under cold running water and drain. Cut off each stem about ½ inch (1.5 cm) from each cherry. Place the prepared cherries in the jar (do not pack them down) and add the alcohol; 10 cherry pits, coarsely crushed in a mortar and wrapped in a piece of thin cloth, can be added at this time if desired.

Seal the jar and leave the cherries to macerate in the alcohol for 2 months in a kitchen cabinet (they should not be exposed to light) before proceeding with the recipe.

After maceration, remove the bag of cherry pits (if using) and use a small ladle to remove a generous ¾ cup (2 d*l*) of liquid from the jar. Place this in a bowl with the sugar and cherry liqueur, stir to dissolve the sugar completely, and then pour this mixture back into the jar. Seal the jar and shake it gently, inverting the jar once or twice, to mix all of its contents; then leave the cherries to macerate for at least one week more before serving.

Uses: Two to three cherries and some of the alcohol are served in very small glasses to guests as an after dinner drink.

Brandied cherries are also used in making certain chocolates, such as Royal Cherries (Recipe 176) and Chocolate Cherries (Recipe 201).

To Store: If kept in a dark, dry place such as a kitchen cabinet, brandied cherries can be kept for a year. The alcohol acts as a preservative, and fruit and alcohol can be removed as desired, but there must always be enough alcohol remaining in the jar to completely cover the fruit.

Note 1: Pure grain alcohol is pure ethyl alcohol, which is the alcohol in all alcoholic beverages. It is the result of the fermentation of fruits or grains, hence its name. Grain alcohol should not be confused with either wood alcohol (methyl alcohol), which is highly poisonous, or denatured alcohol, which is a mixture of ethyl and methyl alcohols and is also highly poisonous.

In the United States, the alcoholic content of a beverage is expressed in "proof," which is simply the percentage of alcohol multiplied by 2. Hence, a liquid which contains 45% alcohol by volume is called 90 proof.

The higher the alcoholic content, the longer the brandied fruits can be preserved. It is therefore preferable to use 120 proof (60°) grain alcohol when making them, although anything down to 90 proof (45°) can be used. Do not use alcohol of less than 90 proof (45°). If you are lucky enough to find grain alcohol of 180 to 200 proof (90° to 100°), you can dilute it with water to obtain the strength you want by using the following formula:

$$\frac{\text{volume} \times \text{proof or percent alcohol}}{\text{proof or percent desired}} \quad = \quad \text{total volume}$$

Total volume − original volume = amount of water to add

For example, if you have 1 cup (250 ml) of 180 proof (90°) alcohol and want to make 120 proof (60°) alcohol, you do the following calculation:

U.S. measures	Metric measures
$\dfrac{1 \text{ cup} \times 180}{120} = 1\frac{1}{2} \text{ cups total}$	$\dfrac{250 \text{ ml} \times 90}{60} = 375 \text{ ml total}$
1½ cups − 1 cup = ½ cup water to add	375 ml − 250 ml = 125 ml water to add

Note 2: More sugar may be added if the brandied fruit seems to be too strong; this is especially true if 120 proof (60°) alcohol was used. Do the recipe as described; then after the fruit has sat the required time with the sugar, taste the liquid. Up to 1½ cups (150 g) more sugar may be added for every 2 generous cups (½ l) alcohol used, but it is best not to add more than that or the liquid will taste terribly sweet. Allow to sit another week or 10 days at least before serving. It should be noted that brandied fruits taste less "alcoholic" the longer they sit.

127

Brandied Raspberries (Framboises à l'Eau-de-Vie)

(Photo page 157)

PREPARATION	10 minutes
MACERATION	About 10 weeks
INGREDIENTS	*For a 1-quart (1-l) jar* 2½ pints (600 g) raspberries 2 generous cups (½ l) pure, 90 to 120 proof (45° to 60°) grain alcohol (see Note 1 after Recipe 126) A pinch of cinnamon *or* 1 clove (optional) ½ cup (100 g) granulated sugar (see Note 2 after Recipe 126)
UTENSILS	A 1-quart (1-l) jar, preferably with a wire latch (see photo) Mixing bowl

Making the Brandied Raspberries: Fill the jar with fruit which has been rapidly rinsed under cold running water and thoroughly drained. Only perfectly ripe, firm, unbruised fruit should be used, and they should be placed gently in the jar not packed down. Add the cinnamon or clove, if using, and the alcohol.

Seal the jar and leave the fruit to macerate for 2 months before proceeding with the recipe. While macerating, the jar should be kept away from the light and at room temperature (in a kitchen cabinet for example).

After macerating, use a ladle to remove a generous ¾ cup (2 dl) of liquid from the jar, place this in a bowl, and add the sugar. Stir until the sugar has dissolved completely and then pour the liquid back into the jar. Seal the jar and shake it gently, turning it upside down once or twice to mix its contents. Place the jar back in the kitchen cabinet for at least another week before serving.

Uses: Brandied raspberries can be served as an after dinner drink, by placing two or three of the raspberries and a little of their liquid in very small glasses.

They can also be used in making certain chocolates (see Recipe 202 for Chocolate Raspberries).

The alcohol from the jar can be mixed with a little cherry syrup to make a delicious cocktail or added to a fruit salad to enliven its taste.

To Store: If kept in a dark, dry place such as a kitchen cabinet, brandied raspberries can be kept for a year. The alcohol acts as a preservative, and fruit and alcohol can be removed as desired, but there must always be enough alcohol remaining in the jar to completely cover the fruit.

128
Black Currant Liqueur
(Liqueur de Cassis)

PREPARATION	20 minutes
DRAINING TIME	40 minutes
MACERATING	At least 2 months
COOKING TIME	5 minutes
COOLING TIME	1 hour
INGREDIENTS	*For 1⅔ pints (8 dl)* 3¾ cups (600 g) fresh black currants, stems removed 2 black currant leaves 2 generous cups (5 dl) pure, 90 to 120 proof (45° to 60°) grain alcohol (see Note) 2½ cups (500 g) granulated sugar Scant 1⅓ cups (3 dl) water
UTENSILS	A 1-quart (1-l) jar with wire closing latch (see photo, page 157) Large strainer 2 mixing bowls Saucepan Candy thermometer A 1-quart (1-l) bottle (approximate capacity)

Making the Liqueur: Wash and drain the black currants. Place them in a jar with the currant leaves and add the alcohol. Seal the jar and leave to macerate for at least 2 months before proceeding with the recipe. Keep the jar away from the light—in a kitchen cabinet, for example.

After macerating, place a large strainer over a mixing bowl and pour the contents of the jar into the strainer. Do not press the currants in the sieve, but rather leave them alone so that the flavored liquid can drain naturally into the bowl. Leave to drain for at least 40 minutes; after this time, you should have about a generous 1⅔ cups (4 dl) of liquid in a bowl. The drained currants and leaves should be discarded.

In a saucepan, place the sugar and water, bring to a boil, and cook over high heat for about 5 minutes, or until the syrup registers 230–234°F (110–112°C) on a candy thermometer. Remove from the heat and leave to cool completely (about 1 hour).

Pour the cooled syrup into the strained liquid from the black currants; then pour the mixture back and forth between the mixing bowl and saucepan until the black currant liquid and sugar syrup are completely combined without stirring (stirring tends to make the sugar crystalize). The liqueur is now ready to serve.

To Store: Store the black currant liqueur in a well-stoppered bottle or jar in a closed cabinet (away from the light) at room temperature. The liqueur can be kept for a good year, but after that time its beautiful deep purple color begins to turn brown.

Uses: This liqueur is delicious served as an after dinner drink. It also makes a nice before dinner drink when mixed with dry white wine, or even Beaujolais.

Black currant liqueur can be used to flavor ice cream and sherbet or in candy making to flavor fondant.

Note: Pure grain alcohol is pure ethyl alcohol, which is the alcohol in all alcoholic beverages. It is the result of the fermentation of fruits or grains, hence its name. Grain alcohol should not be confused with either wood alcohol (methyl alcohol), which is highly poisonous, or denatured alcohol, which is a mixture of ethyl and methyl alcohols and is also highly poisonous.

In the United States, the alcoholic content of a beverage is expressed in "proof," which is simply the percentage of alcohol multiplied by 2. Hence, a liquid which contains 45% alcohol by volume is called 90 proof.

The higher the alcoholic content, the longer the brandied fruits can be preserved. It is therefore preferable to use 120 proof (60°) grain alcohol when making them, although anything down to 90 proof (45°) can be used. Do not use alcohol of less than 90 proof (45°). If you are lucky enough to find grain alcohol of 180 to 200 proof (90° to 100°), you can dilute it with water to obtain the strength you want by using the following formula:

$$\frac{volume \times proof\ or\ percent\ alcohol}{proof\ or\ percent\ desired} = total\ volume$$

Total volume − original volume = amount of water to add

For example, if you have 1 cup (250 ml) of 180 proof (90°) alcohol and want to make 120 proof (60°) alcohol, you do the following calculation:

U.S. measures	Metric measures
$\dfrac{1\ cup \times 180}{120} = 1\frac{1}{2}$ cups total	$\dfrac{250\ ml \times 90}{60} = 375\ ml$ total

1½ cups − 1 cup = ½ cup water to add | 375 ml − 250 ml = 125 ml water to add

129

Tropical Fruit Salad (Salade de Fruits Exotiques)

(Photo page 198)

This recipe is given here as a supplement to the other fruit recipes. The comments made about tropical fruits may sometimes be of interest for sherbet making or when using these fruits in other desserts. The following is, in fact, not really a recipe, but more a general outline of a procedure you can adapt to make your own tropical fruit salads. The amounts of the tropical fruits are not given, since this is up to you and to the availability of these fruits in your area. Tropical fruits can be used exclusively to make the salad or in combination with other more common fruits, depending on your taste. In general, allow about 4 to 5 ounces (125 to 150 g) of combined ingredients per serving (i. e., a pound of prepared fruit plus sugar will serve four).

Prepare the basic fruit sauce and add the fruits of your choice to it; it is preferable to make the salad a day in advance and leave to macerate overnight before serving. Some fruits, like bananas and kiwis, being used for decoration, should be added to the salad only at the last minute. In general, two or three tropical fruits mixed with the basic fruit sauce make a varied and delicious salad; the quantity and variety of the fruit employed depends on your taste.

INGREDIENTS

For Basic Fruit Sauce for a salad serving 10 to 12
A 1-quart (1-*l*) jar of Apricots in Light Syrup (Recipe 122)
1 pineapple weighing approximately 2¼ pounds (1 kg)
4 medium oranges
½ cup (100 g) granulated cane sugar

UTENSILS

Electric blender
Mixing bowl
Knife

Making the Basic Fruit Sauce: Drain the apricots and place them with a little of their syrup in the blender and blend until smooth. This apricot puree will be the basis of your fruit sauce. Pour the puree into a bowl.

Peel the pineapple and squeeze the juice in the pineapple skin into the bowl with the apricot puree; core the pineapple and slice it; then cut the slices into small wedges and add them to the bowl of puree as well.

Wash the oranges, cut off and discard the two ends of each orange, but do not peel them. Slice each orange very thinly; then cut each slice into quarters. Place the pieces of orange into a bowl with the cane sugar and leave overnight before mixing them with the apricot–pineapple mixture.

The Tropical Fruits: See the introductory comments on choice and amounts of tropical fruits to use in the salad. (See photo to help identify the fruits themselves.)

Guava: The guava is first green, then it turns yellow with slightly reddish marbling when ripe. It is a flavorful fruit and slightly acid. Peel the fruit as you would an apple and then slice it into the salad; add a little nutmeg to the salad at the same time.

Kiwi: This small oval fruit has a soft, peach-like, brown exterior but is bright green with brilliant, black seeds inside. It is very rich in vitamin C and is ripe when soft to the touch. It can be eaten by cutting it in half and scooping out the pulp or peeled and cut into slices. When sliced, it is added to the basic fruit sauce given earlier; a few slices should be placed on top of the salad at the last minute to decorate.

Kumquat: This is a familiar fruit to many people but an exotic treat to others. Kumquats are orange-like fruits about the size of an olive, which are generally eaten whole, skin and all. Fresh kumquats should be cut in half and left to soak in a bowl with a little white rum for 30 minutes before adding them to the salad. Canned kumquats in thick syrup can be used, in which case they are drained, cut in half, and added directly to the other ingredients used to make the salad (some of their syrup can be added to the salad if the fruit sauce seems too acid).

Limes: Limes, which are a nice addition to punches and can be used to make sherbet (Recipe 8), are squeezed like lemons. Their juice is added to the basic fruit sauce described above.

Litchi or Leechi: Litchis are generally small, about the size of a strawberry, with reddish-brown, hard, exterior skins. Once the skin is peeled off, the fruit itself is soft and white with a smooth, brown seed in its center. Only the white pulp is eaten. Place the peeled litchis in a bowl with a little white rum for 30 minutes before adding them to the fruit salad. If canned litchis are used, simply drain them and cut them in half over the salad bowl.

Tropical Fruit Salad, Recipe 129
1.   Limes
2.   Yellow Passion Fruit
3.   Red Bananas
4.   Mangosteens
5.   Rambutans
6.   Mangos
7.   Guavas
8.   Brown Passion Fruit
9.   Pineapples
10.   Kiwis

Mango: Mangos, which generally weigh from ½ pound (250 g) to 1 pound 5 ounces (600 g), vary in color depending on the variety employed. They are often apricot-yellow and are soft to the touch when ripe. If purchased unripe, they should be left at room temperature (not refrigerated) to ripen. To use, peel off the skin and cut the pulp surrounding the central pit into small cubes. Add these cubes to the salad or use the mango for making Mango Sherbet (Recipe 14).

Mangosteen: Not to be confused with mangos, the mangosteen is reddish-brown outside and soft to the touch when ripe. It is peeled and eaten much like a tangerine or cut open with a knife to expose the sweet whitish pulp which can be added to the other fruits used in making tropical fruit salad.

Papaya: Papayas are the size and shape of a somewhat elongated melon. Some varieties are green when ripe but most turn yellow or orange. The fruit is peeled and sliced, and when added to a tropical fruit salad, add a little port or lemon juice at the same time to highlight the fruit's taste.

Passion Fruit: There are two common varieties of this fruit; one with a reddish skin and one with a yellow skin. The reddish variety is the more flavorful of the two, although they can be used interchangeably. The fruit is generally about the size of a lemon, and the skin becomes wrinkled and indented all over when the fruit is ripe. Passion fruit can be stored at room temperature to ripen if not purchased ripe. When ripe, cut the fruit in half and scoop out the very soft pulp, which is filled with seeds; this pulp, seeds and all, can be eaten as it is, or it can be worked through a sieve to eliminate the seeds, as when making sherbets (Recipe 12).

For salads, work the pulp through a sieve as well, and mix the strained juice with an equal amount of cane sugar. The resulting passion fruit sauce can be used instead of the basic fruit sauce given initially or simply added to the basic fruit sauce when making tropical fruit salads.

Rambutan: When peeled, this fruit looks almost identical to a litchi, but when still in its skin, it is easily distinguishable because of the soft, hair-like protrusions that cover its exterior. The fruit is peeled and used like litchis.

Red Banana: Generally smaller and firmer than ordinary bananas, red bananas should be firm but never hard when used in salads. To use them, simply peel and slice them as you would any other banana, adding them to the salad just before serving.

To Serve: Tropical fruit salad can be served in a variety of unusual and decorative ways. A pineapple or melon (a watermelon can be used if serving a large party) can be cut in half and hollowed out; then filled with the fruit salad to serve. The pulp of the pineapple or melon is added to the salad before serving. The salad can also be served in seashells, champagne glasses, in individual bowls or in a large serving bowl as shown in the photo.

200

Chapter 6

COOKING SUGAR, JAMS, AND FRUIT JELLIES

RECIPES

130. Cooking Sugar (Cuisson du Sucre) ♨

131. Basic Jam Recipe (Recette de Base) ♨ ♨

132. Apricot Jam (Confiture d'Abricots) ♨ ♨

133. Cherry–Currant Jam (Confiture de Cerises–Groseilles) ♨ ♨

134. Strawberry Jam (Confiture de Fraises) ♨ ♨

135. Raspberry Jam (Confiture de Framboises) ♨ ♨

136. Peach Jam (Confiture de Pêches) ♨ ♨

137. Plum Jam (Confiture de Prunes) ♨ ♨

138. Rhubarb Jam (Confiture de Rhubarbe) ♨ ♨

139. Bitter Orange Marmalade (Confiture d'Oranges Amère) ♨ ♨

140. Lemon Marmalade (Confiture de Citrons) ♨ ♨

141. Sweet Orange Marmalade (Confiture d'Oranges Douce) ♨ ♨

142. Caramel-Apple Sauce (Confiture de Pommes-Caramel) ♨ ♨

143. Red Currant Jelly (Gelée de Groseilles) ♨ ♨

144. Basic Fruit Jelly Recipe (Pâtes de Fruits) ♨

145. Apricot Jellies (Pâte d'Abricots)
146. Pineapple Jellies (Pâte d'Ananas Frais)
147. Banana–Apple Jellies (Pâte de Bananes–Pommes)
148. Carrot Jellies (Pâte de Carottes)
149. Black and Red Currant Jellies (Pâte de Cassis–Groseilles)
150. Cherry Jellies (Pâte de Cerises)
151. Quince Jellies (Pâte de Coings)
152. Fig Jellies (Pâte de Figues)
153. Strawberry Jellies (Pâte de Fraises)
154. Raspberry Jellies (Pâte de Framboises)
155. Raspberry–Red Currant Jellies (Pâte de Framboises–Groseilles)
156. Passion Fruit Jellies (Pâte de Fruits de la Passion)
157. Red Currant Jellies (Pâte de Groseilles)
158. Melon Jellies (Pâte de Melon)
159. Orange Jellies (Pâte d'Oranges)
160. Fresh Peach Jellies (Pâte de Pêches Fraîches)
161. Canned Peach Jellies (Pâte de Pêches au Sirop)
162. Pear Jellies (Pâte de Poires)
163. Apple Jellies (Pâte de Pommes)
164. Grape Jellies (Pâte de Raisins)
165. Rhubarb Jellies (Pâte de Rhubarbe)

130
Cooking Sugar (Cuisson du Sucre)
(*Photo page 207*)

As sugar cooks, it goes through various stages—gloss, thread, blow, and so on until it turns to caramel. Each stage indicates an increase in the density, and in the temperature, of the sugar syrup.

The easiest way to judge whether the correct stage has been reached is to use a candy thermometer that can stand temperatures up to 392°F (200°C) without breaking. The greatest problem with a candy thermometer is that it may not be exact; thermometers of this type can be off by as much as 3 to 4°F (2°C). For this reason, when using a candy thermometer do not let the thermometer touch the bottom of the saucepan or the temperature of the syrup will seem higher than it really is. Also, remember that since the thermometer may not be exact anyway and because the sugar you use may contain more or less impurities in it, which will change the temperature slightly, you should always cook the syrup a little longer after it has reached the degree indicated to make sure that it has in fact cooked enough. For example, sugar cooked to 311°F (155°C) will crack under your teeth, whereas if it is only 307°F (153°C) it may still stick to them a little bit.

In the table given below, the different stages of cooked sugar are described, with both the temperatures and the tests used to verify them. Each stage corresponds to a different use in confectionery, so I suggest that you practice cooking sugar and testing the cooking stages a few times. That way, you will be able to make all the recipes for jams and all the candies in this book without the least hesitation or difficulty.

PREPARATION	5 minutes
COOKING TIME	5 to 15 minutes
INGREDIENTS	2½ cups (500 g) granulated sugar ⅔ cup (1½ dl) water 10 drops lemon juice
UTENSILS	Medium, heavy-bottomed saucepan (preferably stainless steel) Wooden spoon *or* spatula Skimmer Small bowl Ordinary teaspoon Pastry Brush Candy thermometer (optional)

Cooking the Sugar: Place the sugar and water in a heavy-bottomed saucepan and set over moderate heat. If cooking with gas, make sure that the flame does not go beyond the edges of the saucepan.

Fill a small bowl with cold water and a few ice cubes and place it, as well as an ordinary teaspoon, on a table or other surface next to the saucepan.

Heat the syrup, stirring with a wooden spoon or spatula; then, just before it boils, stir in the lemon juice. As soon as the syrup boils, stop stirring, but clean the sides of the saucepan with a clean, moist pastry brush; any impurities contained in the sugar will rise to the surface and stick to the sides of the pot.

Now start testing for the various stages the sugar will go through. Compare the table entries with the respective photos on page 207.

| Name | Temperature | | Aspect and *Uses* |
	°F	°C	
GLOSS	214°	101°	The surface of the syrup is covered with large bubbles.
LARGE GLOSS	217°	103°	The bubbles become much smaller.

For the following stages it will be necessary to take a little syrup out of the saucepan with the teaspoon. With a sharp downward movement, shake the teaspoon so that the syrup falls in the bowl of ice water; then lift it out of the water with your thumb and index finger. Change the water in the bowl every time you make a test because the syrup must fall into pure, very cold, water.

Name	°F	°C	Aspect and Uses
THREAD	223°	106°	Little sticky threads will form as you separate your thumb and index finger. (Photo 1) *Final cooking of jams.*
BLOW	228/234°	109/112°	Dip a skimmer into the syrup; then lift it out and blow hard through the holes—little bubbles of sugar will form. *Syrup for jams and Black Currant Liqueur.*
SOFT BALL	239°	115°	A very soft, flattened ball can be formed with the syrup. *Certain jams.*

Name	Temperature °F	°C	Aspect and *Uses*
FIRM BALL	244°	118°	The ball is firmer, but still somewhat soft—it holds its shape better. (Photo 2) *Caramelized Almonds and Hazelnuts, Nut brittle powder and paste.*
HARD BALL	257/275°	125/135°	The ball is quite hard and perfectly round (Photo 3) *Soft Caramels—257° (125°)—Italian meringue and butter cream used in pastries.*
LIGHT CRACK	277/286°	136/141°	The syrup detaches itself from the fingers and sticks to the teeth when chewed.
HARD CRACK	293/302°	145/150°	The film of sugar breaks easily but still sticks to the teeth.
VERY HARD CRACK	311/315°	155/157°	The film of sugar breaks like glass and no longer sticks to the teeth. (Photo 4) *Caramel Apple Sauce, Nougatine, Sugar-Coated Fruit Candies, Spun Sugar.*
LIGHT CARAMEL	320°	160°	The sugar turns a light golden brown color. (Photo 5) *For caramelizing cream puff pastries and decorative pastry centerpieces.*
DARK CARAMEL	356°	180°	The sugar is mahogany brown. It has to be poured onto an oiled baking sheet to cool quickly enough. (Photo 6) *Caramelized custard.*
	374°	190°	The caramel begins to smoke; it is too late to use it.

Caramel may also be made by cooking the sugar without water (see Recipe 198 for Lenôtre's Caramel).

GENERAL COMMENTS ON JAMS

Utensils Used in Cooking the Jam

Pots or Preserving Pans: The quantities given in the following recipes have been adapted for cooking in a large pot of about a 5-quart (5-*l*) capacity. Preserving pans are larger, the smallest ones generally being of a 10-quart (10-*l*) capacity. The quantities can be doubled, tripled, etc., according to the size of your pan.

It is preferable to use a large, heavy-bottomed, stainless steel pot or preserving pan. Stainless steel has the advantage of not reacting to the acids contained in fruit, so that the fruit and sugar may macerate in the pot being used to cook the jam.

Traditionally, copper preserving pans are used in cooking jams and jellies, and many people consider them the best because they heat quickly and evenly. However, the raw fruit and sugar must *not* be placed in a copper pan to macerate because the fruit juices would attack the copper and toxic compounds could be formed, which would be very dangerous. For this reason, if using a copper preserving pan, allow the fruit and sugar to macerate in a large bowl. When the macerating time is up, place a colander in the preserving pan and drain the fruit. The syrup is thus collected directly in the pan it cooks in; cook the syrup and jam exactly as described in the recipes. There is no danger whatever in *cooking* jam in a copper pan.

Aluminum preserving pans are less expensive than either stainless steel or copper ones. The jam tends to stick to them more easily as it is cooking, however, and some people feel that if the fruit and sugar macerate in an aluminum pan, the taste of the jam is changed slightly. This is a debatable point, and in any case, there is no danger involved if you decide to let the fruit and sugar macerate in an aluminum pan.

A cast iron pot should *never* be used in making jams and jellies. Even while cooking, the fruit juices attack the iron, giving such a terrible taste to the jam that it is completely ruined.

Other Utensils: A candy thermometer is very useful although not essential to making jams and jellies.

A long-handled, wooden spatula or long-handled, metal skimmer should be used for stirring the jam as it cooks.

Although not really a utensil, the stove on which the jam is cooked is very important. I very strongly advise using a gas stove if possible—the heat must constantly be regulated to prevent the jam from splattering or from foaming up and overflowing. For best results, jam should be cooked quickly, over high heat; the longer the fruit cooks, the more its taste is changed. A gas stove can be easily regulated to find the maximum heat for any given jam—the point at which it boils rapidly but does not threaten to overflow or splatter. If an electric stove gets too hot, it cannot be turned down quickly enough. Since it would be ex-

1

2

3

4

5

6

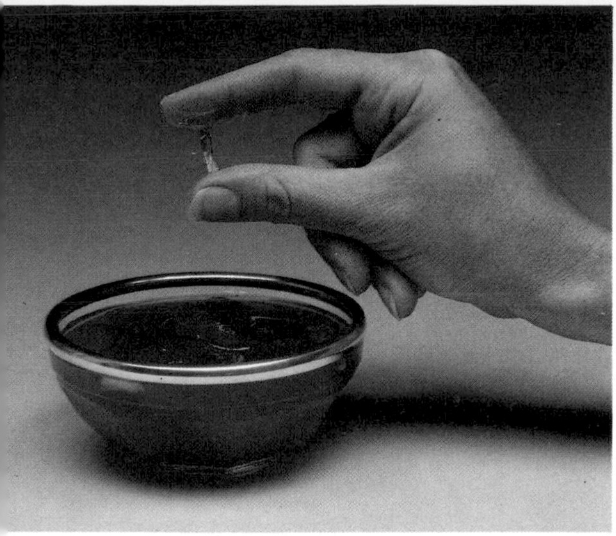

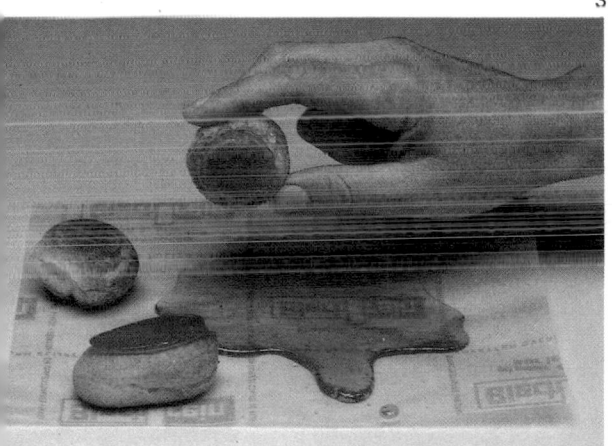

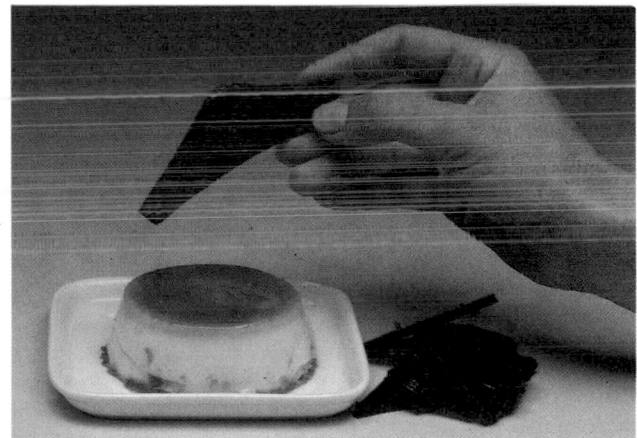

Cooking Sugar, Recipe 130

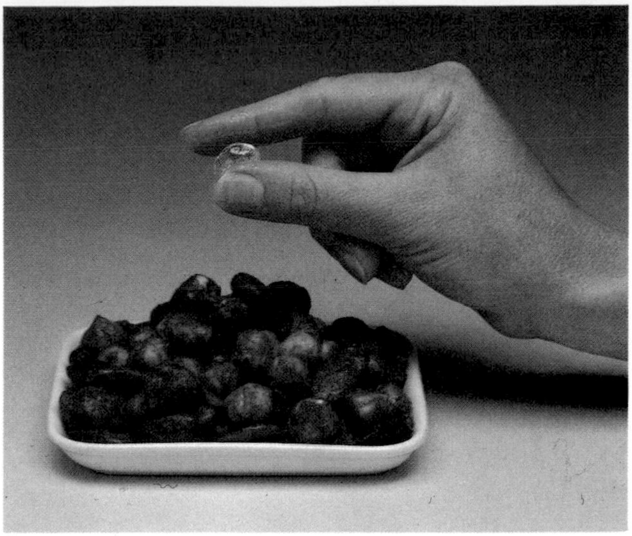

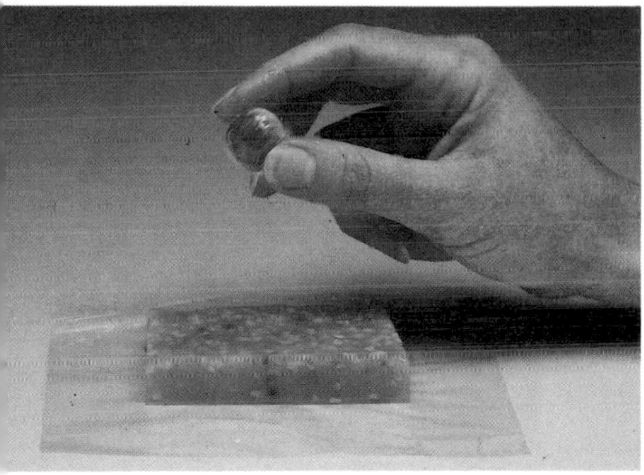

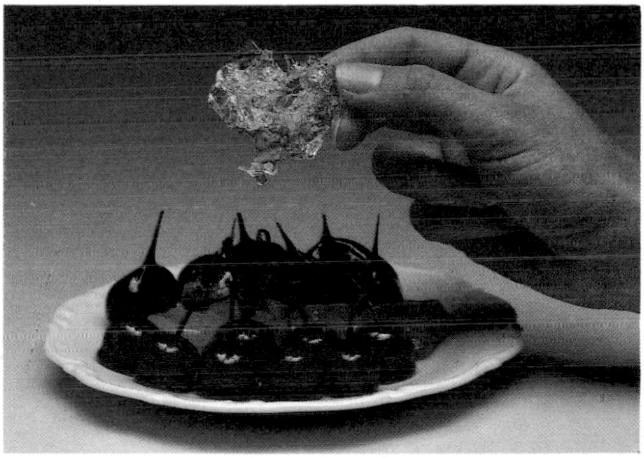

1. *223°F (106°C) Thread*
2. *224°F (118°C) Firm Ball*
3. *257°F (125°C) Hard Ball*
4. *311°F (155°C) Very Hard Crack*
5. *320°F (160°C) Light Caramel*
6. *356°F (180°C) Dark Caramel*

tremely dangerous to try to move a pan full of foaming, splattering jam off the burner, it is best to be very cautious when using an electric stove and to cook the jam a little more slowly, for a little longer time, than risk an accident.

Because cooking jam can be unpredictable, it is always best to have some burn ointment on hand just in case.

Jam Jars

Choosing the Jars: Jars made of tempered glass should be used because they must be able to stand temperatures of about 221°F (105°C) without breaking. I prefer using jars with either screw-on tops or traditional preserving jars with glass covers attached to the jar with a heavy wire hinge. Traditional jam jars, sealed with paraffin or cellophane, etc., may of course be used, but there are several advantages to using jars with tops. The jars seal hermetically; they are easier to store because they can be placed on top of one another; they can be transported without any fear of spilling if they tip over; and once the jar has been opened, it can be tightly closed again so that the taste of the jam does not change.

In order to seal the jar correctly, however, the top must be equipped with a rubber sealing ring, and in order to ensure a perfect seal, the rubber ring must be new. Traditional preserving jars have removable rubber rings, so they present no problems, but if using jars with screw-on tops, make sure that the rubber ring can either be removed or that new tops can be bought separately.

Filling and Sealing the Jars: First the jars must be sterilized. Place them, their tops, and the rubber sealing rings in boiling water for 3 minutes. Then remove them from the water with a fork or a wooden pincer-type implement. Wear a protective pot-holding glove in case some of the boiling water spills. Place the jars upside down on a clean cloth or paper towel to drain—do the same with the tops and sealing rings. If making only 4 to 5 jars of jam, this can be done while the jam is cooking, but if doubling or tripling the recipe, it should be done in advance.

When the jam is cooked, remove the pot or preserving pan from the heat or place it over the pilot light if you have one. With your hand protected by a pot-holding glove, hold a jar over the pan and ladle the jam into it, stirring it slightly as you lift it out of the pan. Or, if you prefer, simply set the jar down on the counter next to the pan and ladle the jam into it. Fill the jar to the brim; then place it on the cloth or towel on which it drained and close the top immediately. If using a screw-on top, screw it on as tight as you can. Make sure the jar is perfectly closed and then turn it upside down; the air contained in it will pass through the boiling hot jam and be immediately sterilized. If using traditional jam jars that are sealed with parrafin or cellophane, do not fill them completely—leave about ½ inch (1.2 cm) between the surface of the jam and the top edge of the jar and wait until the jam is cold before sealing the jars.

131
Basic Jam Recipe (Recette de Base)
(Photo page 219)

I chose this basic recipe because of its short cooking time, which changes the flavor of the fruit less than if it had to cook a long time. However, I have given the recipe two chef's hats for two reasons: first, because it takes a certain amount of experience to be able to tell whether the fruit contains more or less water than average; and second, because you must be very careful not to burn yourself in handling the hot jam when stirring it or putting it into the jars.

PREPARATION	From 15 minutes to 1 hour
MACERATION	12 to 36 hours (see individual recipes)
COOKING TIME	15 minutes
INGREDIENTS	*For 4 to 5 jars* 3 pounds 5 ounces (1.5 kg) fruit pulp (Cup measurements are given with specific recipes) 6 cups (1.2 kg) granulated sugar
UTENSILS	Large, stainless steel pot *or* preserving pan (see General Comments on Jams) Long-handled, wooden spatula Skimmer Large bowl Colander Candy thermometer Ladle 4 to 5 sterilized jam jars (see General Comments on Jams)

Preparing the Fruit: Prepare the fruit by washing, peeling, seeding, and cutting into pieces. Then place the pieces in the preserving pan with the sugar and allow to stand for 12 to 36 hours (see the comments on the choice of preserving pans, page 206). Most fruits must stand for 24 hours, but there are exceptions, and the specific macerating time is given with each specific recipe. For best results, place the fruit and sugar in alternating layers, starting with a layer of fruit and ending with a layer of sugar. The number of layers depends on the amount of jam being made, but for the proportions given here, three layers of each is sufficient.

While the fruit is macerating, the fruit juices will be drawn out by the sugar, the fruit will soften, and a thick sugar syrup will form. If any large undissolved lumps of sugar are left on top of the last layer of fruit, stir them into the rest of the syrup with a wooden spatula or skimmer before proceeding to the next step.

When the macerating time is up and the sugar is dissolved, lift the fruit out of the preserving pan with a skimmer or slotted spoon and place it over a large bowl in a colander. Allow the fruit to drain for 15 to 20 minutes; then add any juice in the bowl to that which is already in the preserving pan.

Cooking the Syrup: Place the preserving pan over high heat and boil the syrup until it reaches 228–230°F (109–110°C) or the Blow stage (see Recipe 130, Cooking Sugar). If the fruit you are using is not ripe or if it seems to be particularly full of water, continue cooking the syrup to the Firm Ball stage or 244°F (118°C).

Cooking the Fruit: When the correct temperature of the syrup is reached, add the fruit immediately. Bring back to a boil and cook for 5 to 15 minutes or until the syrup either reaches the Thread Stage, 222–224°F (106–107°C), or until a drop of syrup "beads" on a cool, dry plate (see Note). The cooking time depends on how ripe the fruit is and how much water it contains. Watch the cooking jam constantly, and adjust the heat when necessary to prevent it from splattering or overflowing; stir often with a wooden spatula or the skimmer to keep the jam from sticking to the bottom of the pan. At the end of the cooking time, remove any foam from the surface of the jam with a skimmer if necessary.

Remove the pan from the heat and ladle the jam immediately into clean jam jars (see the Comments on filling and sealing jam jars, page 208).

To Store: Jam can be stored for up to a year. Once opened, keep in the refrigerator if not used every day. See specific recommendations for each jam.

Comments: Most jams thicken for several days after being put into the jars. If it still seems too liquid, however, it can be cooked again. In order to do this, place a colander over a bowl or in the preserving pan and empty the jars into it. When the syrup has drained off, cook it to 228°F (109°C); add the fruit and continue cooking to 222°F (106°C); then put it back into clean jars.

Note: To see if the syrup "beads," dip the skimmer into it, shake off any excess syrup, and hold the skimmer about 1 to 2 inches (2.5 to 5 cm) above a clean, dry plate. If the drop of syrup that falls onto the plate holds its shape for 2 to 3 seconds at least before collapsing, the syrup is said to "bead" and the jam is done.

132

Apricot Jam
(Confiture d'Abricots)

(Photo page 17)

It is best to use slightly acid varieties of apricots so that the jam will not be too sweet.

PREPARATION	30 minutes
MACERATION	36 hours
COOKING TIME	15 minutes from the time the syrup boils
INGREDIENTS	*For 4 to 5 jars* 3¾ pounds (1.7 kg) firm, slightly acid apricots 6 cups (1.2 kg) granulated sugar 20 pits from the apricots
UTENSILS	Large, stainless steel pot *or* preserving pan Long-handled, wooden spatula Skimmer Large bowl Colander Candy thermometer Ladle 4 to 5 sterilized jam jars Small saucepan Nut cracker Strainer Clean cloth

Preparing the Fruit: Cut the apricots in half lengthwise and remove the pits. Set 20 pits aside for later use. There should be 3 quarts (1.5 kg) of pitted apricot halves. Place them with the sugar in the preserving pan and allow to macerate for 36 hours if using hard apricots that are slightly acid. If using very ripe apricots, 24 hours macerating time is sufficient. For best results, place the apricots and sugar in alternating layers, starting with a layer of fruit and ending with a layer of sugar. For this recipe, three layers of each should be sufficient.

While the apricots are macerating, the juices will be drawn out by the sugar, the fruit will soften, and a thick sugar syrup will form. If any large undissolved lumps of sugar are left on top of the last layer of apricots, stir them into the rest of the syrup with a wooden spatula or skimmer before proceeding to the next step.

When the macerating time is up and the sugar is dissolved, lift the apricots out of the preserving pan with a skimmer or slotted spoon and place it over a large bowl in a colander. Allow the apricots to drain for 15 to 20 minutes; then add any juice in the bowl to that which is already in the preserving pan.

With the nutcracker, crack the 20 apricot pits reserved earlier and remove the small "almond" from their centers. Fill a small saucepan with water, bring to a boil, add the "almonds," lower the heat, and simmer for 20 seconds. Then drain in a strainer and cool rapidly by holding the strainer under cold running water for 1 to 2 seconds. Peel the apricot "almonds" by pressing each one between the thumb and index finger, toward the narrower end; the almond will slip out from its skin and onto the table. When peeled, split each little "almond" in two and lay them on a clean cloth to dry.

Cooking the Jam: Cook the syrup until it reaches the Firm Ball stage, 244°F (118°C). Stir the syrup constantly to prevent it from sticking to the bottom of the pan.

Lower the heat and add the apricot halves and the apricot "almonds" to the syrup. Be very careful because the syrup tends to splatter. Bring the syrup back to a boil; then boil very gently for 9 minutes or until the syrup beads on a plate (see Note). At the end of this time, skim off any foam on the surface of the jam.

Remove the pan from the heat and fill the jam jars (see General Comments on Jam Jars, page 208), distributing the "almonds" as evenly as possible between them.

Note: To see if the syrup "beads," dip the skimmer into it, shake off any excess syrup, and hold the skimmer about 1 to 2 inches (2.5 to 5 cm) above a clean, dry plate. If the drop of syrup that falls onto the plate holds its shape for 2 to 3 seconds at least before collapsing, the syrup is said to "bead" and the jam is done.

133

Cherry–Currant Jam
(Confiture de Cerises–Groseilles)

Since cherries have very little pectin in them, a little red currant juice is added to help the jam set.

PREPARATION	1½ hours
MACERATION	12 hours
COOKING TIME	15 to 17 minutes from the time the syrup boils
INGREDIENTS	*For 6 to 8 jars* 4 pounds (1.8 kg) ripe, sour, cooking cherries 8 cups (1.6 kg) granulated sugar 2½ pints (625 g) red currants
UTENSILS	Large, stainless steel pot *or* preserving pan Long-handled, wooden spatula Skimmer Large bowl Colander Candy thermometer Ladle 4 to 5 sterilized jam jars Cherry pitter Drum sieve *or* food mill

Preparing the Fruit: Remove the stems from the cherries and remove the pits with a cherry pitter. Place them in the preserving pan with the sugar and allow to macerate for 12 hours. For best results, place the cherries and sugar in alternating layers, starting with a layer of cherries and ending with a layer of sugar. For the proportions given here, three layers of each is sufficient.

While the cherries are macerating, the juices will be drawn out by the sugar, the cherries will soften, and a thick syrup will form. If any large undissolved lumps of sugar are left on top of the last layer of cherries, stir them into the rest of the syrup with a wooden spatula or skimmer before proceeding to the next step.

When the macerating time is up and the sugar is dissolved, lift the cherries out of the preserving pan with a skimmer or slotted spoon and place them over a large bowl in a colander. Allow the cherries to drain for 15 to 20 minutes; then add any juice in the bowl to that which is already in the preserving pan.

Remove the stems from the red currants. Then work them through a drum sieve or food mill, a third at a time, to obtain 2 generous cups (500 g) of juice.

Cooking the Jam: Cook the syrup for 7 minutes or until it reaches the Firm Ball stage, 239–244°F (115–118°C).

Add the cherries and cook for 8 to 10 minutes more to the Thread stage, 225°F (107°C).

Add the red currant juice, bring the jam back to a boil, and then remove from the heat. Stir the jam for 3 minutes away from the heat. Then place it in the jam jars (see General Comments on Jam Jars, page 208).

The jam will thicken after 24 hours.

Variation: Cherries in Thick Syrup (Cerises au Sirop Épais)

The currant juice may be omitted from the recipe, but the jam will be very liquid—more like cherries in a thick syrup. A bit too thin to spread on toast, it is nevertheless delicious served with rice pudding or with a variety of ice creams or sherbets; the Loire Valley Sundae (Recipe 65) and the Ruby Sundae (Recipe 67) are two examples.

To store: Cherries in thick syrup can be stored like any other jam.

134
Strawberry Jam (Confiture de Fraises)

(Photo page 219)

PREPARATION	30 minutes
MACERATION	24 hours
COOKING TIME	20 to 30 minutes from the time the syrup boils
INGREDIENTS	*For 1 to 5 jars* 6½ pints (1.6 kg) strawberries 6 cups (1.2 kg) granulated sugar Juice of 1 lemon
UTENSILS	Large, stainless steel pot *or* preserving pan Long-handled, wooden spatula Skimmer Large bowl Colander Candy thermometer Ladle 4 to 5 sterilized jam jars

Preparing the Strawberries: Rinse the strawberries off, remove the stems, and cut any very large ones in half lengthwise. There should be 9 cups (1.5 kg) of cleaned strawberries.

Place the strawberries and sugar in the preserving pan as described in Recipe 131 and allow to macerate for 24 hours.

Cooking the Jam: Drain the strawberries as described in Recipe 131 and add the lemon juice to the syrup. Then cook the syrup for about 10 minutes or until it reaches the Blow stage, 228–234°F (109–112°C).

Add the strawberries, bring the syrup back to a boil, and cook at a moderate boil for 10 to 20 minutes or until the Thread stage, 223°F (106°C). Watch the jam carefully as it tends to foam a great deal and could overflow; so adjust the heat accordingly. The cooking time varies a great deal depending on the amount of water the strawberries give out.

Skim off any thick foam from the surface of the jam at the end of the cooking time.

Remove the pan from the heat and fill the jam jars (see General Comments on Jam Jars, page 208). This jam is a beautiful, deep, red color.

135
Raspberry Jam (Confiture de Framboises)

This is an excellent, very flavorful jam.

PREPARATION	15 minutes
MACERATION	24 hours
COOKING TIME	14 minutes from the time the syrup boils
INGREDIENTS	*For 4 jars* 3 quarts (1.5 kg) raspberries 6 cups (1.2 kg) granulated sugar
UTENSILS	Large, stainless steel pot *or* preserving pan Long-handled, wooden spatula Skimmer Large bowl Colander Candy thermometer Ladle 4 to 5 sterilized jam jars

Preparing the Raspberries: Use only ripe, perfectly healthy raspberries; any that look even slightly bruised or moldy should be discarded. Remove any stems and rinse the berries off rapidly under cold running water.

Place the raspberries and sugar in the preserving pan as described in Recipe 131 and leave to macerate for 24 hours (see Note).

Cooking the Jam: Drain the raspberries as described in Recipe 131 and cook the syrup for 6 minutes at a rapid boil until it reaches the Blow stage, 230°F (110°C); then add the raspberries and cook 8 minutes more until the syrup reaches the Thread stage, 223°F (106°C). Adjust the heat as necessary to keep the jam from foaming up too much.

At the end of the cooking time, skim off any thick foam remaining on the surface of the jam.

Remove the pan from the heat and fill the jam jars (see General Comments on Jam Jars, page 208).

Note: The raspberries may not give out enough juice while macerating; a great deal of sugar will remain unmelted in this case. If this happens, place the preserving pan over low heat just long enough to melt the sugar (this will happen very quickly), stirring gently once or twice. Then drain the fruit and cook exactly as described.

136
Peach Jam (Confiture de Pêches)

PREPARATION	30 to 45 minutes
MACERATION	12 hours
COOKING TIME	20 to 25 minutes from the time the syrup boils
INGREDIENTS	*For 3 to 4 jars* 4 pounds 6½ ounces (2 kg) ripe peaches 5½ cups (1.1 kg) granulated sugar ½ a vanilla bean Juice of ½ a lemon
UTENSILS	Large, stainless steel pot *or* preserving pan Long-handled, wooden spatula Skimmer *or* colander Candy thermometer Large pot Ladle 2 large bowls 4 to 5 sterilized jam jars

Preparing the Peaches: First, peel the peaches. To do this, bring a large pot of water to a boil, add the peaches, and parboil for 15 seconds. Then lift them out of the pot with a skimmer or drain them in a colander, and cool them by placing them in a large bowl or basin of cold water. The skins will come off easily.

If using clingstone peaches, cut the flesh off the pit. Try to cut the flesh off in wedges by cutting toward the pit and then working each wedge free with the knife by twisting it and slicing the wedge off as close to the pit as possible.

If using freestone peaches, simply cut the peach in half by cutting along the crease that runs around each peach lengthwise; then twist the halves in opposite directions with your hands to loosen the pit and separate the halves. Cut each half into wedges.

When the peaches have been peeled and sliced, there should be 6½ cups (1 kg 500 g) for making the jam. Place them with the sugar in the preserving pan as described in Recipe 131 and allow them to macerate for 12 hours.

Cooking the Jam: Drain the peaches as described in Recipe 131 and cook the syrup for 12 to 15 minutes or until it reaches the Blow stage, 230°F (110°C). Regulate the heat since it tends to foam and splatter if cooked too fast.

Add the peaches and the vanilla bean, bring the syrup back to a boil, and cook for 5 to 10 minutes or until the Thread stage, 225°F (107°C). Skim the surface of the jam if necessary, and then stir in the lemon juice. Immediately remove the jam from the heat and fill the jars (see General Comments on Jam Jars, page 208).

217

137
Plum Jam
(Confiture de Prunes)

Small, yellow plums are best for this recipe because they do not discolor while macerating, but other plums may be used as well.

PREPARATION	30 to 40 minutes
MACERATION	24 hours
COOKING TIME	10 to 16 minutes from the time the syrup boils
INGREDIENTS	*For 4 to 5 jars* 4 pounds (1.8 kg) plums 6 cups (1.2 kg) granulated sugar
UTENSILS	Long-handled, wooden spatula Skimmer Large bowl Colander Candy thermometer Ladle 4 to 5 sterilized jam jars

Preparing the Plums: Cut the flesh off the pits and then measure the plums; there should be 9 cups (1.5 kg) for making the jam.

Place the fruit and sugar in the preserving pan and allow to macerate for 24 hours. For best results, place the plums and sugar in alternating layers, starting with a layer of plums and ending with a layer of sugar. For this recipe, three layers of each should be sufficient.

Cooking the Jam: Drain the fruit and cook the syrup as described in Recipe 131 for 10 minutes or until it reaches the Blow stage, 223–234°F (111–112°C).

Add the plums, bring the syrup back to a boil, and cook for 3 to 6 minutes or until the Thread stage, 223°F (106°C). Do not cook over too high a heat as the jam tends to foam a great deal and will stick to the bottom of the pan if not watched carefully.

At the end of the cooking time, skim off any thick foam left on the surface of the jam.

Remove the pan from the heat and fill the jam jars (see General Comments on Jam Jars, page 208).

Strawberry Jam, Recipe 134

138

Rhubarb Jam (Confiture de Rhubarbe)

PREPARATION	20 minutes
MACERATION	24 hours
COOKING TIME	15 minutes from the time the syrup boils
INGREDIENTS	*For 4 to 5 jars* 6 pounds 10 ounces (3 kg) rhubarb with partial leaves 5 cups (1 kg) granulated sugar Juice of 1 lemon
UTENSILS	Paring knife Large, stainless steel pot *or* preserving pan Long-handled, wooden spatula Skimmer Large bowl Colander Candy thermometer Large pot Ladle 4 to 5 sterilized jam jars

Preparing the Rhubarb: Cut off the leaves and the ends of the stems from the rhubarb. Strip off the skin using a paring knife; then cut the stems into pieces 1¼ to 1½ inches (3 to 4 cm) long and measure them. There should be 13 cups (1 kg 500 g) for making the jam.

Bring a large pot of water to a boil, add the rhubarb, leave for 30 seconds over high heat, and then drain. Place the rhubarb and sugar in the preserving pan as described in Recipe 131 and allow to macerate for 24 hours.

Cooking the Jam: Drain the rhubarb and cook the syrup as described in Recipe 131 for 10 minutes or until it reaches the Blow stage, 228°F (109°C).

Add the rhubarb and lemon juice and cook at a rapid boil for 4 minutes—the syrup should then be quite thick and form crater-like bubbles. At this point the jam is done. At the end of the cooking time, skim off any thick foam on the surface of the jam.

Remove the pan from the heat and fill the jam jars (see General Comments on Jam Jars, page 208).

Comment: This jam is tricky because it does not really set and thicken for 24 hours, so the ordinary temperature and "bead" tests do not really apply. The cooking time and aspect of the bubbling jam are therefore the best guides.

Assorted Fruit Jellies: Apricot Jellies, Recipe 132; Strawberry Jellies, Recipe 153

139
Bitter Orange Marmalade
(Confiture d'Oranges Amère)

(Photo page 177)

PREPARATION	15 minutes
COOLING TIME	15 minutes
COOKING TIME	30 minutes to poach the fruit 30 minutes to cook the marmalade
INGREDIENTS	*For 4 to 5 jars* 3 pounds 5 ounces (1.5 kg) oranges (preferably non-treated) 1 lemon 6 cups (1.2 kg) granulated sugar Scant 1⅓ cups (3 d*l*) water
UTENSILS	Large, stainless steel pot *or* preserving pan Long-handled, wooden spatula Skimmer Large bowl Colander Candy thermometer Ladle 4 to 5 sterilized jam jars Shallow glass *or* china dish Food processor *or* large knife

Preparing the Fruit: Wash and brush the oranges and lemon clean under warm running water. Place them in the preserving pan and cover them with cold water. Bring to a boil and cook for 30 minutes. Then drain in a colander and cool under cold running water for about 15 minutes. Discard the water in which they cooked.

Place the oranges and lemon in a shallow glass or china dish to cut them into thick slices—pour any juice they give out into a bowl. Discard any seeds as well as both ends of each fruit.

Coarsely chop the sliced fruit in a food processor or by hand with a large knife. If you like finding large pieces of orange in marmalade, save a few slices and quarter them.

When the oranges and lemon have been chopped, pour them into a colander placed over the bowl containing their reserved juice and allow to drain completely.

Cooking the Marmalade: While the fruit is draining, place the sugar and water in the preserving pan and bring slowly to a boil, so that the sugar has time to melt completely. Then boil rapidly for about 3 minutes or until the syrup reaches the Soft Ball stage, 239°F (115°C). Add the juice from the bowl and bring back to a boil; then cook for about 5 minutes or until the syrup reaches the Blow stage, 234°F (112°C). Add the chopped fruit and boil for 15 to 20 minutes more or until a drop of syrup "beads" on a plate (see Note to Recipe 131).

Remove the pan from the heat and fill the jam jars (see General Comments on Jam Jars, page 208).

140
Lemon Marmalade
(Confiture de Citrons)

PREPARATION	15 minutes
COOLING TIME	15 minutes
COOKING TIME	30 minutes to poach the lemons 20 minutes to cook the marmalade (see Note)
INGREDIENTS	*For 4 to 5 jars* 3 pounds 5 ounces (1.5 kg) lemons (preferably non-treated) 6 cups (1.2 kg) granulated sugar Scant 1⅓ cups (3 d*l*) water
UTENSILS	Large, stainless steel pot *or* preserving pan Long-handled, wooden spatula Skimmer Large bowl Colander Candy thermometer Ladle 4 to 5 sterilized jam jars Shallow glass *or* china dish Food processor *or* large knife

Preparation: Follow the directions for Bitter Orange Marmalade (Recipe 139) using the ingredients given here.

Note: After the chopped lemons have been added to the syrup, however, it takes only about 10 minutes rather than 15 to 20 for the jam to "bead" on a plate.

141
Sweet Orange Marmalade
(Confiture d'Oranges Douce)

PREPARATION	30 minutes
MACERATION	24 hours
COOKING TIME	2 hours to poach the oranges 5 to 10 minutes to cook the marmalade
INGREDIENTS	*For 5 jars* 13 cups (3 *l*) water 3 pounds 5 ounces (1.5 kg) oranges (preferably non-treated) *For poaching the oranges* 2 cups (400 g) granulated sugar 2 generous cups (5 d*l*) water *For making the marmalade* 6 cups (1.2 kg) granulated sugar Generous 1⅔ cups (4 d*l*) water
UTENSILS	Large, stainless steel pot or preserving pan Long-handled, wooden spatula Skimmer Large bowl Colander Candy thermometer Ladle 4 to 5 sterilized jam jars Food processor *or* large knife

Preparing the Oranges: Place 13 cups (3 *l*) water in the preserving pan, bring to a boil, and add the whole oranges. Boil for 3 minutes, then drain in a colander, and cool under cold running water. Cut the oranges into very thin slices; discard any seeds as well as both ends of each orange.

Place the granulated sugar and water for poaching the oranges in the preserving pan and bring to a boil. Add the orange slices and simmer over very low heat for 2 hours. Be very careful not to let the liquid boil while the oranges are poaching as that would make the orange skins tough.

When it is time, remove the pan from the heat and allow the oranges to macerate in their cooking liquid for 24 hours.

Cooking the Marmalade: Drain the oranges for about 15 minutes. The liquid in which they were poached will not be used in this recipe, but it is delicious added to fresh fruit salad, so save it.

Coarsely chop the drained orange slices in a food processor or do it by hand with a large knife. If you like finding large pieces of orange in marmalade, save a few slices and quarter them.

Place the granulated sugar and the water for making the marmalade in the preserving pan and bring slowly to a boil to give the sugar time to melt completely. Then boil rapidly for 3 minutes or until the Blow stage, 230°F (110°C). Add the chopped oranges, bring back to a boil, and cook for 3 to 5 minutes or until the syrup reaches the Thread stage, 221°F (105°C).

Remove the pan from the heat and fill the jam jars (see General Comments on Jam Jars, page 208).

142
Caramel–Apple Sauce
(Confiture de Pommes–Caramel)

(Photo page 177)

This is really more like an apple sauce than a jam and is excellent served with rice pudding or as a dessert itself accompanied by Vanilla Sauce (Recipe 99). More sugar may be used than indicated here, according to taste.

PREPARATION	30 minutes
COOKING TIME	40 minutes
COOLING TIME	30 minutes
INGREDIENTS	*For 4 to 5 jars*
	Approximately 4½ pounds (2 kg) cooking apples
	Juice of ½ a lemon
	Scant 1⅓ cups (3 d*l*) water
	3½ cups (700 g) granulated sugar
	½ a vanilla bean, split in half lengthwise
	or ¾ teaspoon cinnamon
UTENSILS	Large bowl
	Small saucepan
	Sieve
	Bowl
	Wooden spoon or spatula
	Preserving pan
	Pastry brush
	Candy thermometer
	Ladle
	4 to 5 sterilized jam jars

Preparing the Apples: Peel and core the apples; place the peels and cores in a small saucepan. When the apples are peeled, cut each one into 6 wedges, place them in a large bowl, and add the lemon juice.

Add the water to the apple peels and cores, bring to a boil, then lower the heat, and simmer for 4 minutes.

Cooking the Caramel and Making the Apple Sauce: Hold a sieve over the preserving pan and strain the cooking liquid from the peels and cores through it, pressing the peels with a wooden spoon or spatula to extract as much liquid from them as possible. Add the sugar to the liquid in the pan and bring slowly to a boil, stirring with a wooden spoon or spatula until the sugar melts. If any sugar sticks to the sides of the pan, clean it off with a moistened pastry brush.

When the syrup has come to a boil, raise the heat and boil rapidly for about 10 minutes or until it reaches the Very Hard Crack stage, 313°F (156°C), stirring occasionally. As soon as the syrup begins to turn the color of caramel, add the apples and the vanilla or cinnamon. Stir them into the syrup carefully.

After 5 minutes, lower the heat and cook at a very slow boil for 20 to 25 minutes. The cooking time may be considerably more or less than this, depending on the quality of the apples. Cook them less if they begin to fall apart; more if they give out a lot of water. Try not to stir them, as this could break the pieces of apple, but gently shake the pan from time to time.

When the apples are cooked, remove the pan from the heat and fill the jam jars (see General Comments on Jam Jars, page 208).

To Store: Since this preserve does not contain as much sugar as other jams, it will keep for only 4 months.

143
Red Currant Jelly (Gelée de Groseilles)

PREPARATION	15 minutes
COOKING TIME	15 minutes
COOLING TIME	15 minutes
INGREDIENTS	*For 4 to 5 jars* 5½ pints (1.25 kg) red currants 5 cups (1 kg) granulated sugar 1 generous cup (2.5 d*l*) water
UTENSILS	Large, stainless steel pot *or* preserving pan Long-handled, wooden spatula Skimmer Large bowl Colander Candy thermometer Ladle 4 to 5 sterilized jam jars Food mill or drum sieve Electric mixer with paddle (optional) Mixing bowl (optional)

Making the Jelly: Clean the currants and work them through a food mill or drum sieve as described for Frozen Fruit Purees (Recipe 125). There should be about 5⅓ cups (1 kg) of currant juice puree for this recipe.

In the preserving pan, place the sugar and water and bring to a boil. Then cook rapidly until the syrup reaches the Light Crack stage, 277°F (136°C). Add the currant juice and bring back to a boil—203°F (95°C)—stirring constantly. Then remove the pan from the heat.

With a wooden spatula, stir the jelly for 15 minutes, away from the heat. If preferred, the jelly may be poured into a mixing bowl (preferably metal) and mixed with an electric mixer equipped with a paddle and set on very low speed.

When it is time, fill the jam jars (see the comments on filling and sealing jam jars, page 208).

To Store: This jelly can be kept for a month at room temperature and for several months in the refrigerator after being opened. Like other jellies, it can be kept for a good year before being opened.

Comment: This jelly can be made using frozen red currants. Allow them to thaw completely before making the juice.

GENERAL COMMENTS ON FRUIT JELLIES
(PÂTES DE FRUITS)

The Jellies Themselves: Fruit jellies (pâtes de fruits) are a candy-like preparation composed essentially of sugar and fruit pulp. The fruit pulp contains various minerals and vitamins: vitamin A is found especially in citrus fruits, bananas, apricots, carrots, and melons; vitamin C in citrus fruits, both black and red currants, strawberries, and melons. These vitamins are destroyed by prolonged cooking so it is important to try to limit the cooking time as much as possible.

Apples, pears, quinces, and apricots contain large quantities of pectin, which makes them jell more easily than other fruits. For this reason, until relatively recently, these were the only fruits used in making fruit jellies, which were basically ordinary jam made without the addition of any pectin and cooked for at least 20 to 30 minutes, sometimes far longer, until the "jam" had cooked down enough to solidify when cold. It was then cut into little cubes to be served as one would candies.

Aside from the obvious limitation of flavors, this prolonged cooking had other disadvantages as well: the fruit was so overcooked that most of its original taste had either been lost or completely transformed; they were terribly sweet; and any vitamins contained in the fruit had been completely destroyed.

Today, pectin can be extracted industrially from apples. Since its jelling capacity is increased in the presence of fruit acids, citric acid is extracted from lemons and used in combination with the pectin to aid in the jellification of fruit jellies.

A commercial jelling agent is sold in France for use in making homemade jams. I have tested it and come up with a satisfactory way of using it in making fruit jellies and have even developed some entirely new recipes in the process! Because jelling agents in different countries have somewhat different characteristics, tests were made with American jelling agents for this American edition of my book. So the fruit jelly recipes were again adapted for use with Certo, a liquid jelling agent, widely available in America, which was found to give the best results among the American products.

Utensils Used in Pureeing the Fruit

(*Photo page xix*):   Generally speaking, fruits used in making fruit jellies are pureed before they are cooked. I recommend using either a food processor or an electric blender for doing this most efficiently, although a drum sieve or food mill can be used instead. The advantage of the food processor over the blender is that it does not grind the food as finely so little pieces of the fruit can still be found in the finished jellies.

In some cases, however, the food processor or blender cannot be used. This applies to fruits with a lot of seeds, such as passion fruit, black and red currants, and grapes. For these fruits, an electric juice extractor (juicer), which works like a centrifuge, gives the best results since it effectively separates the seeds and skins from the juice. A drum sieve or food mill may also be used for these fruits, although the resulting juice is not as clear as when a juicer is used because of the

230

presence of more pulp. The finished jellies will be less transparent in this case, but the taste will be the same.

Utensils Used in Cooking the Jellies

Pots or Saucepans: The pot or saucepan used for cooking the fruit pulp and sugar should have a heavy bottom. It may be made of any metal with the exception of iron, which would give a terrible taste to the jellies. Stainless steel is best because it tends to stick the least.

   Because the jelly mixture does tend to stick to the bottom of the saucepan as it cooks, it is a good idea to have a second one on hand so that the jelly can be transferred to it in case it starts to burn.

   For the proportions given in the following recipes, a saucepan with a 2½ to 3-quart (2½ to 3-*l*) capacity should be used.

Other Utensils: A straight-edged, wooden spatula is used for stirring the jelly as it cooks as well as for scraping along the bottom of the saucepan frequently to keep the jelly from sticking.

   If possible, it is preferable to use a gas stove, which allows for better heat control than an electric stove. The jelly should be cooked over as high a heat as possible without making it splatter or overflow. As it cooks, the jelly thickens and begins to pop and splatter, and the heat often has to be adjusted to control this.

Utensils Used in Molding the Jellies: Traditionally, fruit jellies are molded by making a frame with four, large, metal rulers, which are about ½ to ¾ inch (1.2 to 2 cm) wide on each side, placed on a sheet of nonstick parchment paper (see photo for Caramels, page 00). Other sorts of frames may of course be used, such as a metal flan ring or a frame such as the one shown in the photo on page 00 measuring 8 × 12 inches (20 × 30 cm) and 1½ inches (4 cm) high, with a metal "ruler" which can be moved along the frame according to the amount of jelly to be poured into it. If necessary, a weight can be placed against the "ruler" to make sure it doesn't move while the jelly is being poured.

   This frame is in stainless steel, and two different kinds of fruit jellies can be made in it at the same time, as pictured. It can also be used in making caramels or even certain cakes using relatively stiff batters, such as Génoise (Recipe 107) or Orange–Almond Pastry (Recipe 112) because the frame can be used in the oven.

   Professionally, I use a much larger version of this very frame in confectionery but had these smaller ones made for home use at the suggestion of my daughter who found them so practical. When unavailable, either the thick metal rods or rulers mentioned earlier, and pictured on page 000, or a small brownie pan simply lined with nonstick parchment paper work very well for making fruit jellies. The inside measurements of a brownie pan or a frame made with thick metal rulers should be approximately 8 × 6 inches (20 × 15 cm) for making one batch of fruit jellies.

144
Basic Fruit Jelly Recipe (Pâtes de Fruits)
(Photo page 220)

Fruit jellies will keep for up to 2 months without losing any of their flavor.

PREPARATION   10 to 40 minutes, depending on the fruit

COOKING TIME   4 to 9 minutes, depending on the fruit

COOLING TIME   2 to 3 hours

INGREDIENTS   *For approximately 40 to 50 fruit jellies*
1 pound 2 ounces (500 g) fruit pulp
   (Cup measurements are given with specific recipes)
Syrup from canned fruits
   (Used only with certain fruits—see specific recipes)
3 cups (600 g) granulated sugar
1 tablespoon (15 g) butter
2 pouches or 1 bottle of liquid, pectin-based, jelling agent (Certo)

For coating (optional)
Coarse, granulated sugar

UTENSILS   Nonstick parchment paper
Rectangular metal frame, flan ring, metal rods *or* small brownie pan (see Utensils for Molding Fruit Jellies, page 231)
Drum sieve, food mill, electric blender, food processor *or* electric juicer
Large, heavy-bottomed saucepan, preferably stainless steel, with 2½ to 3-quart (2½ to 3-*l*) capacity
Straight-edged, wooden spatula

Preparing the Fruit: Wash, peel, and seed the fruit as necessary. Most fruits are then pureed (see indications given with specific recipes). Some fruits are used as they are and others are mixed with syrup from canned fruit. Because of their relatively neutral taste, pear, peach, or apricot syrups are the best; they can even be mixed together.

Preparing the Mold and Jelling Agent: On a baking sheet or other surface that can stand high temperatures without cracking or warping, place a sheet of

232

nonstick parchment paper and set the metal frame, flan ring, or metal rulers on it; or simply line a small brownie pan with parchment paper.

If using the jelling agent in a bottle, simply open the bottle; if using pouches, cut them open and stand them upright in a large jar or measuring cup so that they will be ready for use.

Cooking the Fruit Jelly: In a large saucepan, place the fruit pulp or fruit pulp–syrup mixture and the sugar. Bring to a rapid boil over high heat, stirring constantly with the spatula. Once a full, rolling boil is reached, start the cooking time; this will be from 4 to 9 minutes, always at a rapid boil and stirring constantly, depending on the fruit used (specific cooking times are given in specific recipes). Add the butter halfway through the cooking time.

When it is time, remove the saucepan from the heat and immediately add the liquid jelling agent; stir vigorously for a few seconds to be sure that it is completely mixed into the jelly mixture.

To Mold, Cut, and Serve the Fruit Jellies: As soon as the jelling agent has been stirred in, pour the boiling hot fruit jelly into the frame or brownie pan (see photo). Allow to set and cool completely, which will take at least 2 to 3 hours.

When the jelly is completely cold, run the blade of a knife all around the edge to detach it from the frame or paper; then cut it into squares about ¾ inch (2 cm) on a side. Lift off the frame; then roll the squares one at a time in granulated sugar (preferably large grained). This step is not absolutely necessary; it does, however, keep the jellies from sticking to each other if piled on top of each other when served and makes them more attractive.

The fruit jellies can be placed in individual paper cases and served in a wooden box or a basket, or they can simply be piled on top of each other on a plate.

To Store: The uncut jellies will keep for 2 months wrapped in the nonstick parchment paper it is molded on, placed in a box, and kept in a cool cellar or the refrigerator. If kept in the refrigerator, the jelly picks up a little moisture but keeps its shine better.

Once cut and rolled in sugar, the jellies will keep for a week in a closed container in the refrigerator; it is preferable to place them in individual paper cases if they are to be stored in this way to keep them from sticking together; these homemade fruit jellies are much softer than commercial ones.

♛

145
Apricot Jellies (Pâte d'Abricots)

(Photo pages 17 and 220)

PREPARATION	10 to 20 minutes
COOKING TIME	6 to 7 minutes
COOLING TIME	2 to 3 hours
INGREDIENTS	*For approximately 40 to 50 jellies* Apricot halves from a 1-quart (1-*l*) jar of Home Canned Apricots (Recipe 122) *or* 1 pound 5 ounces (600 g) fresh apricots (see Note) 2 pouches or 1 bottle of liquid jelling agent 3 cups (600 g) granulated sugar 1 tablespoon (15 g) butter
UTENSILS	Nonstick parchment paper Rectangular metal frame, flan ring, metal rods *or* small brownie pan Electric blender *or* food processor Large, heavy-bottomed saucepan, preferably stainless steel, with 2½ to 3-quart (2½ to 3-*l*) capacity Straight-edged, wooden spatula

Preparing the Apricots: If using canned apricots, drain them; save their syrup for making other fruit jellies. There should be 2 generous cups (500 g) of drained apricot halves for making the jelly.

If using fresh apricots, split them in half and remove the pits. There should be 1 quart (500 g) of seeded halves for making the jelly.

Puree the apricots in a food processor, or set aside a quarter of them and puree the rest in a blender. In this case, finely chop the reserved apricots with a knife.

Preparing the Mold and Jelling Agent: Follow the directions given in Recipe 144.

Cooking the Jellies: Follow the directions given in Recipe 144. Canned apricots should be cooked for 6 minutes; fresh apricots for 7 minutes. Then mold, cut, and serve.

Note: As in making apricot jam, it is best to use slightly acid apricots in making this fruit jelly.

234

146
Pineapple Jellies (Pâte d'Ananas Frais)

Pineapple jellies are almost transparent and have a very nice consistency.

PREPARATION	15 minutes
COOKING TIME	7 minutes
COOLING TIME	2 to 3 hours
INGREDIENTS	*For 40 to 50 jellies*
	A 3 pound 5 ounce (1.5 kg) fresh, ripe pineapple
	3 cups (600 g) granulated sugar
	1 tablespoon (15 g) butter
	2 pouches or 1 bottle liquid jelling agent
UTENSILS	Nonstick parchment paper
	Rectangular metal frame, flan ring, metal rods *or* small brownie pan
	Food mill *or* food processor
	Large, heavy-bottomed saucepan, preferably stainless steel, with 2½ to 3-quart (2½ to 3-*l*) capacity
	Straight-edged, wooden spatula

Preparing the Pineapple: Peel and core the pineapple; then cut it into chunks. There should be 4½ cups (600 g) of pineapple chunks for making the jelly. Squeeze the skins to extract as much juice as possible, and add it to the pineapple.

Puree the pineapple in a food processor or grind it through a food mill using the largest grill. Do not use a blender; it destroys the fibers of the pulp and changes the taste.

Preparing the Mold and Jelling Agents: Follow the directions given in Recipe 144.

Cooking the Jellies: Follow the directions given in Recipe 144. Cook the jelly for 7 minutes, then mold, cut, and serve.

147
Banana–Apple Jellies
(Pâte de Bananes–Pommes)

These jellies are delicious. Since bananas will not jell by themselves, a cooking apple is needed.

PREPARATION	10 minutes
COOKING TIME	6 minutes
COOLING TIME	2 to 3 hours
INGREDIENTS	*For 40 to 50 jellies* 1 pound 2 ounces (500 g) bananas 1 large cooking apple ⅔ cup (1.5 d*l*) syrup from canned fruit 3 cups (600 g) granulated sugar 1 tablespoon (15 g) butter 2 pouches or 1 bottle liquid jelling agent
UTENSILS	Nonstick parchment paper Rectangular metal frame, flan ring, metal rods *or* small brownie pan Electric blender *or* food processor Large, heavy-bottomed saucepan, preferably stainless steel, with 2½ to 3-quart (2½ to 3-*l*) capacity Straight-edged, wooden spatula

Preparing the Fruit: Peel and slice the bananas. There should be 2 cups (250 g) sliced bananas for making the jelly.

Peel and core the apple. Then cut it into pieces and place it in the electric blender or food processor. Add the fruit syrup and blend until smooth; then add the banana slices and blend just long enough to puree the bananas. Do not allow the mixture to become foamy and increase in volume.

Preparing the Mold and Jelling Agent: Follow the directions given in Recipe 144.

Cooking the Jellies: Contrary to Recipe 144, the butter should be added at the beginning of the cooking time rather than halfway through since this fruit jelly tends to stick to the bottom of the saucepan. Otherwise, follow the Basic Fruit Jelly Recipe, cooking the jelly 6 minutes.

To Mold, Cut, and Serve:　Follow the directions given in Recipe 144. This particular jelly has a somewhat grainy appearance. If not cut and coated with sugar, the surface of the finished jelly will crystallize after a few days, so it is not necessary to roll them in sugar unless they are to eaten immediately.

To Store:　Unlike most fruit jellies, Banana–Apple Jellies can be kept for only 2 weeks.

148
Carrot Jellies (Pâte de Carottes)

Carrot jellies have a wonderful, subtle taste as well as being a beautiful color.

PREPARATION	10 minutes
COOKING TIME	6 minutes
COOLING TIME	2 to 3 hours
INGREDIENTS	*For approximately 40 to 50 jellies* 1 pound 2 ounces (500 g) carrots ⅔ cup (15 c*l*) syrup from canned fruit 3 cups (600 g) granulated sugar 1 tablespoon (15 g) butter 2 pouches or 1 bottle liquid jelling agent
UTENSILS	Nonstick parchment paper Rectangular metal frame, flan ring, metal rods, *or* small brownie pan Electric blender *or* food processor Large, heavy-bottomed saucepan, preferably stainless steel, with 2½ to 3-quart (2½ to 3-*l*) capacity Straight-edged, wooden spatula

Preparing the Carrots: Peel the carrots and cut them into slices; there should be 3⅓ cups (400 g) of sliced carrots for making the jellies.

Place the carrots and fruit syrup in an electric blender or food processor and blend until a smooth puree is formed.

Preparing the Mold and Jelling Agent: Follow the directions given in Recipe 144.

Cooking the Jellies: Follow the directions given in Recipe 144. Cook the jelly for 6 minutes. Then mold, cut, and serve.

Assorted Fruit Candies: Stuffed Prunes, Recipe 197; Stuffed Dates, Recipe 180; Stuffed Cherries, Recipe 181; Stuffed Walnuts, Recipe 182; Stuffed Almonds, Recipe 183; Almond Squares, Recipe 185

149
Black and Red Currant Jellies (Pâte de Cassis–Groseilles)

Red currants are added to the black ones to give these jellies a more delicate taste than if only black currants were used.

PREPARATION	20 minutes
COOKING TIME	5 minutes
COOLING TIME	2 to 3 hours
INGREDIENTS	*For approximately 40 to 50 jellies*
	1 pint (320 g) black currants
	1¼ pints (320) red currants
	3 cups (600 g) granulated sugar
	1 tablespoon (15 g) butter
	2 pouches or 1 bottle liquid jelling agent
UTENSILS	Nonstick parchment paper
	Rectangular metal frame, flan ring, metal rods, *or* small brownie pan
	Food mill
	Large, heavy-bottomed saucepan, preferably stainless steel, with 2½ to 3-quart (2½ to-3*l*) capacity
	Straight-edged wooden spatula

Preparing the Currants: Remove the stems from the currants and puree them separately by working them through a food mill (see method in Recipe 125 for Frozen Fruit Purees). There should be 1 generous cup (250 g) of each kind of currant puree.

Preparing the Mold and Jelling Agent: Follow the directions given in Recipe 144.

Cooking the Jellies: Follow the directions given in Recipe 144. Cook the jelly for 5 minutes, making sure you scrape across the bottom of the saucepan with the spatula to keep the jelly from sticking. Then mold, cut, and serve.

150
Cherry Jellies (Pâte de Cerises)

Use ripe cooking cherries, which are sour even when ripe, for doing this recipe; sweet "eating" cherries have very little taste when cooked.

PREPARATION	30 minutes
COOKING TIME	7 minutes
COOLING TIME	2 to 3 hours
INGREDIENTS	*For approximately 40 to 50 jellies*
	1½ pound (700 g) ripe cooking cherries
	3 cups (600 g) granulated sugar
	1 tablespoon (15 g) butter
	2 pouches or 1 bottle liquid jelling agent
UTENSILS	Nonstick parchment paper
	Rectangular metal frame, flan ring, metal rods, *or* small brownie pan
	Drum sieve, food mill, electric blender, *or* food processor
	Large, heavy-bottomed saucepan, preferably with 2½ to 3-quart (2½ to 3-*l*) capacity
	Cherry pitter
	Straight-edged, wooden spatula

Preparing the Cherries: Remove the stems and pits from the cherries; then puree them. A food processor gives the best results in this case, although any of the other appliances may be used.

Preparing the Mold and Jelling Agent: Follow the directions given in Recipe 144.

Cooking the Jellies: Follow the directions given in Recipe 144. Cook the jelly for 7 minutes. Then mold, cut, and serve.

151
Quince Jellies
(Pâte de Coings)

PREPARATION	25 to 30 minutes
COOKING TIME	4 minutes
COOLING TIME	2 to 3 hours minimum
INGREDIENTS	*For approximately 40 to 50 jellies* 1 pound 2 ounces (500 g) ripe quinces ½ a lemon 2 generous cups (5 dl) cold water (approximately) Zest from ½ orange, finely chopped 3 cups (600 g) granulated sugar 1 tablespoon (15 g) butter 2 pouches or 1 bottle of liquid jelling agent
UTENSILS	Skimmer Nonstick parchment paper Rectangular metal frame, flan ring, metal rods, *or* small brownie pan Drum sieve *or* food mill Large, heavy-bottomed saucepan, preferably stainless steel, with 2½ to 3-quart (2½ to 3-*l*) capacity Straight-edged, wooden spatula

Preparing the Fruit: Wash but do not peel the quinces and the lemon and cut each one into four pieces. Place the pieces of quince and lemon in a saucepan, barely cover with water [this takes approximately 2 generous cups (5 dl) water] and bring to a boil. Boil uncovered for 15 minutes; then remove from the heat. Lift the pieces of lemon out of the pot with a skimmer or slotted spoon and discard them.

Lift the quinces out of the pot with a skimmer or slotted spoon and work them through a sieve or food mill, using a fine grill. Add the resulting puree to the cooking liquid still in the saucepan. Add the chopped orange zest to the pot as well.

Preparing the Mold and Jelling Agent: Follow the directions given in Recipe 144.

Vanilla-Flavored Caramels, Recipe 188; Orange-Flavored Caramels, Recipe 189;
Chocolate-Flavored Caramels, Recipe 191

Cooking the Jellies: Follow the directions given in Recipe 144. Cook the jelly for 4 minutes, adding the butter in the beginning of the cooking time rather than halfway through because this jelly tends to stick easily to the bottom of the saucepan. Then mold, cut, and serve.

Note: Frozen quinces may be used for making quince jellies.

To freeze the quinces, wash and dry but do not peel them. Place them on a large plate or platter (do not pile them on top of each other) and then place the platter in the freezer. After 24 hours, place them in a plastic bag, 3 or 4 to a bag; close the bags tightly and place back in the freezer. Work quickly so the quinces do not begin to thaw.

The quinces can be kept frozen for 3 months. Before using them, place them for 24 hours in the refrigerator to thaw.

152
Fig Jellies (Pâte de Figues)

Honey is added to the fig jellies to keep them from crystallizing.

PREPARATION	15 minutes
COOKING TIME	5 minutes
COOLING TIME	2 to 3 hours
INGREDIENTS	*For approximately 40 to 50 jellies* 7 ounces (200 g) dried figs (9 figs) Scant 2 cups (450 g) syrup from canned fruit 2½ cups (500 g) granulated sugar ⅓ cup (100 g) honey 2 pouches or 1 bottle liquid jelling agent
UTENSILS	Nonstick parchment paper Rectangular metal frame, flan ring, metal rods, *or* small brownie pan Electric blender *or* food processor Large, heavy-bottomed saucepan, preferably stainless steel, with 2½ to 3-quart (2½ to 3-*l*) capacity Straight-edged, wooden spatula

Preparing the Figs: Remove the little hard stem from each fig, then cut them into pieces. There should be about 1½ cups (200 g) cut up figs for making the jellies.

Place the figs and fruit syrup in a blender or food processor and blend until a smooth puree is formed. Pour the mixture into a saucepan, whisking if necessary to make sure the figs and syrup are perfectly blended.

Preparing the Mold and Jelling Agent: Follow the directions given in Recipe 144.

Cooking the Jellies: Follow the directions given in Recipe 144. Cook the jelly for 5 minutes, adding the honey when the sugar is added. There is no butter in Fig Jellies.

Mold, cut, and serve.

153
Strawberry Jellies (Pâte de Fraises)

(Photo page 220)

PREPARATION 10 to 20 minutes

COOKING TIME 6 to 9 minutes

COOLING TIME 2 to 3 hours

INGREDIENTS *For approximately 40 to 50 jellies*
2½ pints (625 g) strawberries
3 cups (600 g) granulated sugar
1 tablespoon (15 g) butter
2 pouches or 1 bottle liquid jelling agent

UTENSILS Nonstick parchment paper
Rectangular metal frame, flan ring, metal rods, *or* small brownie pan
Food processor, food mill, *or* electric blender
Large, heavy-bottomed saucepan, preferably stainless steel, with 2½ to 3-quart (2½ to 3-*l*) capacity
Straight-edged, wooden spatula

Preparing the Strawberries: Use only firm, ripe (red) strawberries. Wash them and remove the stems; discard any strawberries with soft, discolored spots on them. There should be 3¾ cups (600 g) cleaned strawberries for making the jellies.

Coarsely puree the strawberries in a food processor or work them through a food mill with a coarse (large-holed) grill. A blender may be used, but blend only for a few seconds so that the puree is not too fine.

Preparing the Mold and Jelling Agent: Follow the directions given in Recipe 144.

Cooking the Jellies: Follow the directions given in Recipe 144. The cooking time varies between 6 and 9 minutes, depending on the amount of water contained in the strawberries. When ready, the jelly will fall very slowly from the skimmer in large, almost sheet-like drops. Try to avoid overcooking as the beautiful color of the strawberries will darken and become dull if they are cooked too long. Mold, cut, and serve.

Note: Strawberry Jellies may be made with Frozen Strawberry Puree (Recipe 125). In this case, place the frozen puree in the blender (do *not* allow the puree to thaw) and blend until smooth. Then proceed as with freshly pureed strawberries, cooking for 6 minutes as described in Recipe 144.

154
Raspberry Jellies (Pâte de Framboises)

PREPARATION	10 minutes
COOKING TIME	6 minutes
COOLING TIME	2 to 3 hours
INGREDIENTS	*For approximately 40 to 50 jellies* 2¼ pints (550 g) raspberries 3 cups (600 g) granulated sugar 1 tablespoon (15 g) butter 2 pouches or 1 bottle liquid jelling agent
UTENSILS	Nonstick parchment paper Rectangular metal frame, flan ring, metal rods, *or* small brownie pan Large, heavy-bottomed saucepan, preferably stainless steel, with 2½ to 3-quart (2½ to 3-*l*) capacity Straight-edged, wooden spatula

Preparing the Raspberries: Remove any stems from the raspberries—use only perfectly healthy ones for making the jellies. It is not necessary to wash them; there should be 4 cups (500 g) of raspberries for making the jellies.

Preparing the Mold and Jelling Agent: Follow the directions given in Recipe 144.

Cooking the Jellies: Follow the directions given in Recipe 144. Cook the jelly for 6 minutes. When the raspberries and sugar have been placed in the saucepan, begin heating slowly until the raspberries have given out some of their juice, then raise the heat, bring to a rapid boil, and continue the recipe as described. The raspberries will turn into a puree as they cook.

Mold, cut, and serve.

155

Raspberry–Red Currant Jellies
(Pâte de Framboises–Groseilles)

PREPARATION	15 minutes
COOKING TIME	6 minutes
COOLING TIME	2 to 3 hours
INGREDIENTS	*For approximately 40 to 50 jellies* 1¼ pint (300 g) raspberries 1½ pints (350 g) fresh or frozen red currants 3 cups (600 g) granulated sugar 1 tablespoon (15 g) butter 2 pouches or 1 bottle liquid jelling agent
UTENSILS	Nonstick parchment paper Rectangular metal frame, flan ring, metal rods, *or* small brownie pan Food mill *or* electric juicer Large, heavy-bottomed saucepan, preferably stainless steel, with 2½ to 3-quart (2½ to 3-*l*) capacity Straight-edged, wooden spatula

Preparing the Fruit: Remove any stems from the raspberries and currants—use only perfectly healthy fruit for making jellies. It is not necessary to wash the raspberries, but the currants should be rinsed off rapidly under cold running water.

There should be 2 cups (250 g) raspberries for making the jellies.

The red currants should be pureed as described in the recipe for Frozen Red Currant Puree (Recipe 125). It is not necessary to measure the red currant puree for this recipe. Frozen red currants may be used instead of fresh ones. In this case allow them to thaw completely before pureeing them.

Preparing the Mold and Jelling Agent: Follow the directions given in Recipe 144.

Cooking the Jellies: Follow Recipe 144. Cook the jelly for 6 minutes. Then mold, cut, and serve. The raspberries will turn into a puree as they cook.

156
Passion Fruit Jellies (Pâte de Fruits de la Passion)

These are the best fruit jellies of all, beautiful to look at and delicious to eat. So try them, even though passion fruits are expensive. It is preferable to use those with a brown skin and reddish flesh, although yellow ones may be used as well. Don't be put off by the wrinkled appearance of the fruit–this is a sign that it is ripe and perfectly juicy inside.

PREPARATION	25 minutes
COOKING TIME	6 minutes
COOLING TIME	2 to 3 hours
INGREDIENTS	*For approximately 40 to 50 jellies* 2¼ pounds (1 kg) passion fruits 1⅓ cups (300 g) syrup from canned fruit 3 cups (600 g) granulated sugar 2 pouches or 1 bottle liquid jelling agent
UTENSILS	Nonstick parchment paper Rectangular metal frame, flan ring, metal rods, *or* small brownie pan Food mill *or* electric juicer Large, heavy-bottomed saucepan, preferably stainless steel, with 2½ to 3-quart (2½ to 3-*l*) capacity Straight-edged, wooden spatula Fine mesh strainer (if using a food mill)

Preparing the Passion Fruits: Cut each fruit in half and scoop out the pulp and seeds with a small spoon. Work the pulp through a food mill with a fine grill and then through a fine mesh strainer, or use an electric juicer to obtain the juice. A juicer is preferable because it does not crush the seeds the way a food mill does.

Discard the seeds. Measure the juice; there should be about 1⅓ cups (300 g) of juice for making the jellies.

Preparing the Mold and Jelling Agent: Follow the directions given in Recipe 144.

Cooking the Jellies: Follow the directions given in Recipe 144. Cook the jelly for 6 minutes; there is no butter in passion fruit jellies. Then mold, cut, and serve.

157
Red Currant Jellies (Pâte de Groseilles)

PREPARATION	20 minutes
COOKING TIME	6 minutes
COOLING TIME	2 to 3 hours
INGREDIENTS	*For approximately 40 to 50 jellies* 3 pints (750 g) red currants 3 cups (600 g) granulated sugar 1 tablespoon (15 g) butter 2 pouches or 1 bottle liquid jelling agent
UTENSILS	Nonstick parchment paper Rectangular metal frame, flan ring, metal rods *or* small brownie pan Food mill *or* electric juicer Large, heavy-bottomed saucepan, preferably stainless steel, with 2½ to 3-quart (2½ to 3-*l*) capacity Straight-edged, wooden spatula

Preparing the Currants: Clean and puree the currants as described in Recipe 125.

Preparing the Mold and Jelling Agent: Follow the directions given in Recipe 144.

Cooking the Jellies: Follow the directions given in Recipe 144. Cook the jelly for 6 minutes. Cook over moderate heat rather than high heat, however, and watch it closely, as this jelly tends to foam up and overflow if cooked over too high a heat.

Mold, cut, and serve.

158
Melon Jellies (Pâte de Melon)

The quality of these jellies depends absolutely on the quality of the melon used. Make sure it is perfectly ripe; otherwise the jellies will have very little taste.

PREPARATION	15 minutes
COOKING TIME	4 minutes
COOLING TIME	2 to 3 hours
INGREDIENTS	*For approximately 40 to 50 jellies* 1 ripe, medium muskmelon or cantaloupe, weighing 1 pound 5 ounces (600 g) Generous ½ cup (130 g) syrup from canned fruit 2½ cups (500 g) granulated sugar 1 tablespoon (15 g) butter 2 pouches or 1 bottle liquid jelling agent
UTENSILS	Nonstick parchment paper Rectangular metal frame, flan ring, metal rods, *or* small brownie pan Food processor *or* electric blender Large, heavy-bottomed saucepan, preferably stainless steel, with 2½ to 3-quart (2½ to 3-*l*) capacity Straight-edged, wooden spatula

Preparing the Melon: Cut the melon in quarters, remove the seeds with a spoon, then cut off the rind, or scoop the pulp off the rind with a spoon. There should be about 1½ cups (320 g) of pulp (cut into chunks) for making the jellies.

Place the melon pulp in a food processor or blender, add the fruit syrup, and blend until smooth.

Preparing the Mold and Jelling Agent: Follow the directions given in Recipe 144.

Cooking the Jellies: Follow the directions given in Recipe 144. Cook the jelly for 4 minutes. Then mold, cut, and serve.

159
Orange Jellies (Pâte d'Oranges)

Orange jellies have lots of flavor and a nice texture because of the pieces of orange peel in them.

PREPARATION	15 minutes
COOKING TIME	5 minutes
COOLING TIME	2 to 3 hours
INGREDIENTS	*For approximately 40 to 50 jellies* 1 large orange (preferably nontreated) 1⅓ cups (3 d*l*) fresh orange juice 2½ cups (500 g) granulated sugar 1 tablespoon (15 g) butter 2 pouches or 1 bottle liquid jelling agent
UTENSILS	Nonstick parchment paper Rectangular metal frame, flan ring, metal rods, *or* small brownie pan Food processor *or* electric blender Large, heavy-bottomed saucepan, preferably stainless steel, with 2½ to 3-quart (2½ to 3-*l*) capacity Straight-edged, wooden spatula Small saucepan

Preparing the Orange: Fill a small saucepan with water, bring to a boil, then add the whole orange, and boil for 10 seconds. Drain and cool under cold running water; then cut the orange into slices. Discard both ends and the seeds. Cut each slice into four pieces, place in a food processor or blender, and reduce to a coarse puree. If using a blender, be careful not to blend too long (no more than 5 seconds) so that the pieces of peel are not ground too small. Add the orange juice and blend just long enough to blend the juice and pulp together.

Preparing the Mold and Jelling Agent: Follow the directions given in Recipe 144.

Cooking the Jellies: Follow the directions given in Recipe 144. Cook the jelly for 5 minutes. Then mold, cut, and serve.

160
Fresh Peach Jellies (Pâte de Pêches Fraîches)

PREPARATION	20 minutes
COOKING TIME	6 minutes
COOLING TIME	2 to 3 hours
INGREDIENTS	*For approximately 40 to 50 jellies* 1 pound 2 ounces (500 g) peaches 2 fresh apricots 3 cups (600 g) granulated sugar 1 tablespoon (15 g) butter 2 pouches or 1 bottle liquid jelling agent
UTENSILS	Nonstick parchment paper Rectangular metal frame, flan ring, metal rods, *or* small brownie pan Food processor *or* electric blender Large, heavy-bottomed saucepan, preferably stainless steel, with 2½ to 3-quart (2½ to 3-*l*) capacity Straight-edged, wooden spatula Large bowl of cold water

Preparing the Fruit: Fill a large saucepan with water and bring to a boil; add the peaches and parboil for 15 seconds. Then drain and place the peaches in a large bowl of cold water. Peel the peaches—the skin will now come off easily.

If using clingstone peaches, cut the flesh off the pit. Scrape the pits with the knife to remove any pulp attached to them.

If using freestone peaches, simply cut the peach in half along the crease which runs around each peach lengthwise, then twist the halves in opposite directions with your hands to loosen the pit, and separate the halves.

Cut the apricots in half and remove the pits.

Place the pulp from the peaches and the apricot halves, as well as any juice from the peaches, in a food processor or blender and blend until a smooth puree is formed.

Preparing the Mold and Jelling Agent: Follow the directions given in Recipe 144.

Cooking the Jellies: Follow the directions given in Recipe 144. Cook the jelly for 6 minutes. then mold, cut, and serve.

253

161
Canned Peach Jellies (Pâte de Pêches au Sirop)

PREPARATION	10 minutes
COOKING TIME	6 minutes
COOLING TIME	2 to 3 hours
INGREDIENTS	*For approximately 40 to 50 jellies* A 1-quart (1-*l*) can or jar of Home Canned Peaches (Recipe 124) 3 cups (600 g) granulated sugar 1 tablespoon (15 g) butter 2 pouches or 1 bottle liquid jelling agent

UTENSILS	Nonstick parchment paper
	Rectangular metal frame, flan ring, metal rods, *or* small
	    brownie pan
	Food processor *or* electric blender
	Large, heavy-bottomed saucepan, preferably stainless
	    steel, with 2½ to 3-quart (2½ to 3-*l*) capacity
	Straight-edged, wooden spatula

Preparing the Peaches: Drain the peaches; save the syrup for use in other fruit jelly recipes. There should be 2 cups (500 g) of peaches for making the jellies. Puree the peaches in a food processor or blender.

Preparing the Mold and Jelling Agent: Follow the directions given in Recipe 144.

Cooking the Jellies: Follow the directions given in Recipe 144. Cook the jelly for 6 minutes. Then mold, cut, and serve.

162
Pear Jellies (Pâte de Poires)

Pear jellies taste like the very essence of pear.

PREPARATION	20 minutes
COOKING TIME	5 minutes
COOLING TIME	2 to 3 hours
INGREDIENTS	*For approximately 40 to 50 jellies*
	1½ pounds (700 g) ripe pears
	½ a vanilla bean
	3 cups (600 g) granulated sugar
	1 tablespoon (15 g) butter
	2 pouches or 1 bottle liquid jelling agent
UTENSILS	Nonstick parchment paper
	Rectangular metal frame, flan ring, metal rods, *or* small brownie pan
	Food processor *or* electric blender
	Large, heavy-bottomed saucepan, preferably stainless steel, with 2½ to 3-quart (2½ to 3-*l*) capacity
	Straight-edged, wooden spatula

Preparing the Pears: Peel the pears, cut them into quarters, and remove the cores. There should be 3½ cups (500 g) of pulp for making the jellies.

Cut the vanilla bean in half lengthwise and scrape out the soft pasty substance from the inside with the tip of a knife. Discard the skin of the vanilla bean.

Place the pears in a food processor, add the vanilla paste, and grind to a coarse puree, or place three-quarters of the pears in a blender with the paste, blend to a puree, and then chop the rest of the pears with a knife so that there will be little pieces of pear in the jellies.

Preparing the Mold and Jelling Agent: Follow the directions given in Recipe 144.

Cooking the Jellies: Follow the directions given in Recipe 144. Cook the jelly for 5 minutes. Then mold, cut, and serve.

163
Apple Jellies (Pâte de Pommes)

Apple jellies are the hardest to make because the poaching time can vary a great deal depending on how much water the apples contain. These jellies have a very light, refreshing, apple taste.

PREPARATION	20 to 25 minutes
COOKING TIME	5 minutes
COOLING TIME	2 to 3 hours
INGREDIENTS	*For approximately 40 to 50 jellies* 1½ pounds (700 g) tart cooking apples (3 large apples) 2 generous cups (5 d*l*) water Juice of ½ a lemon ½ a vanilla bean, split in half lengthwise 3 cups (600 g) granulated sugar 1 tablespoon (15 g) butter 2 pouches or 1 bottle liquid jelling agent Large sieve
UTENSILS	Nonstick parchment paper Rectangular metal frame, flan ring, metal rods, *or* small brownie pan Large sieve Large, heavy-bottomed saucepan, preferably stainless steel, with 2½ to 3-quart (2½ to 3-*l*) capacity Straight-edged, wooden spatula

Preparing the Apples: Peel and core the apples; then cut them into thin slices. There should be about 5½ cups (500 g) of peeled, sliced apples for making the jellies.

Place the apples in a large saucepan with the water, lemon juice, and vanilla bean. Bring to a boil and poach gently for 3 to 10 minutes; remove from the heat as soon as the apples are soft.

Drain the apples in a large sieve. Discard the cooking liquid and the vanilla bean.

Preparing the Mold and Jelling Agent: Follow the directions given in Recipe 144.

Cooking the Jellies: Follow the directions given in Recipe 144. Cook the jelly for 5 minutes. Then mold, cut, and serve.

164
Grape Jellies (Pâte de Raisins)

PREPARATION	20 minutes
COOKING TIME	6 minutes
COOLING TIME	2 to 3 hours
INGREDIENTS	*For approximately 40 to 50 jellies* 1¾ pounds (800 g) grapes, either black or white (see Note) 3 tablespoons grenadine syrup (optional) 3 cups (600 g) granulated sugar 1 tablespoon (15 g) butter 2 pouches or 1 bottle liquid jelling agent
UTENSILS	Nonstick parchment paper Rectangular metal frame, flan ring, metal rods, *or* small brownie pan Food mill *or* electric juicer Large, heavy-bottomed saucepan, preferably stainless steel, with 2½ to 3-quart (2½ to 3-*l*) capacity Straight-edged, wooden spatula

Preparing the Grapes: Remove the grapes from their stems, and work them through a food mill with a fine grill or use a juicer. There should be 2 generous cups (5 d*l*) of juice for making the jellies. If using black grapes, the color may be enhanced by adding the grenadine syrup to the juice.

Preparing the Mold and Jelling Agent: Follow the directions given in Recipe 144.

Cooking the Jellies: Follow the directions given in Recipe 144. Cook the jelly for 6 minutes, adjusting the heat when necessary, as this jelly foams a great deal and will overflow if not watched very carefully. Then mold, cut, and serve.

Note: Any kind of grape may be used in making fruit jellies, but the delicate taste of most table grapes tends to be lost in the cooking process. For this reason, it is best to use Concord grapes or else slightly acid, underripe grapes in making these jellies.

165
Rhubarb Jellies (Pâte de Rhubarbe)

PREPARATION	45 minutes
COOKING TIME	6 minutes
COOLING TIME	2 to 3 hours
INGREDIENTS	*For approximately 40 to 50 jellies* 2¼ pounds (1 kg) rhubarb with partial leaves 3 cups (600 g) granulated sugar 1 tablespoon (15 g) butter 2 pouches or 1 bottle liquid jelling agent
UTENSILS	Colander Nonstick parchment paper Rectangular metal frame, flan ring, metal rods, *or* small brownie pan Food processor *or* electric blender Large, heavy-bottomed saucepan, preferably stainless steel, with 2½ to 3-quart (2½ to 3-*l*) capacity Straight-edged, wooden spatula

Preparing the Rhubarb: Cut off the leaf and the base of each stalk of rhubarb. With a paring knife, strip off the thin stringy skin and then cut each stalk into ¾-inch (2-cm) pieces.

Fill a large saucepan with water, bring to a boil, add the rhubarb, and parboil for 30 seconds; then drain in a colander and cool under cold running water (this will help the rhubarb keep its color).

Place the rhubarb in a food processor or blender and run the machine just long enough to form a coarse puree.

Preparing the Mold and Jelling Agent: Follow the directions given in Recipe 144.

Cooking the Jellies: Follow the directions given in Recipe 144. Cook the jelly for 6 minutes. Then mold, cut, and serve.

Chapter 7

CANDIES

RECIPES

166. Half-Candied Pineapple Slices (Ananas en Tranches Semi-Confites)

167. Half-Candied Orange Peels (Écorces d'Oranges Semi-Confites)

168. Half-Candied Orange Slices (Tranches d'Oranges Semi-Confites)

169. Rock Candy Coating (Candi)

170. Shiny Sugar Coating (Enrobage au Sucre Cuit)

171. Almond Paste (Pâte d'Amandes)

172. Walnut–Almond Paste (Pâte d'Amandes aux Noix)

173. Date Paste (Pâte de Dattes)

174. Candied Orange or Tangerine Wedges (Oranges Déguisées ou Clémentines Déguisées)

175. Candied Pineapple Wedges (Ananas Déguisés)

176. Royal Cherries (Cerises Royales)

177. Candy Chestnuts (Marrons Déguisés)

178. Strawberries Coated with Fondant (Fraises Déguisées au Fondant)

179. Stuffed Prunes (Pruneaux Déguisés)

180. Stuffed Dates (Dattes Déguisées)

181. Stuffed Cherries (Cerises Déguisées)

182. Stuffed Walnuts (Noix Déguisées)

183. Stuffed Almonds (Amandes Déguisées)

184. Candy Half Moons (Demi-Lunes Candis)

185. Almond Squares (Pavés Candis)

186. Disneyland Peanut Brittle (Nougat de Disneyland)

187. Caramelized Almonds or Hazelnuts (Amandes ou Noisettes Caramélisées)

188. Vanilla-Flavored Caramels (Caramels à la Vanille)

189. Orange-Flavored Caramels (Caramels à l'Orange)

190. Coffee-Flavored Caramels (Caramels au Café)

191. Chocolate-Flavored Caramels (Caramels au Chocolat)

192. Florentines (Florentins de Mégève)

GENERAL COMMENTS ON MAKING CANDIES

Making candies is not difficult, so it gives children the perfect opportunity to help in the kitchen. They can help make most of the basic preparations as well as caramels and fruit candies. In general, children can participate in any preparation that does not involve the cooking of sugar—the only dangerous procedure because of its extremely high temperatures and the risk of being burned.

Utensils

(Photo page xix):   A candy thermometer is necessary for cooking sugar, although traditional methods for testing may be used instead (see Cooking Sugar, page 203).

A food processor or electric blender is needed for making Almond Paste and similar preparations. Although either appliance can be used, the food processor is preferable.

Individual paper cases in white pleated paper are used for serving most candies.

Nonstick parchment paper is used in making a great many candies, so be sure to have a good supply on hand. It is often used with a metal frame as in making caramels (see photo, page 242). If you do not have metal rulers such as those pictured or a frame such as that used in making fruit jellies (see photo, page 220), a small rectangular cake or brownie pan lined with parchment paper can be used instead.

Cellophane, usually sold for covering jam jars, is ideal for wrapping finished caramels.

A large selection of containers with covers, such as the type in which cottage cheese comes or large yoghurt pots, can be used for storing basic ingredients such as Almond Paste, Half-Candied Orange Slices, and other similar preparations. For partially finished or finished candies, however, plastic or glass containers that can be hermetically sealed should be used.

Although a freezer is not necessary for making candies, it saves a great deal of time because basic preparations can be cooled three times as fast in the freezer as in the refrigerator.

Basic Ingredients

Any fruits or nuts used in candy making should be of the highest quality.

Confectioner's sugar is often called for; if you do not have any on hand, granulated sugar or lump sugar can be placed in an electric blender and ground until it forms a fine powder. The result will be perfect.

Chocolate and fondant are used in a few candy recipes. For a detailed discussion of them, see General Comments on Making Chocolates (page 313).

166
Half-Candied Pineapple Slices
(Ananas en Tranches Semi-Confites)

The classic recipe for making candied pineapple takes a week, so I am proposing this simplified recipe which is better adapted for home use.

PREPARATION	15 minutes
COOKING TIME	2 hours
MACERATION	24 hours
DRYING TIME	24 to 48 hours
INGREDIENTS	*For 18 to 20 slices* 2 cans of pineapple slices, each weighing 1 pound 4 ounces (567 g) (18 to 20 pineapple slices) 2 generous cups (5 d*l*) water 1½ cups (300 g) granulated sugar
UTENSILS	Large saucepan with cover [2½-quart (2½-*l*) capacity] Large strainer Nonstick parchment paper Cake rack 4 small glasses *or* bowls Plastic wrap

Candying the Pineapple: Drain the pineapple slices; the juice will not be used in this recipe, but it can be saved in the refrigerator and served as a refreshing drink.

In a large saucepan, place the water and sugar, bring to a boil, and then add the pineapple slices; they will barely be covered by the syrup. Lower the heat and simmer, uncovered, for 2 hours. It is very important that the syrup never boil, so check from time to time—if necessary, place the pot on an asbestos mat or other heat-diffusing device.

When the pineapple has finished cooking, cover the saucepan and remove from the heat. Allow the pineapple to macerate in the pot for 24 hours.

Drying the Pineapple Slices: When the pineapple has finished macerating, drain for 5 to 10 minutes (the cooking liquid can be saved and used to sweeten a fruit salad).

Place a sheet of nonstick parchment paper on a table or other flat surface. Set a cake rack on four small glasses or bowls over the parchment paper; the glasses or bowls will permit air to circulate under the rack as well as over it.

Place the pineapple slices on the cake rack—do not pile them on top of each other or let them touch. They can nevertheless be placed very close to each other if necessary to fit them all on the cake rack. Allow them to dry for 24 to 48 hours. During this time any excess syrup will drip off onto the parchment paper.

To Store: When the pineapple slices have finished drying, wrap each one individually in a piece of plastic wrap and place them in a closed container in the refrigerator. They will keep for 2 weeks.

Uses: Half-Candied Pineapple Slices are used in making the Molded Raspberry and Champagne Dessert (Recipe 73), Molded Hawaiian Dessert (Recipe 72), Port Royal Frozen Soufflé (Recipe 80), Gatines-Style Chocolate Truffles (Recipe 226), and Pineapple Sherbet (Recipe 4).

Half-Candied Orange Peels
(Écorces d'Orange Semi-Confites)

The peels of oranges that have been squeezed to make orange juice may be used in this recipe. In this case, rinse off the peels, and then use a knife to remove any bits of membrane, pulp, and so on, still attached to the peels.

PREPARATION	15 minutes
COOKING TIME	2 hours
MACERATION	12 hours
DRYING TIME	6 to 12 hours
COOKING TIME	10 minutes if coated
INGREDIENTS	*For 1½ cups (265 g) candied strips plus 6 large pieces (105 g) candied peel* 4 medium-sized, thick-skinned oranges (preferably non-treated) 2 generous cups (½ *l*) water 1½ cups (300 g) granulated sugar *For the coating (optional)* ⅓ cup (50 g) powdered (ground) almonds ⅓ cup (50 g) confectioner's sugar
UTENSILS	Knife Small saucepan Colander Large saucepan with cover Wooden spoon *or* spatula Baking sheet Flexible-blade spatula Paper towel Electric blender *or* food processor (optional) Large jar with lid

Preparing the Peels: Rinse the oranges off under warm running water and wipe them dry. Slit the peel all around the orange, going from top to bottom; then make a second slit all around the orange at right angles to the first slit. The peel will thus be divided into four equal sections, pointed at the top and bottom.

Remove the sections of peel with your fingers or with a knife if the orange does not peel easily; if using a knife, try not to cut the flesh of the orange because you can use it to make Candied Orange Wedges (Recipe 174).

Set aside 6 of the sections of peel and cut the remaining ones into thin slices.

Candying the Peels: Fill a small saucepan with water, bring to a boil, and add all the orange peel, both sliced and whole. Parboil for 10 minutes; then drain in a colander.

Place 2 generous cups (½ *l*) of water and the sugar in a large saucepan and bring to a boil, stirring with a wooden spoon or spatula so that the sugar will melt completely. As soon as the syrup boils, add the orange peels, lower the heat, and simmer uncovered for 2 hours.

When the cooking time is up, cover the pot, remove from the heat, and allow the peels to macerate for 12 hours.

Coating the Candied Peels (Optional):   If you wish to eat the candied peels by themselves or coat them in chocolate, they should first be coated in the following way.

Allow the peels to drain for 6 to 12 hours, preferably on a rack set on small glasses or bowls to allow the air to circulate.

Preheat the oven to 400°F (200°C).

Carefully mix the powdered almonds and confectioner's sugar together—this mixture is called *Tant-pour-Tant* (Half-and-Half).

Spread the Half-and-Half on a baking sheet and place in the oven for 10 minutes, toward the middle of the oven if it heats from the bottom or toward the bottom of the oven if it heats from the top.

While the Half-and-Half is in the oven, place the orange peels on a paper towel to remove any last drops of syrup from them.

When the time is up for the Half-and-Half, grind it to a powder in either an electric blender or food processor or rub it through a drum sieve. Place the powdered Half-and-Half in a large jar, add the orange peels, close the jar, and shake to cover the peel.

To Store Uncoated Peels: Place the candied peels and their syrup in a closed container in the refrigerator. Remove peel from the syrup as needed and drain before using. The peel will keep at least 1 month in the syrup.

To Store Coated Peels: Leave the peels in the jar with the Half-and-Half, tightly closed in the refrigerator. They will keep this way for 1 month.

Uses: Half-Candied Orange Peels are used in making Florentines (Recipe 192), various chocolates, and for decorating various ice cream desserts and candies. The large pieces are also used in making Candy Half Moons (Recipe 184).

168
Half-Candied Orange Slices
(Tranches d'Oranges Semi-Confites)

PREPARATION	20 minutes
COOKING TIME	1 to 1½ hours
MACERATION	24 hours
INGREDIENTS	*For approximately 2 generous cups (580 g) of candied slices (40 slices)*
	4 oranges weighing a total of 1 pound 5 ounces (600 g)—preferably nontreated
	2 generous cups (½ l) water
	1½ cups (300 g) granulated sugar
UTENSILS	Vegetable brush
	Sharp knife or slicing machine
	Saucepan with cover
	Strainer
	Large jar with lid

Preparing the Oranges: Wash the oranges under warm running water, brushing them with a vegetable brush as you do so.

Cut the oranges into thin, regular slices (about 10 slices each, not counting the end pieces). Discard both ends of each orange as well as any seeds.

Candying the Orange Slices: Place the water and sugar in a large saucepan and bring to a boil. Add the orange slices, lower the heat, and simmer for 1 to 1½ hours. Do not allow the liquid to boil.

When the time is up, cover the pot, remove from the heat, and allow the oranges to macerate for at least 24 hours before using.

Drain the slices in a strainer only when they are to be used, not before.

To Store: Place the orange slices and their cooking liquid in a tightly covered jar and store in the refrigerator. They will keep for 2 to 4 weeks. Simply remove slices from the jar when needed, cover the jar once more, and place it back in the refrigerator.

Uses: Half-Candied Orange Slices are used in making the Riviera Duja (Recipe 210), as well as some ice cream desserts such as the Pré Catelan Sundae (Recipe 57) and the Frozen Grand Marnier Dessert (Recipe 76).

169
Rock Candy Coating (Candi)

It is extremely important that all the utensils used in making this recipe be absolutely clean; otherwise, the recipe itself is very simple.

PREPARATION	10 minutes
COOKING TIME	5 minutes
COOLING TIME	3 hours
MACERATION	12 hours
CRYSTALLIZATION	4 hours
INGREDIENTS	40 stuffed or candied fruits and nuts (see Recipes 179–183) 2½ cups (500 g) granulated sugar Generous ¾ cup (2 dl) water
UTENSILS	Large saucepan Pastry brush Large lidded jar with a 1-quart (1-l) capacity Shallow baking dish or platter, just large enough to hold the candied fruits Cake rack 4 small glasses or bowls Nonstick parchment paper Individual paper cases

Making the Sugar Syrup: Make the sugar syrup the same day you make the candied fruits, i.e., 2 days before serving them.

In a large saucepan, place the sugar and water and bring to a boil, stirring to make all the sugar dissolve. The impurities will come to the surface and be deposited on the sides of the saucepan. With a moist pastry brush, wipe the sides of the saucepan clean.

As soon as the syrup has come to a rolling boil, remove from the heat and allow to cool for 10 minutes. Pour the syrup into a large, 1-quart (1-l) jar, put the lid on the jar, and allow the syrup to cool completely at room temperature for at least 3 hours. It is best to let it sit overnight if possible, but do not allow it to sit any longer than 24 hours.

While the syrup is cooling, be careful not to move it or it might crystallize in the jar.

Coating the Candies: Into a shallow baking dish or platter just large enough to hold all the candied fruits, pour enough syrup to cover the bottom with a thin layer (see photo, page 239).

Arrange the candied fruits neatly in the platter, then very gently pour in the rest of the syrup. Place a cake rack or another platter on top of the candies to keep them from floating—they should be completely covered by the syrup.

Do not touch or move the platter, and leave the candies to macerate in the syrup for at least 12 hours.

Drying the candies: Hold the candies in place with the cake rack and pour the syrup out of the platter into a large saucepan (see Comment).

Place the cleaned cake rack on top of four small glasses or bowls over a sheet of parchment paper; if the rack has "feet" it is unnecessary to use the glasses or bowls.

Place the candied fruit on the grill and allow to drain for 4 hours: 2 hours on one side and 2 hours on the other. During this time the syrup on them will crystallize into very fine rock candy.

Allow the candies to dry for 24 hours if you intend to store them. Otherwise they may be eaten the day they are made, served in individual paper cases.

To Store: The hard Rock Candy Coating protects the fruits and keeps them soft and creamy for more than a month. Keep them in their paper cases, in a tightly closed box.

Comment: After being used to coat the candied fruits, the syrup can be re-used in the following manner:

Add a generous ¾ cup (2 d*l*) of water to the syrup in a saucepan, bring to a boil, then remove from the heat. This makes 28° Sugar Syrup, which can be stored in a jar in the refrigerator and used in making sherbets, ice creams, and other desserts (see 28° Sugar Syrup, Recipe 1).

170
Shiny Sugar Coating (Enrobage au Sucre Cuit)

PREPARATION	10 minutes
COOKING TIME	5 minutes
COOLING TIME	15 to 30 minutes
INGREDIENTS	*For coating 40 candies* ⅓ cup (7.5 c*l*) water 1¼ cup (250 g) granulated sugar 10 drops lemon juice 5 to 10 drops food coloring (optional) 40 stuffed or candied fruits and nuts (see Recipes 179–183) *For serving* A grapefruit, pineapple, *or* 40 paper cases
UTENSILS	Baking sheet *or* large platter, covered with nonstick parchment paper 40 toothpicks Small saucepan Candy thermometer Dish towel

Cooking the Sugar: Before cooking the sugar, prepare the baking sheet by oiling it lightly (if using a platter, place a sheet of nonstick parchment paper on it).

Also insert a toothpick into each of the candies to be coated (see photos of various coated stuffed fruits and candied pineapple wedges, pages 239 and 317).

Place the water and sugar in the saucepan and bring to a boil. After 3 minutes, add the lemon juice and the food coloring if using any. (This is indicated in specific recipes.) Continue boiling for another 2 minutes or until the sugar has reached the Very Hard Crack stage (see page 205), 311°F (155°C). The sugar must reach this stage; if not cooked enough, the sugar coating will be sticky; if cooked too much, it will turn to caramel.

Coating the Pieces: As soon as the sugar is cooked, remove the saucepan from the heat and set it down at a tilt by placing a folded dish towel under one side of it. Dip each fruit or nut into the sugar syrup; try not to get any syrup on the toothpick. Quickly lift the piece out of the sugar, giving a gentle up and down movement with your wrist so that the excess syrup will be pulled back into the syrup still in the pot. Lightly rub the piece against the edge of the saucepan to keep it from dripping as you remove it from the pot, and set it down on the bak-

271

ing sheet or parchment paper. The sugar coating will harden in a few minutes.

If the syrup begins to cool too much and stiffen in the saucepan, simply reheat it again until it reaches the proper consistency.

To Serve: When the coated candied fruits and nuts have cooled completely (15 to 30 minutes), they can be served either by sticking them into a grapefruit or a pineapple with the toothpicks (see photo, page 317) or by placing them in little paper cases and removing the toothpicks. Remove the toothpick by pulling on it as you push against the candy with another toothpick or fork; the shiny sugar coating will become dull if you touch it with your fingers.

To Store: When coated in this way it is best to eat the candies the day they are made. They will keep uncovered for only 12 hours, and if kept in a tightly closed box for only 24 hours. In any case they should be kept in a dry place. On a humid day or in the refrigerator, the sugar will begin to melt and become sticky.

Note: Any leftover sugar syrup can be used to make a spun sugar decoration, if you have something it can be used for the same day.

Spun Sugar Decoration (Décor en Sucre Filé)

Allow the sugar syrup to cool to 185°F (85°C), or if it has cooled too much, heat it to that temperature.

Cover a clean table with several sheets of nonstick parchment paper—make sure the whole table is covered and that you have lots of room to work.

Lightly oil a long stainless steel knife and lay it across two tall jars or decanters about 8 inches (20 cm) tall. The tip of the knife should be pointing toward you.

Place the saucepan with the syrup on one side of the knife. Dip a fork into it and lift it rapidly over the knife, then back over the knife again toward the pot. Dip it back into the syrup whenever necessary to keep some on the fork. Use a wide, quick movement; the filaments of sugar will drape themselves over the blade of the knife. Work quickly but carefully so that the sugar does not splatter—remember that it is still burning hot.

When the sugar filaments have cooled and hardened, lift them all off the blade of the knife and form a nest or half-circle to place on the dessert you wish to to decorate.

Uses: Spun sugar can be used to decorate various ice creams, Sherbet-Filled Pineapple Dessert (Recipe 90), sundaes, fruit salads, snow eggs (*oeufs á la neige*), floating islands, and many other desserts.

171
Almond Paste (Pâte d'Amandes)

Almond paste is used in making stuffed fruits and various chocolates. Also called marzipan, it can be colored, shaped like different miniature fruits, or eaten as it is.

PREPARATION	20 minutes
COOKING TIME	2 minutes to peel fresh almonds
RESTING TIME	1 to 2 hours
INGREDIENTS	*For approximately 2 cups, tightly packed (500 g) almond paste (a scant ½ cup (100 g) is sufficient for stuffing 12 fruits)*

Using whole shelled almonds
Generous 1¾ cups (275 g) shelled almonds
1⅔ cup (250 g) confectioner's sugar
1 egg white, lightly beaten

Using powdered (ground) almonds
2 cups (250 g) powdered (ground) almonds
1⅔ cup (250 g) confectioner's sugar
1 to 2 egg whites, lightly beaten

Coloring (Optional)
A few drops red, green, or yellow food coloring or coffee extract

UTENSILS
Medium saucepan
Strainer
Clean cloth
Electric blender *or* food processor
2 mixing bowls
Wooden spoon *or* spatula

USING WHOLE SHELLED ALMONDS

Peeling the almonds: Fill a saucepan with water and bring to a boil.

Rapidly rinse the almonds off under running water and then drop them in the boiling water. Bring the water back almost to a boil and then remove the pot from the heat; leave the almonds in the hot water for 2 minutes, then drain them in a strainer, and cool rapidly under cold running water.

Peel the almonds by pressing each one between the thumb and index finger, toward the narrower end; the almond will slip out from its skin and onto the table. When all the almonds are peeled, rinse them off once more under cold water and place them on a clean cloth and pat dry.

Making the Almond Paste: Place the peeled almonds, the confectioner's sugar, and half the egg white in a mixing bowl. Stir with a wooden spoon or spatula until evenly mixed; then grind to a fine paste in a food processor or electric blender, a third at a time. If coloring the almond paste, add a few drops of food coloring or coffee extract at this time; 2 to 3 drops will make pastel colors, more will be necessary for darker colors.

After each third has been ground (and colored), place it in a clean mixing bowl. When done, form all of the almond paste into one ball; if too dry and crumbly to do so, add a little more egg white, kneading it in with your hands. The finished almond paste should be relatively soft and smooth but not sticky. This is why only half the egg white was added in the beginning—depending on the amount of oil contained in the almonds it may or may not be necessary to add any more.

USING POWDERED (GROUND) ALMONDS

Making the Almond Paste

With a Food Processor or Blender: Place the powdered almonds, confectioner's sugar, and one lightly beaten egg white in the food processor or blender, and add the food coloring or coffee extract if using any. Grind until a fine paste is formed, adding more egg white if necessary—in any case, more egg white will be needed if using powdered almonds than if using freshly ground ones because powdered almonds have very little oil left in them.

By Hand: If using powdered almonds, the almond paste may also be made by hand. Simply place the powdered almonds and confectioner's sugar in a mixing bowl and stir with a wooden spoon or spatula until mixed together. Then gradually stir in the egg white until the mixture can be formed into a relatively soft but not sticky ball. Add the food coloring or coffee extract if using, and knead the almond paste until a homogenous color is formed.

Comment: If you add too much egg white by accident, the almond paste can be made more firm by adding a little more confectioner's sugar.

To Store: Allow the almond paste to rest for 1 to 2 hours in the mixing bowl. Then place it in a tightly closed plastic bag or jar in the refrigerator; it will keep for 2 to 3 months. Simply remove the amount needed whenever necessary, and replace the rest back in the refrigerator.

172
Walnut–Almond Paste (Pâte d'Amandes aux Noix)

PREPARATION	20 minutes
RESTING TIME	1 to 2 hours
INGREDIENTS	*For approximately 2 cups, tightly packed (500 g)* 1 generous cup (110 g) walnut meats Generous ⅔ cup (110 g) blanched almonds 1⅔ cup (250 g) confectioner's sugar 1 egg white, lightly beaten (see Note)
UTENSILS	Food processor *or* electric blender Mixing bowl Electric mixer with paddle, wooden spoon, *or* spatula

Making the Walnut–Almond Paste: Place a third each of the walnut meats, almonds, and confectioner's sugar in the food processor or blender and grind, adding the egg white, little by little. Add no more than a third of the egg white to each batch. When a fine paste is formed, place it in a mixing bowl and proceed in the same way with the other two-thirds of the ingredients.

If using a food processor, you may make all the paste at once if your machine is large enough.

When all the walnut–almond paste has been placed in the bowl, beat it until smooth with an electric mixer equipped with a paddle or by hand with a wooden spoon or spatula. If the mixture seems too soft and sticky, add more confectioner's sugar. If too crumbly and dry, add more egg white. If making Walnut Wonders (Recipe 205), the paste should be quite stiff; knead it with your hands to make sure it will not get sticky, and add a little more confectioner's sugar if it does.

To Store: Allow the walnut–almond paste to rest for 1 to 2 hours in the mixing bowl. Then store it in a tightly closed jar or plastic bag in the refrigerator. It will keep for 2 to 3 months.

Uses: Walnut–Almond Paste is used in making Walnut Wonders (Recipe 205), Stuffed Walnuts (Recipe 182), and Lutetia Pistacios (Recipe 206).

Note: If using shelled almonds and peeling them yourself as described in Recipe 171 for Almond Paste, half an egg white is sufficient.

173

Date Paste (Pâte de Dattes)

PREPARATION	10 minutes
RESTING TIME	1 to 2 hours
INGREDIENTS	*For 1⅓ cups, tightly packed (400 g) date paste (⅓ cup, tightly packed (100 g) is sufficient for stuffing 12 dates)* ¼ pound (125 g) dates Generous ¼ cup (50 g) Half-Candied Orange Peel in strips (Recipe 167) Generous ⅔ cup (100 g) powdered (ground) almonds 1⅔ cup (250 g) confectioner's sugar 1 egg white, lightly beaten
UTENSILS	Knife Food processor *or* electric blender Mixing bowl Wooden spoon, spatula *or* plastic scraper

Making the Date Paste: Remove the pits from the dates. Then chop them coarsely, as well as the strips of orange peel. Place in the food processor or blender and grind, gradually adding the powdered almonds and half of the confectioner's sugar. If using a blender, it is best to blend only half of these measurements at a time, making the date paste in two batches.

The paste will be more or less finely ground, as well as more or less soft and crumbly, depending on the amount of moisture contained in the dates. Begin adding the egg white little by little; add no more than half at this point.

When the egg white has been mixed into the paste, remove it from the food processor or blender and place it in the mixing bowl.

Gradually add the second half of the confectioner's sugar, beating it in with a wooden spoon or spatula or cutting it in with a plastic scraper.

The finished date paste should be soft but not too sticky; you should be able to take a small piece of it and roll it into a ball between the palms of your hands. If it seems too dry and compact, add a little more, or all, of the remaining egg white, as needed. If too sticky, add a little more confectioner's sugar.

To Store: Allow the date paste to rest for 1 to 2 hours in the mixing bowl before storing it in the refrigerator in a tightly closed jar or plastic bag. It will keep for 2 weeks.

Uses: Date paste is used in making Stuffed Dates (Recipe 180) and Oriental Dates (Recipe 204).

Chocolate Coating, Recipe 193; Eiffel Towers, Recipe 207

GENERAL COMMENTS ON FRUIT CANDIES
(FRUITS DÉGUISÉS)

There are two basic types of fruit candies (see photo, page 239):

1) Fresh fruits, candied or half-candied fruits, or fruits preserved in alcohol (orange or tangerine wedges, half-candied pineapple wedges, brandied cherries) which have been coated with a Shiny Sugar Coating (Recipe 170). Variations of this are Candy Chestnuts (Recipe 177) and Strawberries Coated with Fondant (Recipe 178).

2) Candied fruits, dried fruits, or nuts, which have been stuffed with Almond Paste, Walnut–Almond Paste, or Date Paste. Stuffed fruits can either be eaten as they are or coated with Rock Candy Coating (Recipe 169) or a Shiny Sugar Coating (Recipe 170).

Storing: The length of time fruit candies can be kept varies greatly.

Candies coated with Rock Candy Coating will keep for 1 month in a closed box in a dry place (do *not* place them in the refrigerator).

Candies coated with Shiny Sugar Coating can be kept no more than 12 hours in a dry place (*not* in the refrigerator); they should therefore be eaten the day they are made.

Uncoated stuffed fruits will keep for a week in the refrigerator.

174
Candied Orange or Tangerine Wedges
(Oranges Déguisées ou Clémentines Déguisées)

PREPARATION	30 minutes
DRYING TIME	2 hours before coating
COOKING TIME	5 minutes
COOLING TIME	15 to 20 minutes
INGREDIENTS	*For 15 to 18 candies* 2 oranges *or* 4 tangerines 1¼ cup (250 g) granulated sugar ⅓ cup (7.5 c*l*) water Juice of ½ a lemon 5 drops red food coloring

Duja, Recipe 195; Harlequin Duja, Recipe 209

Cake rack
                                  Saucepan
                                  Candy thermometer (optional)
                                  Dish towel
                                  Lightly oiled baking sheet *or* nonstick parchment paper
                                  20 individual paper cases

Preparing the Fruit: Peel the skin off the oranges or tangerines; be careful not to break through the thin membrane that protects the flesh. Carefully separate the wedges; discard any with broken membranes as the sugar will not stick to them. Tangerines usually present no problem, but it is best to have an extra orange on hand if using oranges, since there can be quite a lot of waste.

Allow the separated wedges to dry on a cake rack for 2 hours.

Coating the Wedges: Place the sugar and water in a small saucepan, bring to a boil, add the lemon juice, and boil until the syrup reaches the Very Hard Crack stage (see page 205), 311°F (155°C). This takes about 5 minutes from the time the syrup boils.

Remove the saucepan from the heat and set it at a tilt by placing a folded dish towel under one side.

Take an orange or tangerine wedge by one end. Dip the other end into the syrup, coating it a little more than halfway up. Be *very* careful not to touch the syrup with your fingers because it is boiling hot. Lift the wedge out of the syrup, scrape it lightly against the edge of the saucepan to prevent it from dripping, and place it on the oiled baking sheet or the parchment paper.

When all the wedges are half coated, place the saucepan back over the heat, add the food coloring to the syrup with a spoon, and stir gently until the syrup comes back to a boil.

Take an orange or tangerine wedge by the coated end and dip the other end into the red syrup, coating it just halfway up this time. Remove it from the syrup as described above and place it on the baking sheet or parchment paper to cool.

To Serve: When the sugar coating has hardened, place each candied wedge in an individual paper case and arrange on a platter to serve. These candies should be eaten the day they are made.

Note: If you have leftover syrup, it can be molded in oiled chocolate molds or any other small "mold," such as small clam shells, to make hard sugar candies; or you can make Spun Sugar Decorations (page 272) with it to decorate an ice cream, sherbet, or fruit salad you plan to serve the same day.

175
Candied Pineapple Wedges (Ananas Déguisés)
(*Photo page 317*)

The pineapple wedges should be quite dry when making this recipe, otherwise the sugar coating will stay sticky rather than hardening.

PREPARATION	25 minutes
DRYING TIME	40 minutes before coating
COOLING TIME	15 to 20 minutes
INGREDIENTS	*For 40 candies*
	5 Half-Candied Pineapple Slices (Recipe 166)
	Shiny Sugar Coating (Recipe 170)
	5 to 10 drops of yellow food coloring (optional)
	For serving
	A grapefruit, pineapple, or 40 paper cases
UTENSILS	Baking sheet or large platter, covered with nonstick parchment paper
	40 toothpicks
	Small saucepan
	Candy thermometer
	Dish towel
	Cake rack

Drying the Pineapple: Preheat the oven at its lowest setting for 15 minutes.

Cut each pineapple slice into 6 to 8 wedges, depending on the size of the slices. Place the wedges on a cake rack (do not allow them to touch each other), place the cake rack in the oven, close the oven door, and turn the oven off. Allow the pineapple wedges to dry in the turned-off oven for 40 minutes.

Coating the Pineapple Wedges: Follow the directions given in Recipe 170 for Shiny Sugar Coating to make the sugar syrup, coat the pineapple wedges, and serve the finished candies.

To Store: Candied pineapple wedges are best eaten the day they are made, but they can be kept on a platter for 12 hours in a dry place or for 24 hours in a tightly closed box. Do not place them in the refrigerator.

176
Royal Cherries
(Cerises Royales)

PREPARATION	15 minutes
DRAINING TIME	15 minutes
COOKING TIME	5 minutes
COOLING TIME	15 to 30 minutes
INGREDIENTS	*For 40 candies* 40 Brandied Cherries (Recipe 126) 1 tablespoon cornstarch 1⅓ cups (250 g) granulated sugar ⅓ cup (7.5 cl) water Juice of ½ lemon 40 drops red food coloring
UTENSILS	2 clean cloths or dish towels Small saucepan Lightly oiled baking sheet *or* platter with nonstick parchment paper Candy thermometer (optional) 40 individual paper cases

Preparing the Cherries: Remove the cherries from their alcohol and drain them on a clean cloth or dish towel for about 15 minutes. Make sure that their stems are still tightly attached.

Spread a second cloth or dish towel on the table and sprinkle it all over with the cornstarch. Place the cherries on the towel; then gather up an end of the towel in each hand and roll the cherries around in the cornstarch by lifting up first one end of the towel, then the other. This will make the cherries perfectly dry.

Coating the Cherries: Place the sugar and water in a small saucepan and bring to a boil. After allowing the syrup to boil for 3 minutes, add the lemon juice and food coloring and continue cooking for about 2 minutes more or until the syrup reaches the Very Hard Crack stage (see page 205), 311°F (155°C).

Quickly roll the cherries one last time in the towel as described above; then hold them by their stems and coat them in the syrup, following the directions given in Recipe 170 for Shiny Sugar Coating. Be sure to dip the cherries straight into the syrup and lift them straight out—do not allow them to turn on their stems.

To Serve: When the cherries have cooled completely, lift them off the baking sheet or parchment paper and place them in individual paper cases to serve. They must be eaten the day they are made.

To Store: Royal Cherries will keep for only 6 hours in a dry place since the alcohol in them tends to dissolve the sugar coating. Do not place them in the refrigerator.

177
Candy Chestnuts (Marrons Déguisés)
(Photo page 317)

PREPARATION	30 minutes
COOKING TIME	10 minutes
COOLING TIME	1½ to 4 hours
INGREDIENTS	*For 24 candies* 3½ tablespoons (50 g) softened butter ⅔ cup tightly packed (200 g) sweetened chestnut paste Cornstarch or confectioner's sugar to sprinkle over the working surface *For the syrup* 1¾ ounces (50 g) semi-sweet chocolate 1¼ cups (250 g) granulated sugar ⅔ cup (1.5 d*l*) water 1 tablespoon (15 g) butter Juice of ½ a lemon
UTENSILS	Large mixing bowl Wooden spoon *or* spatula Ruler Plate Small saucepan and mixing bowl *(bain-marie)* *or* double boiler Medium saucepan Wire whisk Large platter *or* cake rack Tin can approximately 6 inches (15 cm) high 12 forks *or* 24 toothpicks (with 24 pieces of cork or clothespins) Dish towel Nonstick parchment paper 24 individual paper cases

Forming the Chestnuts: Take the butter from the refrigerator at least 30 minutes before using to be sure that it will be quite soft.

Place the chestnut paste in a large mixing bowl and beat in the butter with a wooden spoon or spatula. When the mixture is perfectly smooth and homogenous, place it in the refrigerator to stiffen for 30 to 40 minutes.

Lightly sprinkle the working surface with cornstarch or confectioner's sugar. Divide the chestnut mixture into three equal parts. Place them on the working surface and roll each one into a long sausage shape. Sprinkle with a little more cornstarch or confectioner's sugar if necessary to keep the mixture from sticking to the table.

When the three "sausages" have been made, cut each one evenly into 8 pieces, using a ruler for greater accuracy in measuring. Roll each little piece into a ball, then pinch the top of each ball with your thumb and index finger to make it chestnut shaped (see photo).

Place the mock chestnuts on a plate and put them in the freezer for 1 hour or in the refrigerator for 3 to 4 hours to harden.

Making the Syrup: Put a little water in a small saucepan and set a small mixing bowl in it; the bottom of the bowl should not touch the water—this is a *bain-marie*. Or, put a little water in the bottom half of a double boiler and set the top half in place.

Break the chocolate into the mixing bowl or double boiler, place the *bain-marie* or double boiler over the heat, and bring the water to a boil. As soon as the water boils remove the pot from the heat and allow the chocolate to melt.

When the chocolate has completely melted, place the sugar and water into a second, larger saucepan and bring to a boil. Pour the hot syrup into the melted chocolate, whisking the chocolate vigorously as you do so. When the syrup and chocolate are perfectly mixed together, pour the resulting chocolate syrup back into the saucepan in which the sugar syrup was prepared. Add the butter and bring to a boil, stirring almost constantly with a wooden spoon or spatula.

When the chocolate syrup has boiled for 1 minute, add the lemon juice. When you do, the syrup will bubble violently and foam up to the edge of the pot. Adjust the heat if necessary to keep the syrup from overflowing, but cook it over as high a heat as possible for 9 minutes more. The syrup will steam and thicken during this time; continue to stir frequently. When the syrup is done, it should be thick enough to coat the wooden spatula.

Preparing the Chestnuts for Coating: While the chocolate syrup is cooking, prepare the utensils that will be used in coating the chestnuts.

Place the platter on top of the tin can; the platter should be large enough to hold the 12 forks next to each other.

Stick the prongs of the forks into the bases of 12 of the chestnuts; do not stick the prongs straight toward the pointed top of the chestnuts, but at an angle (see photo). Push the chestnut onto the fork as far as possible without having the prongs stick out the side of the chestnut.

After coating, the chestnuts will be placed in individual paper cases, so set these out as well.

If you wish to present the chestnuts stuck into a grapefruit or a pineapple, as shown in the photo, and alternating with Candied Pineapple Wedges (Recipe 175), stick a toothpick into each one. Point the toothpick straight toward the top of the chestnut and push it in as far as possible. In this case, place the cake rack, rather than the platter, on top of the tin can. After dipping the chestnuts into the syrup as described below, slide the free end of the toothpick between the bars of the cake rack and stick it into a piece of cork, or slide it through the bars and clamp it in place with a clothespin.

Coating the Chestnuts: When the chocolate syrup has finished cooking, remove the saucepan from the heat and set it at a tilt by placing a folded dish towel under one side. Dip each chestnut rapidly into the syrup, leaving a ring of uncoated chestnut around the fork or toothpick (see photo). Lift the coated chestnut out of the syrup (a long filament will form at the end of it) and lay the fork across the platter with the chestnut sticking out over the edge as shown in the photo or set the toothpick on the cake rack as described above.

The sugar coating will harden very quickly so the same forks can be used to coat the other chestnuts. When hardened after a few minutes, cut the long filament off of each chestnut so that there is just a little point at the end of each one; then place the candies in individual paper cases. Do not touch the sugar coating with your fingers as it will become dull if you do.

If using toothpicks, do not leave the coated chestnuts too long at room temperature because they will soften and their weight will pull them off the toothpicks. As soon as the sugar coating hardens, cut off the filament, stick the finished candies into the grapefruit or pineapple, and place in the refrigerator.

If necessary, the chocolate syrup can be reheated any time during the coating process.

To Store: Candy chestnuts will keep for 24 hours in the refrigerator. During this time they harden, but after 24 hours the sugar coating begins to melt and become sticky.

Note: Leftover syrup can be molded in lightly oiled chocolate molds or small clam shells to make little hard sugar candies, called "sweet cockles" *(coques-doux)*, a favorite with French children.

178
Strawberries Coated with Fondant
(Fraises Déguisées au Fondant)

These are delicious, but very fragile; they must be eaten within 2 to 3 hours after being made.

PREPARATION	10 minutes
COOKING TIME	10 minutes to heat fondant
COOLING TIME	30 minutes
INGREDIENTS	*For 25 candies*
	25 large ripe strawberries with stems totaling about 1 pint (250 g)
	Generous ⅔ cup (250 g) Plain Fondant (Recipe 194)
	4 to 5 teaspoons water
	For dipping (optional)
	Granulated sugar
UTENSILS	Mixing bowl and saucepan *(bain-marie) or* double boiler
	Wooden spoon *or* spatula
	Yoghurt thermometer
	Baking sheet and nonstick parchment paper *or* a soup plate
	25 individual paper cases

Preparing the Strawberries: Try to choose strawberries all the same size and shape (preferably round with a pointed end, rather than flattened varieties).

To clean them, brush them off with a dry pastry brush. Do not wash them and do not remove the stems.

Preparing the Fondant: Melt the fondant in a *bain-marie* or double boiler as described on page 319. The fondant should be heated to no more than 86°F (30°C). Dilute the fondant slightly with the water, stirring it in with a wooden spoon or spatula.

Coating the Strawberries: Place a sheet of nonstick parchment paper on a baking sheet, or fill a large soup plate with granulated sugar. Hold each strawberry by its stem and dip it into the fondant until it is coated three-quarters of the way up. Then either lay the coated strawberry down directly on the parchment paper or dip the coated tip of the strawberry in the granulated sugar and lay the strawberry down in the sugar.

To Serve: Allow the fondant to harden completely; then place each strawberry in a little paper case and serve.

179
Stuffed Prunes (Pruneaux Déguisés)
(*Photo page 239*)

PREPARATION	15 minutes
DRYING TIME	12 to 24 hours (optional)
INGREDIENTS	*For 12 stuffed prunes*
	Scant ½ cup (100 g) white or green Almond Paste (Recipe 171)
	12 prunes, pits removed
UTENSILS	Knife
	Ruler
	12 individual paper cases

Stuffing the Prunes: With your hands, roll the Almond Paste into a sausage shape on the table; the "sausage" should be 9 inches (24 cm) long. With a ruler and knife, measure and cut it into 12 pieces ¾ inch (2 cm) long each. Shape each little piece into an oval.

Take each prune and spread it open along the slit which was made when removing the pit. Place an oval of Almond Paste in the center of each prune; then press the sides of the prune around the stuffing to hold it in place.

Decorate the Almond Paste that is still visible by making a crisscross design on it with the tip of a sharp knife (see photo).

To serve: The Stuffed Prunes may be served as they are or allowed to dry for 12 to 24 hours and coated with either a Rock Candy Coating (Recipe 169) or a Shiny Sugar Coating (Recipe 170).

Serve in individual paper cases.

To Store: The Stuffed Prunes can be kept for varying amounts of time depending on whether they are coated or not and which coating is used. (See General Comments on Fruit Candies, page 279).

180
Stuffed Dates (Dattes Déguisées)

(*Photo page 239*)

PREPARATION	15 minutes
DRYING TIME	12 to 24 hours (optional)

INGREDIENTS	*For 12 stuffed dates*
	⅓ cup (100 g) Date Paste (Recipe 173)
	   or scant ½ cup (100 g) White or Green Almond Paste
	   (Recipe 171)
	12 dates, pits removed

UTENSILS	Knife Ruler 12 individual paper cases

Stuffing the Dates: With your hands, roll the date or almond paste into a sausage shape on the table; the "sausage" should be 9 inches (24 cm) long. With a ruler and knife, measure and cut it into 12 pieces ¾ inch (2 cm) long each. Shape each little piece into an oval.

Take each date and spread it open along the slit which was made when removing the pit. Place an oval of date or almond paste in the center of each date and press the sides of the date around the stuffing to hold it in place.

Decorate the date or almond paste that is still visible by making a crisscross design on it with the tip of a sharp knife (see photo).

To Serve: The stuffed dates may be eaten as they are or allowed to dry for 12 to 24 hours and coated with either a Rock Candy Coating (Recipe 169) or a Shiny Sugar Coating (Recipe 170).
Serve in individual paper cases.

To Store: The stuffed dates can be kept for varying amounts of time depending on whether they are coated or not and which coating was used. (See General Comments on Fruit Candies, page 279).

181

Stuffed Cherries (Cerises Déguisées)

(Photo page 239)

PREPARATION	15 minutes
DRYING TIME	12 to 24 hours (optional)
INGREDIENTS	*For 12 stuffed cherries* Scant ½ cup (100 g) white or yellow Almond Paste (Recipe 171) 12 large candied cherries
UTENSILS	Knife Ruler 12 individual paper cases

Stuffing the Cherries: Cut the cherries in half.

With your hands, roll the almond paste into a sausage shape on the table; the "sausage" should be 9 inches (24 cm) long. With a ruler and knife, measure and cut it into 12 pieces ¾ inches (2 cm) long each.

Press half a cherry against each of the flat sides of the pieces of almond paste. Make sure the cherries stick to the paste.

To Serve: The stuffed cherries may be eaten as they are, or allowed to dry for 12 to 24 hours and coated with either a Rock Candy Coating (Recipe 169) or a Shiny Sugar Coating (Recipe 170).

Serve in individual paper cases.

To Store: The stuffed cherries can be kept for varying amounts of time depending on whether they are coated or not and which coating was used. (See General Comments on Fruit Candies, page 279).

182
Stuffed Walnuts (Noix Déguisées)
(Photo page 239)

PREPARATION	15 minutes
DRYING TIME	12 to 24 hours (optional)

INGREDIENTS	*For 12 stuffed walnuts*
	Scant ½ cup (100 g) Walnut–Almond Paste (Recipe 172)
	    or scant ½ cup (100 g) coffee-colored Almond Paste
	    (Recipe 171)
	24 walnut meats

UTENSILS	Knife Ruler 12 individual paper cases

Stuffing the Walnuts: With your hands, roll the walnut–almond paste or almond paste into a sausage shape on the table; the "sausage" should be 9 inches
(24 cm) long. With a ruler and knife, measure and cut it into 12 pieces ¾ inch (2
cm) long each.

Press a walnut meat against each of the flat sides of the pieces of walnut–
almond or almond paste. Make sure the nut meats stick to the paste.

To Serve: The stuffed walnuts may be eaten as they are, or allowed to dry for 12
to 24 hours, and coated with either a Rock Candy Coating (Recipe 169) or a Shiny
Sugar Coating (Recipe 170).

Serve in individual paper cases.

To Store: The stuffed walnuts can be kept for varying amounts of time depending on whether they are coated or not and which coating is used. (See General
Comments on Fruit Candies, page 279).

183
Stuffed Almonds (Amandes Déguisées)
(Photo page 239)

PREPARATION	15 minutes
DRYING TIME	12 to 24 hours (optional)
INGREDIENTS	*For 12 stuffed almonds* Scant ½ cup (100 g) Almond Paste (Recipe 171) 12 whole blanched almonds
UTENSILS	Knife Ruler 12 individual paper cases

Making the Candies: With your hands, roll the almond paste into a sausage shape on the table; the "sausage" should be 9 inches (24 cm) long. With a ruler and knife, measure and cut it into 12 pieces ¾ inch (2 cm) long each.

Shape each piece of almond paste into an oval. With the tip of the knife, cut a slit lengthwise in each oval and place an almond in the slit. Press the almond paste against the sides of the almond to hold it in place; the edge of the almond should still be visible, sticking up out of the slit.

Decorate the almond paste by drawing a few lines in it with the tip of the knife (see photo).

To Serve: The stuffed almonds may be eaten as they are or allowed to dry for 12 to 24 hours and coated with either Rock Candy Coating (Recipe 169) or Shiny Sugar Coating (Recipe 170).

Serve in individual paper cases.

To Store: The stuffed almonds can be kept for varying amounts of time depending on whether they are coated or not and which coating is used. (See General Comments on Fruit Candies, page 279).

184
Candy Half Moons (Demi-Lunes Candi)

PREPARATION	30 to 40 minutes
DRYING TIME	12 to 24 hours
COATING TIME	12 hours
INGREDIENTS	*For approximately 30 candies* Scant ½ cup (80 g) Half-Candied Orange Peel in strips (Recipe 167) 1 generous cup tightly packed (300 g) Almond Paste (Recipe 171) Confectioner's sugar to dust almond paste *For decoration* 3 large pieces (50 g) Half-Candied Orange Peel (Recipe 167) Rock Candy Coating (Recipe 169)
UTENSILS	Electric blender *or* food processor Mixing bowl Wooden spoon *or* spatula Clean sheet of plastic Rolling pin Ruler Round cookie cutter 1½ inches (4 cm) in diameter Knife Cake rack

Preliminary Preparations: Make the sugar syrup for the Rock Candy Coating (Recipe 169).

Chop the half-candied strips of orange peel in the blender or food processor.

Break the almond paste into several pieces, place them in a mixing bowl, and add the chopped orange peel. Blend the almond paste and orange peel together with a wooden spoon or spatula.

Making the Candies: When the chopped orange peel and almond paste have been well mixed together, form the mixture into a ball, dust it lightly with confectioner's sugar, and place it on a clean sheet of plastic. With a rolling pin, roll the almond paste out to a thickness of about ½ inch (1.2 cm). Dust the almond paste lightly with confectioner's sugar whenever necessary to keep it from sticking to the rolling pin.

Use the cookie cutter to cut the almond paste into circles; then cut each circle in half with a knife.

Take any scraps left over from cutting out the circles and form them into a ball; then roll out and cut as described above so that there will be no waste.

Decorating and Coating the Candies: Cut the large pieces of half-candied orange peel into as many squares or lozenges as you have half circles and place one on each candy.

Place the decorated candies on a cake rack to dry for 12 to 24 hours; then coat them with Rock Candy Coating as described on page 270.

To Store: Once coated, the candy half moons will keep for 1 month in a tightly closed box in a dry place. Do not place them in the refrigerator.

185
Almond Squares (Pavés Candis)
(Photo page 239)

PREPARATION	30 to 40 minutes
RESTING TIME	2 to 3 hours
DRYING TIME	12 to 24 hours
COATING TIME	12 hours
INGREDIENTS	*For approximately 30 candies*
	¾ teaspoon kirsch or calvados
	1 drop green food coloring
	2 drops yellow food coloring
	⅓ cup (50 g) chopped almonds
	1 generous cup tightly packed (300 g) Almond Paste (Recipe 171)
	Confectioner's sugar to dust almond paste
	2 tablespoons 28° Sugar Syrup (Recipe 1)
	or 1 tablespoon granulated sugar dissolved in 1 tablespoon hot water
	Rock Candy Coating (Recipe 169)
UTENSILS	Small bowl
	Wooden spoon *or* spatula
	Baking sheet
	Clean sheet of plastic
	Rolling pin
	2 sets of cardboard rulers (optional)
	Pastry brush
	Knife
	Cake rack

Preliminary Preparations: Prepare the sugar syrup for the Rock Candy Coating (Recipe 169).

Preheat the oven to its lowest setting for 15 minutes.

In a small bowl, place the kirsch or apple brandy and the green and yellow food coloring. With a wooden spoon or spatula, stir until the mixture is a uniform color; then add the chopped almonds. Stir until all the bits of almond are the same color.

Spread the colored almonds out on a baking sheet and place in the oven to dry for 15 minutes. Remove the baking sheet from the oven and allow the almonds to cool.

Making the Squares: While the almonds are cooling, lightly dust the almond paste with confectioner's sugar and place it on a clean sheet of plastic. Use a rolling pin to roll it out into a square about ½ inch (1.2 cm) thick. To roll the almond paste out perfectly square, two sets of cardboard rulers can be piled up to a height of ½ inch (1.2 cm) and the almond paste rolled out between them.

When the almond paste has been rolled out to the correct thickness, moisten the entire surface with the 28° syrup or the mixture of sugar and water using a pastry brush.

Sprinkle the moistened almond paste with the colored almonds, tapping them lightly so that they stick to the surface of the paste. Allow to rest for 2 to 3 hours.

When the time is up, turn the almond-covered paste upside down onto the working surface (the chopped almonds should be on the bottom). Using a sharp knife, cut it into approximately 30 squares about 1 inch (2.5 cm) on a side.

Drying and Coating the Almond Squares: Turn the squares right side up and place them on a cake rack to dry for 12 to 24 hours; then coat them with a Rock Candy Coating (Recipe 169).

To Store: The coated almond squares will keep for 1 month in a tightly closed box in a dry place. Do not place them in the refrigerator.

186
Disneyland Peanut Brittle (Nougat de Disneyland)

This is made with salted peanuts; children love it and it is very inexpensive.

PREPARATION	30 minutes (including 20 minutes to make caramel)
COOLING TIME	10 minutes
INGREDIENTS	*For Lenôtre's Caramel (Recipe 198)* 2 cups (400 g) granulated sugar 20 drops lemon juice *Other ingredients* 1 tablespoon (15 g) butter 1 cup (150 g) salted peanuts
UTENSILS	Saucepan Straight-edged, wooden spatula Baking sheet Flexible-blade, metal spatula Large knife

Making the Peanut Brittle: Make the caramel following the directions for Lenôtre's Caramel (Recipe 198) using the measurements given here.

When the caramel is made, remove the saucepan from the heat, stir in the butter, and add the peanuts. Mix the peanuts into the caramel with the straight-edged, wooden spatula, making sure that all the peanuts are coated.

Lightly oil a baking sheet and pour the caramel–peanut mixture onto it, then spread it out in an even layer with a flexible-blade, metal spatula, which has also been lightly oiled. The layer should be the thickness of a peanut—do not leave them piled on top of each other.

Allow the peanut brittle to cool for 5 minutes. Then turn it over and allow to cool for 5 minutes on the other side.

If the peanut brittle is still soft after the 10-minute cooling period, cut it with the flexible-blade spatula; but if it has hardened, use a large knife to cut it into squares or rectangles.

Serve the peanut brittle as it is.

To Store: Peanut brittle will keep for 1 month in a tightly closed box in a dry place. Do not place it in the refrigerator. If the weather is humid, it will become sticky.

Uses: This peanut brittle can be coarsely ground in a food processor or blender and mixed with Peanut Butter Ice Cream (Recipe 30) when it comes from the ice cream freezer.

187
Caramelized Almonds or Hazelnuts
(Amandes ou Noisettes Caramélisées)

PREPARATION	15 minutes
COOKING TIME	10 minutes
INGREDIENTS	*For 10½ ounces (300 g) caramelized almonds* 1⅓ cups (200 g) shelled almonds ½ cup (100 g) granulated sugar 2 tablespoons water ½ a vanilla bean, split in half lengthwise 1 tablespoon (15 g) butter *For ½ pound (250 g) caramelized hazelnuts* 1⅓ cup (200 g) shelled hazelnuts Generous ⅓ cup (75 g) granulated sugar 1½ tablespoons water ½ a vanilla bean, split in half lengthwise 1 tablespoon (15 g) butter
UTENSILS	Baking sheet Drum sieve, fine grill, *or* clean cloth Medium saucepan Candy thermometer (optional) Wooden spoon or spatula 2 forks

Preliminary Preparations: If using hazelnuts, remove their thin brown skins as follows.

Preheat the oven to 350°F (175°C).

Spread the hazelnuts on the baking sheet and heat them in the oven for 7 minutes. Remove them from the oven and place them on a drum sieve or fine grill. Remove their skins by rubbing them against it. The skin can also be removed by wrapping them in a clean cloth or dish towel and rubbing the nuts together inside it.

It is unnecessary to remove the skins from the almonds; on the contrary, their skin gives a very good taste to this candy.

Caramelizing the Nuts: Place the sugar, water, and vanilla bean in a saucepan. Bring slowly to a boil, stirring until the sugar has melted; then boil rapidly for 2 to 3 minutes or until the syrup reaches the Firm Ball stage (see page 205), 244°F (118°C).

Nougatine and Nougatine Crumble, Recipe 197; Trianons, Recipe 220

Remove the saucepan from the heat and add the nuts to the syrup. Stir gently with a wooden spoon or spatula to coat all the nuts—the mixture will begin to look sandy (see photo, page 340). Continue stirring gently for 30 seconds.

Place the saucepan back over moderate heat, stirring gently. The sugar will slowly melt and caramelize. As this happens, roll the nuts in the caramel with the wooden spoon or spatula; the nuts will begin to color and make a dry clicking sound as they touch each other. Do not let the mixture smoke—if it does, immediately lower the heat.

When all the sugar has caramelized and the nuts are coated, remove the saucepan from the heat and stir in the butter. When the butter has been mixed in, pour the contents of the saucepan out onto an oiled baking sheet, spreading it out with the wooden spoon.

Allow the caramelized nuts to cool for a few minutes, using two forks to stir them and turn them over. When the caramel has hardened, separate any nuts that are sticking to each other.

To serve: The caramelized almonds or hazelnuts can be eaten as they are or coated with chocolate (see Recipe 193 for Chocolate Coating).

To Store: The caramelized nuts will keep for 2 weeks in a hermetically closed box in the refrigerator or in a cool dry place. If kept in the refrigerator, you must be sure that the box they are kept in is *very* tightly closed; if exposed to humidity, the nuts will soften and taste stale.

♔

188
Vanilla-Flavored Caramels (Caramels à la Vanille)
(Photo page 242)

*In this recipe I have included a detailed description concerning the molding,
cutting, wrapping, and storing of all sorts of caramels.*

PREPARATION	15 minutes
COOKING TIME	9 to 10 minutes
COOLING TIME	1½ hours
INGREDIENTS	*For 14 ounces (400 g) of caramels* ⅓ cup chopped almonds 1 generous cup (250 g) very sweet crème fraîche or heavy cream (see Dictionary of Terms) ½ a vanilla bean, split in half lengthwise 3 tablespoons (60 g) honey 1¼ cups (250 g) granulated sugar 1 tablespoon (15 g) butter
UTENSILS	Shallow baking dish Medium saucepan Straight-edged, wooden spatula Candy thermometer (optional) Small bowl Ordinary teaspoon Metal frame, thick metal rulers, small brownie pan *or* rectangular dish 6 x 8 inches (15 x 20 cm) Nonstick parchment paper Large knife Plastic scraper (optional) 20 squares of cellophane 6 inches (15 cm) on a side

Cooking the Cream: Preheat the broiler for 10 minutes.

Place the chopped almonds in a shallow baking dish and grill them for a few
seconds—they should turn barely golden brown.

Place the crème fraîche or heavy cream in a medium saucepan and bring to
a boil, stirring with a wooden spoon or spatula. When the cream boils, add the
vanilla bean, honey, and sugar. After the cream comes back to a boil, boil
rapidly for 9 to 10 minutes or until the mixture has reached the Hard Ball stage
(see page 205), 253°F (125°C). If your saucepan has a very heavy, thick bottom,

302

cook the cream to only 253°F (123°C) since the pot will retain the heat and the cream will continue cooking away from the heat.

When the correct temperature has been reached, remove the pot from the heat, lift out the vanilla bean, and stir in the butter and almonds.

Molding the Caramels: First test to see whether the cream has cooked enough.

Fill a small bowl with very cold water. Use an ordinary teaspoon to lift a little cream (about the size of a hazelnut) out of the saucepan; then dip it into the cold water. Leave the spoon in the water for a few seconds; then feel the caramel with your fingers. It will now be the consistency it will be once it has all cooled off. If it seems too soft, cook it a little longer before molding it.

Lightly oil a frame like the one shown in the photo on page 220 picturing fruit jellies; or oil four metal rulers and place the frame or rulers on a sheet of nonstick parchment paper (see photo, page 242) forming a mold 6 × 8 inches (15 × 20 cm); or line a small brownie pan or rectangular dish with parchment paper. Pour the hot caramel into the mold and allow to cool for 1½ hours at room temperature.

If at the end of this time the caramel still seems too soft, scrape it off the parchment paper with a plastic scraper and place it in a clean saucepan. Bring to a boil, stirring constantly—scrape off any caramel that sticks to the sides of the saucepan with a wooden spatula and mix it into the rest of the cooking caramel. Allow the caramel to boil for 2 minutes. Then mold again as described above.

Cutting and Wrapping the Caramels: Lightly oil the working surface as well as a large knife. Lift off the mold or rulers, cutting around the edge of the caramel if necessary to detach it. Turn the parchment paper upside down so that the caramel is resting directly on the oiled working surface and then peel off the paper.

Cut the caramel into bands 4 inches (10 cm) long and about ⅝ inch (1.5 cm) wide. There should be about 20 to 26 strips of caramel. If any caramel sticks to the knife as you are cutting it, scrape it off with a smaller knife. Re-oil the knife whenever necessary.

To wrap the caramels, cut the cellophane squares in half (cellophane squares sold for sealing jam jars are perfect for this). Place a caramel strip toward one edge of the cellophane and roll it up toward the other edge. Twist the ends of the cellophane to seal in the caramel (see photo). The strips can then be unwrapped and cut into squares as needed.

If you prefer, you may simply wrap the entire block of caramel in plastic wrap and cut off little squares of caramel when needed.

To Store: The caramel will keep for 2 weeks in a closed plastic container in the refrigerator.

189
Orange-Flavored Caramels
(Caramels à l'Orange)

(Photo page 242)

PREPARATION	15 minutes
INFUSING TIME	10 minutes
COOKING TIME	15 minutes
COOLING TIME	1½ hours
INGREDIENTS	*For 14 ounces (400 g) caramels*

For the infusion
Generous ½ cup (115 g) granulated sugar
3 tablespoons water
Zest of 1 orange, very finely chopped

For the cream
1 generous cup (250 g) very sweet crème fraîche or heavy
    cream (see Dictionary of Terms)
3 tablespoons (60 g) honey
1 generous cup (235 g) granulated sugar
1 tablespoon (15 g) butter

UTENSILS

Shallow baking dish
Medium saucepan
Straight-edged, wooden spatula
Candy thermometer (optional)
Small bowl
Small saucepan
Ordinary teaspoon
Metal frame, thick metal rulers, small brownie pan, *or*
    rectangular dish 6 x 8 inches (15 x 20 cm)
Nonstick parchment paper
Large knife
Plastic scraper (optional)
20 squares of cellophane 6 inches (15 cm) on a side

Making the Orange Infusion: Place the sugar, water, and chopped orange zest in a small saucepan and bring to a boil. Then remove from the heat, cover the saucepan, and allow to infuse for 10 minutes

304

Cooking the Cream: Place the crème fraîche or heavy cream in a medium saucepan and bring to a boil, stirring constantly. Then add the honey and sugar, bring back to a boil, and boil rapidly, stirring from time to time, for about 5 minutes or until the mixture almost reaches the Soft Ball stage (see page 204), 239°F (115°C). Stir in the orange infusion, making sure that the little pieces of zest are mixed into the cream evenly.

Bring the contents of the saucepan back to a boil. Boil rapidly for 8 to 10 minutes or until the cream reaches the Hard Ball stage (page 205), 257°F (125°C). If using a very heavy-bottomed saucepan, cook the cream to only 253°F (123°C).

Remove the saucepan from the heat and stir in the butter.

To Mold, Cut, Wrap, and Store the Caramels: Follow the directions given in Recipe 188 for Vanilla-Flavored Caramels.

190
Coffee-Flavored Caramels (Caramels au Café)

PREPARATION	10 minutes
COOKING TIME	9 to 10 minutes
COOLING TIME	1½ hours
INGREDIENTS	*For 14 ounces (400 g) of caramels* 1 generous cup (250 g) very sweet crème fraîche or heavy cream (see Dictionary of Terms) 1¼ cup (250 g) granulated sugar ⅓ cup (100 g) honey ¾ teaspoon coffee extract *or* 1½ teaspoons instant coffee dissolved in 1½ teaspoons hot water 1 tablespoon (15 g) butter
UTENSILS	Shallow baking dish Medium saucepan Straight-edged, wooden spatula Candy thermometer (optional) Small bowl Ordinary teaspoon Metal frame, thick metal rulers, small brownie pan, *or* rectangular dish 6 x 8 inches (15 x 20 cm) Nonstick parchment paper Large knife Plastic scraper (optional) 20 squares of cellophane 6 inches (15 cm) on a side

Cooking the Cream: Place the cream in a medium saucepan and bring to a boil. Then add the sugar and honey, bring back to a boil, and boil rapidly, stirring from time to time, for 9 to 10 minutes or until the mixture reaches the Hard Ball stage (see page 205), 257°F (125°C). If using a very heavy-bottomed saucepan, cook to only 253°F (123°C).

Remove the saucepan from the heat, stir in the coffee extract or instant coffee mixture, and add the butter.

To Mold, Cut, Wrap, and Store the Caramels: Follow the directions given in Recipe 188 for Vanilla-Flavored Caramels.

191

Chocolate-Flavored Caramels (Caramels au Chocolat)

(Photo page 242)

PREPARATION	10 minutes
COOKING TIME	8 minutes
COOLING TIME	1½ hours
INGREDIENTS	*For 1 pound 5 ounces (600 g) caramels* 1 generous cup (250 g) very sweet crème fraîche or heavy cream (see Dictionary of Terms) 7 ounces (200 g) semi-sweet chocolate, cut into pieces 1¼ cup (250 g) granulated sugar ⅓ cup (100 g) honey 1 tablespoon (15 g) butter
UTENSILS	Shallow baking dish Medium saucepan Straight-edged, wooden spatula Candy thermometer (optional) Small bowl Ordinary teaspoon Metal frame, thick metal rulers, small brownie pan, *or* rectangular dish 6 x 8 inches (15 x 20 cm) Nonstick parchment paper Large knife Plastic scraper (optional) 20 squares of cellophane 6 inches (15 cm) on a side

Cooking the Cream: Place the crème fraîche or heavy cream in a medium saucepan and bring to a boil. Then add the chocolate, sugar, and honey, bring back to a boil, and boil for 8 minutes or until the Hard Ball stage (see page 205), 257°F (125°C). If using a very heavy-bottomed saucepan, cook to only 253°F (123°C).

While the cream is cooking, stir constantly, and halfway through the cooking time lower the heat and cook at a gentle boil because the chocolate thickens the mixture and it may stick to the bottom of the saucepan.

When the correct temperature is reached, remove the pot from the heat and stir in the butter.

To Mold, Cut, Wrap, and Store the Caramels: Follow the directions given in Recipe 188 for Vanilla-Flavored Caramels.

192

Florentines (Florentins de Megève)

(Photo page 259)

PREPARATION	30 minutes
COOKING TIME	15 minutes
COOLING TIME	3 hours
COATING TIME	10 minutes
INGREDIENTS	*For 20 to 30 florentines*
	Generous ½ cup (100 g) strips of Half-Candied Orange Peel (Recipe 167)
	¼ cup (40 g) whole candied cherries
	Generous ⅔ cup (160 g) crème fraîche or heavy cream (see Dictionary of Terms)
	Generous ⅔ cup (150 g) granulated sugar
	8 teaspoons (50 g) honey
	1 generous cup (100 g) slivered almonds
	For the coating
	7 ounces (200 g) semi-sweet chocolate
UTENSILS	Baking sheet
	Nonstick parchment paper (optional)
	20 to 30 metal tartlet rings, 2⅜ to 3⅛ inches (6 to 8 cm) in diameter (see Note)
	Medium saucepan
	Ordinary tablespoon
	Glass *or* small bowl
	Wooden spoon *or* spatula
	Flexible-blade, metal spatula
	Sheet of plastic *or* flat, plastic boxtop

Preliminary Preparations: Preheat the oven to 350°F (175°C).

Lightly oil the baking sheet or line it with nonstick parchment paper. Butter the tartlet circles and arrange them on the baking sheet. The baking sheet should be perfectly flat—if it is warped, the almond mixture will run out under the tartlet circles when baking.

Coarsely chop the strips of orange peel and the candied cherries.

Making the Almond Mixture: In a medium saucepan, place the cream, sugar, and honey. Bring to a boil and cook at a rapid boil stirring constantly, for about 3 minutes or until the Firm Ball stage (see page 205), 244°F (118°C) is reached.

Stir in the chopped orange peel and cherries as well as the slivered almonds and remove the saucepan from the heat.

Baking the Almond Mixture: Place a generous tablespoon of the almond mixture in each tartlet circle if using the 3⅛ inch (8 cm) size or a level tablespoon of the mixture if using the 2⅜ inch (6 cm) size.

Fill a glass or small bowl with cold water, dip an ordinary tablespoon into it, then flatten the mounds of almond mixture with the wet spoon. Since the mixture will spread out while baking, it is not necessary to spread it around evenly in the rings; simply press out the mound in the middle. The almond mixture should be soft for filling the rings. If it starts to cool and harden too much, reheat it to soften it again.

Place the baking sheet in the oven and bake the florentines for 10 to 11 minutes. As soon as they come from the oven, remove the tartlet rings using a pot holder, and press on the florentine with the back of the spoon to keep it from lifting off the baking sheet as you lift off the ring. Allow the florentines to cool completely on the baking sheet.

The florentines should be allowed to cool for at least 3 hours before being coated with chocolate. If desired, they may be placed in a tightly closed box in a cool, dry place (not in the refrigerator) for several days before coating them.

Coating the Florentines. Melt the chocolate as described in the recipe for Chocolate Coating (Recipe 193).

Cover two baking sheets with sheets of plastic or use plastic box tops or other firm support in nontoxic plastic.

Using a flexible-blade, metal spatula, spread a layer of chocolate over the smooth (bottom) side of each florentine; then turn it over and place it, chocolate-side down, on the plastic. Press it down firmly to eliminate any air pockets; the chocolate will thus be spread evenly over the bottom of the florentine and will be shiny when dry.

Place the florentines, still on the sheet of plastic, in the refrigerator to cool them off for 10 minutes—but no longer—otherwise they will begin to absorb humidity from the refrigerator and become soft and sticky.

To Store: Remove the florentines from the refrigerator and separate them from the sheet of plastic. Place them in a metal or plastic box that closes tightly and store them in a cool, dry place (not in the refrigerator). They will keep for 2 weeks.

Note: The exact size of the rings is not important, but rings without bottoms, not tartlet pans, *must* be used.

Chapter 8

CHOCOLATES

RECIPES

193. Chocolate Coating (Enrobage au Chocolat)   ♟

194. Fondant (Fondant Neutre—Utilisation)   ♟

195. Duja (Duja)   ♟

196. Nut Brittle Powder or Paste (Praliné-Noisettes ou Praliné-Amandes)   ♟

197. Nougatine and Nougatine Crumble (Nougatine et Craquelin Nougatine)   ♟ ♟ ♟

198. Lenôtre's (Dry Cooked) Caramel (Caramel Cuit à Sec)   ♟ ♟

199. Fruit-Flavored Fondant Candies (Boules de Fondant au Coulis de Fruit)   ♟

200. Black Currant Fondant Candies (Boules de Fondant au Cassis)   ♟

201. Chocolate Cherries (Cerises au Chocolat)   ♟ ♟

202. Chocolate Raspberries (Framboises au Chocolat)   ♟ ♟

203. Chocolate Thistles (Chardons Surprise)   ♟ ♟ ♟

204. Oriental Dates (Dattes Orientales)   ♟

205. Walnut Wonders (Noix Merveilleuses)   ♟ ♟

206. Lutetia Pistacios (Pistaches de Lutèce)   ♟

207. Eiffel Towers (Tours Eiffel)   ♟

208. Jura Chocolates (Boules du Jura)   ♟

209. Harlequin Duja (Duja Arlequin)

210. Riviera Duja (Duja Côte d'Azur)

211. Paris Delights (Finesses de Paris)

212. Chocolate Almonds (Amandes au Chocolat)

213. Hazelnut Squares (Carrés Noisettes)

214. Charlies (Charlies)

215. Nut Brittle Boulders (Rochers Pralinés)

216. Mocha Pleasures (Plaisirs Moka)

217. Tea Pleasures (Plaisirs Thé)

218. Sultans (Sultans)

219. Norman-Style Chocolate Truffles (Truffes Normandes)

220. Trianons (Trianons)

221. Calvados-Flavored Chocolate Truffles (Truffes au Calvados)

222. Caramel-Flavored Chocolate Truffles (Truffes au Caramel)

223. Cusenier Chocolate Truffles (Truffes au Cusenier)

224. Shiny Chocolate Truffles (Truffes Brillantes)

225. Ardeche-Style Truffles (Truffes de l'Ardèche)

226. Gatines-Style Chocolate Truffles (Truffes des Gatines)

227. Lenôtre Truffles (Truffes Maison)

GENERAL COMMENTS ON MAKING CHOCOLATES

As with making candies in general, making chocolates is easy, and children can participate in almost all stages of their preparation, including decorating them. The only preparations that children should not do are those involving the cooking of sugar, which are dangerous because of the extremely high temperatures and the risk of being burned.

UTENSILS

(*Photo page xix*)

You must have either several double boilers or else a number of stainless steel mixing bowls of different sizes that can be set into saucepans over hot water to make a *bain-marie.*

A yoghurt thermometer is needed to control the temperature when melting chocolate or fondant.

A food processor or electric blender is needed for making nut brittle powder and paste, duja, and other similar preparations. Although either appliance can be used, the food processor is preferable.

A pliable plastic or rubber scraper is very useful in scraping melted chocolate, fondant, and various creams from saucepans, bowls, or jars so that there is no waste.

A pastry bag is indispensable for making certain soft chocolates; make sure that you have a large selection of nozzles ranging from 1/16 to ¾ inch (2 mm to 2 cm) in diameter as well as a relatively small, star-shaped nozzle.

As with candies, chocolates are often served in individual paper cases. In most cases, ordinary ones made of white pleated paper are fine, but when making certain chocolate truffles in which the truffle cream is squeezed from a pastry bag directly into the paper cases, it is best to use those made of brown parchment paper.

Nonstick parchment paper is often called for, so be sure to have plenty on hand.

A large selection of containers with covers, such as the type in which cottage cheese comes, are useful for storing basic ingredients such as duja, nut brittle powder, and so on. For partially finished or finished chocolates, however, plastic or glass containers that can be hermetically sealed should be used.

Although a freezer is not necessary for making chocolates, it saves a great deal of time because basic preparations can be cooled three times as fast in the freezer as in the refrigerator.

Basic Ingredients

Chocolate: Only the best-quality chocolate should be used in making these recipes, so it is a good idea to try several different brands, taste them, and melt them to make sure that they don't become grainy when used in cooking. The differences in price among different brands are often justified.

Two basic kinds of chocolate are called for in this book: semi-sweet (dark) chocolate and milk chocolate. In fact, professionals use a special kind of chocolate called "covering chocolate" for dipping and making chocolate coating. This chocolate contains a very high percent of cocoa butter, which means that the finished chocolates are very shiny. Unfortunately, it is much too difficult to use in home candy making since it must be melted, worked, and then hardened several times before finally being melted and held at a constant temperature— between 86 and 90°F (30 to 32°C)—during the actual coating process.

I have found that using semi-sweet chocolate combined with a little cooking oil or shortening, which is very easy to use, gives results that are not quite as spectacular as those of professionals but are nevertheless very satisfying.

Milk chocolate has a very different composition from semi-sweet chocolate because the milk has replaced some of the cocoa, but it can be used exactly like semi-sweet chocolate for making chocolate centers as well as for dipping and making chocolate coating. The choice of one or the other is simply a matter of taste.

Other Ingredients: Crème fraîche or heavy cream is used in many recipes. Great care must be taken, especially in making chocolate truffles, to use only cream which is very fresh and sweet, not acid. Otherwise, the taste will be affected and the cream will curdle when cooked.

Fondant is also an important basic ingredient. It can either be bought in specialty stores or made at home (see Recipe 194). In either case, its consistency can vary considerably, so when adding liquid to it, it is a good idea to add a little less than the amount indicated in the recipe and test it. If it is not liquid enough for the recipe in question, add a little more liquid, but keep in mind that it is better for it be a little too firm than a little too liquid because it is very difficult to make it thicker again once it is too thin.

Note: In order to reduce the amount of time spent in making the chocolates in this book, their size is slightly larger than those I make professionally; in fact, they can be made three times larger than the size indicated here. In this case, use a ¾-inch (2-cm) nozzle on the pastry bag [the size indicated in the recipes is generally closer to ½ inch (1.2 cm)] and use large individual paper cases (# 10).

314

193
Chocolate Coating (Enrobage au Chocolat)
(Photo page 277)

This chocolate coating is not as shiny nor as thin as that made by professionals (see General Comments on Making Chocolates, page 313). Nevertheless, it is perfectly adapted for home use and permits the making of a great variety of homemade chocolate candies.

PREPARATION   5 minutes

COOKING TIME   10 minutes

COOLING TIME   30 minutes

INGREDIENTS   *For coating 10 to 50 chocolates*
                           7 ounces (200 g) semi-sweet chocolate
                               or 7 ounces (200 g) milk chocolate
                           2 tablespoons tasteless cooking oil, cocoa butter, *or*
                               melted vegetable shortening

UTENSILS   Small, metal, mixing bowl and small saucepan (*bain-
                               marie*)
                               or double boiler
                           Wooden spoon *or* spatula
                           Yoghurt thermometer
                           Dish towel (optional)
                           Fork
                           Sheet of plastic *or* nonstick parchment paper
                           Knife

Recommendations: If the chocolate coating is made with cooking oil, it will be easier to work with than if it is made with cocoa butter or vegetable shortening.

Also, since the chocolate can be melted and reused several times, you can plan to make a large number of chocolates—double or triple the measurements given here. It won't go bad, and will make it easier later. After coating each batch of candies but before putting the chocolate away, be sure to clean the inside edges of the mixing bowl or double boiler with a plastic scraper.

Melting the Chocolate: Place a little water in a small saucepan or the bottom of a double boiler; then set a mixing bowl in the saucepan to make a *bain-marie* or put the top half of the double boiler in place. The water should not touch the bottom of the bowl or double boiler.

Bring the water to a boil; then remove the *bain-marie* or double boiler from the heat. Break the chocolate into pieces, and place the pieces of chocolate and the oil, cocoa butter, or shortening in the bowl or double boiler. Cover and allow to melt for 2 minutes. Then stir with a wooden spoon or spatula. If there are any hard pieces of chocolate left, cover and wait until all of them have melted completely, stirring occasionally.

Do not leave the *bain-marie* or double boiler on the heat. The water might boil, and although the chocolate will melt faster, it will dry out too much, get too hot, and not make as nice a coating.

Another very important point: Do not let even one drop of water get into the chocolate or it will harden immediately and be completely useless.

Coating the Candies: Check the temperature of the chocolate with a yoghurt thermometer—it should be no more than 90°F (32°C) when used for coating. Allow to cool if necessary.

If it is not too hot, the chocolate may be left over the hot water. It is easier to coat the candies, however, if the top of the double boiler or the mixing bowl is set at a tilt by placing a folded dish towel under one edge of it on the table. The chocolate may be warmed, if necessary, by placing it back over the hot water from time to time.

Drop a candy into the melted chocolate, turn it over with a fork to coat all sides, and then lift it out by placing the fork under it. As you lift it out of the chocolate, make a gentle up and down movement with your wrist so that the excess chocolate on the candy will be pulled back into the chocolate still in the bowl or double boiler. Lightly scrape the bottom of the fork against the edge of the pot or bowl so that the chocolate won't drip; then slide the candy onto a sheet of plastic or nonstick parchment paper with the tip of a knife.

Allow the candies to cool for 30 minutes in the refrigerator before serving.

To Store: The chocolate used for coating will keep for a week in the refrigerator, left simply in the bowl or double boiler in which it was melted.

As for the candies, they will keep for various lengths of time, depending on their ingredients (see specific recipes).

Note: Any leftover chocolate coating may be molded in a lightly oiled mold or container and eaten like a chocolate bar.

194

Fondant (Fondant Neutre)

(Photo page 157)

Fondant is used in making a number of chocolates and a few candies. It is used as it is or diluted slightly with a liquid, the amount of which varies, depending on the consistency of the fondant.

PREPARATION   15 minutes including cooling time

COOKING TIME   5 to 10 minutes

INGREDIENTS   *For 1½ cups tightly packed (550 g) plain fondant*
                     2½ cups (500 g) granulated sugar
                     1 generous cup (½ l) water
                     ½ teaspoon lemon juice

UTENSILS   Saucepan
                     Candy thermometer (optional)
                     Marble table top, slab *or* large, flat porcelain platter
                     Wooden spatula
                     Metal spatula
                     Glass jar with cover

Making the Fondant: Place the sugar, water, and lemon juice in a saucepan, bring to a boil, and boil rapidly until the syrup reaches the Soft Ball stage (see page 204), 234°F (112°C). This takes about 5 to 10 minutes.

Pour the syrup onto a clean, cool surface, preferably marble—if you have neither a marble table top nor a marble slab, a porcelain platter may be used instead.

Allow the syrup to cool for 1 minute. Then begin working it with a wooden spatula in a back and forth or figure eight motion. Scrape the edges toward the center from time to time, working the entire surface of the melted sugar. It will slowly turn white and be more difficult to work. After about 15 minutes, when it is completely opaque and begins to look mat and somewhat pasty in texture as the spatula is pulled through it, the fondant is ready. Scrape it up from the table with a metal spatula and pack it into a glass jar.

To Store: Fondant will keep indefinitely in a tightly closed glass jar in the refrigerator or other cool place.

How To Use Fondant (Fondant Neutre—Utilisation)

PREPARATION	10 minutes
COOKING TIME	10 minutes
COOLING TIME	1 hour

INGREDIENTS	*For 25 to 30 candies*
	About ½ jar or ¾ cup tightly packed (275 g) Fondant
	1 to 3 tablespoons water,
	    or 28°Sugar Syrup (Recipe 1)
	    or alcohol,
	    or pureed fruit

UTENSILS	Small saucepan and mixing bowl (*bain-marie*) *or* double boiler Wooden spoon *or* spatula Yoghurt thermometer 30 individual paper cases

Preparing the Fondant: Place the jar of fondant in a small saucepan or in the bottom of a double boiler and fill the pot with water until it comes to within 1 inch (2.5 cm) of the top of the jar. Remove the jar from the pot and bring the water to a boil. Then remove the pot from the heat, place the jar of fondant in the hot water, and leave there for 5 minutes to soften it and make it easier to remove from the jar.

Using a wooden spoon or spatula, remove the fondant from the jar and place it in the mixing bowl or the top half of the double boiler. If desired, the fondant may be measured before placing it in the bowl or double boiler, but an approximate amount is sufficient for using it as described here.

Set the mixing bowl over the hot water in the saucepan to make a *bain-marie* or set the top of the double boiler in place. Place over low heat, and as soon as the fondant is warm, add the liquid called for in the specific recipe being followed. Stir in the liquid until a homogenous mixture is formed; then heat the fondant until it reaches 140°F (60°C) or the temperature indicated in the specific recipe if it differs from this. Remove the *bain-marie* or double boiler from the heat (see photo, page 157).

Making the Candies: Arrange the paper cases on a platter. Pour the hot fondant—140°F (60°C)—from the bowl or double boiler or use a spoon to fill the paper cases. Make sure the fondant lands in the middle of the cases, otherwise they tend to tip. The fondant will harden on cooling.

In certain recipes, such as Chocolate Raspberries (Recipe 202), the paper cases are first lined with a layer of chocolate. In this case allow the fondant to cool to 86°F (30°C) before pouring it into the cases.

To Store: The finished candies will keep in the refrigerator for a week.

195
Duja (Duja)
(Photo page 278)

PREPARATION	25 minutes
COOKING TIME	15 minutes
COOLING TIME	15 minutes
INGREDIENTS	*For 4 cups (560 g) of duja* 1 cup (150 g) blanched, whole almonds 1 cup (150 g) shelled hazelnuts 1 cup (150 g) confectioner's sugar
UTENSILS	Roasting pan *or* shallow baking dish Drum sieve *or* ordinary sieve Food processor *or* electric blender Mixing bowl Wooden spoon *or* spatula

Preliminary Preparations: Preheat the oven to 350°F (175°C).

Place the almonds and hazelnuts in a roasting pan or shallow baking dish and roast them in the oven for 15 minutes. Watch the nuts carefully; they should turn golden but not brown because if they color too much they will have a burnt taste.

When the nuts have colored sufficiently, remove them from the oven and rub the hot hazelnuts on a drum sieve or in an ordinary sieve to remove their skins. Allow the almonds and hazelnuts to cool for 15 minutes.

Making the Duja: In the food processor or electric blender, place about 20 almonds, 20 hazelnuts, and 2 generous tablespoons of confectioner's sugar. Grind or blend—in a few seconds the mixture will become powdery and then perhaps somewhat pasty, depending on the amount of oil contained in the nuts. Empty this first batch into a mixing bowl.

Repeat the operation as many times as is necessary to use up all the nuts. Any leftover confectioner's sugar should be stirred into the mixture in the mixing bowl and a wooden spoon or spatula. The finished duja will be a powdery mixture (see photo).

To Store: The duja will keep for 2 to 3 weeks in a tightly closed container in the refrigerator.

To Freeze: The duja can also be placed in a plastic bag, which is then tightly closed and placed in the freezer. It will keep for 3 months. Before using it, however, be sure to let it thaw out for 24 hours in the refrigerator.

Uses: Duja is used in making Riviera Duja (Recipe 210), Paris Finesses (Recipe 211), Harlequin Duja (Recipe 209), Jura Chocolates (Recipe 208), and Lenôtre Truffles (Recipe 227).

196

Nut Brittle Powder or Paste
(Praliné-Noisettes ou Praliné-Amandes)

(Photo page 340)

PREPARATION	15 minutes
COOKING TIME	20 minutes
COOLING TIME	1 hour
INGREDIENTS	*For 5 cups (750 g) powdered nut brittle or 2½ cups (750 g) nut brittle paste* 3⅓ cups (500 g) shelled almonds *or* hazelnuts 2½ cups (500 g) granulated sugar Generous ½ cup (12.5 c*l*) water
UTENSILS	Shallow baking dish (if using hazelnuts) Drum sieve, ordinary sieve, *or* dish towel (if using hazelnuts) Saucepan Candy thermometer Wooden spoon *or* spatula Baking sheet Nonstick parchment paper (optional) Food processor *or* electric blender Jars with lids

Cooking the Nut Brittle: If using hazelnuts, preheat the oven to 350°F (175°C).

Warm the hazelnuts by placing them in a shallow baking dish and placing them in the oven for 7 minutes. At the end of this time, take them from the oven and remove their skins by rubbing them on the mesh of a drum sieve or an ordinary sieve or by wrapping them in a clean dish towel and rubbing them vigorously together.

If you are using almonds, this first step can be omitted.

Place the sugar and water in a large saucepan and boil until the sugar reaches the Firm Ball stage, 248°F (120°C) (see page 205). This takes about 5 to 10 minutes. Add the nuts and remove the pot from the heat. With a wooden spoon or spatula, slowly stir the mixture until the sugar has a grainy, sandy appearance. Put the saucepan back over medium heat for about 10 to 15 minutes to melt the sugar again, constantly stirring and scraping the bottom of the saucepan to keep the sugar from sticking. Cook until the sugar is a dark caramel color.

Pour the mixture out onto a baking sheet which has been lightly oiled or lined with nonstick parchment paper. Allow to cool for 1 hour; then break the nut brittle into small pieces.

Grinding the Nut Brittle: Place the pieces of nut brittle in a food processor or blender and grind them. Depending on how long it is ground, the nut brittle will become grainy or will be transformed into a paste. It can be used in any of the four following forms, each representing a grinding time longer than the one before it:

1) Coarsely ground: for decorating various candies and cakes.
2) Finely ground: for use in ice creams and various dessert creams.
3) Grainy paste: for filling chocolates with firm centers.
4) Soft creamy paste: for filling chocolates with soft, almost liquid, centers.

The coarsely ground and finely ground types are in fact produced with the same amount of grinding. It takes only a few seconds of grinding to transform the pieces of nut brittle into a powder, but there are inevitably some relatively large pieces left in it. To separate these large pieces (those used in decorating) from the finely ground powdered nut brittle, simply empty the contents of the food processor or blender into a bowl and shake the bowl gently. The large pieces will come to the top and can be removed with a spoon.

To Store: Place the coarsely ground and finely ground nut brittles in tightly closed jars as soon as they are ready. They will keep for 3 months in a dry place.

Allow the nut brittle pastes to cool for 12 hours before placing in tightly covered jars. They will keep for 3 months in the refrigerator. If the nut brittle paste is to be mixed with melted chocolate, be sure to remove it from the refrigerator and leave it at room temperature for 12 hours before using it, otherwise the mixture will harden immediately.

Uses: Nut Brittle Powder can be used with Vanilla Ice Cream (Recipe 27), Nut Brittle Ice Cream (Recipe 38), Snowball (Recipe 75), and Ice Cream on a Stick (Recipe 96).

Nut Brittle Paste can be used with Hazelnut Squares (Recipe 213), Chocolate Almonds (Recipe 212), Charlies (Recipe 214), Nut Brittle Boulders (Recipe 215), and Lenôtre Truffles (Recipe 227).

197

Nougatine and Nougatine Crumble
(Nougatine et Craquelin Nougatine)

(Photo page 298)

This is a difficult preparation which calls for a certain amount of strength on the part of the person making it if it is to be flattened properly. In fact, professionals use a special roller (a laminoir) made of solid iron, which is very heavy. Here an ordinary rolling pin is used, so you must press on it very hard and lean on it; for this reason the nougatine is rolled out in small quantities at a time. Be sure that you have all the utensils ready to use before starting this recipe.

PREPARATION	45 minutes
COOKING TIME	15 minutes
COOLING TIME	15 minutes

INGREDIENTS

For 20 small circles 1½ inches (4 cm) in diameter, 40 squares ¾ inch (2 cm) on a side, and approximately 1¼ cups (220 g) of nougatine crumble
1 cup (150 g) chopped almonds

For Lenôtre's Caramel
1¾ cups (350 g) granulated sugar
10 drops lemon juice

UTENSILS

To roll out and cut the nougatine
Putty knife
2 baking sheets
Rolling pin
Large knife
Round cookie cutter 1½ inches (4 cm) in diameter

Other utensils
Roasting pan *or* shallow baking dish
Bowl
Small, heavy-bottomed saucepan
Straight-edged, wooden spatula
Mortar and pestle *or* food processor

Preliminary Preparations: Preheat the oven to 350°F (175°C).

Oil all the utensils to be used in rolling out and cutting the nougatine, including the baking sheets and rolling pin, because the warm nougatine is very sticky.

Place the chopped almonds in a roasting pan or shallow baking dish and place them in the oven for 6 minutes or until they turn a pale, gold color. Then remove them from the oven, place them in a bowl, and turn the oven down to 300°F (150°C).

Cooking the Nougatine: Make a light-colored Lenôtre's Caramel following the directions given in Recipe 198. It is very important not to let the caramel color too much. If the sugar sticks to the wooden spoon or spatula too much, use another one—do not scrape the sugar off the first one.

When the caramel has been made, remove the saucepan from the heat and stir in the roasted almonds. Then immediately pour the mixture onto one of the oiled baking sheets.

Rolling out the Nougatine: Spread the caramel–almond mixture in an even layer over the baking sheet with the putty knife—it should be about ⅜ inch (1 cm) thick. Then place it in the oven with the door ajar. The nougatine should remain soft in order to roll it out correctly.

Using the putty knife, detach a quarter of the nougatine from the rest, place it on the other, cold, oiled, baking sheet, place it on the working surface, and immediately begin rolling it out. Place both hands on the cylindrical part of the rolling pin. Lean on it with all your weight, pressing and rolling in quick little jerks to flatten the nougatine. After being rolled out, the nougatine should be very thin (see photo).

Cutting the Nougatine: The flattened nougatine should be cut into shapes very quickly. First, cut out 10 little squares with the oiled knife; the squares should be approximately ¾ inch (2 cm) on a side.

Then, using the oiled cookie cutter, cut out as many circles as possible, tapping the cutter hard with the rolling pin in order to cut the nougatine.

The nougatine cools and hardens very quickly. Separate the squares and circles from the scraps and place the scraps back in the oven to soften again.

Using the putty knife, detach a second quarter of the nougatine from the rest that is still in the oven; then close the oven door and repeat the rolling out and cutting processes as described above. Do the same with the third and fourth quarters and with the scraps which will have softened again until you have cut out 40 squares and 20 circles.

Making the Nougatine Crumble: After all the squares and circles have been made, use what is leftover to make the nougatine crumble. Simply take all the hardened scraps and grind them coarsely using a mortar and pestle or a food processor.

Separate the large pieces of nougatine crumble from the small ones by placing all of the ground crumble in a bowl and shaking the bowl gently. The large pieces will come to the surface and can be scooped out with a spoon.

The large pieces of nougatine crumble are used for decorating various chocolates and the small ones for chocolate fillings and ice creams. There will be a little more than ½ cup (100 g) of large crumble and about ⅔ cup (120 g) of small crumble.

To Store: The nougatine will keep for 1 month in a tightly closed container in a dry place (the nougatine crumble can be stored in a tightly closed jar). Since any humidity will make the nougatine sticky, it should be placed in the container as soon as it is cool and hard and kept in a cool dry place, not in the refrigerator.

Note: If you have a plate warmer which can be kept very warm but not hot enough to melt the nougatine completely, it can be used to keep the nougatine soft, rather than placing the nougatine in the oven.

198
Lenôtre's (Dry-Cooked) Caramel (Caramel Cuit à Sec)

Although this is not really a difficult recipe, it has been given two chef's hats be-cause this caramel, cooked without water, must be watched very carefully in order to keep the sugar from burning. This kind of caramel is indispensable in making Caramel Ice Cream, Disneyland Peanut Brittle, Nougatine, and Caramel-Flavored Chocolate Truffles.

PREPARATION	10 minutes
COOKING TIME	20 to 25 minutes
COOLING TIME	Variable, depending on the utilization of the caramel
INGREDIENTS	1 cup (200 g) granulated sugar 10 drops lemon juice
UTENSILS	Small, heavy-bottomed saucepan Straight-edged, wooden spatula

Making the Caramel: Place the saucepan over low heat and add a quarter of the sugar. Stir constantly, scraping the edge of the spatula against the bottom of the saucepan. At first the sugar will become very grainy, and then it will slowly begin to melt.

When this first quarter has melted completely, add the second quarter of sugar. It will get very lumpy at first, but these lumps will melt. When all the lumps have completely melted, add the third quarter of the sugar and proceed exactly as described above, finally adding the fourth quarter when the third has completely melted.

It is very important not to add any new sugar until all the lumps from the pre-vious batch have completely disappeared. It takes about 5 minutes for each ad-dition of sugar to melt.

When all the sugar has melted, add the lemon juice. Remove the caramel from the heat as soon as the desired color is reached; just after all the sugar has melted, it will be a rich, golden, cinnamon color, but depending on the recipe either this relatively light color or a deep mahagony, reddish color will be called for. Do not let the caramel get too dark, however, as this will give it a burnt taste.

Note: Although this is done over low heat, it does not have to be too low. The essential thing is that the caramel be cooked over a small flame and that the flame must never go beyond the edges of the saucepan or it will burn the sugar stuck to the sides of the pot.

If the sugar piles up on one side and looks as if it is going to harden there, tip that side of the pot toward the flame until it melts, stirring constantly.

199

Fruit-Flavored Fondant Candies
(Boules de Fondant au Coulis de Fruit)

PREPARATION	20 minutes
COOKING TIME	10 minutes
COOLING TIME	1 hour
INGREDIENTS	*For 25 to 30 candies* About ½ jar or ¾ cup tightly packed (275 g) Fondant (Recipe 194) ⅓ cup (50 g) cleaned raspberries, strawberries, red currants, *or* black currants 3½ ounces (100 g) semi-sweet chocolate 2 teaspoons tasteless cooking oil
UTENSILS	Yoghurt thermometer Small strainer Wooden spoon *or* spatula Ordinary teaspoon 2 mixing bowls and saucepans (*bain-marie*) *or* 2 double boilers 30 individual paper cases Platter

Preliminary Preparations: Heat the fondant as described in the How to Use Fondant (page 319). As it becomes warm, place the fruit in a small strainer over the fondant and rub it through the strainer directly into the fondant, which will color and become more liquid. Stir the fondant until the color becomes uniform; then heat it to 140°F (60°C). At first the fondant will be pale in color and opaque. Then, as the correct temperature is reached, it will darken in color and become transparent.

Melt the chocolate and add the oil to it as described in Recipe 193 for Chocolate Coating.

Open the paper cases and place them on a patter.

Making the Candies: When the fondant and chocolate are ready, fill each little paper case with about 2 teaspoons of flavored fondant—the case should be ¾ full. Then cover the fondant in each case with about a teaspoon of melted chocolate, which should come to the edge of the case. Lift the edge of the platter with a light tapping motion to make sure the chocolate spreads out evenly over the candies.

Place the candies in the refrigerator and allow to cool for at least 1 hour before serving.

To Store: These candies will keep for 1 week in a tightly closed box in the refrigerator.

Note: The fruit creams are also delicious just as they are without the chocolate covering.

200
Black Currant Fondant Candies
(Boules de Fondant au Cassis)

PREPARATION	20 minutes
COOKING TIME	10 minutes
COOLING TIME	1 hour
INGREDIENTS	*For 25 to 30 candies* About ½ jar or ¾ cup tightly packed (275 g) Fondant (Recipe 194) 4 teaspoons Black Currant Liqueur (Recipe 128—see Note) 3½ ounces (100 g) semi-sweet chocolate 2 teaspoons tasteless cooking oil
UTENSILS	Wooden spoon *or* spatula Yoghurt thermometer 2 mixing bowls and saucepans (*bain-marie*) *or* 2 double boilers Platter 30 individual paper cases

Preliminary Preparations: Open the paper cases and place them on a platter.

Heat the fondant and add the liqueur to make it more liquid, as indicated in How to Use Fondant (page 319).

At first the fondant will be opaque, but as it reaches the correct temperature, it will darken in color and become transparent.

Melt the chocolate and add the cooking oil, as indicated in Recipe 193 for Chocolate Coating.

Making the Candies: When the fondant and chocolate are ready, fill each little paper case with about 2 teaspoons of flavored fondant; each case should be three-quarters' full. Then cover each candy with about 1 teaspoon of melted chocolate so that the cases are filled to the brim. Lift the edge of the platter containing the candies, and with a light tapping motion, make the chocolate spread evenly over the candies.

Place the finished candies in the refrigerator to cool for at least 1 hour before serving.

To Store: These candies will keep for 1 week in a tightly closed box in the refrigerator.

Note: This recipe can be varied by using other fruit liqueurs such as cherry, raspberry, and so on, in place of the Black Currant Liqueur.

For children, the fondant may be flavored with fruit syrups or other flavored syrups, such as grenadine, mint, or aniseed.

201

Chocolate Cherries (Cerises au Chocolat)

(Photo page 157)

It is best to allow these candies to rest for a week before eating them so that the alcohol in the cherries has time to dissolve the fondant.

PREPARATION	40 minutes
COOKING TIME	15 minutes
RESTING TIME	24 hours to 1 week
INGREDIENTS	*For 40 to 50 cherries* 40 to 50 Brandied Cherries (Recipe 126) About ½ jar or ¾ cup tightly packed (275 g) Fondant (Recipe 194) 4 teaspoons alcohol from the cherries *For chocolate coating* 9 ounces (250 g) semi-sweet chocolate 1 tablespoon tasteless cooking oil
UTENSILS	2 small saucepans and mixing bowls (*bains-marie*) *or* 2 double boilers Wooden spoon *or* spatula Yoghurt thermometer Dish towel Fork Grill *or* cake rack Shallow baking dish Sheet of plastic *or* nonstick parchment paper Knife Clean dish towel 50 individual paper cases Platter

Preliminary Preparations: The cherries should be at least 2 months' old. Drain them on a grill or cake rack placed over a shallow baking dish.

Heat the fondant and add the alcohol from the cherries to make it more liquid, as described in How to Use Fondant (page 319). Heat the fondant to between 149°F and 158°F (65 to 70°C) so that it will be liquid enough to dip the cherries into.

While the fondant is heating, place the cherries on a clean dish towel and pat them dry. Be careful not to pull their stems off.

Open the paper cases and place them on a platter.

Dipping the Cherries: Holding each cherry by the stem, dip it into the fondant, being careful to leave a small, uncoated ring around the stem (see photo). Lift the cherry out of the fondant, scraping it lightly against the edge of the mixing bowl or double boiler to keep the fondant from dripping, and place it on the nonstick parchment paper. The cherries will dry and harden in a few minutes.

If necessary, reheat the fondant, stirring as it heats, and add a little more alcohol if it begins to stiffen while dipping the cherries.

If the cherries you are using have no stems, follow the directions given in Recipe 202 for Chocolate Raspberries.

Coating the Cherries: Melt the chocolate and add the cooking oil as described in Recipe 193 for Chocolate Coating.

Dip each fondant-coated cherry into the chocolate—move it very gently up and down in the chocolate to prevent air bubbles from forming. The chocolate should come up to the stem. Lift the cherry out of the chocolate, but do not scrape it against the edge of the bowl or double boiler; the extra chocolate will help seal the candy better.

Place each chocolate-coated cherry in a paper case as soon as it is lifted out of the chocolate.

Place the finished candies in the refrigerator to harden for 24 hours. Then check the chocolate coating—if there are no holes in it, keep the cherries for a week before eating them—if there are holes in the chocolate, eat them as quickly as possible because they will not keep.

To Store: If the cherries are well coated, they will keep for 2 weeks in a tightly closed box in the refrigerator.

202
Chocolate Raspberries (Framboises au Chocolat)
(Photo page 157)

PREPARATION	40 minutes
COOKING TIME	15 minutes
COOLING TIME	45 minutes
RESTING TIME	24 hours to 1 week
INGREDIENTS	*For 45 to 50 raspberries* 45 to 50 Brandied Raspberries (Recipe 127) 12¼ ounces (350 g) semi-sweet chocolate About ½ jar or ¾ cup tightly packed (275 g) Fondant (Recipe 194) 2 tablespoons alcohol from the raspberries
UTENSILS	2 small saucepans and mixing bowls (*bains-marie*) *or* 2 double boilers Wooden spoon *or* spatula Yoghurt thermometer Dish towel Fork Sheet of plastic *or* nonstick parchment paper Knife Grill *or* cake rack Shallow baking dish 50 individual paper cases Platter Pastry brush

Preliminary Preparations: Open the paper cases and place them on a platter.

The raspberries should be at least 2 months' old. Pick the smallest ones and drain them on a grill or cake rack placed over a shallow baking dish.

Melt the chocolate according to the directions given in Recipe 193 for Chocolate Coating. With a pastry brush generously coat the paper cases with a layer of chocolate on the bottom and sides (see photo). Place the chocolate-coated cases in the refrigerator for 30 minutes to harden.

Making the Candies: Remove the chocolate-coated cases from the refrigerator and place a raspberry in each one. If the raspberries are large and come up more than three-quarters of the way up the paper case, cut them in half and place them cut side down in the cases (in this case you will need only 25 raspberries).

333

Heat the fondant as described in How to Use Fondant (page 319), but do not let it heat past 86°F (30°C). Stir in the alcohol—if necessary add a little more than indicated; the fondant should be liquid enough at this low temperature to be poured easily from a spoon into the paper cases.

Fill each paper case with the fondant, almost covering the raspberries but not quite (see photo). There should still be room in the case to cover the raspberries with a layer of chocolate.

Place the candies in the refrigerator for 15 minutes when the fondant has been added to all of them.

Reheat the chocolate if necessary to bring it back to 86°F (30°C) as described in Recipe 193. Place about 1 teaspoon of melted chocolate in each paper case— the cases should then be filled to the brim. Lift the edge of the platter with a light tapping motion to make the chocolate spread evenly over the candies.

Place the finished candies in the refrigerator for 24 hours. At the end of this time, check the chocolate covering—if there are any holes in it, eat the candies as soon as possible because they will not save. If there are no holes in the chocolate, save the candies for 1 week before eating them—like chocolate cherries (Recipe 201), they are even better if allowed to sit.

To Store: If the chocolate coating is perfect, these candies will keep for 2 weeks in a tightly closed box in the refrigerator.

203

Chocolate Thistles (Chardons Surprise)

(Photo page 300)

PREPARATION	30 minutes
COOKING TIME	5 minutes
COOLING TIME	40 minutes to 2 hours
INGREDIENTS	*For 50 to 60 candies*
	1 generous cup tightly packed (320 g) white or green Almond Paste (Recipe 171)
	Confectioner's sugar or potato starch to sprinkle work surface
	2 tablespoons 28° Sugar Syrup (Recipe 1) *or* 1 tablespoon granulated sugar dissolved in 1 tablespoon hot water
	For chocolate coating
	7 ounces (200 g) semi-sweet chocolate
	Unsweetened cocoa powder (optional)
	For truffle cream
	¼ cup (60 g) crème fraîche or heavy cream (see Dictionary of Terms)
	5¼ ounces (150 g) semi-sweet chocolate
UTENSILS	Mixing bowl and small saucepan (*bain-marie*) *or* double boiler
	Rolling pin
	Ruler
	Pastry bag with ⅝-inch (1.5-cm) nozzle
	Pastry brush
	Knife
	60 individual paper cases
	Platter

Making the Rolls: Make the truffle cream according to the directions given on page 259. Set aside and allow to cool, as described, while you roll out the almond paste.

Sprinkle the work surface with confectioner's sugar or potato starch. Then roll out the Almond Paste into a rectangle 8 by 12 inches (20 by 30 cm). Trim the edges to make them square and divide the rectangle lengthwise into three bands, approximately 2½ inches (6 cm) wide each.

335

When the truffle cream has cooled to the proper temperature, fill the pastry bag with it and press out a long sausage of truffle cream about a third of the way in from one edge of each band of almond paste (see photo).

With a pastry brush, moisten the almond paste on both sides of each "sausage" with the sugar syrup.

Starting from the edge furthest away from the "sausage," roll the almond paste over the truffle cream pressing the second edge lightly over the first to make it stick (see photo); then turn the finished roll over so that the seam is on the bottom.

Place the three finished rolls in the refrigerator for 1 hour or in the freezer for 20 minutes.

Coating the Rolls and Cutting: Melt the chocolate in a *bain-marie* or double boiler as described in Recipe 193 for Chocolate Coating—make sure the chocolate does not heat past 95°F (35°C).

Remove the rolls from the refrigerator and, using a pastry brush, paint them with the chocolate, starting on the bottom side and tapping lightly with the brush to make little spikes like those on a thistle. While the chocolate is still soft, a little unsweetened cocoa powder may be sprinkled over it.

When coating the rolls, the chocolate may begin to cool too much; if this happens and it begins to harden on the brush, simply heat it until it reaches 90°F (32°C) again, leaving the brush in it so that the chocolate on it will melt as well.

When the rolls are all coated with chocolate, place them in the refrigerator for 10 to 15 minutes or until the chocolate has hardened completely.

While the rolls are cooling, arrange the paper cases on a platter.

When the chocolate coating is hard, remove the rolls from the refrigerator and cut them into slices about ⅝ inch (1.5 cm) thick with a sharp knife that has been dipped into hot water and wiped dry. Place each slice in a paper case and keep the chocolate thistles in the refrigerator until ready to serve.

To Store: The finished chocolate thistles will keep for 2 weeks in a tightly closed box in the refrigerator.

Assorted Truffles: Mocha Pleasures, Recipe 216; Sultans, Recipe 218; Cusenier Chocolate Truffles, Recipe 223; Caramel-Flavored Chocolate Truffles, Recipe 222; Ardeche-Style Truffles, Recipe 225; Gatines-Style Chocolate Truffles, Recipe 226; Calvados-Flavored Chocolate Truffles, Recipe 221; Lenôtre Truffles, Recipe 227

204

Oriental Dates (Dattes Orientales)

PREPARATION	20 minutes
COOKING TIME	10 minutes
COOLING TIME	30 minutes to 2 hours
INGREDIENTS	*For 40 to 50 dates* 1⅓ cups (400 g) Date Paste (Recipe 173) 2 teaspoons aniseed-flavored liqueur Cornstarch or potato starch to sprinkle work surface *For chocolate coating* 9 ounces (250 g) bitter chocolate 4½ teaspoons walnut or peanut oil Approximately ⅓ cup (50 g) confectioner's sugar
UTENSILS	Mixing bowl 2 wooden spoons *or* spatulas Nonstick parchment paper Ruler Knife Mixing bowl and small saucepan (*bain-marie*) *or* small double boiler Shallow dish *or* soup plate Fork 40 or 50 individual paper cases

Forming the Dates: In a mixing bowl place the Date Paste and stir in the aniseed liqueur with a wooden spoon or spatula.

Sprinkle the work surface with cornstarch or potato starch. Place a sheet of nonstick parchment paper on a platter.

Divide the flavored Date Paste into two equal parts; then roll each one into a slightly flattened sausage shape on the work surface; each sausage should be about ¾ inch (2 cm) thick.

Form each slice into the shape of a date and place them all on the parchment paper. Then place the platter of "dates" in the freezer for 30 minutes or in the refrigerator for 2 hours.

Coating the Dates: Melt the chocolate and add the walnut oil as describe in Recipe 193 for Chocolate Coating. Place the confectioner's sugar in a shallow dish or soup plate.

338

Remove the dates from the freezer or refrigerator. Place a little melted chocolate in the palm of your hand and roll a date in it to cover it with a very thin coating of chocolate. Then place it in the confectioners's sugar, and using a fork, gently roll the date in the sugar.

Place the finished dates in individual paper cases and place in the refrigerator until ready to serve.

To Store: The dates will keep for 2 weeks in a tightly closed box in the refrigerator.

If not eaten immediately, it is best to keep them in confectioner's sugar and to place them in the paper cases only when ready to serve them.

205
Walnut Wonders (Noix Merveilleuses)
(Photo page 320)

PREPARATION	30 minutes
COOKING TIME	5 minutes
COOLING TIME	1½ hours
INGREDIENTS	*For 40 to 50 candies* Cornstarch or potato starch to sprinkle over work surface 1 scant cup tightly packed (250 g) Walnut–Almond Paste (Recipe 172) ½ cup tightly packed (175 g) Fondant (Recipe 194) 2 teaspoons water 40 to 50 walnut meats *For chocolate coating* 9 ounces (250 g) semi-sweet chocolate 4½ teaspoons walnut (or peanut oil) *or* vegetable shortening
UTENSILS	Ruler Knife Grill or cake rack 2 mixing bowls and saucepans (*bains-marie*) *or* 2 double boilers Yoghurt thermometer 2 platters Ordinary teaspoon Fork Nonstick parchment paper

Preliminary Preparations: Lightly sprinkle the work surface with cornstarch or potato starch. Divide the Walnut–Almond Paste into two equal parts and use your hands to roll each one into a slightly flattened sausage shape ¾ inch (2 cm) thick. Cut each "sausage" into slices ⅜ to ½ inch (1 to 1.2 cm) thick.

Put these slices on a grill or cake rack and place in the freezer for 30 minutes or in the refrigerator for 2 hours.

Making the Candies: In a *bain-marie* or double boiler, heat the fondant and dilute it with the water as described in How to Use Fondant (page 319). Do not let it heat past 86°F (30°C).

Nut Brittle Paste, Recipe 196; Chocolate Almonds, Recipe 212;
Nut Brittle Boulders, Recipe 215

Remove the grill with the walnut–almond slices from the refrigerator and place it over a shallow dish or platter. With an ordinary teaspoon, spoon enough fondant over each slice to coat the top and sides; if the fondant is not liquid enough to do this, stir in a little water. The fondant that drips off the candies can be mixed back in with the fondant in the *bain-marie* or double boiler.

As each slice is coated with fondant, place a walnut meat on it—this must be done while the fondant is still soft. When all the candies have been coated, allow them to drain and harden for 30 minutes.

Melt the chocolate and add the oil or shortening as described in Recipe 193 for Chocolate Coating.

Place a sheet of nonstick parchment paper on a platter.

When the candies have finished draining, place each one on a fork and dip it delicately into the melted chocolate. Only the bottom and sides should be coated with the chocolate—the top should stay white (see photo). The simplest way to do this is to dip first one end of the candy into the chocolate, then, holding the walnut between your thumb and index finger, gently turn the candy around and dip the other end into the chocolate. Do not hold the candy by the sides as the fondant will melt when you touch it.

When all the candies have been dipped in the chocolate, place them in the refrigerator for at least 1 hour before serving.

To Store: Walnut wonders will keep for 2 weeks in a tightly closed box in the refrigerator.

206

Lutetia Pistacios (Pistaches de Lutèce)

(Photo page 320)

PREPARATION	30 minutes
COOKING TIME	5 minutes
COOLING TIME	1½ hours
INGREDIENTS	*For 40 to 50 candies* ⅓ cup (50 g) shelled, unsalted pistacios 1 scant cup (250 g) Walnut–Almond Paste (Recipe 172) 4 teaspoons kirsch Cornstarch or potato starch (optional) *For chocolate coating* 7 ounces (200 g) white chocolate 4½ teaspoons tasteless cooking oil
UTENSILS	Nut chopper, food processor, *or* blender Mixing bowl Wooden spatula *or* spoon Pastry bag with ⅝-inch (1.5-cm) nozzle (optional) Small baking sheet *or* platter Nonstick parchment paper Small mixing bowl and saucepan (*bain-marie*) *or* double boiler Ordinary teaspoon and tablespoon Fork 50 individual paper cases

Forming the Candies: Coarsely chop the pistacios using a nut chopper, food processor, or blender. Place the Walnut–Almond Paste in a mixing bowl and stir in the chopped pistacios and the kirsch with a wooden spoon or spatula.

Place a sheet of parchment paper on a baking sheet or platter and stick the corners down with a little of the pistacio mixture.

If the pistacio mixture is very soft, place it in a pastry bag and squeeze out little mounds onto the parchment paper.

If the mixture is firm enough, sprinkle a little cornstarch or potato starch over the working surface, divide the pistacio mixture into two equal parts, and roll each one into a long sausage shape about ¾ inch (2 cm) thick. Cut the sausage into slices about ⅜ to ½ inch (1 to 1.2 cm) thick, form the slices into little balls, and place them on the parchment paper.

Place the pistacio balls in the freezer for 20 minutes or in the refrigerator for 1 hour.

Coating the Candies: Melt the white chocolate in a *bain-marie* or double boiler and add the oil exactly as in Recipe 193 for Chocolate Coating. Do not let the temperature rise above 86°F (30°C).

Place a little of the melted chocolate in an ordinary tablespoon and roll a pistacio ball in it. Place the coated ball on the parchment paper. Coat 5 balls this way. Then, starting with the first one again, roll them all in the white chocolate a second time. Just after each one receives its second coating, tap it with a fork to make the chocolate stick up in little points (see photo).

Continue coating the candies this way, 5 at a time. Then place them in the refrigerator for at least 30 minutes before placing them in individual paper cases and serving.

To Store: Lutetia pistacios will keep for 2 weeks in a tightly closed box in the refrigerator.

207
Eiffel Towers (Tours Eiffel)
(Photo page 277)

PREPARATION 20 to 30 minutes

COOKING TIME 10 minutes

COOLING TIME 15 minutes

INGREDIENTS

For 40 to 50 candies
1 cup (160 g) shelled hazelnuts
⅓ cup (70 g) granulated sugar
4½ teaspoons water
½ a vanilla bean, split in half lengthwise

For Chocolate coating
7 ounces (200 g) semi-sweet chocolate
4½ teaspoons tasteless cooking oil

UTENSILS

Baking sheet
Drum sieve, fine mesh strainer, *or* clean dish towel
Platter
Nonstick parchment paper
Small saucepan
Straight-edged, wooden spatula
Small mixing bowl and saucepan *(bain-marie)* or double
    boiler
Wooden spoon *or* spatula
Yoghurt thermometer
Fork
Knife

Preliminary Preparations: Preheat the oven to 370°F (175°C).

Place the hazelnuts on a baking sheet and roast in the oven for 7 minutes. Then to remove their skins, rub the nuts against the mesh of a drum sieve or fine mesh strainer or wrap them in a clean dish towel and rub them together vigorously. Leave the oven on for later use.

Remove the baking sheet from the oven and oil it lightly.

Place a sheet of nonstick parchment paper on a platter or on a second baking sheet. This is for placing the finished candies on.

Making the Candies: In the saucepan, place the sugar, water, and vanilla bean. Bring to a boil and boil rapidly uncovered for 3 minutes or until the syrup reaches the Firm Ball stage (see page 205), 244°F (118°C)

Remove the saucepan from the heat and add the hazelnuts. Stir gently with a straight-edged, wooden spatula—the mixture will become grainy and look somewhat like sand. This takes about 30 seconds to a minute.

Place the saucepan back over moderate heat, stirring constantly. Gradually the sugar will begin to melt again and caramelize. Roll the nuts around in the sugar to coat them, and scrape off any sugar that sticks to the spatula against the sides of the saucepan. Do not allow the mixture to smoke—lower the heat if necessary. When the nuts are done they will be coated lightly with caramel and make a dry clicking sound as they hit each other.

Pour the coated nuts out onto the oiled baking sheet. Oil your fingers and stick 3 nuts together, then place a fourth one on top of them, forming a little pyramid (see photo). Place the finished "towers" on the parchment paper.

During the time it takes to form the candies, the ones left on the baking sheet may dry and harden, so place the baking sheet back in the oven from time to time, to keep the caramel soft and sticky.

Allow the finished candies to cool for 15 minutes at room temperature (not in the refrigerator).

Coating the Candies: Melt the chocolate, add the oil, and dip the candies into it to coat them as described in Recipe 193 for Chocolate Coating. Place the finished chocolates in the refrigerator for 15 minutes to harden the chocolate before serving.

To Store: The chocolate-coated Eiffel Towers will keep for 2 weeks in a tightly closed box in the refrigerator. The candies may be eaten without being coated with chocolate. In this case they will keep for 2 weeks in a tightly closed box in a dry place. Do not place them in the refrigerator or the caramel will absorb humidity and become sticky.

208

Jura Chocolates (Boules du Jura)

PREPARATION	20 minutes
COOKING TIME	10 minutes
COOLING TIME	20 minutes
INGREDIENTS	*For 50 to 60 candies* 3½ ounces (100 g) semi-sweet chocolate 1¾ cups (250 g) Duja (Recipe 195) *For coating* 7 ounces (200 g) semi-sweet chocolate 4½ teaspoons tasteless cooking oil Generous ½ cup (100 g) large Nougatine Crumble (Recipe 197)
UTENSILS	Small mixing bowl and saucepan (*bain-marie*) *or* double boiler Large mixing bowl Pastry bag with ½-inch (1.2-cm) nozzle *or* 2 ordinary teaspoons Baking sheet Nonstick parchment paper Soup bowl 60 individual paper cases

Forming the Candies: In a *bain-marie* or double boiler, melt 3½ ounces (100 g) of chocolate as described in Recipe 193 for Chocolate Coating.

Place the Duja in a large mixing bowl and add the melted chocolate. The mixture should be quite firm—if too soft, place it in the refrigerator for 10 minutes.

Line a baking sheet with a sheet of parchment paper; then fill the pastry bag with the Duja–chocolate mixture and form 50 to 60 little mounds about the size of a walnut on the parchment paper. If you prefer, you can make the mounds by taking a teaspoon of the mixture on one spoon and scraping it off onto the parchment with a second teaspoon.

Place the mounds in the refrigerator for 20 minutes.

Coating the Candies: Pour the nougatine crumble into a soup bowl.

Melt the chocolate for coating and add the oil as described in Recipe 193 for Chocolate Coating.

Rapidly form the little mounds of candy into balls between the palms of your hands. Dip each one into the chocolate to coat it as described on page 316.

Then, while the chocolate is still soft, roll the candy in the Nougatine Crumble. Place the finished candies in individual paper cases.

To Store: Jura chocolates will keep for 2 weeks in a tightly closed box in the refrigerator.

209
Harlequin Duja (Duja Arlequin)
(Photo page 278)

PREPARATION	30 minutes
COOKING TIME	20 minutes
COOLING TIME	2 hours
INGREDIENTS	*For 70 to 80 candies* 3½ ounces (100 g) milk chocolate 3 cups (400 g) Duja (Recipe 195) 3½ ounces (100 g) semi-sweet chocolate Generous ¼ cup (50 g) large Nougatine Crumble (Recipe 197) *For chocolate coating* 5¼ ounces (150 g) semi-sweet chocolate 2 teaspoons tasteless cooking oil
UTENSILS	Metal frame or small brownie pan 6½ × 8 inches (16 × 20 cm) Baking sheet Nonstick parchment paper Small mixing bowl and saucepan (*bain-marie*) *or* double boiler Wooden spoon *or* spatula Plastic scraper Flexible-blade, metal spatula Large sharp knife 80 individual paper cases

Molding the Candy: Place a sheet of nonstick parchment paper on a baking sheet and place the metal frame on top of it, or line a small brownie pan with the parchment paper.

In a *bain-marie* or double boiler, melt the milk chocolate; then add a scant 1½ cups (200 g) of Duja to it. Mix together with a wooden spoon or spatula.

Pour the mixture into the metal frame or brownie pan. Even out the surface with a plastic scraper. Then place in the refrigerator for 30 minutes.

In the same *bain-marie* or double boiler, melt the semi-sweet chocolate, add the remaining scant 1½ cups (200 g) of Duja, mix well together, and pour the mixture over the first, hardened layer in the mold.

While this second layer is still soft, sprinkle the Nougatine Crumble over half of it—use a flexible-blade, metal spatula to form a barrier across the middle and prevent the crumble from getting on the other half.

Place in the refrigerator for 1 hour to harden.

Cutting the Candies: The photo shows clearly the two different layers of this candy, as well as the finished, cut candies. The top half of the metal frame shows the candy that has not been sprinkled with Nougatine Crumble—the recipe was doubled for making this photo.

When the molded candy has completely hardened, slide the blade of a knife around the edges of the mold; then lift off the mold. If a brownie pan was lined with paper, carefully lift the paper out of the pan with the candy on it and set it down on the table.

Cut the candy, both the part with the crumble and that without it, into bands ¾ inch (2 cm) wide; then cut the bands into squares or trapezoids.

Place the candies covered with the crumble in individual paper cases.

Melt the semi-sweet chocolate for the coating, add the oil, and coat the remaining, uncovered candies, with the chocolate as described in Recipe 193 for Chocolate Coating. When coated, place these candies in individual paper cases as well and serve.

To Store: Harlequin Duja will keep for 2 weeks in a tightly closed box in the refrigerator.

Note: It is not absolutely necessary to coat the uncovered candies with chocolate. They may be eaten as they are if preferred.

210

Riviera Duja (Duja Côte d'Azur)

PREPARATION	30 minutes
COOKING TIME	10 minutes
COOLING TIME	30 minutes
INGREDIENTS	*For 50 to 60 candies* Generous ⅓ cup (100 g) Half-Candied Orange Slices (Recipe 168) 3½ ounces (100 g) milk chocolate 1¾ cups (250 g) Duja (Recipe 195) *For decoration* 8 ounces (225 g) milk chocolate 5 large pieces (80 g) Half-Candied Orange Peel (Recipe 167)
UTENSILS	Small mixing bowl and saucepan (*bain-marie*) *or* double boiler Medium-sized mixing bowl Wooden spoon *or* spatula 60 individual paper cases Yoghurt thermometer Pastry bag with ¼-inch (6-mm) nozzle Pastry bag with ⅛-inch (3-mm) nozzle *or* cone made with nonstick parchment paper Scissors Baking sheet *or* platter

Making the Candies: Finely chop the Half-Candied Orange Slices, but do not chop them so fine as to make a puree out of them.

In a *bain-marie* or double boiler, melt the milk chocolate. Place the Duja in a mixing bowl and add the melted chocolate to it. Then gently stir in the chopped orange slices with a wooden spoon or spatula. The mixture should be barely warm—no more than 86°F (30°C).

Place the paper cases on a baking sheet or platter. Fill a ¼-inch (6-mm) nozzled pastry bag with the mixture and fill the cases three-quarters' full. If preferred, the mixture can simply be spooned into the paper cases by taking a spoonful of it on one spoon and scraping it into the case with another spoon.

Place the garnished paper cases in the refrigerator for 30 minutes or until the mixture is firm.

Decorating the Candies: Cut each large piece of Half-Candied Orange Peel into 12 lozenges.

In the *bain-marie* or double boiler, melt the chocolate for the decoration. Do not allow it to heat past 86°F (30°C).

Fill a ⅛-inch (3-mm) nozzled pastry bag with melted chocolate or make a paper cone with some nonstick parchment paper. Fill it with the chocolate and cut off the tip. Squeeze just enough chocolate into each paper case to cover the Duja mixture in it. The chocolate can also be spooned into the paper cases.

From time to time, lift the edges of the platter and make a gentle tapping motion to spread the chocolate evenly over the candies.

Place one lozenge of candied peel on top of each candy while the chocolate is still soft; then place in the refrigerator until ready to serve.

To Store: These candies will keep for 2 weeks in a tightly closed box in the refrigerator.

211

Paris Delights (Finesses de Paris)

PREPARATION	20 minutes
COOKING TIME	10 minutes
COOLING TIME	1½ hours
INGREDIENTS	*For 40 candies* 3½ ounces (100 g) milk chocolate 1¾ cups (250 g) Duja (Recipe 195) *For chocolate coating* 7 ounces (200 g) milk chocolate 4½ teaspoons tasteless cooking oil
UTENSILS	Mixing bowl and saucepan (*bain-marie*) *or* double boiler Baking sheet Nonstick parchment paper Wooden spoon *or* spatula Metal frame or small brownie pan 4¾ × 8 inches (12 × 20 cm) Plastic scraper Large, sharp knife 40 individual paper cases

Making and Molding the Candy: Place a sheet of nonstick parchment paper on a baking sheet and place a metal frame on top of it, or line a small brownie pan or other rectangular mold with the paper.

In a *bain-marie* or double boiler, melt the milk chocolate as described on page 315. Add the Duja and stir it in gently with a wooden spoon or spatula. Pour the mixture into the mold and smooth the surface with a plastic scraper.

Place in the refrigerator for 30 minutes.

Cutting and Coating the Candies: When the mixture has hardened, slide the blade of a knife around the edge of the frame and lift it off, or carefully lift the parchment paper out of the brownie mold with the candy on it and set it down on the table. Cut the candy into 8 bands, ⅝ inch (1.5 cm) wide and 8 inches (20 cm) long. Then cut the bands into lozenges.

Do not discard the triangles that are formed at the ends of each band—simply stick them together, two by two, to form lozenges. Place the cut candies back in the refrigerator for 30 minutes.

In a *bain-marie* or double boiler, melt the milk chocolate, add the oil, and coat the lozenges as described in Recipe 193 for Chocolate Coating.

Place the coated candies in the refrigerator for 30 minutes to harden; then place them in individual paper cases to serve.

To Store: These chocolates will keep for 2 weeks in a tightly closed box in the refrigerator.

212

Chocolate Almonds (Amandes au Chocolat)
(Photo page 340)

PREPARATION	15 minutes
COOKING TIME	5 minutes
COOLING TIME	1 hour
INGREDIENTS	*For 50 to 60 chocolates* 1 cup (300 g) Nut Brittle Paste (Recipe 196) 3 ounces (90 g) milk chocolate 60 Caramelized Almonds (Recipe 187)
UTENSILS	Small mixing bowl and saucepan (*bain-marie*) *or* double boiler Wooden spoon *or* spatula Plastic scraper Pastry bag with star-shaped nozzle or ½-inch (1.2-cm) round nozzle Platter *or* baking sheet Nonstick parchment paper 60 individual paper cases

Making the Candies: In a *bain-marie* or double boiler, melt the chocolate as described on page 315.

When the chocolate has melted, add the Nut Brittle Paste, stirring it in with a wooden spoon or spatula. The mixture should be relatively firm in order to hold its shape when squeezed from the pastry bag. If it seems too soft, place it in the refrigerator for about 15 minutes and scrape the mixture from the sides of the bowl with a plastic scraper, more or less forming a ball in the bowl with the mixture.

Place a sheet of nonstick parchment paper on a platter or baking sheet. Fill the pastry bag with the chocolate mixture and squeeze it out into large almond shapes (see photo). Place a Caramelized Almond on top of each one. If the chocolate mixture seems to be softening too much in the pastry bag, form the almond shapes directly in individual paper cases, then decorate them with the Caramelized Almonds.

Place the finished candies in the refrigerator for at least 1 hour before serving. If they were made on the parchment paper, they may either be placed in individual paper cases when hard or simply served on a plate.

To Store: These candies will keep for only 1 week in a tightly closed box in the refrigerator. After that, the Caramelized Almonds begin to soften and taste stale.

213
Hazelnut Squares (Carrés Noisettes)

PREPARATION	20 to 30 minutes
COOKING TIME	10 minutes
COOLING TIME	1½ hours
INGREDIENTS	*For 50 squares* 1 cup (150 g) shelled hazelnuts 3 ounces (90 g) semi-sweet *or* milk chocolate 1 cup (300 g) Hazelnut Brittle Paste (Recipe 196) *For chocolate coating* 7 ounces (200 g) milk chocolate 4½ teaspoons tasteless cooking oil
UTENSILS	Drum sieve, fine mesh strainer, *or* clean dish towel Electric blender, food processor, *or* nut chopper *For method 1* Small frame and baking sheet or brownie pan 4 × 8 inches (10 × 20 cm) Nonstick parchment paper Knife *For method 2* Pastry bag with ½-inch (1.2-cm) nozzle 50 individual paper cases Platter *or* baking sheet

Preliminary Preparations: Preheat the oven to 350°F (175°C).

Place the hazelnuts in the oven for 8 minutes. Then as soon as they come from the oven, rub them against the mesh of a drum sieve or fine mesh strainer, or simply wrap them in a clean dish towel and rub them together vigorously to remove their skins.

Set 50 hazelnuts aside. Finely chop the rest in a blender, food processor, or nut chopper, but do not reduce them to a powder. Place the chopped nuts on a drum sieve or in a strainer to separate them from any powder; there should be approximately ⅓ cup (60 g) of chopped nuts left.

Making the Candies: In a *bain-marie* or double boiler, melt the chocolate for the candy as described on page 315. Stir in the Nut Brittle Paste and then the chopped hazelnuts. The candies can then be formed in either of the following ways.

355

Method 1. *In a Mold:*   Place a sheet of nonstick parchment paper on a baking sheet or platter and place a metal frame (like those used for Fruit Jellies, see photo, page 220) on top of the paper or line a small brownie pan with the paper. Pour the candy mixture into the mold and allow to cool for at least 1 hour. When the mixture has hardened, slide the blade of a knife around the edge of the frame and lift the frame off the candy, or lift the paper with the candy on it carefully out of the brownie pan. Cut the candy into squares approximately ¾ inch (2 cm) on a side.

Melt the chocolate for the Coating, add the oil, and coat the candies as described in Recipe 193 for Chocolate Coating. While the chocolate coating is still soft, decorate each candy with one of the hazelnuts reserved earlier.

Method 2. *In paper cases:*   When made in paper cases, the candies are not coated with chocolate.

If the candy mixture is very soft, let it stiffen for 15 to 30 minutes, then fill a pastry bag with it, and squeeze the mixture into the paper cases arranged on a platter or baking sheet. The mixture may also be spooned into the paper cases, by taking a spoonful of it on one teaspoon and scraping it into the case with a second spoon.

From time to time, lift the edge of the platter or baking sheet and with a gentle tapping motion spread the candy mixture evenly in the cases. Decorate each candy with one of the hazelnuts reserved earlier. Place the finished candies in the refrigerator for at least 1 hour to harden before serving.

To Store: These nut candies will keep for 2 weeks in a tightly closed box in the refrigerator.

Note: Walnut meats may be used instead of hazelnuts. In this case it is not necessary to roast them and remove their skins. Save the nicest nut meats for the decoration.

214
Charlies (Charlies)

PREPARATION	20 minutes
COOKING TIME	5 minutes
COOLING TIME	1 hour
INGREDIENTS	*For 50 candies* 1 generous cup (100 g) slivered almonds 1 cup (300 g) Nut Brittle Paste (Recipe 196) 3 ounces (90 g) milk chocolate
UTENSILS	Baking sheet Small mixing bowl Wooden spoon *or* pestle Spatula Medium-sized mixing bowl and saucepan (*bain-marie*) *or* double boiler Pastry bag with ⅜-inch (1-cm) nozzle 50 individual paper cases

Preliminary Preparations: Preheat the broiler.

Place the slivered almonds on the baking sheet and place them under a medium-heat broiler for a few seconds—watch them carefully so that they don't color too much—they should be a rich, golden brown.

Set aside one-third of the grilled almonds (try to pick out the prettiest ones).

Place the rest of the grilled almonds in a mixing bowl, crush them coarsely with a pestle or wooden spoon, and then add the Nut Brittle Paste. Mix together with a wooden spoon or spatula.

Making the Candies: In a *bain-marie* or double boiler, melt the chocolate; then add it to the nut brittle mixture.

Fill a pastry bag with the mixture and fill 50 paper cases three-quarters' full. Decorate the candies with the grilled almonds reserved earlier.

Place in the refrigerator to harden for at least 1 hour before serving.

To Store: Charlies will keep for 2 weeks in a tightly closed box in the refrigerator.

215

Nut Brittle Boulders (Rochers Pralinés)

(Photo page 340)

PREPARATION	15 minutes
COOKING TIME	10 minutes
COOLING TIME	1 hour
INGREDIENTS	*For 35 boulders* 2 ounces (60 g) milk chocolate 1 cup (300 g) Nut Brittle Paste (hazelnut or almond) (Recipe 196) or 2 generous cups of Duja (Recipe 195) Generous ½ cup (100 g) large Nougatine Crumble (Recipe 197)
UTENSILS	Small mixing bowl and saucepan (*bain-marie*) *or* double boiler Wooden spoon *or* spatula Pastry bag with ⅝-inch (1.5-cm) nozzle Baking sheet Nonstick parchment paper Soup bowl 35 individual paper cases

Making the Candies: In a *bain-marie* or double boiler, melt the chocolate (see page 315). Add the Nut Brittle Paste, stirring it in gently with a wooden spoon or spatula.

Place a sheet of nonstick parchment paper on a baking sheet—stick the corners of the paper down with a little of the chocolate mixture.

Fill the pastry bag with a little of the chocolate mixture.

Fill the pastry bag with the chocolate mixture and squeeze out 35 mounds about the size of a walnut onto the paper. You may simply spoon the mixture onto the paper if you prefer by taking a spoonful of the mixture on one teaspoon and scraping it off onto the paper in a little mound using a second teaspoon. If the mounds spread out a little, that's all right.

Place the baking sheet in the refrigerator for 30 minutes to let the mixture harden; then form each little mound into a ball between the palms of your hands.

Place the Nougatine Crumble in a soup bowl and roll the balls in it to coat them on all sides (see photo). Place the finished candies in the refrigerator for 30 minutes more to harden. Then place in individual paper cases to serve.

To Store: Nut Brittle Boulders will keep for 2 weeks in a tightly closed box in the refrigerator.

ENERAL COMMENTS ON CHOCOLATE TRUFFLES
(Truffes)

The chocolate truffle cream used in the recipes that follow is not hard to make, but its quality depends greatly on the use of only the best ingredients. The cream, especially, should be perfectly fresh and without any acidity which would make it curdle when brought to a boil.

When making chocolate truffles, it is always best to use a yoghurt thermometer to check the temperature of the truffle cream before shaping it. When shaping the chocolates (usually using a pastry bag), it should be between 68 and 77°F (20 to 25°C), or room temperature. The proportion of chocolate to liquid ingredients in the truffle recipes are those I generally use, but for those who prefer either stiffer or creamier truffles, they can simply increase the amount of chocolate or reduce it, respectively; the more chocolate, the stiffer the truffle cream. In any case, the chocolate is generally broken into small pieces and mixed with the other ingredients away from the heat (see specific instructions in the recipes that follow).

Once the chocolate truffles are made, they should be served within a week. Since they are not coated with a hard chocolate coating, they soften very quickly; store them in the refrigerator and take them out just before serving (they should be eaten within 30 minutes of the time they come from the refrigerator).

216
Mocha Pleasures (Plaisirs Moka)
(Photo page 337)

PREPARATION	15 minutes
COOKING TIME	10 minutes
COOLING TIME	30 to 50 minutes

INGREDIENTS	*For 35 truffles*
	6½ tablespoons (100 g) crème fraîche *or* heavy cream
	  (see Dictionary of Terms)
	3 tablespoons milk
	2 teaspoons instant coffee
	7 ounces (200 g) semi-sweet chocolate broken into pieces
	70 sugar coffee beans
	  (see Dictionary of Terms)

UTENSILS	Saucepan with cover Wooden spoon *or* spatula Wire whisk Yoghurt thermometer Pastry bag with ⅛-inch (3-mm) nozzle 35 individual paper cases

Making the Truffle Cream: Place the crème fraîche or heavy cream in a saucepan and bring to a boil stirring constantly. Then add the milk and bring back to a boil. Remove the saucepan from the heat and add the instant coffee and the chocolate. Cover the pot and save for about 3 minutes to allow the chocolate to melt; after that time, use a wooden spoon or spatula to stir the ingredients until a smooth mixture is formed (this should happen easily at this stage). Leave the truffle cream to cool for about 30 to 50 minutes before shaping (see General Comments on Chocolate Truffles, page 359).

Making the Truffles: When the truffle cream is ready, beat it lightly about 20 times with a wire whisk, wait 2 minutes, and then spoon it into a pastry bag fitted with a ⅛-inch (3-mm) nozzle. Squeeze enough truffle cream into each paper case to fill it no more than half way, place a sugar coffee bean in the center of each one, and then finish filling the case with truffle cream, topped with another sugar coffee bean. Then place them in the refrigerator to harden before serving.

To Store: Once hardened, the truffles can be placed in a tightly sealed container and kept for a week in the refrigerator.

217

Tea Pleasures (Plaisirs Thé)

PREPARATION	15 minutes
COOKING TIME	10 minutes
COOLING TIME	1 hour
INGREDIENTS	*For 45 truffles* ⅔ cup (150 g) crème fraiche or heavy cream (see Dictionary of Terms) 2 tablespoons water 5 teaspoons (25 g) butter 1½ tablespoons (10 g) tea 10 ounces (280 g) semi-sweet chocolate, in pieces
UTENSILS	2 saucepans with covers Wooden spoon *or* spatula Strainer Mixing bowl Yoghurt thermometer Pastry bag with a star-shaped nozzle 45 paper cases

Making the Truffle Cream: Place the cream in a saucepan and bring to a boil stirring constantly; then add the water and butter. Keep the mixture boiling and stir in the tea; then cover the pot and remove from the heat. Leave the ingredients to infuse together for 3 minutes (or 5 minutes if you prefer a stronger tea taste). Then pour the contents of the saucepan through a strainer into a mixing bowl, and pour the strained ingredients into a clean saucepan and bring to a boil. Once boiling, remove the saucepan from the heat and immediately add the chocolate. Cover the saucepan and leave for 3 minutes so the chocolate will melt; then stir with a wooden spoon or spatula to form a smooth mixture (this should happen easily at this stage). Leave the truffle cream to cool for about 1 hour before proceeding to shape the truffles (see General Comments on Chocolate Truffles, page 359).

Making the Truffles: Open the paper cases and place them on a platter.
   Once the truffle cream is ready to shape, beat it lightly with a wire whisk about 20 times and wait 2 minutes before spooning it into a pastry bag fitted with a star-shaped nozzle. Squeeze the truffle cream out evenly to fill the paper cases; then place the truffles in the refrigerator to harden.

To Store: Once hardened, the truffles can be kept in a tightly sealed container for 1 week in the refrigerator.

218
Sultans (Sultans)
(Photo page 337)

PREPARATION	15 minutes, one day in advance 15 minutes for the truffle cream
COOLING TIME	Approximately 30 minutes
INGREDIENTS	*For 50 truffles* Scant 1½ cups (3 d*l*) water Scant ½ cup (80 g) raisins 1½ tablespoons rum Generous ½ cup (125 g) crème fraîche or heavy cream (see Dictionary of Terms) 9 ounces (250 g) milk chocolate, broken into pieces
UTENSILS	Small saucepan Small bowl with cover Large saucepan with cover Yoghurt thermometer Wooden spoon *or* spatula Knife Pastry bag with star-shaped nozzle 50 paper cases Platter *or* baking sheet

Preliminary Preparations: The day before making the truffle cream, bring the water to a boil in a saucepan, remove from the heat, and stir in the raisins. Leave the raisins to swell in the water for 15 minutes, then drain completely, and place them in a bowl with the rum. Cover the bowl and leave it at room temperature until the next day.

Making the Truffle Cream: When ready to make the truffle cream, place the crème fraîche or heavy cream in a saucepan and bring to a boil, stirring constantly. Once the cream boils, remove the saucepan from the heat and add the pieces of chocolate. Cover the pot and leave for 3 minutes to allow the chocolate to melt. Then stir the mixture with a wooden spoon or spatula until perfectly smooth (the ingredients should mix easily at this stage). Leave the truffle cream to cool for 30 minutes in the refrigerator before proceeding to shape the chocolates; remove it from the refrigerator at the end of this time so that it won't get too cold (see General Comments on Chocolate Truffles, page 359).

Making the Truffles: Open the paper cases and place them on a platter or baking sheet.

Take about 50 whole raisins and save them for decorating the truffles. Use a knife to chop the remaining raisins; then whisk them into the truffle cream. After whisking, leave the truffle cream at room temperature for 2 minutes. Then spoon it into a pastry bag fitted with a star-shaped nozzle and squeeze out the cream to fill the paper cases. Top each truffle with one of the whole raisins reserved earlier (see photo). Place the chocolates in the refrigerator to harden.

To Store: Once the chocolates have hardened they will keep in a tightly sealed container for 1 week in the refrigerator.

219

Norman-Style Chocolate Truffles (Truffes Normandes)

PREPARATION	15 minutes
COOKING TIME	10 minutes
COOLING TIME	30 minutes

INGREDIENTS

For 40 to 50 truffles or 1 cup (275 g) Norman-Style Truffle Cream
3 tablespoons (50 g) crème fraîche or heavy cream (see Dictionary of Terms)
5 teaspoons (25 g) butter
¼ a vanilla bean, split open lengthwise
¼ cup (50 g) granulated sugar
1 egg yolk
2¾ ounces (80 g) semi-sweet chocolate broken into pieces
2¾ ounces (80 g) milk chocolate broken into pieces

For decoration
50 caramelized hazelnuts

UTENSILS

Large saucepan with cover
Wire whisk
Mixing bowl
Wooden spoon *or* spatula
Baking sheet
Nonstick parchment paper
Yoghurt thermometer
Pastry bag with star-shaped nozzle
50 paper cases

Making the Truffle Cream: Place the crème fraîche or heavy cream in a saucepan and bring to a boil, stirring constantly with a wire whisk. Then add the butter, vanilla bean, and half of the sugar. Continue whisking over the heat until the mixture comes back to a boil; then remove from the heat.

Place the remaining sugar in a mixing bowl with the egg yolk and whisk until the mixture whitens; this will take about 30 seconds, and all the sugar should dissolve. Pour the beaten egg yolk–sugar mixture into the saucepan with the other ingredients, whisking rapidly to combine all the ingredients together. Place the saucepan over medium heat for about 5 seconds, whisking constantly; then remove from the heat. Take out the vanilla bean, add the chocolate, and cover the pot. Leave for 3 minutes to allow the chocolate to melt, and then stir with a wooden spoon or spatula to make a smooth mixture (this should be easy to do at this stage). Leave the cream to cool for 30 minutes in the refrigerator, then remove it so it will not be too cold to form the truffles (see General Comments on Chocolate Truffles, page 359).

Making the Truffles: Cover a baking sheet with a piece of nonstick parchment paper (stick the corners of the paper down with a little of the truffle cream). Spoon the truffle cream into a pastry bag fitted with a star-shaped nozzle and squeeze it out into about 40 to 50 rose-like mounds. Top each little mound with a caramelized hazelnut. Then place the truffles in the refrigerator to harden. Once hard, place each truffle in an individual paper case to serve or store.

To Store: Once hardened, the truffles can be kept in a tightly sealed container for 1 week in the refrigerator.

Uses: The Norman-Style Truffle Cream is also used to make Trianon Chocolate Truffles (Recipe 220) and Wafer Rounds Filled with Truffle Cream (Recipe 116).

220
Trianons (Trianons)

(Photo page 298)

PREPARATION	15 minutes
COOLING TIME	30 minutes for the Norman-Style Truffle Cream
INGREDIENTS	*For 30 trianons* Generous ¾ cups (240 g) Norman-Style Truffle Cream (Recipe 219) 120 squares of Nougatine (Recipe 197)
UTENSILS	Baking sheet Nonstick parchment paper Pastry bag with ⅝-inch (1.5-cm) nozzle

Making the Trianons: Cover a baking sheet with a piece of nonstick parchment paper (stick the corners of the paper down with a little of the truffle cream). Place 30 squares of the Nougatine on the paper. Spoon the truffle cream into a pastry bag fitted with a ⅝-inch (1.5-cm) nozzle and squeeze out a little mound of it onto each nougatine square (see photo). Use the remaining squares to make a "roof" over each little mound of truffle cream, using 3 squares to cover each one (see photo).

Place the finished chocolates in the refrigerator to harden for 15 minutes but no more since the Nougatine will soften and become sticky from the direct exposure to the humidity in the refrigerator.

To Store: After the 15-minute hardening time, place the trianons in a box that can be tightly sealed and store them in the refrigerator; if the box closes very well, they can be kept this way for 1 week.

221

Calvados-Flavored Chocolate Truffles (Truffes au Calvados)

(Photo page 337)

PREPARATION	30 minutes
COOKING TIME	10 minutes
COOLING TIME	30 minutes to 1½ hours
INGREDIENTS	*For 35 truffles* 7 ounces (200 g) milk chocolate 3 tablespoons (50 g) crème fraîche or heavy cream (see Dictionary of Terms) 2½ tablespoons (35 g) granulated sugar 2 tablespoons calvados (see Note) *For decoration (Method 1)* Scant ½ cup (50 g) unsweetened cocoa powder *For decoration (Method 2)* 3½ ounces (100 g) milk chocolate 3½ ounces (100 g) semi-sweet chocolate 2 teaspoons tasteless cooking oil
UTENSILS	2 Mixing bowls and saucepans (*bains-marie*) or 2 double boilers Wooden spoon or spatula Ordinary spoon Mixing bowl Small saucepan Pastry bag with ⅛-inch (3-mm) nozzle (optional) Baking sheet Nonstick parchment paper Vegetable grater with large holes Yoghurt thermometer Dish towel Fork Sheet of plastic *or* nonstick parchment paper Knife 35 paper cases Platter

Making the Truffle Cream: Melt the 7 ounces of milk chocolate to be used in the truffle cream in a *bain-marie* or double boiler as described for Chocolate Coating (page 315).

Place the crème fraîche or heavy cream in a small saucepan, bring to a boil, stir in the granulated sugar, and then pour this mixture onto the melted chocolate, stirring to mix well. The resulting mixture should be perfectly smooth. Stir in the calvados and leave the truffle cream to cool to room temperature (see General Comments on Chocolate Truffles, page 359).

Making the Truffles: There are two ways of making and serving the truffles made with the cream given here.

Method 1.   The first and simplest method is to whisk the cooled truffle cream lightly, then spoon it into a pastry bag fitted with a ⅛-inch (3-mm) nozzle, and squeeze it out into the paper cases. Then dust the surface of each truffle with a little unsweetened cocoa powder.

Method 2.   The second method of shaping the truffles is to leave the truffle cream in the refrigerator to stiffen slightly for 30 minutes so that it can be shaped into balls.

Line a baking sheet with nonstick parchment paper (stick the corners of the paper down with a little of the truffle cream). Then either spoon the truffle cream into a pastry bag fitted with a ⅛-inch (3-mm) nozzle and squeeze it out onto the parchment paper to make about 35 walnut-sized mounds, or take a teaspoon of the cream and scrape it onto the paper with a second teaspoon to form the mounds. Place the baking sheet in the refrigerator to harden the chocolate for 30 to 50 minutes.

Meanwhile, using a vegetable grater with large holes, grate the milk chocolate used for the decoration into a shallow dish or soup plate.

Prepare the chocolate coating using the amounts of semi-sweet chocolate and cooking oil given here but following the directions in Recipe 193 for Chocolate Coating.

Open the paper cases and place them on a platter.

When the mounds of chocolate have hardened, take one from the refrigerator and roll it rapidly between the palms of your hands to form a ball and then quickly dip it in the chocolate as described in Recipe 193 for Chocolate Coating. Lift the truffle out of the chocolate and place it in the plate of chocolate shavings. When five truffles are in the plate, roll them in the shavings using a fork, turning and coating them with shavings on all sides; then lift them out of the shavings and place them in individual paper cases. Continue in this manner until all the truffles have been dipped and coated with shavings.

To Store: The finished truffles will keep for 1 week in a tightly closed box in the refrigerator.

Note: An interesting variation of this recipe can be made with Scotch whiskey instead of calvados. These "Scotch truffles" are made exactly as described here by replacing the calvados with Scotch and using semi-sweet chocolate rather than milk chocolate when making the truffle cream.

222

Caramel-Flavored Chocolate Truffles
(Truffes au Caramel)

(Photo page 337)

PREPARATION	30 minutes
COOKING TIME	10 minutes
COOLING TIME	30 minutes

INGREDIENTS	*For 50 to 60 truffles*
	Scant ⅔ cup (140 g) crème fraîche or heavy cream
	   (see Dictionary of Terms)
	Generous ⅓ cup (9 cl) milk
	½ cup (100 g) granulated sugar
	5¼ ounces (150 g) semi-sweet chocolate, broken into
	   pieces
	3½ ounces (100 g) milk chocolate, broken into pieces
	
	For Lenôtre's Caramel (Recipe 198)
	½ cup (100 g) granulated sugar
	5 drops lemon juice
	
	For decoration
	1 generous cup (100 g) Grilled Slivered Almonds (Recipe
	   118)
	
	or
	Generous ½ cup (100 g) large Nougatine Crumble (Recipe 197)
	Generous ½ cup (50 g) Grilled Slivered Almonds (Recipe
	   118)

UTENSILS	Candy thermometer Saucepan Wooden spoon *or* spatula Wire whisk Pastry bag with a ⅜-inch (1-cm) nozzle 60 to 70 individual paper cases

Making the Truffle Cream: Make the caramel as described in Recipe 198 for Lenôtre's Caramel, using the amounts of sugar and lemon juice listed here. Once the caramel has been made, remove it from the heat and, using a ther-

369

mometer to monitor the temperature, let it cool to 212°F (100°C) while preparing the other ingredients that will be mixed with it.

Place the crème fraîche or heavy cream in a saucepan and bring to a boil stirring constantly. Then add the milk and sugar and bring back to a boil. Once this mixture boils, pour it into the caramel, stirring constantly over low heat to combine all the ingredients. Then remove from the heat and immediately add the chocolate and cover the saucepan. Leave for 3 minutes to allow the chocolate to melt; then stir the mixture with a wooden spoon or spatula to make a smooth cream. Leave the cream to cool for 30 to 50 minutes before shaping the truffles (see General Comments on Chocolate Truffles, page 359).

Making the Truffles: After the cream has been allowed to cool, whisk it gently about 20 times. Then wait 2 minutes and spoon it into a pastry bag fitted with a ⅜-inch (1-cm) nozzle. Squeeze the cream out to fill 60 to 70 paper cases; the top of each truffle can be decorated with either Grilled Slivered Almonds or half of the truffles can be made and decorated as described, but the remaining truffle cream can be mixed with half of the Nougatine Crumble and shaped and decorated with the rest of the Nougatine Crumble (see photo).

To Store: The chocolates can be kept in a tightly sealed container for 1 week in the refrigerator.

370

223

Cusenier Chocolate Truffles (Truffes au Cusenier)
(*Photo page 337*)

PREPARATION   30 minutes

COOKING TIME   10 minutes

COOLING TIME   30 minutes for the truffle cream
                       40 minutes to 1 hour to harden

INGREDIENTS   *For 50 truffles*
                       ½ cup (120 g) crème fraîche or heavy cream
                           (see Dictionary of Terms)
                       10½ ounces (300 g) semi-sweet chocolate, broken into
                           pieces
                       2 tablespoons Cusenier or other orange-flavored liqueur

                       For the Coating
                       7 ounces (200 g) milk chocolate
                       2 teaspoons cooking oil

                       For decoration
                       ⅓ cup (50 g) confectioner's sugar

UTENSILS   Saucepan with cover
                       Wooden spoon or spatula
                       Mixing bowl
                       Yoghurt thermometer
                       Baking sheet
                       Nonstick parchment paper
                       Pastry bag with ⅝-inch (1.5-cm) nozzle
                       Shallow dish *or* soup bowl
                       50 individual paper cases
                       Fork

Making the Truffle Cream: Place the crème fraîche or heavy cream in a saucepan and bring to a boil stirring constantly. Then remove from the heat and immediately add the chocolate. Cover the saucepan and leave for 5 minutes to allow the chocolate to melt. After the time is up, stir the chocolate with a wooden spoon or spatula to make a smooth cream; then pour the mixture into a mixing bowl and stir in the liqueur little by little. Leave the truffle cream to cool in the refrigerator for 30 minutes, removing it from the refrigerator so it will not cool off too much (see General Comments on Chocolate Truffles, page 359).

Making the Truffles: Line a baking sheet with nonstick parchment paper (stick the corners down with a little of the truffle cream). Spoon the cooled truffle cream into a pastry bag fitted with a ⅝-inch (1.5-cm) nozzle, and squeeze it out in long lines on the parchment paper. Place the baking sheet in the refrigerator for 40 minutes to 1 hour to harden the chocolate; then remove from the refrigerator and cut the lines of chocolate into pieces 1¼ inches (3 cm) long. Place the pieces back in the refrigerator while preparing the chocolate coating.

Melt the chocolate for the coating and add the oil as described in Recipe 193 for Chocolate Coating.

Place the confectioner's sugar in a shallow dish or soup bowl.

Open the paper cases and place them on a platter.

When everything is ready for coating the chocolates, remove the chocolates 10 at a time from the refrigerator, leaving the others in the refrigerator while coating the first 10, and so on. Dip a chocolate in the melted chocolate as described in the recipe for Chocolate Coating (page 315), then lift it out, and place in the confectioner's sugar. When 10 of the chocolates have been dipped, roll them in the confectioner's sugar, using a fork, and place them in individual paper cases.

When all the truffles have been coated and decorated, place them in the refrigerator to harden.

To Store: The truffles will keep for 1 week in a tightly sealed container in the refrigerator, although it is best to place them in a little extra confectioner's sugar if keeping them for any length of time.

224

Shiny Chocolate Truffles (Truffes Brillantes)

PREPARATION	30 minutes
COOKING TIME	15 minutes
COOLING TIME	30 minutes
INGREDIENTS	*For 35 truffles* 7 ounces (200 g) semi-sweet chocolate, preferably in bars Generous ⅓ cup (90 g) crème fraîche *or* heavy cream (see Dictionary of Terms) 1 tablespoon (15 g) butter 2 teaspoons Grand Marnier *For decoration* 35 pistacio halves
UTENSILS	Large saucepan with cover Skimmer Strainer *or* colander Knife Wooden spoon *or* spatula 2 mixing bowls Rubber scraper Yoghurt thermometer Wire whisk Pastry bag with ⅛-inch (3mm) nozzle 35 paper cases Platter

Making the Truffle Cream: Bring a large saucepan of water to a boil.

Place the chocolate bars on a skimmer, dip them into the boiling water for 2 to 3 seconds, then lift them out, and drain them in a strainer or colander. (If you don't have chocolate bars, use whole 1 ounce squares.) Cut the chocolate into about 20 pieces. This initial operation (like the use of two mixing bowls in the instructions that follow) is important in order to obtain shiny truffles.

Pour the water out of the saucepan, clean the pot, and place the crème fraîche or heavy cream in it. Bring the cream to a boil stirring constantly, then remove from the heat, add the pieces of chocolate, cover the pot, and leave for 3 minutes to allow the chocolate to melt. After this time, gently heat the pot, stirring its contents to make a smooth mixture; then pour the resulting cream into a mixing bowl. Stir in the butter and Grand Marnier. Then pour the contents of the mixing bowl into another bowl, scraping everything from the sides of the first bowl with a rubber scraper so there will be no waste.

Leave the cream in this second bowl and place in the refrigerator for 20 to 30 minutes to cool, but at the end of this time remove it from the refrigerator so it will not cool too much for shaping the truffles (see General Comments on Chocolate Truffles, page 359).

Making the Truffles: When the cream is at the right temperature, whisk it gently about a dozen times; then spoon it into a pastry bag fitted with a ⅛-inch (3-mm) nozzle. Squeeze the truffle cream out to fill the paper cases and decorate the top of each one with half a pistacio.

Place the chocolates back in the refrigerator to harden.

To Store: Once hardened, the truffles can be kept for 1 week in a tightly sealed container in the refrigerator.

225
Ardeche-Style Truffles
(Truffes de l'Ardèche)
(Photo pages 77 and 337)

PREPARATION	20 minutes
COOKING TIME	5 minutes
COOLING TIME	2½ hours
INGREDIENTS	*For 50 to 60 truffles* ¼ pound (125 g) butter ⅓ cup (125 g) Fondant (Recipe 194) ⅔ cup tightly packed (200 g) chestnut paste (see note) 4½ ounces (125 g) semi-sweet chocolate 3 tablespoons (30 g) unsweetened cocoa powder
UTENSILS	Large mixing bowl Wooden spoon *or* spatula Electric mixer (optional) Mixing bowl and saucepan (*bain-marie*) *or* double boiler Baking sheet Nonstick parchment paper Pastry bag with ½-inch (1.2-cm) nozzle (optional) Shallow dish *or* soup bowl 50 individual paper cases

Making the Truffle Cream: The butter, Fondant, and Chestnut Paste used to make the truffle cream should all be approximately the same consistency. Take them all from the refrigerator at least 30 minutes ahead of time to soften somewhat before mixing.

Place the butter in a mixing bowl and beat with a wooden spoon or electric mixer until soft and creamy. Still beating, add first the Fondant and then the Chestnut Paste (if the paste is too stiff, beat it first in another bowl to soften it to the consistency of the butter).

Melt the chocolate in a *bain-marie* or double boiler as described in Recipe 193 for Chocolate Coating. Add the melted chocolate to the other ingredients and mix to combine well. If the mixture is too soft to hold its shape, place it in the refrigerator to stiffen for about 30 minutes before shaping. Be sure to scrape the sides of the bowl clean to prevent a crust of cream from forming on them, and cover the bowl before putting it in the refrigerator.

Making the Truffles: Cover a baking sheet with nonstick parchment paper (stick the corners down with a little of the truffle cream).

Spoon the cream into a pastry bag fitted with a ½-inch (1.2-cm) nozzle, and squeeze out about 50 walnut-sized mounds onto the paper. The cream may also simply be spooned onto the paper by taking a spoonful of it on one spoon and scraping it off in a little mound with a second spoon.

Place the chocolates in the refrigerator to harden for about 2 hours or place them in the freezer for 30 minutes.

Place the unsweetened cocoa powder in a shallow dish or soup bowl. Then roll each truffle lightly in it and roll it rapidly between the palms of your hands to form a ball. Roll each finished truffle in the cocoa powder once more before placing it in an individual paper case. Because these truffles soften very quickly, it is best to remove only 10 of them from the refrigerator at a time when forming them.

To Store:　These truffles can be kept in a tightly sealed container with a little extra cocoa powder for 1 week in the refrigerator.

Note:　Chestnut paste (*pâte de marrons*) is available at some specialty shops, imported from France. It is *not* the same as Chestnut Cream (crème de marrons); it is stiffer and denser. Chestnut Cream can nevertheless be used in making these truffles by changing the measurements as follows: Use ⅔ cup (200 g) Chestnut Cream but reduce the amount of butter indicated in the recipe by 5 teaspoons (25 g) and increase the amount of Fondant by 1 tablespoon (25 g).

226

Gatines-Style Chocolate Truffles
(Truffes des Gatines)

(Photo page 337)

PREPARATION	15 minutes
COOKING TIME	5 minutes
COOLING TIME	30 to 50 minutes
INGREDIENTS	*For 40 to 50 truffles* 6½ tablespoons (100 g) crème fraîche or heavy cream 　(see Dictionary of Terms) 1½ tablespoons (25 g) honey 1½ tablespoons sweetened condensed milk 5¼ ounces (150 g) milk chocolate, broken into pieces 5¼ ounces (150 g) semi-sweet chocolate, broken into 　pieces *For decoration* 5¼ ounces (150 g) semi-sweet chocolate (for cases) *Either* ½ cup (100 g) diced Half-Candied Pineapple Slices (Recipe 166) *Or* ½ cup (50 g) chopped walnuts 50 walnut meats
UTENSILS	Saucepan with cover Wooden spoon *or* spatula Mixing bowl and saucepan (*bain-marie*) *or* double boiler Pastry brush Pastry bag with ¼-inch (6-mm) *or* ⅜-inch (1 cm) nozzle 50 paper cases Platter

Making the Truffle Cream: Place the creme fraîche or heavy cream in a saucepan and bring to a boil stirring constantly. Then add the honey and condensed milk and bring back to a boil. Remove from the heat, immediately add the pieces of chocolate, and cover the pot. Leave for 3 minutes to allow the chocolate to melt. Then stir with a wooden spoon or spatula until perfectly smooth (the ingredients should mix easily at this stage). Leave the cream to cool for 30 to 50 minutes before shaping (see General Comments on Chocolate Truffles, page 359).

Making the Truffles: The chocolates can be decorated and garnished with either Half-Candied Pineapple Slices or with walnuts. In any case, before making them, melt 5¼ ounces (150 g) of semi-sweet chocolate in a *bain-marie* or double boiler.

Open the paper cases and place them on a platter. Then, using a pastry brush, coat the inside of each paper case with a thin film of chocolate.

To Garnish and Decorate with Pineapple: Whisk the truffle cream a few times. Then spoon it into a pastry bag fitted with a ¼-inch (6-mm) nozzle and squeeze it out to half fill each of the paper cases. Place a piece of pineapple in the middle of each chocolate, finish filling the paper cases with truffle cream, and then place another piece of pineapple on top to decorate. Place the truffles in the refrigerator to harden.

To Garnish and Decorate with Walnuts: Mix the chopped nuts into the truffle cream. Then spoon the cream into a pastry bag with a ⅜-inch (1-cm) nozzle and squeeze it into the paper cases to fill them. Place a walnut meat on top of each chocolate and place in the refrigerator to harden.

To Store: Once hardened, the truffles can be kept for a week in a tightly sealed container in the refrigerator.

227

Lenôtre Truffles (Truffes Maison)

(Photo page 337)

PREPARATION	15 minutes
COOKING TIME	5 minutes
COOLING TIME	30 minutes
INGREDIENTS	*For 40 to 50 truffles* 6½ tablespoons (100 g) butter ⅓ cup (120 g) Fondant (Recipe 194) Generous ¾ cup (10 g) Duja (Recipe 195) *or* generous ⅓ cup (120 g) Almond Brittle Paste (Recipe 196) 5½ ounces (150 g) semi-sweet chocolate *For coating* 3 tablespoons (30 g) unsweetened cocoa powder
UTENSILS	Large mixing bowl Wooden spoon *or* spatula Mixing bowl and sauce (*bain-marie*) *or* double boiler Rubber scraper Baking sheet Nonstick parchment paper Pastry bag with ⅝-inch (1.5-cm) nozzle (optional) 50 paper cases Platter Shallow dish *or* soup bowl

Making the Truffle Cream: Take the butter and Fondant from the refrigerator to soften for an hour at room temperature. Beat them together in a bowl using a wooden spoon or spatula, then sprinkle in the Duja or Almond Brittle Paste, and mix well.

Melt the chocolate in a *bain-marie* or double boiler as described in Recipe 193 for Chocolate Coating. Then pour it into the bowl with the other ingredients (scrape the sides of the bowl or double boiler with a rubber scraper to make sure there is no waste). Stir well to combine the ingredients; then leave to cool for 30 minutes in the refrigerator but no longer than that so the cream will not be too stiff for shaping (see General Comments on Chocolate Truffles; page 359).

Making the Truffles: Cover a baking sheet with nonstick parchment paper (stick the corners down with a little of the truffle cream). Fill a pastry bag fitted with a ⅝-inch (1.5-cm) nozzle with the truffle cream and squeeze out about 50 walnut-sized mounds onto the paper. The truffle cream may also be spooned onto the paper by taking a spoonful of it and scraping it off onto the paper in a little mound with a second teaspoon.

Place the baking sheet in the refrigerator to harden the chocolate for at least 30 minutes.

Open the paper cases and place them on a platter.

Place the cocoa powder in a shallow dish or soup bowl.

When the mounds are hard, remove them 10 at a time from the refrigerator, roll them rapidly between the palms of your hands to form them into balls, and then roll each one in the cocoa powder before placing it in a paper case.

When all the truffles have been made, place them in the refrigerator to harden.

To Store: The truffles can be kept for 1 week in a tightly closed container in the refrigerator. If keeping them for any length of time, it is best to keep them in a little extra cocoa powder.

CROSS INDEX
Basic Ingredients and Desserts

The following is a list of basic recipes and ingredients included in this book, along with the numbers of the recipes in which they can be used. If, for example, you make Apricot Jam and you find that you have some left, you can consult this listing and see the Apricot Jam is used also in Recipes 82 and 94. Also, if you wanted to know how to make Apricot Jam, you would look at the listing and see Recipe **132** marked in bold type which means that 132 is the basic recipe.

Almond Ice Cream: Recipe 28
Almond Paste: Recipes 91, **171**, 179–185, 203
Almond Pastry: Recipes 78, 82, 83, **111**
Almonds (blanched): Recipes 37, 172, 183, 195
Almonds (chopped): Recipes 185, 188, 197
Almonds (ground): Recipes 28, 110–113, 167, 171, 173
Almonds (slivered): Recipes 47, 61, 63–65, 82, 88, **118**, 192, 214, 222
Almonds (whole, shelled): Recipes 171, 187, 196, 212, 227
Aniseed-Flavored Liqueur: Recipe 204
Apple Cider Sherbet: Recipe **23**
Apple Jellies: Recipe **163**
Apples: Recipes 142, 147, 163
Apricot Jam: Recipes 82, 94, **132**
Apricot Jellies: Recipe **145**
Apricots (canned): Recipes 3, 47, 63, 80, 88, **122**, 129, 145
Apricots (fresh): Recipes 2, 98, 122, 132, 145, 160
Apricot Sauce: Recipes 20, 48, 94
Apricot Sherbet: Recipes **2**, **3**, 71, 82, 86, 88
Ardèche-Style Truffles: Recipe 74, **225**
Armagnac: Recipes 39, 54
Armagnac and Prune Ice Cream: Recipes **39**, 54
Banana Ice Cream: Recipes 29, 97
Bananas: Recipes 5, 29, 60, 97, 147
Bananas (Red): Recipe 129
Banana Sherbet: Recipes **5**, 51
Black Currant Jellies: Recipes 56, **149**

Black Currant Liqueur: Recipes 6, 128, 200
Black Currants: Recipes 6, 125, 128, 149, 199
Black Currant Sauce: Recipes 56, **98**
Black Currant Sherbet: Recipes **6**, 56
Calabash: Recipe 52
Calvados: Recipes 21, 185, 221
Calvados Sherbet: Recipe **21**
Candy Chestnuts: Recipes 20, **177**
Candied Fruits: Recipes 78, 79, 88
Caramel (Dry Cooked): Recipes 31, 186, 197, **198**
Caramel Ice Cream: Recipes **31**, 85, 88, 96, 113
Caramel Sauce: Recipes 27, 38, 45, 62, 70, **102**
Carrot Jellies: Recipe **148**
Carrots: Recipe 148
Certo: Recipes 144–165
Champagne: Recipes 22, 103
Champagne Sherbet: Recipes **22**, 58, 73
Chantilly Cream: Recipes 45, 49, 53, 56, 60, 61, 64, 75, 81, 82, 85–87, **104**, **105**
Cherries (Brandied): Recipes 65, 67, **126**, 176, 201
Cherries (Candied): Recipes 75, 77, 80, 90, 91, 181, 192
Cherries (Canned): Recipes 65, 67, 123
Cherries (Fresh): Recipes 123, 126, 133, 150
Cherry-Currant Jam: Recipe **133**
Cherry Jellies: Recipe **150**
Cherry Liqueur: Recipe 126
Chestnut Cream: Recipes 34, 69, 74
Chestnut Ice Cream: Recipes **34**, 69, 74

Chestnut Paste: Recipes 177, 225
Chocolate (Bitter): Recipe 204
Chocolate (Milk): Recipes 209–215, 219, 221, 226
Chocolate (Semi-Sweet): Recipes 43, 84, 96, 119, 177, 191, 192, 199–203, 205, 207, 209, 213, 216–219, 221, 225–227
Chocolate (White): Recipe 206
Chocolate Coating: Recipes 192, **193**, 207–209, 211, 213, 223
Chocolate Decorations: Recipes 81, 83
Chocolate Granite: Recipe 93
Chocolate Ice Cream: Recipes **32**, 49–51, 93, 95, 96
Chocolate Palm: Recipes 36, 51, 52, **119**
Chocolate Parfait: Recipes 43, 68, 81, 83, 84, 89
Chocolate Sauce (Hot): Recipes 5, 27, 29, 47, 60, 61, 84, 95, **101**
Chocolate Shavings: Recipes 49, 50, 61
Cinnamon (Powdered): Recipes 127, 142
Cocoa Powder: Recipes 32, 49, 101, 203, 221, 225, 227
Coconut Ice Cream: Recipes **36**, 52, 96
Coconuts: Recipes 36, 52, 96
Coffee (Beans): Recipes 25, 33, 42, 53, 216
Coffee (Extract): Recipes 41, 42, 171, 190
Coffee (Instant): Recipes 42, 87, 105, 190, 216
Coffee Granite: Recipes **25,** 92
Coffee Ice Cream: Recipes **33,** 53, 68, 87, 88, 92, 95
Coffee Parfait: Recipes **42,** 70, 81
Cognac: Recipes 44, 88
Cognac Parfait: Recipes **44,** 82
Cream: Recipes 27, 28, 31, 33, 35, 36, 38, 40–44, 101, 102, 104–106, 188–192, 203, 216–219, 226
Cream Puff Pastry: Recipes 95, **108**
Cusenier: Recipe 223
Date Paste: Recipes **173,** 180, 204
Dates: Recipes 173, 180
Disneyland Peanut Brittle: Recipe 30, **186**
Duja: Recipes **195,** 207, 209–211, 227
Egg Whites: Recipes 7, 8, 88, 109–114, 171–173
Egg Yolks: Recipes 27–67, 99, 100, 103, 219
Fig Jellies: Recipe **152**
Figs (Dried): Recipe 152
Fondant: Recipes 178, **194,** 199–202, 205, 225, 227
Food Coloring: Recipes 96, 112, 170, 171, 174–176, 185
French Meringue: Recipes 97, **109**
Fresh Fruit Sauce: Recipes 65, **98**
Fruits: Recipes 63, 98, 125, 129, 131, 144

Fruits (Canned): Recipes 147, 148, 152, 156, 158, 169, 170
Genoise: 88, **107**
Grain Alcohol: Recipes **126**–128
Grand Marnier: Recipes 44, 78, 79, 224
Grand Marnier Parfait: Recipes **44,** 76, 78, 79
Grapefruit: Recipes 16, 91
Grapefruit Sherbet: Recipes **16,** 91
Grape Jellies: Recipe **164**
Grapes: Recipe 164
Grenadine: Recipe 164
Guavas: Recipe 129
Hard Apple Cider: Recipes 23, 25
Hazelnuts: Recipes 38, 187, 195, 196, 207, 213, 219
Honey: Recipes 35, 152, 188–192, 226
Honey Ice Cream: Recipe **35**
Kirsch: Recipes 4, 20, 37, 44, 55, 88, 185, 206
Kirsch Parfait: Recipes **44,** 55, 72
Kiwi: Recipes 12, 129
Kumquats: Recipe 129
Lemon: Recipes 7, 8, 17–20, 22, 91, 102, 130, 134, 136, 138–140, 142, 151, 163, 170, 174, 176, 177, 194, 222
Lemon Marmalade: Recipe **140**
Lemon Sherbet: Recipes **7,** 57, 91
Lime: Recipes 8, 4, 129
Lime Sherbet: Recipe **8**
Litchis: Recipes 6, 129
Mangos: Recipes 14, 48, 129
Mango Sherbet: Recipe **14**
Mangosteens: Recipe 129
Melon Jellies: Recipe **158**
Melons: Recipes 15, 24, 59, 129, 158
Melon Sherbet: Recipes **15,** 59
Meringues: Recipes 61, 84–87
Mineral Water: Recipes 5, 7–9, 12, 21, 22
Nougatine: Recipes 85, **197,** 220
Nougatine Crumble: Recipes 31, 45, 78, 79, 88, 96, **197,** 207, 209, 215, 222
Nut Brittle: Recipes 27, 38, 62, 57, 88, 96, **196,** 212–215, 227
Nut Brittle Ice Cream: Recipes **38,** 62, 70, 96
Orange–Almond Pastry: Recipes 78, 83, 89, **112**
Orange–Flavored Liqueur: Recipe 223
Orange–Flower Water: Recipe 118
Orange Jellies: Recipe **159**
Orange Marmalade: Recipes 139, **141**
Orange Peel (Half-Candied): Recipes 54, 76, 83, **167,** 173, 184, 192, 210
Oranges: Recipes 9, 22, 57, 91, 100, 112, 129, 139, 141, 159, 167, 168, 174
Orange Sauce: Recipes 50, **100**
Orange Sherbet: Recipes **9,** 76, 83, 91

Orange Slice (Half-Candied): Recipes 57, 76, 79, 89, **168,** 210
Orange Zest: Recipes 151, 189
Papayas: Recipes 48, 129
Passion Fruit: Recipes 12, 129, 156
Passion Fruit Jellies: Recipe **156**
Passion Fruit Sherbet: Recipes 12, 52
Peaches (Canned): Recipes 18, 47, **124,** 161
Peaches (Fresh): Recipes 17, 124, 136, 160
Peach Jam: Recipe **136**
Peach Jellies: Recipes **160, 161**
Peach Sherbet: Recipes **17, 18**
Peanut Butter Ice Cream: Recipe 30
Peanuts: Recipe 186
Pear Jellies: Recipe **162**
Pears (Canned): Recipes 19, 20, 47, **124**
Pears (Fresh): Recipes 124, 162
Pear Sauce: Recipes 34, **98**
Pear Sherbet: Recipes **19, 20,** 69, 74
Petit Fours: Recipe 113
Pineapple (Canned): Recipes 4, 166
Pineapple (Fresh): Recipes 90, 129, 146
Pineapple (Half-Candied Slices): Recipes 4, 55, 58, 72, 73, 77, 80, 90, **166,** 175, 226
Pineapple Jellies: Recipe 146
Pineapple Sauce: Recipes 5, 12, 29, 36, 72, **98**
Pineapple Sherbet: Recipes **4,** 55, 72, 77
Pistachio Ice Cream: Recipes **37,** 84, 113
Pistachios (Unsalted): Recipes 37, 113, 206, 224
Plum Jam: Recipe **137**
Plums: Recipe 137
Port: Recipes 24, 59
Port Sherbet: Recipes **24,** 59
Prunes: Recipes 39, 179
Prunes (Stuffed): Recipes 54, **179**
Quince Jellies: Recipe **151**
Quinces: Recipe 151
Raisins: Recipe 218
Rambutans: Recipe 129
Raspberries (Brandied): Recipes **127,** 202
Raspberries (Fresh): Recipes 11, 58, 71, 86, 125, 127, 135, 154, 155, 199
Raspberry Jam: Recipe 135
Raspberry Jellies: Recipe **154**
Raspberry Sauce: Recipes 58, 65, 66, 71, 86, **98**
Raspberry Sherbet: Recipes **11,** 58, 66, 68, 71, 73, 86, 96

Red Currant Jellies: Recipes 149, **157**
Red Currant Jelly: Recipes 13, 63, 67, **143**
Red Currants: Recipes 6, 13, 46, 66, 125, 133, 143, 149, 155, 157, 199
Red Currant Sauce: Recipes 6, 46, **98**
Red Currant Sherbet: Recipes **13,** 67
Rhubarb: Recipes 138, 165
Rhubarb Jam: Recipe **138**
Rhubarb Jellies: Recipe **165**
Rice: Recipe 94
Rock Candy Coating: Recipes **169,** 180–185
Rum: Recipes 5, 29, 44, 218
Rum Parfait: Recipes **44,** 77, 80
Sabayon Sauce: Recipes 12, 22, **103**
Shiny Sugar Coating: Recipes **170,** 175, 180–183
Strawberries: Recipes 10, 59, 71, 86, 125, 134, 153, 178, 199
Strawberry Jam: Recipe 134
Strawberry Jellies: Recipe 153
Strawberry Sauce: Recipes 59, 71, 86, **98**
Strawberry Sherbet: Recipes **10,** 59, 65, 68, 71, 75, 86, 96
Success Pastry: Recipes 62, 84, 85, 87, **110**
Sugar Coffee Beans: Recipes 33, 53, 70, 87, 88
Sugar Syrup, 28°: Recipes **1,** 2–24, 39, 88, 90, 118, 122–124, 185, 203
Sweetened Condensed Milk: Recipe 226
Tangerines: Recipes 9, 91, 174
Tangerine Sherbet: Recipes **9,** 91
Tea: Recipes 26, 217
Tea Granite: Recipe **26**
Truffle Cream: Recipes 116, 220–224
Tulip Pastries: Recipes 63–67, **117**
Vanilla (Bean): Recipes 27, 40, 99, 114, 136, 142, 162, 163, 187, 188, 207, 219
Vanilla Ice Cream: Recipes **27,** 45–48, 56, 60, 61, 63, 64, 68, 75, 77, 86, 88, 94–96
Vanilla Parfait: Recipes **40, 41,** 75, 81
Vanilla Sauce: Recipes 6, 14, 29, 31, 38, 39, 51, 52, 54, 62, 85, 95, 99
Vanilla Wafer Batter: Recipes 114–117
Vanilla Wafers: Recipe **115**
Walnut–Almond Paste: Recipes **172,** 182, 205, 206
Walnuts: Recipes 172, 182, 205, 226
Whipped Cream: Recipe **106**
Whiskey: Recipe 221

LIST OF PHOTOGRAPHS

Almond squares 239
Apricots in light syrup 17
Apricot jam 17
Apricot jellies 17 and 220
Apricot sherbet 17
Ardeche-style truffles 77 and 337
Baked Alaska 138
Bitter orange marmalade 177
Brandied cherries 157
Brandied raspberries 157
Calvados-flavored truffles 337
Candied pineapple wedges 317
Candy chestnuts 317
Caramel-apple sauce 177
Caramel-flavored chocolate truffles 337
Champagne and raspberry sundae 55
Chocolate almonds 340
Chocolate cherries 157
Chocolate coating 277
Chocolate-flavored caramels 242
Chocolate raspberries 157
Chocolate thistles 300
Chocolate truffles 337
Coffee Liégeois sundae 35
Cooking sugar 207
Cusenier chocolate truffles 337
Duja 278
Eiffel towers 277
Finger wafers 175
Florentines 259
Fondant 157
Fresh fruit sauce 17
Frozen cognac and apricot dessert ii
Frozen Grand Marnier dessert 97
Frozen Raspberry Vacherin 155
Fruit jellies 220
Gatines-style chocolate truffles 337

Harlequin Duja 278
Ivory Coast sundae 35
Juanita banana sundae 35
Lenôtre truffles 337
Loire Valley sundae 58
Lutetia pistacios 320
Melba tulip cookie desserts 58
Mocha pleasures 337
Molded raspberry and champagne dessert 55
Molded vanilla dessert 95
Nougatine and nougatine crumble 298
Nut brittle boulders 340
Nut brittle paste 340
Orange-flavored caramels 242
Passion fruit sundae 38
Perigord crown dessert 77
Port Royal frozen souffle 117
Raspberry tulip 58
Sherbet-filled fruits 38
Sherbet-filled pineapple dessert 136
Snowball 75
Strawberry Jam 219
Strawberry jellies 220
Stuffed almonds 239
Stuffed cherries 239
Stuffed dates 239
Stuffed prunes 239
Stuffed walnuts 239
Sultans 337
Trianons 298
Tropical fruit salad 198
Tulip pastries 175
Two-flavored frozen souffle 115
Vanilla-flavored caramels 242
Wafer rounds
    filled with truffle cream 175
Walnut wonders 320

INDEX

Page numbers in **boldface** type indicate pages with color plates.

Almond ice cream (*glace aux amandes*), 45–46

Almond paste (*pâte d'amandes*), 273–274

Almond pastry (*biscuit aux amandes*), 166–67

Almond squares (*paves candis*), **239**, 295–96

Apple cider sherbet (*sorbet au cidre*), 34

Apple jellies (*pâte de pommes*), **17**, **220**, 256

Apricot jam (*confiture d'abricots*, **17**, 211–12

Apricot jellies (*pâte d'abricots*), 234

Apricot sherbet I (*sorbet aux abricots frais*), 12, **17**

Apricot sherbet II (*sorbet aux abricots au sirop*), 13, **17**

Apricots in light syrup or "au naturel," home canned (*abricots au sirop ou au naturel*), **17**, 187–88

Ardeche-style truffles (*truffes de l'Ardèche*), **77**, **337**, 375–76

Armagnac and prune ice cream (*glace aux pruneaux d'Agen*), 63–64

Auteil-style frozen caramel dessert (*biscuit glace d'Auteuil*), 122

Bain-marie, xiii, 313

Baked Alaska (*omelette norvégiènne*), 127–29, **138**

Baked Alaskan banana dessert (*banane à la Norvégiènne*), 144

Banana–apple jellies (*pâte de bananes-pommes*), 236–37

Banana ice cream (*glace à la banane*), 47–49

Banana sherbet (*sorbet à la banane*), 15

Basic fruit jelly recipe (*pâtes de fruits*), **220**, 232–33

Basic jam recipe (*recette de base*), 209–10

Black currant fondant candies (*boules de fondant au cassis*), 329–30

Black currant liqueur (*liqueur de cassis*), 195–96

Black currant sherbet (*sorbet au cassis*), 16

Black and red currant jellies (*pâte de cassis-groseilles*), 240

Bowls, xiii

Brandied cherries (*cerises à l'eau de vie*), 157, 192–93

Brandied raspberries (*framboises à l'eau de vie*), **157**, 194

Butter, xiii

Calvados-flavored chocolate truffles (*truffes au Calvados*), **337**, 367–68

Calvados sherbet (*sorbet au Calvados*), 32

Candied orange or tangerine wedges (*oranges deguisées ou clementines deguisées*), 279–80

Candied pineapple wedges (*ananas deguisés*), 281, **317**

Candies, general comments on making, 263; *see also* Fruit candies

Candy chestnuts (*marrons deguisés*), 284–86, **317**

Candy half moons (*demi-lunes candi*), 293–94

Canned peach jellies (*pâte de pêches au sirop*), 254

Caramel-apple sauce (*confiture de pommes-caramel*), **177**, 227–28

Caramel flavored chocolate truffles (*truffes au caramel*), **337**, 369–70

Caramelized almonds or hazelnuts (*amandes ou noisettes caramelisées*), 299–301

Caramel sauce (*sauce au caramel*), 151

Carrot jellies (*pâte de carottes*), 238

Champagne Sabayon sauce (*Sabayon au champagne*), 152

Champagne sherbet (*sorbet au champagne*), 33

Chantilly cream (*Chantilly*), 153

Charlies (*Charlies*), 357

Cherry–currant jam (*confiture de cerises–groseilles*), 213–14 variation of, 214

Cherry jellies (*pâte de cerises*), 241

Chestnut cream (*crème de marrons*), xiv

Chestnut ice cream (*glace aux marrons*), 56

Chestnut paste (*pâte de marrons*), xiv

Chocolate almonds (*amandes au chocolat*), **340**, 354

Chocolate cherries (*cerises au chocolat*), **157**, 331–32

Chocolate-coated ice cream on a stick, 142–43

Chocolate coating (*enrobage au chocolat*), **277**, 315–16

Chocolate-flavored caramels (*caramels au chocolat*), **242**, 307

Chocolate ice cream (*glace au chocolat*), 53

Chocolate palms and other chocolate ornaments (*décors en chocolat*), 181–82

Chocolate raspberries (*framboises au chocolat*), **157**, 333–34

Chocolates, general comments on making, 313 basic ingredients for, 313–14

Chocolate thistles (*chardons surprise*), **300**, 335, 336

Coconut ice cream (*glace à la noix de coco*), 59

Coffee-flavored caramels (*caramels au café*), 306

Coffee-flavored Chantilly cream (*Chantilly au café*), 154

Coffee granité, 37

Coffee ice cream (*glace fin moka*), 54

Combination desserts, general comments on molded, 93

Cooking sugar (*cuisson du sucre*), 203–05, **207**

Coupe; *see* Sundae

Cream:
Chantilly (*Chantilly*), 153
coffee-flavored Chantilly (*Chantilly au café*), 154
truffle, 176
whipped (*crème fouettée*), 156

Cream puff pastry (*pâte à choux*), 160–61

Crème de marrons (chestnut cream), xiv

Crème fraiche, xiv

Cusenier chocolate truffles (*truffes au Cusenier*), **337**, 371–72

Date paste (*pâte de dattes*), 276

Decorating, notes on, 7

Disneyland peanut brittle (*nougat de Disneyland*), 297

Duja, **278**, 321–22

Eggs, xiv
whites of, xiv–xv

Eiffel towers (*Tours Eiffel*), **277**, 345–46

Fig jellies (*pâte de figues*), 245
Finger wafers (*langues de chat*), 174, **175**
Flan rings, xv
Florentines (*florentins de Megève*), **259**, 308–09
Flour, xv
Fold, xv
Fondant (*fondant neutre*), **157**, 318
how to use (*utilisation*), 319
Freezer, ice cream;
choosing an, 1–2
using the, 2–4
French meringue (*meringue française*), 162–63
Fresh fruit sauce (*coulis de fruits*), **17**, 147
Fresh peach jellies (*pâte de pêches fraiches*), 253
Frozen Chocolate and Orange Dessert (*biscuit glace du Roussillon*), 120
Frozen chocolate dessert (*chocolate frappé*), 139
Frozen coffee dessert (*café frappé*), 137
Frozen coffee vacherin (*vacherin fin moka*), 125–26
Frozen Cognac and apricot dessert (*biscuit glace de Cognac*), **ii**, 118–19
Frozen desserts:
general comments on, 1–7
general comments on, cake or pastry based, 116
Frozen fruit puree (*purée de fruits*), 190–91
Frozen Grand Marnier dessert (*rosace glacée au Grand Marnier*), **97**, 105–06
Frozen Grand Marnier Soufflé (*soufflé au Grand Marnier*), 108–09
Frozen Martinique dessert (*rosace glacée de la Martinique*), 107
Frozen nut brittle delight (*glace praline-delices*), 98
Frozen rice pudding with apricots (*riz du mas du juge*), 140
Frozen Soufflés:
general comments on, 108
Frozen strawberry or raspberry vacherin (*vacherin aux fraises ou aux framboises*), 123–24, **155**
Fruit candies, general comments on, 279
Fruit-flavored fondant candies (*boules de fondant au coulis de fruit*), 328–29

Gatines-style chocolate truffles (*truffes des Gatines*), **337**, 377–78
Gatines-style spice cake (*pain d'espices des Gatines*), 185–86
Génoise, 158–59
Glace; *see* Ice cream, combination desserts

Granité:
Coffee (*au café*), 37
Tea (*au thé*), 39
Grapefruit sherbet (*sorbet au pamplemousse*), 27
Grape jellies (*pâte de raisins*), 257
Grilled slivered almonds (*amandes effilées et grillées*), 180
Guava, 199

Half-candied orange peels (*écorces d'orange semi-confites*), xvii, 266–67
Half-candied orange slices (*tranches d'oranges semi-confites*), 268
Half-candied pineapple slices (*ananas en tranches semi-confites*), 264–65
Harlequin duja (*duja Arlequin*), **278**, 348–49
Hazelnut squares (*carrés noisettes*), 355–56
Home canned cherries in light syrup or "au naturel" (*cerises au sirop ou au naturel*), 188
Home canned pears or peaches in light syrup (*pêches au sirop*), 189
Honey ice cream (*glace au miel*), 57
Hot chocolate sauce (*sauce à profiteroles*), 150
Hydrometer, 11

Ice cream:
almond (*aux amandes*), 45–46
armagnac and prune (*aux pruneaux d'Agen*), 63–64
banana (*à la banane*), 47–49
chestnut (*aux marrons*), 56
chocolate (*au chocolat*), 53
coconut (*à la noix de coco*), 59
coffee (*fin moka*), 54
general comments on, 42
honey, (*au miel*), 57
Lenôtre's special caramel (*au caramel Lenôtre*), 51–52
nut brittle (*au praline noisettes*), 62
peanut butter (*aux cacahuètes*), 50
pistachio (*à la pistache*), 60
vanilla (*à la vanille*), 42–44
Individual chocolate parfait desserts (*parfait au chocolat individuel*), 130

Individual frozen Grand Marnier soufflés (*soufflé au Grand Marnier individuel*), 110

Jam:
apricot (*confiture d'abricots*), 211–12
basic recipe for (*recette de base*), 209–10
cherry-currant (*confiture de cerises-groseilles*), 213–14
general comments on, 206–08
peach (*confiture de pêches*), 217

plum (*confiture de prunes*), 218
raspberry (*confiture de framboises*), 216
rhubarb (*confiture de rhubarbe*), 221
strawberry (*confiture de fraises*), 215
Jam jars, 208
Jelly:
apple (*pâte de pommes*), 256
apricot (*pâte d'abricots*), 234
banana-apple (*pâte de bananes-pommes*), 236–37
basic fruit (*pâtes de fruits*), 232–33
black and red currant (*pâte de cassis-groseilles*), 240
canned peach (*pâte de pêches au sirop*), 254
carrot (*pâte de carottes*), 238
cherry (*pâte de cerises*), 241
fig (*pâte de figues*), 245
fresh peach (*pâte de pêches fraiches*), 253
general comments on, 230–31
grape (*pâte de raisins*), 257
melon (*pâte de melon*), 251
orange (*pâte d'oranges*), 252
passion fruit (*pâte de fruits de la passion*), 249
pear (*pâte de poires*), 255
pineapple (*pâte d'ananas frais*), 235
quince (*pâte de coings*), 243–44
raspberry (*pâte de framboises*), 247
red currant (*gelée de groseilles*), 229
red currant (*pâte de groseilles*), 250
rhubarb (*pâte de rhubarbe*), 258
strawberry (*pâte de fraises*), 246
Jura chocolate (*boules du Jura*), 347–48

Kiwi, 199
Kumquat, 199

Lemon marmalade (*confiture de citrons*), 224
Lemon sherbet (*sorbet au citron*), 18
Lenôtre's (dry-cooked) caramel (*caramel cuit à sec*), 327
Lenôtre's special caramel ice cream (*glace au caramel Lenôtre*), 51–52
Lenôtre truffles (*truffes maison*), **337**, 379–80
Limes, 199
Lime sherbet (*sorbet au citron vert*), 19
Litchi or leechi, 199
Lutetia pistachios (*pistaches de Lutèce*), **320**, 343–44

Madeleines, 183–84
Mango, 200

Mango sherbet (*sorbet aux mangues*), 25
Mangosteen, 200
Marmalade,
  bitter orange (*confiture d'oranges amère*), 222–23
  lemon (*confiture de citrons*), 224
  sweet orange (*confiture d'oranges douce*), 225–26
Medicis frozen pistachio dessert (*biscuit glacé Medicis*), 121
Melon jellies (*pâte de melon*), 251
Melon sherbet (*sorbet au melon*), 26
Mocha pleasures (*plaisirs moka*), 337, 360
Molded Dessert:
  apricot and raspberry (*sorbet abricots framboises*), 99
  chestnut and pear (*glace marron-poires*), 96
  Hawaiian (*bombe Hawai*), 100
  raspberry and champagne (*sorbet champagne-framboises*), **55, 101**
  vanilla (*glaces panachées à la vanille*), 93–94, **95**
Molds, ice cream, 4 5
Mousse, frozen banana (*mousse glacée à la banane*), 49

Norman-style chocolate truffles (*truffes normande*), 364–65
Nougatine and nougatine crumble (*nougatine et craquelin nougatine*), **298**, 324–26
Nut brittle boulders (*rochers pralines*), **340**, 358
Nut brittle ice cream (*glace au praline noisettes*), 62
Nut brittle powder or paste (*praline-noisettes ou praline-amandes*), 322–23, **340**

Orange-almond pastry (*biscuit orange aux amandes*), 168–69
Orange-flavored caramels (*caramels à l'orange*), **242**, 304–05
Orange-flower water, xv
Orange jellies (*pâte d'oranges*), 252
Orange marmalade, bitter (*confiture d'oranges amère*), **177**, 222–23
Orange or tangerine sherbet (*sorbet à l'orange ou à la mandarine*), 20
Orange sauce (*sauce à l'orange*), 149
Oriental dates (*dattes orientales*), 338–39

Papaya, 200
Parchment paper, xv
Parfaits:
  alcohol-flavored (*à l'alcool*), 71–72
  chocolate (*au chocolat*), 70
  coffee (*au café*), 69

coffee-flavored vanilla (*à la vanille parfumé au café*), 68
  general comments on, 65
  vanilla (*à la vanille*), 65–67
Paris delights (*finesses de Paris*), 352–53
Passion fruit, 200
Passion fruit jellies (*pâte de fruit de la passion*), 249
Passion fruit sherbet (*sorbet aux fruits de la passion*), 23
Pastry:
  almond (*biscuit aux amandes*), 166–67
  cream puff (*pâte à choux*), 260–62
  orange-almond (*biscuit orange aux amandes*), 168–69
  success (*fond de succès*), 164
  tulip (*tulipes*), 178–79
Pâte de marrons (chestnut paste), xiv
Peach jam (*confiture de pêches*), 217
Peach sherbet I (*sorbet aux pêches fraiches*), 28
Peach sherbet II (*sorbet aux pêches au sirop*), 29
Peanut butter ice cream (*glace aux cacahuètes*), 50
Pear jellies (*pâte de poires*), 255
Pear sherbet I (*sorbet aux poires de conserve maison*), 30
Pear sherbet II (*sorbet aux poires au sirop*), 31
Perigord crown dessert (*couronne perigourdine*), 77, 102
Pineapple jellies (*pâte d'ananas frais*), 235
Pineapple sherbet (*sorbet à l'ananas au sirop*), 14
Pistachio ice cream (*glace à la pistache*), 60–61
Plum jam (*confiture de prunes*), 218
Port Royal frozen soufflé (*soufflé Port Royal*), 111–12, **117**
Port sherbet (*sorbet au Porto*), 36
Powdered (ground) almonds, xvi
Profiteroles (*profiteroles*), **141**
Provençal Petit fours (*biscuits de Provence*), 170–71

Quince jellies (*pâte de coings*), 243–44

Rambutan, 200
Raspberry jam (*confiture de framboises*), 216
Raspberry jellies (*pâte de framboises*), 247
Raspberry-red currant jellies (*pâte de framboises-groseilles*), 248
Raspberry sherbet (*sorbet aux framboises*), 22
Red currant jelly (*gelée de groseilles*), 229
Red currant jellies (*pâte de groseilles*), 250

Red currant sherbet (*sorbet aux groseilles*), 24
Rhubarb jam (*confiture de rhubarbe*), 221
Rhubarb jellies (*pâtes de rhubarbe*), 258
Ribbon, xvi
Riviera duja (*duja côte d'Azur*), 350–51
Rock candy coating (*candi*), 269–70
Royal cherries (*cerises royales*), 282–83

Sauce:
  caramel (*sauce au caramel*), 151
  caramel-apple (*confiture de pommes-caramel*), 227–28
  champagne Sabayon (*Sabayon au champagne*), 152
  fresh fruit (*coulis de fruits*), 147
  hot chocolate (*sauce à profiteroles*), 150
  orange (*sauce à l'orange*), 149
  vanilla (*sauce à la vanille*), 148
Sherbet:
  apple cider (*au cidre*), 34
  apricot I (*aux abricots frais*), 12
  apricot II (*aux abricots aux sirop*), 13
  banana (*à la banane*), 15
  black currant (*au cassis*), 16
  Calvados (*au Calvados*), 32
  champagne (*au champagne*), 33
  grapefruit (*au pamplemousse*), 27
  lemon (*au citron*), 18
  lime (*au citron vert*), 19
  mango (*aux mangues*), 25
  melon (*au melon*), 26
  orange or tangerine (*à l'orange ou à la mandarine*), 20
  passion fruit (*aux fruits de la passion*), 23
  peach I (*aux pêches fraiches*), 28
  peach II (*aux pêches au sirop*), 29
  pear I (*aux poires de conserve maison*), 30
  pear II (*aux poires au sirop*), 31
  pineapple (*à l'ananas au sirop*), 14
  port (*au porto*), 36
  raspberry (*aux framboises*), 22
  red currant (*aux groseilles*), 24
  strawberry (*aux fraises*), 21
Sherbet-filled fruits (*fruits givres*), 38, 134–35
Sherbet-filled pineapple dessert (*sorbet à l'ananas dans le fruit*), 131–33, **136**
Shiny chocolate truffles (*truffes brillantes*), 373–74
Shiny sugar coating (*enrobage au sucre cuit*), 271–72
Sirop à 28 Baumé, 11
Snowball (*boule de neige*), **75**, 103–04
Sorbet—*See* Sherbet